LOCOMOTION PAPERS

# The
# Aldeburgh Branch

*by*
*Peter Paye*

# THE OAKWOOD PRESS

British Library Cataloguing in Publication Data
A Record for this book is available from the British Library
ISBN 978 0 85361 723 5

Typeset by Oakwood Graphics.
Repro by PKmediaworks, Cranborne, Dorset.
Printed by Information Press Ltd, Eynsham, Oxford.

*Note*
Much of the rolling stock used on the Aldeburgh branch was also used on many other ex-Great Eastern Railway branches. For this reason the plans and dimensions published in the author's earlier titles have not been repeated in this volume.

**By the same author and published by Oakwood Press:**

*The Snape Branch (2005)*
*The Hadleigh Branch (2006)*
*The Jersey Eastern Railway (2007)*
*The Framlingham Branch (2008)*
*The Wisbech & Upwell Tramway (2009)*
*The Bishop's Stortford, Dunmow and Braintree Branch (2010)*
*The Mellis & Eye Railway (2012)*

*Front cover:* 'F6' class 2-4-2T No. 67230 has topped the 1 in 58 gradient from Saxmundham Junction and passes the Junction up branch fixed distant signal as she makes for Leiston and Aldeburgh. The two-coach train is formed of Gresley LNER 4-compartment non-gangway brake/third to diagram 64 or 65 and Gresley LNER lavatory composite. No. 67230 was regularly outbased at Aldeburgh or Framlingham sheds when allocated to Ipswich. *The late Dr I.C. Allen*

*Rear cover:* Extract from Ordnance Survey One-Inch maps, sheets 137 and 150 (published 1946), showing the Aldeburgh branch and its environs. *Crown Copyright*

*Title page:* 'F6' class 2-4-2T No. 67230 in fully lined-out livery approaching Thorpeness Halt with a Saxmundham to Aldeburgh train formed of Gresley LNER brake/third with four compartments to diagram 64 or 65 built 1926 to 1930, then Gresley composite with 2 x first compartments/lavatory/5 x third class compartments to diagram 215, with the final vehicle a non-corridor third with eight compartments. *The late Dr I.C. Allen*

Published by The Oakwood Press (Usk), P.O. Box 13, Usk, Mon., NP15 1YS.
E-mail:   sales@oakwoodpress.co.uk
Website:  www.oakwoodpress.co.uk

# Contents

Richard Garrett's Aveling & Porter 0-4-0 shunting locomotive *Sirapite* standing in the sunshine on the loop road at Leiston on 19th December, 1961. The locomotive served at Garrett's works from 1929 until withdrawal in 1962. It has since been restored to working order and is back in operation for special occasions at Leiston. The footbridge No. 1110A spanning the main single line and goods yard is in the background.          *J.H. Meredith*

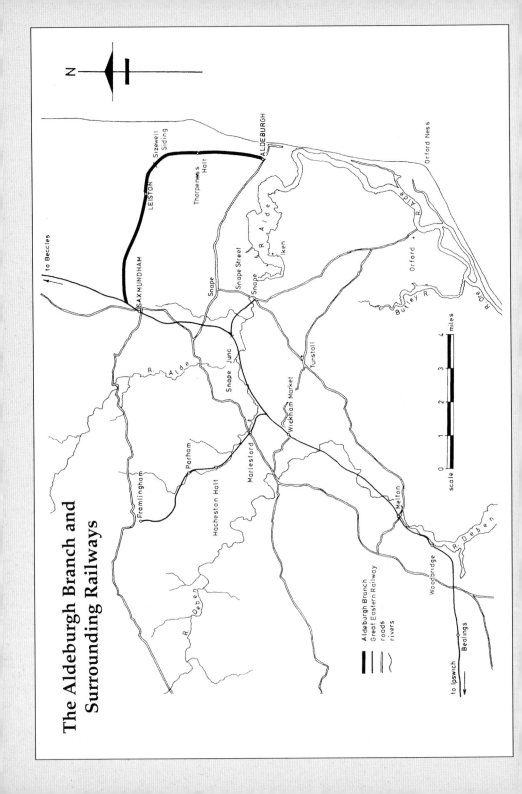

# The Aldeburgh Branch and Surrounding Railways

N

to Beccles

to Ipswich

Bealings

SAXMUNDHAM

LEISTON

Sizewell Siding

Thorpeness Halt

ALDEBURGH

Orford Ness

R. Alde

Iken

Orford

Butley R.

R. Ore

Snape

Snape Street

Snape

Snape Junc.

R. Alde

Tunstall

Wickham Market

Framlingham

Parham

Hacheston Halt

Marlesford

Melton

Woodbridge

R. Deben

R. Deben

scale

0  1  2  3  4 miles

Aldeburgh Branch
Great Eastern Railway
roads
rivers

# Introduction

The Aldeburgh branch, unlike many of the lines inherited or built by the Great Eastern Railway (GER), was not solely reliant on agricultural traffic for the major portion of its receipts. Much of the revenue came from the engineering works established at Leiston in 1778 by Richard Garrett, initially making blades and agricultural equipment for local farmers. Over the years the family business flourished and the management was taken over by his son Richard. Unfortunately there was no position for the younger son, Newson, who initially went to London to seek his fortune. In 1840, at the behest of brother Richard, 29-year-old Newson returned to Suffolk to set up a maltings business at Snape on the banks of the River Alde, some five miles south of Leiston. Before the advent of the railway Richard Garrett, father and son, had dispatched much of their products through Slaughden Quay, near Aldeburgh, whilst Newson had ready access to the River Alde for the import and export of barley and malt. The reliance on and delays incurred using the existing primitive road and water transport was of constant concern but salvation came with the creation of the Halesworth, Beccles & Haddiscoe Railway in 1851, which opened for passenger traffic on 4th December, 1854. Such was the success of the venture that a southern extension to Woodbridge to join up with a planned Eastern Union Railway line from Ipswich was soon mooted, the chief promoters being Sir Samuel Morton Peto and Richard Cobbold, the Ipswich brewer and banker.

The Garrett brothers were influential in the area to be served by the new railway and as both would gain from the venture and in return offer traffic to the undertaking, it was of no surprise that Richard Garrett was appointed to the preliminary Board of the embryonic re-titled East Suffolk Railway (ESR). When the Bill received the Royal Assent on 3rd July, 1854, the statute included branch lines to Richard Garrett's manufactory at Leiston and Newson Garrett's maltings at Snape Bridge as well as a third line to Framlingham, the latter to appease the burghers of that town after the Duke of Hamilton had objected to the railway passing through his estate at Easton. Like the people of Framlingham, the influential inhabitants of the coastal port of Aldeburgh on the German Ocean, later North Sea, were concerned at the possible loss of trade. The town, known as Aldborough until the 1880s, had since the demise of the principal port Dunwich, further to the north, assumed a maritime activity with the export of corn and wool and import of coal and timber, as well as fishing. However with constant coastal erosion the port had succumbed to nature and a vast shingle bank had subsequently blocked the harbour so that vessels could only access the town by way of the rivers Ore and Alde to Slaughden Quay, a long, winding and time consuming course. Although much of the trade declined Aldeburgh was establishing itself as a fashionable resort for the gentry; it was thus essential for the railway to serve the town and the extension to Aldeburgh was authorized on 19th April, 1859. The East Suffolk main line together with the branches to Leiston, Framlingham and Snape opened for traffic on 1st June, 1859, the latter only for freight, and the section on to Aldeburgh was subsequently opened on 12th April, 1860.

From the outset the Aldeburgh branch was operated by the Eastern Counties Railway, in conjunction with the ESR until 1862, when the Great Eastern Railway assumed control. Initially the new company made few innovations, passenger traffic was chiefly local in character, whilst freight increased

Sunshine and shade. 'J15' class 0-6-0 No. 65459 stands under the overall roof at Aldeburgh after the arrival of the 12.30 pm train from Saxmundham on 26th July, 1953.          *The late R.E. Vincent*

considerably as Garrett's works expanded production, augmented by agricultural, fish and coal traffic. As the years progressed so Aldeburgh's importance as a coastal holiday destination increased and weekend excursion tickets were issued to the resort. From 1906 through coaches were worked from Liverpool Street to and from Aldeburgh, with the vehicle or vehicles being attached and detached from main line services at Saxmundham. After the London & North Eastern Railway (LNER) took over in 1923 the through coaches continued, enhanced by another innovation introduced by the company in the summer months from June 1929: the 'Eastern Belle' Pullman train from Liverpool Street to Aldeburgh and return which visited the branch once a week, when passengers could travel in luxury and spend a few hours by the sea. Other East Anglian resorts were visited on other days of the week but this service and the through coaches were discontinued with the outbreak of hostilities in 1939.

The restrictions of the war seriously hampered movements but much military traffic was handled. The halcyon years were never repeated, and except for a few excursion trains to and from Ipswich and Felixstowe, passenger traffic was again local in character. Despite the attempts by the LNER to encourage rail travel, when British Railways, Eastern Region took over from 1st January, 1948 the popularity of Aldeburgh as a holiday resort could not be compared with Clacton or Great Yarmouth. The population had barely increased in the previous two decades and although the upper and middle class clientele continued to enjoy the attractions, passenger numbers were hardly encouraging to the new management. The internationally famous Aldeburgh Festival, now firmly established in the world of arts, was also founded in 1948 by the joint efforts of Benjamin Britten, Peter Pears and Eric Crozier with initial performances held in Aldeburgh parish church, the Baptists' chapel and the Jubilee Hall. It was hoped the festival would bring an increase in branch passenger revenue but as the festival's reputation grew so the arena of activities spread to the splendid churches at Framlingham, Blythburgh and Orford and audiences tended to travel by car. As the repertoire expanded the venues were considered too fragmented and a central location was required. In the meantime branch freight traffic was on the decline; the abolition of petrol rationing resulted in farmers and growers sending increasing tonnages by road, added to which Garrett's were transferring allegiance to the new mode of transport.

With a view to economy, diesel-multiple-units (dmus) took over passenger working in June 1956 and yet further reductions came in January 1959, when all workings were accommodated within a 12 hour shift. Diesel locomotives took over freight services and from 30th November of the same year freight facilities were withdrawn from Aldeburgh and Thorpeness. The early 1960s offered some hope for the branch when the impending provision of nuclear power stations on the shores of the North Sea at Sizewell was announced and ultimately Sizewell A and Sizewell B were commissioned in 1966 and 1995 respectively with some construction traffic being conveyed by rail and spent nuclear flasks being dispatched away to Sellafield. Conversely the establishment of the Aldeburgh Festival at the converted Snape Maltings, opened from 1967, meant the further decline of Aldeburgh branch passenger traffic and the service was withdrawn on 10th September, 1966. Leiston public delivery siding closed for freight traffic on 7th May, 1984 but the truncated section between Saxmundham and Sizewell siding remains in use for the sporadic flask traffic from Sizewell A, which was shut down on 31st December, 2006, Sizewell B which has a life span to 2035 although Electricité de France (EDF) have announced a strategic target of 20 years extension beyond that date, and possible utilization should the new Sizewell C power station be built. Since February 2009 plans for this twin unit reactor have appeared positive as on 18th October, 2010 the British Government confirmed Sizewell was one of eight sites considered suitable for a future nuclear power station. Various plans have been mooted for the reopening of the branch to Aldeburgh but future historians will have to report the event.

This then is the 'old testament' of the Aldeburgh branch from conception to the present day. I have attempted to trace the history of the line and details have been checked with available documents, but apologies are offered for any errors which might have occurred.

*Peter Paye*
*Bishop's Stortford*

Metropolitan-Cammell two-car dmu No. E79066/E79282 standing at Aldeburgh on 6th September, 1966, the last week of passenger train operation. The Aldeburgh station sign is exposed to the daylight as the overall roof had long been removed. Note the fading white paint on the brickwork of the wall and the decorative arches. *G.R. Mortimer*

# Chapter One

## A Branch Railway to Leiston

The River Alde rising near Brundish in the undulating hills of mid-Suffolk is an insignificant and reluctant stream until it reaches Snape Bridge, five miles as the crow flies from the North Sea. Thereafter it broadens out taking a seven mile-long meandering course past the ports of Iken and then Aldeburgh, where within a hundred yards of the coast it turns south to Slaughden Quay within the shadow of a forbidding unique quatrefoil Martello Tower. After another two miles the Alde confusingly changes its name to the River Ore and the southward course continues for another 10 miles passing a lengthy shingle bar before reaching the German Ocean or North Sea at Orford Ness. The seaside resort and fishing village of Aldeburgh, previously known as Aldborough meaning Old Fort, since 1948 associated with the famed Aldeburgh Festival, was once on the site of an old burh or defensive place with a wide inlet to the north, which has long been drained. Despite the disadvantage of the long approach the river provided a good shelter for small vessels. The small half-timbered brick and flint moot hall, built in Tudor times as the market hall, and later serving as a gaol, ammunition store and council chambers, now stands almost on the shingle beach where fishermen draw up their boats, for much of the Tudor town has disappeared into the sea. Shipbuilding was the chief industry in the 16th and 17th centuries with amongst others Sir Francis Drake's vessels *Greyhound* and *Pelican*, later renamed *Golden Hind*, products of local craftsmen. The shipbuilding declined when the Johnson family shipbuilders moved the business to Blackwall on the River Thames. Legitimate trading gave way to lucrative smuggling in the 18th century, when it was said the parson was the only man in the town not associated with the illicit trade. Aldeburgh had gained a charter in 1529, was a Parliamentary borough from 1571, and returned two members of Parliament, the right to vote being vested in the freemen of the town. In Georgian times the town was described as 'small and poor', latterly being considered a rotten borough and lost its representation in the 1832 Reform Act.

As decades evolved writers were attracted to the town, including Wilkie Collins and Edward Fitzgerald. Carlisle approved of Aldeburgh's shingle beaches and clear water and E.M. Forster enjoyed the bleakness of the locality. A broadcast talk by Forster about Aldeburgh drew Benjamin Britten to the area and in a converted windmill at Snape he wrote the opera 'Peter Grimes' before moving to Aldeburgh in 1947. The flint church of St Peter and St Paul was host to strolling players who performed plays in the nave. George Crabbe, the poet clergyman, born in the town in 1754, preached as a curate in the elaborately carved pulpit. Crabbe's grandfather was customs collector for the area and it was from George Crabbe that Britten took the story of Peter Grimes. Benjamin Britten, who died in 1976, is buried in the churchyard and a stained glass memorial window in the church to his memory was designed by John Piper. Elizabeth Garrett Anderson, daughter of Newson Garrett, was Britain's first woman doctor and a leading campaigner for women's rights who, after her death in 1917, was buried in the church. She grew up in Aldeburgh and was mayor of the town in 1908, the first female mayor in Britain, succeeding her father, who had been mayor in 1889.

Richard Garrett was established as blacksmith at the inland village of Leiston in 1778 and his son Richard expanded the business into the manufactory of agricultural implements. His two sons were to follow far different careers for the elder, Richard, continued the expansion of the Leiston establishment, whilst the younger, Newson, after a short sojourn in London, returned to inaugurate the maltings at nearby Snape and develop Aldeburgh as a watering place. Both were to encourage the railway to serve this remote area of East Suffolk.

The coming of the railways into East Anglia began in earnest with the incorporation of the Eastern Counties Railway (ECR) on 4th July, 1836; the 1835 Prospectus made a point of the reduced travel time from London to Aldeburgh from 10 hours 58 minutes to 6 hours 16 minutes. With the share capital of £1,600,000 the company was granted powers to construct a 126 mile line from Shoreditch in East London to Norwich and Yarmouth via Colchester, Ipswich and Eye. By September £58,100 of shares had been sold but there was great concern that only a twelfth of the capital raised was of local origin. Construction of the railway commenced in late March 1837 at the London end only, as incomplete negotiations with landowners prevented a start being made concurrently at Norwich and Ipswich. The problems continued when landowners along the proposed route demanded higher compensation, and by October 1838, with 40 per cent of the capital called, only nine miles of railway was under construction. With creditors urgently pressing, action was necessary to prevent total ruin and by April 1839 Lancashire proprietors, who had taken a majority stake in the undertaking, forced a decision to terminate the line at Colchester.

The first public trains ran from a temporary terminus at Mile End to Romford on 20th June, 1839, with extensions at each end to Shoreditch and Brentwood opening for traffic on 1st July, 1840. Robert Stephenson was engaged by the ECR Directors to give engineering advice but he could only confirm that another £520,000 was required to complete the railway to Colchester. Mutinous shareholders were almost bludgeoned into meeting the calls for outstanding shares and application was made to Parliament for a further £350,000 share capital in 1840. With these assets and the added borrowing powers authorized by the 1840 Act, construction of the final section progressed. Eventually the line was opened to Colchester for goods traffic on 7th March, and for passenger trains on 29th March, 1843. The 51 mile line had taken seven years to construct at a cost of nearly £2½ million, the works alone amounting to £1,631,000 had exceeded the original estimate for the whole project from London to Yarmouth.

The ECR Directors' decision to terminate the project at Colchester was of particular concern to the merchants and traders of Ipswich and Norwich, who were fearful of isolation from the railway network and probable loss of trade. Some of the ECR shareholders from Norfolk and Suffolk alarmed by the slow progress and decision of April 1839, obtained a rule nisi in the Bail Court to force the fulfillment of the company's contract with the public, but this was overruled in 1840 when Parliament refused to extend the ECR powers beyond

July of that year. Local factions in Norfolk then decided to take action by planning a railway linking Norwich with Yarmouth and this received the Royal Assent in 1842 to be followed in the following year by a projected line from Norwich to Brandon. By now Ipswich traders and businessmen were fearful of economic isolation. The situation was aggravated by the ECR plan to join up with the Norwich to Brandon line at Thetford, with the main line by-passing Ipswich altogether and leaving the town at the end of a branch line from Hadleigh.

Objections were raised but ignored and so the traders and merchants of Ipswich produced their own scheme for a line linking the town with the ECR at Colchester. Peter Schuyler Bruff, who had already worked on surveys for the original ECR route from London, prepared the plans. The leading advocate of the Ipswich scheme was John Chevallier Cobbold, a member of the wealthy Ipswich banking and brewing family, who was a member of the original ECR Board of Directors. As well as connecting Ipswich with Colchester, the promoters of the scheme also intended to continue with a line running north to Norwich, and the new company entitled the Eastern Union Railway (EUR) was incorporated on 19th July, 1844.

In the meantime the ECR plans for a route to Thetford were abandoned but a group of businessmen in Bury St Edmunds were concerned the town would also be isolated from the developing railway network. In February 1844, the ECR Directors received a deputation who wished to salvage their plans but were advised the company was unwilling to extend their line beyond Colchester. The townsfolk subsequently promoted their own line, the East & West Suffolk Railway and were advised the EUR would not oppose the railway provided the route went from Bury St Edmunds to Ipswich via Hadleigh and not interfere with the direct line from Ipswich to Colchester.

The development of railways in Norfolk and Suffolk was the subject of a special investigation by the Railway Department of the Board of Trade and in a final report of 4th March, 1845 full support was given to the EUR scheme to Ipswich and for the extension to Norwich. The tract of land north-west of Ipswich towards Bury St Edmunds finally received the attention of railway developers with the passing on 21st July, 1845 of the Act authorizing the construction of the Ipswich and Bury St Edmunds Railway. With an initial capital of £400,000 the new concern appeared nominally independent but was, however, an extension of the EUR, with no less than six EUR Directors appointed to a Board totalling 15 members. The Colchester to Ipswich section of the EUR was opened to goods traffic on 1st June and passenger traffic on 15th June, 1846, whilst the extension to Bury St Edmunds was opened to goods traffic on 7th December and to passenger traffic on 24th December, 1846. In the same year Cornelius Welton, a land agent and surveyor from Wickham Market, hoped to provide a section of East Suffolk with a railway, producing plans for a line passing through Ashbocking and Clopton from where a branch was to run to Framlingham.

Meanwhile, in the autumn of 1845 a proposed railway to Hadleigh, backed by the EUR, had effectively stemmed the competitive desire of the ECR to build a duplicate line from Colchester into East Anglia. However, much to the annoyance of the Ipswich company, the ECR had not abandoned the goals of Norwich and Yarmouth, but had taken steps to reach Norfolk via an alternative route. On the same day the ECR was incorporated in 1836, a rival company the Northern & Eastern Railway (N&ER), received the Royal Assent to build a line over the 53 miles from Islington to Cambridge financed by a share capital of £1,200,000. The N&ER like the ECR soon encountered financial difficulties and it was 1839 before construction commenced and even then only with the sanction of the ECR. To conserve finances the N&ER route was diverted from Tottenham via Stratford, where running powers were permitted into the ECR Shoreditch terminal. Like the ECR the new line was built to a gauge of 5 feet, and despite abandonment of the route north of Bishop's Stortford by Act of Parliament in 1840, had reached the Hertfordshire market town on 16th May, 1842, at a cost of over £25,000 per mile. In 1843 the N&ER secured an extension Act for a line to Newport, some 10 miles nearer Cambridge but on 23rd December of that year the ECR agreed terms on a 999 years lease for the company from 1st January, 1844. Once the lease was in force the ECR lost no time obtaining powers linking Newport to the Norwich and Brandon Railway at Brandon on 4th July, 1844. The N&ER line, along with the existing ECR line, was converted to standard gauge of 4 ft 8½ in. in the late summer of the same year and after a formal opening the previous day, the entire line from Bishop's Stortford to a temporary terminus at Norwich (Trowse) commenced public service on 30th July, 1845.

The southern railway approach to Norwich was surveyed by Joseph Locke and built by the EUR. It ran from a junction with the Bury St Edmunds line at Haughley direct to the Norfolk capital via Diss. The line was opened in stages, initially for goods traffic to Finningham from 7th June, 1848, then to Burston for goods on 11th June and passengers from 2nd July, 1849, with completion throughout by 7th November of the same year. Thus while the main routes from London to Norwich via Cambridge and Ipswich were established, a vast acreage of East Suffolk was devoid of railways.

The genesis of the branch railway to Leiston and ultimately to Aldeburgh began in 1851 when a local venture, the Halesworth, Beccles & Haddiscoe Railway (HB&HR) obtained powers to construct a line connecting the river ports of Halesworth and Beccles with the Reedham to Lowestoft line of the Norfolk Railway. The statute authorized the raising of £150,000 in 7,500 £20 shares to finance the scheme and the first Directors were Edward Leathes, Andrew Johnson, Frederick William Farr and Richard Till. The following year it was empowered to enter into a working agreement with the Norfolk company and subsequently, after construction by Peto & Betts, opened to goods on 20th November and to passenger traffic on 4th December, 1854. From the outset the railway was operated by the ECR, which had leased the Norfolk Railway in 1848, and by June 1855 the company was able to show a modest profit of £528. In the meantime the HB&HR Directors, encouraged by the backing they had received and endorsed by the Earl of Stradbroke, Lord Lieutenant of the County of Suffolk, proposed a southward extension to Woodbridge to join up with the EUR. The EUR connection from Ipswich, originally authorized in the Ipswich & Bury Railway (Woodbridge Extension)

Act of 1847, was never built, and so these plans were also dusted down and resurrected in the hope the combined railways would provide a through route to the Suffolk capital and chief port of the county. At the same time it was proposed to re-title the HB&H undertaking as the East Suffolk Railway. Sir Samuel Morton Peto, who had ambitious schemes afoot to elevate the status of Lowestoft, immediately recognized that the new line would provide a more direct access to London than the existing routes via Norwich. He quickly became the principal subscriber and subsequently offered to lease the whole line for 14 years on a cost not exceeding £10,000 per mile, with 3½ per cent paid during construction.

The original intention had been to route the Halesworth to Woodbridge extension via the town of Framlingham but the Duke of Hamilton had objected to the railway passing through his estate at Easton and so the proposed line was routed further to the east. The proposals for both the EUR and ESR schemes, together with plans and books of reference were deposited with the Parliamentary Private Bill Office on 30th November, 1853, with copies sent to parish councils affected by the planned railways. Included in the ESR proposal were branch railways to serve Richard Garrett's engineering works at Leiston and Newson Garrett's maltings at Snape Bridge, it being envisaged that both would provide lucrative traffic for the line. As early as 1846 Richard Garrett, in evidence to the Parliamentary Committee, stressed the importance of railway transport to the expansion of his business – annual tonnage of fuel and raw materials entering his works amounting to 4,600 to 4,800 tons and goods leaving 3,600 to 3,800 tons. A third branch was to serve the town of Framlingham. In addition to Garrett, who lived at Carlton Hall near Saxmundham, local backers for the Leiston branch included Frederick Wentworth and the Honorable Arthur Thelluson of Aldeburgh, who were keen for the branch railway to be extended to the coastal town.

The ECR Directors objected to the schemes and sent their General Manager to public meetings to argue against the proposals. The new line would in effect drain traffic from the Ipswich to Norwich main line via Haughley, which the ECR, after taking steps to destroy it when in EUR hands, now controlled. Realizing they were losing the arguments, the ECR officers then astutely altered their strategy and agreed to work the new East Suffolk line, but without the financial guarantees applicable to the original Halesworth to Haddiscoe section, thus ensuring a controlling power.

The vesting of all the assets of the Halesworth, Beccles & Haddiscoe Railway to the newly titled East Suffolk Railway was duly authorized by the East Suffolk Railway Act (17 and 18 Vict. cap. cxix), which received the Royal Assent on 3rd July, 1854. The statute also sanctioned the extension of the main line authorized in 1851 on to Woodbridge and the construction of three branch railways or tramways, the first from a junction at Saxmundham to Leiston with an extension on to the Manufactory of Richard Garrett at Leiston and the second from a junction with the main line in the Parish of Campsea Ash to Framlingham. The third branch railway or tramway commenced by a junction with the main line in the Parish of Farnham in the County of Suffolk and terminated in the Parish of Tunstall near Snape Bridge, As with the other

ANNO DECIMO SEPTIMO & DECIMO OCTAVO

# VICTORIÆ REGINÆ.

❋❋❋❋❋❋❋❋❋❋❋❋❋❋❋❋❋❋❋❋❋❋❋❋❋❋❋❋❋❋❋❋❋❋❋❋❋❋❋❋❋❋❋❋❋❋

## *Cap.* cxix.

An Act for making a Railway in Deviation and Extension of the *Halesworth, Beccles, and Haddiscoe* Railway from *Westhall Low Common* to *Woodbridge*, and certain Branches therefrom, and for changing the Name of the Company to the *East Suffolk* Railway Company.

[3d *July* 1854.]

WHEREAS an Act was passed in the Session of Parliament held in the Fourteenth and Fifteenth Years of the Reign of Her present Majesty, called "The *Halesworth, Beccles, and Haddiscoe* Railway Act, 1851," whereby the *Halesworth, Beccles, and Haddiscoe* Railway Company were incorporated and authorized to make a Railway from the *Lowestoft* Railway at *Haddiscoe* in the County of *Norfolk*, by *Beccles*, to *Halesworth*, with a short Branch to the *Lowestoft* Railway in the Parish of *Haddiscoe*, and such Railway is now in course of Construction between the Terminus at *Haddiscoe* and a Place called *Westhall Low Common* in the Parish of *Westhall* in the County of *Suffolk*: And whereas the making of a Railway in Extension of the said Railway from *Westhall Low Common* aforesaid to near the Town of *Woodbridge* in the County of *Suffolk*, with Branch Railways or Tramways therefrom to *Leiston*, *Snape Bridge*, and *Framlingham*, would be of great public and local Advantage; and the said *Halesworth, Beccles,*

14 & 15 Vict. c. xxvi.

[*Local.*]          21 G          *and*

East Suffolk Railway Act of 3rd July, 1854, which amongst other things sanctioned the building of the Leiston branch.

branches three years were permitted for the compulsory purchase of land for the Leiston branch and five years for the completion of works.

The share capital of the new company for the new schemes was £450,000 formed of £150,000 shares of the former Haddiscoe company and £300,000 new shares. The company was authorized to borrow £50,000, when all shares had been subscribed for and once half of the original capital was actually paid up. The first Directors of the company were Edward Leathes, Andrew Johnston, Richard Till, James Peto, Holland Thomas Birkett and George Teed. George Berkley of 24 Great George Street, Westminster, London and designer of Fenchurch Street station in the city was appointed company Engineer. The EUR line from Ipswich to Woodbridge was authorized by the Eastern Union Railway Act, which received the Royal Assent on 16th July, 1854.

On 22nd February, 1855 Sir Samuel Morton Peto estimated the cost of the Halesworth to Woodbridge line at £194,686 2s. 6d., or £8,812 per mile, with the principal stations at Halesworth, Yoxford, Saxmundham and Framlingham and cheaply built minor stations at Melton, Campsea Ashe, Leiston, Snape and Bramfield. The 5 miles 52 chains Framlingham branch was costed at £8,064 per mile compared with an exorbitant £10,601 12s. 7d. for the relatively short Snape branch and £6,109 for the short line to Leiston. At a subsequent meeting of the Special Joint Committee of the ECR, the Norfolk Railway and the EUR held on 11th May, 1855, G.P. Bidder, the ESR Consulting Engineer, reported that the final costs of the proposed lines were not yet available. This, despite having submitted a written report from his office at 24 Great George Street, Westminster on 5th May, 1855 with the estimated cost of the line and three branches concurring with the figure given by Peto in February. The meeting considered the facts of the report. The total cost of the Saxmundham to Leiston line was re-estimated at £22,032 2s. 8d. for the 3 miles, 4 furlongs, 8 chains and 50 links-long route engulfing 26 acres of land.

The district served by the ESR was approximately 450 square miles bordered on the east by the coast, whilst 15 miles to the west was the EUR linking Ipswich with Norwich. At the northern extremity were the towns of Lowestoft and Bungay and to the south the River Deben. The land acreage was 493,471, whilst the population in the 1851 census was recorded as 104,760. It comprised a highly fertile agricultural district with many nobility and gentry and a number of watering places, including Aldeburgh and Southwold, which were well situated and capable of much improvement. Bidder was of the opinion it was an 'absolute condition' that only the main line should be considered as priority with the branches as an optional extra. The three members of the Joint Committee, R. Moseley, General Manager, Charles Capper, outdoor manager and A.G. Church, coaching superintendent, begged to differ, and considered the main line would be best served by the feeder lines all being constructed together.

The ECR had initially considered taking over the ESR but at the ECR shareholders meeting on 13th July, 1855, Mr Bruce, a Director, opposed the idea saying the ECR shareholders would lose money if the takeover were made. He was severely critical of the report made by the ECR officers on the prospects for the East Suffolk line, saying they had omitted Aldeburgh and Snape when calculating the effects of local ports on the railway. He also claimed that the estimate of 104,760 persons in the catchment area of the railway was 15 per cent too high. David Waddington, the ECR Chairman, countered saying 'if they did not construct the line other parties would'. Mr Lewin, a shipper of flour from Woodbridge stated he had traded for the past 40 years and fully advocated the building of the railway. After further discussion Bruce won the day and the shareholders were sent further information on the line so they could reach a decision. The shareholders duly endorsed the doubts of Bruce and rejected the takeover, leaving the ESR to finance the building of the railway. The Directors of the Norfolk Railway also met on the same day and reported that the cost of constructing the ESR would reach £10,000 per mile.

The ESR issued its Prospectus on 1st September, 1855 and estimated revenue of £48,014, by comparing the amount of trade in East Suffolk with that in other areas already served by railways. It stressed passenger revenue would be £22,261 and goods receipts £25,753, whilst operating costs were expected to be 46 per cent of receipts with debt interest on the construction of the line a mere 5 per cent. The initial working profit of 54 per cent was, however, to be largely swallowed up paying off miscellaneous debts. Local traffic alone was expected to pay a 5 per cent dividend. The ESR Prospectus still expressed the promoters' desire for the ECR to take over the concern but because of the ECR shareholders' decision, the ESR Directors begged the ECR to help. J.C. Cobbold, the EUR Chairman whose company was already controlled by the ECR, was delegated as an intermediary to convey the request. The ECR Directors, however, refused to contribute towards the construction of the ESR and the local Directors were forced to raise the sum of £600,000, a figure £150,000 in excess of the share capital authorized by the 1854 Act.

The ECR authorities initially had no qualms with Sir Samuel Morton Peto's subscription to the ESR Woodbridge extension, but when in 1856 two newly authorized companies backed by Peto, the Yarmouth & Haddiscoe (Y&H) and the Lowestoft & Beccles Railway (L&B), accepted his proposals to lease them for 21 years at 6 per cent, their suspicions were aroused. At the same time Peto was showing an interest in making a line from Pitsea, on the London Tilbury and Southend Railway, which he already leased, to Colchester from where running powers would be sought over the EUR to Woodbridge. By such means it was possible for a competitive service to run from London to Yarmouth and Lowestoft in direct opposition to the ECR. Fortunately the Pitsea to Colchester line was never constructed, but the process of amalgamating the Y&H and L&B with the ESR in 1856 was the start of grandiose plans. Later Peto revised his terms with the ECR so that the whole line would be leased for 21 years, with 6 per cent paid from 1st July, 1857, whether open to traffic or not, on the undertaking that double track was provided from Yarmouth to Woodbridge, but leaving the Lowestoft to Beccles and Leiston, Snape and Framlingham branches as single lines. The contract for building the railway and branches was duly awarded to Messrs Peto, Brassey and Betts.

At the half-yearly meeting of shareholders held on the last day of February 1857 at the Angel Inn, Halesworth, Berkley, the company Engineer reported that the main line was laid out and construction well advanced. Negotiations had commenced for the acquisition of land for the Framlingham, Snape and Leiston branches. In early June the *Ipswich Journal* reported that between two and three million bricks intended for the construction of various bridges and stations had been landed at Woodbridge Quay. They had been purchased at Harwich and transported round the coast by barge, having originated from brickyards in the environs of London. At the beginning of July 1857, a 'highly finished' locomotive arrived at Halesworth from Birkenhead to be used on ballasting of the main line between Saxmundham and Woodbridge and also the three branch lines.

Sinclair, the ECR Engineer and Locomotive Superintendent, reported on 7th July, 1857 that he had carefully examined plans for the proposed stations on the ESR at Wickham Market or Campsea Ash, Saxmundham and Yoxford and considered them to be 'skilfully laid out and sufficient for traffic'. By August 1857 all cuttings and embankments on the main line were completed and four-fifths of the bridges had been constructed. Nine miles of the formation had been ballasted and eight miles of track laid but no bridges had been constructed on the Snape and Leiston branches, although fencing had been erected.

In September 1857 the *Ipswich Journal* reported that good progress was being made on the main line, and that a pile of bricks was in place near the site of Campsea Ash station waiting for bricklayers to start work. However, on 19th September a correspondent describing himself as 'your obedient servant an idle man' described a walk he had made along the new line from Wissett near Halesworth in a southerly direction and reported a 'stupendous bridge' was still required where the railway was to pass over the turnpike near Saxmundham. On 7th October the *Suffolk Chronicle* reported a journey along the line when a reporter was conveyed in a horse-drawn wagon from Woodbridge to Ufford Bridge. Here there was a break in the line as 'the land required for the railway had only just been purchased'. The journalist then walked the three miles to Campsea Ash where he joined another train, which took him on to Saxmundham. Yet another journey of inspection from Woodbridge to Saxmundham was offered to a select party on 14th October and the *Ipswich Journal* subsequently reported that the bridges were constructed mostly of iron from Richard Garrett's works at Leiston. As before the party travelled in horse-drawn wagons as far as Ufford Bridge, which where they had to walk the three miles to the site of Wickham Market station before boarding a train of carriages and wagons propelled by a locomotive waiting at the crossing just to the north of the proposed location. The permanent way was laid to within 200 yards of Saxmundham station site and once again the participants had to resort to walking, noting that the line crossed Chantry Road on the level, where there was to be a gatekeeper's lodge, and another crossing over Albion Street before the site of Saxmundham station was reached. To the north of this it was noted the large bridge was under construction over the turnpike, consisting of two brick abutments and four heavy cast-iron girders bolted by 1½ inch horizontal iron bolts. Edward Leathes then joined the party and after rejoining the train they were conveyed back to Snape Junction and over the branch to Snape, where at the extremity was a timber bridge of seven openings, each of 20 ft span across the River Alde. The arrival of the first train was 'greeted by an immense concourse of the inhabitants', after which the passengers inspected Newson Garrett's maltings before participating of a 'splendid cold collation' which had been laid on for the party, now exceeding some 200, including many ladies. The day finished with many speeches extolling the construction of the ESR and comparing it with Peto's construction of over 800 miles of railway in Canada.

At the half-yearly meeting of ESR shareholders, chaired by the Earl of Stradbroke, held at the end of February 1858, George Berkley, the Engineer, reported that the main line was nearly completed, whilst rails were laid along the Snape branch. The other branches were not as advanced, but earthworks and bridges on the Framlingham branch were in a forward state, whilst permanent way materials had been delivered to the Leiston line. At the gathering the Directors optimistically announced the main line and branches to Snape Bridge and Leiston would open in July with the Framlingham branch opening in September 1858. Heavy snow across Norfolk and Suffolk in the first weeks of March effectively delayed progress and when the ECR Directors visited the various new works on the ESR on 3rd and 4th June, 1858, construction was far from complete whilst the connecting EUR line from Ipswich was also unfinished. Owen, the Secretary and Robertson, the superintendent of the line accompanied the ECR Directors, and on the first day travelled to Ipswich by the 4.30 pm express from Shoreditch, whence they journeyed by road to Woodbridge. The next morning the party travelled to see the partially-built station at Campsea Ash (Wickham Market) and where the rails were laid before continuing to Snape. At the same time Peto asked the ECR Directors if the company could supply two old carriages so that workmen could be conveyed to site. The request was agreed subject to payment of a small charge and Moseley, the General Manager, was instructed to arrange a choice of vehicles and transfer them as quickly as possible.

By early August the entire line from Halesworth to Woodbridge and the Leiston and Snape branches were completed, whilst the Framlingham branch required a section of line through Parham to be finished. Cornelius Welton, the ESR land agent, reported early opening was not possible, as the Woodbridge to Ipswich section of the EUR was not expected to be ready for traffic until February or March 1859.

With all concentration on the completion of main line and branches, the proposed extension of the Leiston branch had been advancing and on 20th November, 1858 the *Ipswich Journal* had notified the public that the ESR was about to deposit a Bill for the extension of the line from Leiston to Aldeburgh. By January 1859 the standing order had been passed by the House of Lords. The extension was a natural development as for over a decade signs were apparent that the town was attracting an embryonic holiday trade. In 1844 *White's History, Gazetteer and Directory of Suffolk* advised:

Till the commencement of the present century, Aldborough [*sic*], impoverished and depopulated by the encroachments of the ocean, was hastening to decay; but several families of distinction, wishing for greater degree of privacy and retirement than can be enjoyed in a fashionable watering place, having made it their summer residence, its appearance has, since that period, been totally changed. The deep sands which formerly led to it have given place to excellent turnpike roads; and instead of the clay built cottages, which give the place a squalid appearance, are now seen neat and comfortable dwellings, and several large and handsome mansions, which are the occasional retreat of persons of rank and fortune.

In the early months of 1859 rumour and counter-rumour were rife on the opening date for the ESR main line and its branches. On 5th February it was said the line would be opened completely at the beginning of March as station masters and other officials were appointed, but four days later 'Indignant Shareholder' complained to the *Ipswich Journal* that he understood the line was to be open for goods traffic only. By 19th February, 1859 the press prophesied 'much anxiety would be voiced' at the half-yearly meeting to be held at Halesworth on 25th February, as the railway would not open on 1st March, and June and July were the expected dates for opening to passenger traffic. 'Unless something satisfactory was announced', Sir Samuel Morton Peto would 'have to run the gauntlet of fierce determined opposition from shareholders'.

On Friday 25th February, 1859 as a prelude to the meeting, the company through Mr Lockey, the sub-agent of the contractors Peto, Brassey & Betts, arranged with the ECR to run a special train from Woodbridge to take shareholders and other interested parties to Halesworth. The special formed of an engine and 12 first class coaches conveying, amongst others, Sir Samuel Morton Peto and Mr Wagstaff, the company solicitor, departed at 10.00 am, and stopped initially at Campsea Ash station before traversing the Framlingham branch. After returning to the main line, the train made a momentary halt at Snape Junction so that passengers could view the completed goods line before continuing to Saxmundham. After travelling over the branch to Leiston and back the train continued to Halesworth. At the meeting, chaired by the Earl of Stradbroke, the Secretary W. Day announced that the main line and branches were completed and ready for inspection. It was reported that the ESR had cost £450,000 to construct and it was agreed the company extend the Leiston branch to Aldeburgh as soon as possible, and to this end the standing orders had already been passed and an Act was being sought. The expected cost for the 4½ miles extension was £40,000 and Sir Samuel Morton Peto was willing to operate it on the same terms as the remainder of the line. It was hoped the main line and branches line would open for traffic on 13th March. Notice had been given to the Board of Trade, and by 2nd March, 1859 arrangements were made for two heavy locomotives to be available for the inspecting officer's visit the following Thursday. Sinclair, the ECR locomotive superintendent was also delegated to attend. Then on 3rd March the first locomotive to traverse the entire line from Ipswich to Woodbridge hauled a train of wagons loaded with material for the electric telegraph.

Captain H.W. Tyler conducted the Board of Trade (BOT) inspection of the main line between Woodbridge and Yarmouth, together with the branches to Framlingham, Snape and Leiston, on Thursday 7th March, 1859. The inspector noted the permanent way on the Leiston branch was a mixture of double-headed rails as used on the main line and bridge rails of a lighter weight as used on the Framlingham branch. The earthworks were standing well and Tyler, whilst noting there were no bridges between the junction with the main line and Leiston, found one culvert near Saxmundham had lost its original shape and required regular examination. The stations, junctions and signalling arrangements were 'generally perfect', save that the auxiliary signal at Leiston Junction [*sic*] was to be repositioned so that the signalman had means of knowing whether the signal was operational or not. Clocks were to be supplied to all stations and Tyler required the company to furnish him with a certificate advising the method of safe working of the single lines, including the Leiston branch. Because of the incompleteness of works, the opening of the lines offered for inspection was refused. Within days Berkley, working closely with the contractors, arranged for the remedial works to be put in hand.

At a meeting in London on 22nd March, 1859, Sir Samuel Morton Peto agreed he would lease the Aldeburgh line for 21 years and expected the expansion of Aldeburgh would provide enough traffic for the line to pay its way. Eight days later the subject of warehouses at Halesworth and Saxmundham came up for discussion and the ECR Secretary agreed to raise the issue with his ESR counterpart regarding terms of occupancy and rental. The ECR General Manager also reported on his visit to the ESR and his meeting with Sir Samuel Morton Peto, to discuss through passenger and goods rates.

At a special meeting between the Directors of the ECR and ESR on 8th April, 1859, Sir Samuel Morton Peto was handed copies of the proposed timetables and passenger fares lists and noted the goods cartage rates would be available within a few days. It was agreed that ECR staff appointed to the new stations including Saxmundham and Leiston, would take up their duties for the opening on 1st May, 1859. Indeed all men appointed as station masters, clerks, porters and signalmen were taken on Monday 18th March, 1859 to the various stations by Mr Dutton, superintendent of the line, and advised of their future role. Ironically the EUR management refused to let the new staff travel from Ipswich via Woodbridge and they were forced to travel via Norwich and Haddiscoe to get to the ESR. Although the ECR had taken action to staff the ESR stations, matters at Woodbridge were far from satisfactory, forcing the *Ipswich Journal* of 23rd April, 1859 to remark, 'It is now apparent the line will not open at the end of the month'.

Progress on the remedial works were so advanced that on 26th April, 1859 the ECR announced a special train would run the following day to deliver stores and furniture to all branch stations. Behind the scenes, however, many shareholders as well as local traders, and businessmen were highly critical of the delay in opening the line, as almost two months had passed since the BOT inspection. To quell the growing tide of complaints the company took the unusual step of publishing the extract of a letter dated 3rd May from Berkley, the company Engineer, in the *Ipswich Journal*: 'Captain Tyler has today seen the slight alterations he required to be made to some of the signals have been completed. You will be aware that these were made nearly two months since but we waited until he was in the neighbourhood in inspecting the line from Ipswich to Woodbridge before they could conveniently be seen by Captain Tyler'.

Captain H.W. Tyler had indeed re-inspected the East Suffolk main line and branches and in his report of 5th May noted that all the requirements made in his earlier report had been completed. He had received an undertaking signed by the Chairman and Secretary of the company that only One Engine in Steam would be allowed on the single line branches at any one time. Having received this assurance the inspector duly sanctioned the opening of all lines, including the Leiston branch.

# Chapter Two

# Extension to Aldeburgh

The East Suffolk Railway Act 1859, granting the company powers to extend the line from Leiston to Aldeburgh, received the Royal Assent on 19th April, 1859 (22 Vict. cap. xxviii). The statute authorized the construction of a line commencing by a junction with the Leiston branch of the East Suffolk Railway in the parish of Leiston in the county of Suffolk and terminating in the parish of Aldborough [*sic*] in the same county. The railway was permitted to carry not more than two lines of rails over level crossings of public roads Nos. 30 and 32a in the Parish of Leiston, roads Nos. 2, 7 and 15 in the parish of Aldringham-cum-Thorpe and road No. 4 in the parish of Aldeburgh-cum-Hazlewood and Turnpike Road No. 2 in the parish of Leiston. Stations or lodges for crossing keepers were to be provided at all of these crossings. Clause X of the Act stipulated that if so required by the Board of Trade bridges were to be erected in lieu of level crossings.

Two years were allowed for the compulsory purchase of land and three years for the completion of the works. Clause XIV permitted the ESR to raise additional capital of £40,000 in £10 shares, the said sum being in addition to the £620,000 and £360,000 authorized by the 1854 Act, the East Suffolk Railway Companies Amalgamation Act of 1858 and the East Suffolk Railway (Branch and Capital) Act of 1858, and made the aggregate capital £1,020,000. After the whole share issue had been subscribed and one half been paid up, the company could borrow not exceeding £340,000 on mortgage. If the Aldeburgh extension line was not completed and opened for public traffic within the three years period of the passing of the Act it was not lawful for the company or the Directors to pay any dividend to shareholders on the ordinary capital until the extension railway was completed and opened to the public. As the railway was to cross Crown Lands, clause XXVIII required the company to seek the written authority of the Commissioner of Her Majesty's Woods, Forests and Land Revenues before work could commence.

On 27th April, 1859 it was announced that Mr Lipscombe had been contracted to operate the company cartage in Aldeburgh and that the shunting of company cartage at Saxmundham was to be operated by Mr Lincoln at a cost of £1 10s. 0d. per week. Later on 11th May, Lipscombe was granted the contract to operate cartage from Leiston at 2s. 6d. per ton special, 3s. 4d. per ton first and second class, 4s. 2d. per ton third class and 5s. 0d. per ton fourth and fifth class loads. Up to 20 lb. smalls traffic was conveyed at 2d. each consignment and over 20 lb., 3d. each.

Some time elapsed after Captain Tyler's second inspection before the ECR announced that the ESR main line and branches to Framlingham, Snape and Leiston would be opened to traffic on and from Wednesday 1st June, 1859. Unlike the Framlingham line, the Leiston branch opened without ceremony and an initial service of four trains ran in each direction to and from Saxmundham on weekdays, and two each way on Sundays. Leiston station was located at the

ANNO VICESIMO SECUNDO

# VICTORIÆ REGINÆ.

\*\*\*\*\*\*\*\*\*\*\*\*\*\*\*\*\*\*\*\*\*\*\*\*\*\*\*\*\*\*\*\*\*\*\*\*\*\*\*\*\*\*\*\*\*\*\*\*\*\*\*

## *Cap.* xxviii.

An Act to enable the *East Suffolk* Railway Company to extend their Railway to *Aldborough* in the County of *Suffolk;* and for other Purposes. [19th *April* 1859.]

WHEREAS by "The *East Suffolk* Railway Companies Amalgamation Act, 1858," the Undertakings of the *Yarmouth and Haddiscoe* Railway Company and of the *Lowestoft and Beccles* Railway Company were united to and consolidated with the Undertaking of the *East Suffolk* Railway Company (herein-after called "the Company"), and the Share Capitals of those Companies under the Acts therein recited were amalgamated, the Aggregate of such Share Capital being the Sum of Six hundred and twenty thousand Pounds; and the Company were authorized to borrow One Third of their Share Capital; and Provision is made in such Act for the Lease of the amalgamated Undertaking to Sir *Samuel Morton Peto* Baronet, his Executors, Administrators, and Assigns, and for certain Traffic Arrangements with the *Eastern Counties* Railway Company, with the Assent of the *Norfolk* and *Eastern Union* Railway Companies: And whereas by "The *East Suffolk* Railway (Branch and Capital) Act, 1858," the *East Suffolk* Railway Company were empowered to raise, by the Creation of

21 & 22 Vict. c. cxi.

[*Local.*]                    4 *Q*                                        new north-east corner of the town on the road to Theberton at its junction with Buckleswood Road and some 600 yards north of Garrett's works. To coincide with the opening of the railway, the section of Theberton Road in the town was renamed more appropriately Station Road. The standard gauge tramway connecting the branch line to Garrett's Works made an end-on junction with a siding on the south of the line and crossed Station Road by an ungated level crossing and curved south to cross the main road by a gated level crossing before entering the premises by the main gate. It then ran up the yard to serve the foundry and boiler shop.

The ESR Directors held a banquet at Lowestoft on Tuesday 14th June, 1859 to celebrate the opening of the railway. Sir Samuel Morton Peto chaired and conducted the proceedings, which followed the usual meal and complimentary speeches. Amongst those attending were the Earl of Stradbroke, Lord Paget MP, Horatio Love and J.C. Cobbold, respective Chairmen of the ECR and EUR, together with ECR Engineer Robert Sinclair and Peter Bruff, his counterpart on the EUR. Despite opening for traffic, considerable minor works had yet to be completed and on 22nd June, 1859, the ECR authorities agreed to convey all materials required for completion of the lines over their system free of charge. The Leiston branch had been particularly busy for Richard Garrett & Sons provided a miscellany of items for the new railway from their Leiston Works, including lamp posts, ironmongery and general ironworks to the value of £4,300.

In June 1859 a 9-year-old boy named Spalding was apprehended whilst placing stones on the rails on the Leiston branch. He was taken to Mr Doggett, the Saxmundham station master, who locked up the lad for a few hours and then decided not to prosecute because of his 'tender age'. It later transpired that Spalding, a noted felon, had twice tried to derail trains as he was bored by his work as a sheep minder!

On 6th July, 1859 it was decreed that the Leiston branch trains were to use the bay platform at Saxmundham and not the main line platforms. From the opening day all trains from the branch had been required to stop short of the junction signal at Leiston Junction [sic], even if it was cleared, before proceeding to the station. At the same meeting Moseley the General Manager was instructed to arrange for Mr Long's siding at Saxmundham to be shunted by horse to save the cost of locomotive power. The superintendent also reported that men employed by the contractors Peto, Brassey & Betts, were travelling without tickets on the Leiston branch and the ECR Secretary was directed to write to the contractors for them to apply for passes to selected workers only.

The driver of the 5.45 pm train from Yarmouth approaching Saxmundham on 14th July, 1859 was aghast to find his train diverted from the main line on to the siding occupied by the Leiston branch train but was able to apply the brakes and avoid a collision. At the subsequent local enquiry it was established that the points had remained set for the siding after the arrival of the branch train and not been reset for the main line. The ECR Traffic Committee discussed the matter on 20th July and reprimanded station master Doggett for failing to check the position of the points after the arrival of the branch train. It was also agreed to inform Sir Samuel Morton Peto of the type of points used and suggesting a separate line of rails being laid down from the junction to the station thus obviating the local train occupying the main line, a proposition never acted upon. At the meeting on the 20th it was also agreed to allow the Aldeburgh Harbour Pilots to travel on the branch Parliamentary trains and the 3.00 pm train to Leiston on payment of third class fares (as late as 1883 sixteen pilots were registered at Aldeburgh). The lack of telegraph facilities between Saxmundham and Leiston was next on the agenda and on 20th July, 1859 Sir Samuel Morton Peto was asked to finance the installation of the telegraph to all East Suffolk line stations.

The amount of goods traffic worked to and from the Leiston branch so surprised the ECR authorities that on 3rd August, 1859, the superintendent requested the installation of a siding on the up side of the ESR main line at Saxmundham to enable wagons from the branch to be shunted clear of the main line, so as not to delay services. Meanwhile work continued on the construction of the extension beyond Leiston to Aldeburgh and on 29th August, 1859 over 50 tons of materials were worked through from Halesworth to Leiston. Despite the wagons being hauled by Peto's locomotive, the ECR insisted on charging the ESR a 1d. per ton per mile for the privilege of conveyance over their own railway!

At the end of August 1859 both the ECR goods manager and superintendent reported to its Board that cattle pens had not been provided at Leiston and Saxmundham and furthermore buffer stops were required at Saxmundham to prevent wagons running over the ends of sidings and derailing. In fact the superintendent was so exasperated with the ESR that he reported, 'No loading gauges have been erected anywhere!' The matter was immediately raised with the ESR management and on 14th September, 1859 it was recorded that Sir Samuel Morton Peto had ordered cattle pens for installation at Leiston and Saxmundham and that the other outstanding items would receive immediate attention.

Despite the opening of the railway the expected transfer of general freight traffic from road and water to rail failed to materialize because of the exorbitant rates charged by the ECR. The ESR Directors complained and requested a modification of the cartage rates and on 24th September, 1859 it was agreed that charges for the conveyance of grain, oil cake and manure from Saxmundham to Leiston and Darsham be reduced from 3s. 4d. to 2s. 6d. per ton. Parcel rates were to be reduced by 4d. or 6d. depending on destination.

After action by Peto on 28th September, 1859 authority was given for the electric telegraph to be installed along the branch from Saxmundham to Leiston, the charge payable to the ECR being 3s. per week increasing to 8s. per week, whilst on the main line it was 6s. increasing to 18s. per week. At a meeting on the same day the ECR Way & Works Committee agreed to the urgent repairs to sub-standard trackwork in Saxmundham goods yard.

By 12th October, 1859 the ESR main line was open for traffic night and day, and especially at night for the passage of fish trains from Yarmouth and Lowestoft, and the ECR superintendent reported that it was an urgent requirement to employ extra station staff so that the full benefit of the scheme could be realized. The ESR management readily agreed to the provision of the manpower. Continuous heavy rain later in the month on 31st October, 1859 caused flooding of the line between Saxmundham and Leiston and two trains were cancelled before the water subsided and the service was restored.

Since the opening of the line most of the branch services were worked by tender locomotives and footplate crews constantly complained of the necessity to work trains tender first in one direction. Evidently a turnplate was available at Leiston but with the onset of winter the superintendent, on 9th November, 1859, requested the provision of a turntable at Saxmundham, so that tender-first running could be totally eliminated but no such facility was ever installed. On 7th December, 1859 the ESR announced that the insurance for Saxmundham station buildings was £1,450, which was considered an exorbitant sum. It was agreed to appeal against the rating.

With the introduction of the electric telegraph, on 28th January, 1860 the Directors agreed to the public sending telegrams from stations on the branch. In the same month the National Lifeboat Institute advised the ECR that a new lifeboat had been built for service at the Thorpeness station and asked if the railway company would convey the vessel from London to Leiston. The Directors intimated on 15th February, 1860 that they were happy to convey the vessel for half the usual goods rate. In August 1862 the company conveyed a lifeboat to Wells free of charge!

On 29th February, 1860 it was reported that the parish rates payable by the ESR for the Saxmundham parish had been reduced to £25 per mile per annum. The following month the ECR superintendent required the ESR to complete sundry repairs to the goods yard at Saxmundham after reports of poor track drainage and cart roads full of potholes.

Work on the Aldeburgh extension progressed rapidly despite adverse winter weather and on 3rd March, 1860 the *Ipswich Journal* reported 'with great pleasure' that 'the Aldeburgh branch line is now complete', and would 'open for traffic as soon as the manager thinks proper'. Sir Samuel Morton Peto and other railway officers had recently visited the line and Peto's plant had been used to construct the 2½ mile road extension to the Esplanande at the same time as the branch. The *Ipswich Journal* added 'this will be a great improvement to the town as from the path a view will be obtained of trains passing and re-passing, and likewise extensive views of the German Ocean with steamers and vessels sailing to all parts of the world'. The terminal station was 'substantially built in white brick and covered with a glass roof. It is one of the best on the East Suffolk line, the grounds are tastefully laid out and planted with trees and shrubs with beautiful gravel walks'.

Captain H.W. Tyler conducted the Board of Trade inspection of the extension on 6th April, 1860. He found the railway presented for examination was a single line, four miles in length, extending from the present station at Leiston to the town of Aldeburgh. The inspector after examining the permanent way referred to his report of 7th March, 1859 on the original section of the branch; although the sharpest curve was of 40 chains radius he required the additional installation of iron spikes in addition to wooden trenails to help stabilize the rails on the curves, as a precaution against a derailment. He found three bridges had been provided on the section of line, all constructed of cast-iron girders on masonry abutments. The largest had a span of 24 ft 4 in. and the other two spans were of 12 ft each. Tyler noted the largest girders were of similar dimensions as those used for spans on the East Suffolk main line and 'are hardly so strong by calculation as I would wish to see'. Although they were very stiff under test the inspector had 'every confidence in them as other works on the line'. The two level crossings returned in details furnished by the company were those of parish roads not authorized by the Parliamentary Act, the former at 1 mile 18 chains from Leiston was a public road 'or rather a track' which had been diverted in order that it did not cross the railway as provided for in the Parliamentary plans. An occupational crossing had been added at 2 miles 51 chains from Leiston for the use of Crown Lands, through which the line passed, on a part of the railway which deviated from the line originally laid down. Not far from the same spot was a two chains deviation outside the Parliamentary plans in consequence of an inaccuracy in the original plans. The crossing provided at this point combined the two crossings authorized by Parliament, one on either side of it into one and the 'result is advantageous'. At the terminal station Tyler considered that one corner of the goods shed had been placed too near to the siding, which ran past it. Although it did not affect the safety of the travelling public it caused a risk to the company's servants and the Engineer agreed to make urgent alterations to obviate the problem. After receiving the undertaking that the line would be worked by one engine in steam at any one time Captain Tyler agreed to the line opening for traffic 'without danger to the public'.

On 11th April, 1860 it was reported that the contractor had rented the ballast pit at Aldeburgh from the Lord of the Manor at £10 per annum as the ballast had been suitable for ballasting the railway. Sinclair was asked to report back to the ECR Directors if he found any cause for complaint but none was forthcoming.

It was also announced on 11th April that the line to Aldeburgh would be ready for opening on 12th April, 1860, using the one engine in steam method of working. Both the *Ipswich Journal* and *Suffolk Chronicle* reported the opening on Thursday 12th April, the latter commenting that Captain Tyler's inspection had been so favourable that authority to open had been granted immediately. A service of four trains in each direction on weekdays and two each way on Sundays was provided with connections at Saxmundham to and from Ipswich and Yarmouth and Lowestoft. It was also reported that Newson Garrett had financed the development of a 35 acre housing scheme at Aldeburgh, the estate being designed by Peter Bruff, Engineer of the EUR. The extension to Aldeburgh bisected Station Road by a gated level crossing immediately east of Leiston station and curved round the north flank of the town passing over Valley Road by a girder bridge before crossing open land to the terminus.

Thorpeness fishermen wishing to take advantage of the new railway had approached the ECR in April 1860 requesting that Aldeburgh branch trains stop at Thorpeness gate crossing house to enable inhabitants of the area to use the service and load fish traffic and offload empty boxes. After due discussion the application was refused by the superintendent on 25th April, as it was thought the amount of traffic would not justify the cost of stopping and starting the services there. However, the local rifle corps obtained the concession to pay military fares when attending shooting practice at Aldeburgh. On the same day authority was given for a shunting horse to be allocated to Leiston as the rapid increase in traffic had resulted in the branch engine being unable to complete shunting duties between haulage of the normal train services. Mr Lipscombe announced he was willing to operate the Aldeburgh goods and parcels road service but toll gate charges of 2d. for a single horse and cart were an obstacle and the ESR was to be asked to provide another entrance at Aldeburgh.

In May 1860 the service on the Aldeburgh branch was increased to five trains each way on weekdays but complaints were made that the additional services provided no connection at the junction for onward services on the main line. On an unspecified day in the same month station master Doggett of Saxmundham purchased a ticket to Manningtree but travelled on to London. When the train arrived at Stratford a ticket inspector checked the train and Doggett claimed he had only travelled from Ilford and purchased an excess ticket from there on to London. Unbeknown to him his movements had been monitored and his future career was in question when he was suspended from duty. In the meantime station master Grover of Needham Market was instructed on 23rd May to transfer to Saxmundham with an increase of £20 in annual salary to a new salary of £90 per annum. On 6th June Doggett resigned from the ECR before he was summarily dismissed for 'fare swindle and fraudulent travel'. In the meantime the Earl of Stradbroke suggested that from 1st June, 1860 all traffic receipts were to go to Railway Clearing House for clearance - a suggestion agreed by both the ESR and ECR Directors.

The effects of the railway on the town were soon noted and elaborately reported by the local press. 'During the week the trains have been pouring in company from all parts of the kingdom, every train being laden with excursionists who appeared to enjoy a day by the sea'. As a special train was departing from Saxmundham on 4th July, 1860 one of the carriages was derailed by persons unknown who interfered with the points as the vehicle was passing over them. The ECR subsequently offered a £10 reward for information leading to the prosecution of the culprit. In the meantime on 21st June, 1860 Sinclair, the ECR Engineer, reported that he had visited the East Suffolk line and inspected the surplus land and warehouses. The major lessee appeared to be Newson Garrett with a monopoly holding at the smaller stations. Despite objections to the arrangements at some stations on the main line, there was no objection to the lease of the goods shed at Aldeburgh and the partial lease of the shed at Leiston and a copy of the findings was sent to Sir Samuel Morton Peto. It was agreed on 18th July, 1860 that surplus land at Thorpeness could be leased to interested parties. Along the line at Leiston the former engine shed and associated sidings, which had been superseded by the opening of the locomotive shed at Aldeburgh, had also been declared surplus together with surrounding land. It was agreed to release the land for sale but the ECR wished to retain the former engine shed and sidings. Then on 1st August application was made for an extension to the station sidings at Leiston on land owned by Garrett's. Alterations were also required to the carriage dock at Leiston and both matters were put to Sir Samuel Morton Peto as Chairman of the ESR for a decision.

During his inspection of the ESR in June 1860, Sinclair registered that the granary at Saxmundham was to be declared surplus to requirements and was to be surrendered. However, before any action could be taken Garrett claimed that he owned the granary located opposite the booking office at the junction station, and on a tour of inspection, which included the ESR line on 10th October 1860, the ECR Chairman visited the site with Garrett and after a mutual meeting asked the ECR Secretary to ascertain with the ESR the exact legal agreement regarding the building and its usage.

The superintendent advised the Way & Works Committee on 12th September, 1860 of the difficulty experienced recruiting porters at Leiston as Garrett's workpeople were occupying all available housing. The General Manager was instructed to write to Sir Samuel Morton Peto asking if the ESR Company would erect four cottages for railway staff at the station. After a spate of complaints regarding the mis-management of Aldeburgh station it was agreed on 10th October, 1860 that station master Stubbins was to be dismissed. The new incumbent was, however, far from happy and complained of the condition of the station house where lighting was by oil lamps. On 5th December, 1860 it was agreed that a gas supply would be installed.

At the beginning of December 1860, Newson Garrett requested the provision of a siding commencing from the terminus at Aldeburgh across the turnpike road into a field in his ownership so that building materials for the new housing development could be delivered by rail. After Sinclair had reported on the scheme the ECR authorities agreed to construct the siding, subject to Garrett paying the full costs, and also provided the connection was made to the satisfaction of the ESR engineer. The ECR Directors whilst agreeing to the proposals added a rider on 19th December that 'their trucks would be allowed to pass on the said siding in such a manner as they may direct'. Authority was finally given on 24th April, 1861 at a cost of £30, the work to be allowed to proceed once the money had been received. House passes were however declined. Earlier in February a horse belonging to a Mr Lincoln accessed the railway near Saxmundham through a gate, which had inadvertently been left open by persons unknown, and was run down and killed by a train. On 27th February, 1861 the company summarily dismissed a claim for £30 submitted for compensation.

The Way & Works Committee was advised on 24th April, 1861 that Garrett's had hired teamed horses to move heavy equipment from Leiston station yard to their premises, the cost to 31st December, 1860 being £21 14s. 7d. The ECR proportion of receipts received from the Railway Clearing House for conveyance of the traffic was £90 2s. 2d. The General Manager was asked to investigate whether ECR locomotives could perform the task but discovered the connecting line was a tramway with a 1 in 38 gradient leading from the railway to the works and no suitable locomotive with lightweight axle loading or clearance was available.

In May 1861 Gibbons, the timber merchants of Ipswich, who as well as dealing with local commodities imported supplies from the continent, held a timber sale in the goods yard at Saxmundham paying a rental of £1 for the day. Then on 22nd May, 1861 the goods manager announced that the rate for the conveyance of oranges from London to Leiston would be reduced to £1 2s. 6d. per ton.

Soon after the opening of the line to Leiston the telegraph had been installed from Saxmundham to Leiston, but the superintendent reported the lack of the facility to Aldeburgh caused problems when there was any alteration to train services as station staff at the terminal had no knowledge of any changes. Authority was duly given on 5th June, 1861 for the Electric Telegraph Co. to extend the telegraph along the branch from Leiston to Aldeburgh, the weekly cost of 3s. 0d. being paid to the ECR.

The opening of the railway was supposed to have attracted the conveyance of all but the most local traffic to the branch but on 5th June, 1861 the goods manager reported that much of the traffic from Ipswich to Saxmundham, Leiston and Aldeburgh was going by road, despite the longer journey times. After complaints by traders and farmers and further investigation it was evident that the rail conveyance charges were still considered abnormally expensive and so the Directors decreed the rates were to be lowered to obviate further loss of revenue.

For some time the lack of lock-up facilities for small packages and parcels at Saxmundham had caused inconvenience when the items had to be stored awaiting collection in the goods office or the station booking office. The matter was raised at the Way & Works Committee meeting on both 3rd and 31st July, 1861, when it was resolved that the goods shed was to have a corner lock-up but the ECR insisted the ESR should finance the provision of the building. The provision of the facility was confirmed on 31st July.

The annual Aldeburgh Regatta for 1861 was to be held on 29th July and the organizers duly requested a donation from the ESR and ECR for the event. An application was also made for additional trains to run on the day to convey the expected additional visitors to the town. Rather tersely on 17th July both requests were refused, the ECR voicing the objection for both companies, saying they considered the present facilities were adequate, yet £3 subscription had been donated to the regatta at Wells! The company officials also reported disagreement with Mr Roper at Saxmundham regarding the shunting of wagons to and from his siding. On 14th August the ECR superintendent insisted that any wagons shunted for Roper would be charged at 6d. per wagon.

Serious delays occurred to train services on 30th August, 1861 when the pin holding the locomotive connecting rod fractured as a train was leaving Saxmundham. The connecting rod subsequently fell to the ballast and almost derailed the engine as it dug into the subsoil. Fortunately the train was brought to a halt without incurring any further damage to the permanent way and no staff or passengers reported injuries. The matter was reported to the BOT and on 25th September, 1861, Sinclair was instructed to submit a report on the incident. In the autumn of 1861 Richard Garrett, who resided at Carlton Hall, near Saxmundham, made several approaches to both the ESR and ECR management asking permission to plant conifer trees on surplus land bordering the railway close to his parkland. The matter was finally raised at a Board meeting on 15th January, 1862 and full permission granted subject to the usual provisos.

Early in May 1862 it was learned that Newson Garrett at both Snape and Aldeburgh, and to a lesser extent Richard Garrett at Leiston, were sending grain in ECR sacks by sea. The matter was brought before the ECR Traffic Committee at their meeting on 21st May when it was resolved that ECR sacks could in future only be filled by farmers at stations and forwarded to their destination by rail. Both Garrett brothers were informed of the ruling and asked to return sacks to the railway company. On the same day an application by Garrett for alterations to coal traffic sidings at Leiston was approved subject to Garrett paying the full cost estimated at £40. Earlier in the month on 5th May, 1862 the ECR Board were advised that surplus land at Saxmundham had been sold to Mr Cobbold without the sanction of the Joint Committee. After investigation it was revealed on 27th May, 1862 that the ground opposite Saxmundham station had been sold to Cobbold where he intended to build a restaurant. The matter was referred to the ESR Board and by 18th June Wagstaff of the legal department was investigating further, but before any action could be taken restructuring of railway affairs in East Suffolk overtook events.

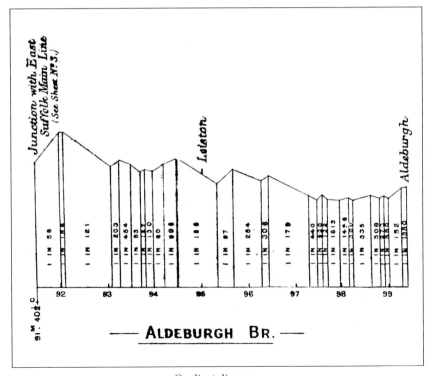

Gradient diagram.

# Chapter Three

# Great Eastern Operation

Having leased or taken over the working of all major railways in East Anglia the ECR was the principal party to a scheme being prepared for the amalgamation of the Eastern Counties, Eastern Union, East Anglian, Newmarket and Norfolk railways into a new undertaking to be known as the Great Eastern Railway. The Act sanctioning the amalgamation - the Great Eastern Railway Act 1862 (25 and 26 Vict. cap. ccxxiii) received the Royal Assent on 7th August, 1862 but took effect retrospectively from July of that year.

With ECR officers taking over the leading positions in the new organization few initial changes were made to Aldeburgh branch services. As a result of the takeover, ESR proprietors were awarded £340,000 in GER 4 per cent debentures and £335,000 in 4½ per cent preference shares, as well as ordinary shares to the value deemed appropriate in future revenue expectations by Captain Galton of the Board of Trade. In return the GER was indemnified against £86,488 contract debt and other liabilities of the company. As a gesture of goodwill, on 20th August, 1862 the new management agreed to donate £5 to the Aldeburgh Regatta Committee probably knowing the success of the event would encourage more to travel by train.

On 25th November, 1863 it was reported that a Mr Barnes had offered to release free of charge a strip of land 13 ft wide to convert an existing footpath to Saxmundham station into a carriage road. The gesture was made provided the GER gave him a building frontage to the carriage road and a triangular piece of land containing 10 rods next to Albion Street, the road from Rendham. The matter was passed to Sinclair for a decision and as the Engineer thought the scheme advantageous to the company the transaction was sanctioned.

Since the opening of the line through to Aldeburgh local factions were keen to extend the railway to the sea front and quayside hoping the connection would generate further traffic and enhance the reputation of the town. The GER management had no interest in the scheme but expressed no objections provided the works did not interfere with the existing railway, its facilities and infrastructure. The company also agreed to work traffic over the new line. The Aldborough Pier and Railway Act (27 and 28 Vict. cap. cccxxvi) subsequently received the Royal Assent on 29th July, 1864 and authorized the construction of

1.  A railway situate in the Parish of Aldborough commencing by a junction with the Aldborough branch of the Great Eastern Railway at or near the termination thereof, and terminating on the shore of the German Ocean at the southern end of the town of Aldborough.
2.  A railway situate wholly in the Parish of Aldborough commencing by a junction with the last mentioned intended railway at or near Marsh Lane, and terminating at or near Hunt's Shipyard in Slaughden.
3   A pier or jetty commencing by a junction with the first mentioned intended railway in the said Parish Of Aldborough in the County of Suffolk and extending seawards in an easterly direction for a distance of five hundred and twenty feet or

thereabouts, provided nonetheless that the said pier or jetty beyond the distance of one hundred yards from the high water mark at Spring Tides shall not be a solid embankment or pier, but an openwork viaduct, with or without a floating pier or landing stage.

Clause 22 of the statute permitted the company to cross road No. 2 in the parish of Aldborough by a level crossing and in addition required them to make and maintain within 150 yds southwards from the road, a road under the railway with the arch over the road not less than 20 ft span and 13 ft in height. The railway was also to cross public road No. 63 in the parish of Aldborough by a bridge having a 25 ft span and 11 ft in height. Within a distance of 110 yds east of the road bridge the railway was permitted to cross another road by level crossing.

Three years were allowed for the compulsory purchase of the land and five years for the completion of works. Clause 28 stipulated the limits of the pier and the space lying between the pier and the shore, and a line running parallel with the pier at a distance 300 yds from the north side of the pier, and a straight line drawn due north and south at a distance of 300 yds from the east end of the pier, and a line running parallel with the first mentioned line at a distance 300 yds from the south side of the pier. Clause 46 permitted the company to enter into a working agreement with the GER for working the pier and jetty and railway; the conveyance of part or all traffic, the division or apportionment of rates and tariffs, the supply of rolling stock, the management maintenance and repair of pier or jetty or railway and cost apportioned thereto. If such action was taken clause 47 stipulated that the railway and GER would be considered as one railway for rates and tariffs.

To finance construction the company was authorized to raise £20,000 in £10 shares and to borrow £6,666 when the whole capital had been subscribed and half actually paid up. The first Directors of the Alborough Pier & Railway Co. were Gerrard Thomas Worthington Ferrand, Newson Garrett, Frederick Nash, Lieutenant Colonel Arthur J. Bethell Thelluson and the Reverend William Tate, the latter the writer of the hymn, *If he shall hold no Cure of Souls*. The Engineer was Peter Schuyler Bruff, Engineer of the Eastern Union Railway, the Tendring Hundred Railway and surveyor to the Bury St Edmunds & Thetford Railway. A model of a proposed harbour refuge at Aldeburgh to his design was shown at the Great Exhibition in 1851, although the Bill seeking authorization failed because of the intended methods of administration and finance. The scheme brought Bruff into contact with Newson Garrett and the two were involved with this and other land development schemes in the town. In 1860 Bruff's eldest daughter Elizabeth married Garrett's son, Lieutenant Newson Garrett of the Bengal Artillery.

The original concept of Saxmundham as a simple wayside station with little siding accommodation showed considerable lack of forethought especially as the branch from Leiston quickly generated goods traffic to and from Garrett's, and then fish and agricultural traffic to and from Aldeburgh. The railway company was totally embarrassed as complaints of delay multiplied when wagons were sent to other stations waiting accommodation at Saxmundham before transfer to the branch. Sinclair was asked to investigate and obviate the problem and on 14th June, 1865 duly submitted proposals for additional sidings at an estimated cost of £1,456.

At the end of July 1865 Newson Garrett wrote to the GER Board stating that the corporation of Aldeburgh had thoughts of establishing a market in the town three days a week, for the sale of meat, poultry and fish and asked if the GER would carry passengers from local stations at single fare for the return journey. The matter was raised on 2nd August but a fortnight later the General Manager replied that the Directors were unable to grant the issue of market tickets at such cheap rates. Despite the apparent reluctance to attract additional traffic *Measom's Guide to the Great Eastern Railway* for 1865 extolled the virtues of Aldeburgh as a fashionable seaside resort reporting, 'The Great Eastern Railway branch line is rapidly improving the town, and from the salubrity of the air, and the convenience of the shore for sea-bathing, it has lately become a fashionable resort during the summer'.

In the spring of 1866 an offer was received from a Mr Crampion to purchase a strip of land totalling an area of 5½ perches forming a slope between a public road at the side of proposed almshouses at Saxmundham. The subject was raised at the Traffic Committee meeting on 9th May when Davis, the Engineer, said that the GER had the expense of maintaining and fencing the plot. He considered the land of no operational value to the company and as it had cost the company £400 per acre the plot could be released to Crampion for £14. The prospective purchaser was, however, only offering £2 and the matter was passed to the General Manager to resolve. The land was finally released for an undisclosed sum after further negotiation.

In the early weeks of 1868 the Land Agent reported that Messrs Cowell & Son, who were constructing a new road connecting Mill Lane to Albion Street, Saxmundham, had asked the Engineer whether the 20 ft width of the thoroughfare was satisfactory to the GER authorities. The matter was raised at a meeting of the Traffic Committee on 22nd April, when the Land Agent reminded the members that the meeting of 9th December, 1863 had decided that the width should be 25 ft but the recent erection of the police station had now rendered this impossible. Messrs Cowell & Son had agreed to the other stipulated terms and to the purchase of a small triangular strip of GER land for £15. If the Directors agreed to the alteration in width of the road Cowell would undertake to dedicate it to public use. The Directors agreed to the proposal on the undertaking that the road was built to a width of 25 ft where possible and on 30th July, 1868 the GER leased a portion of land to accommodate the wider thoroughfare, which later became Alma Place.

A proposal to reduce the number of staff working on the Aldeburgh branch, made after investigation by Mr Blood on 10th November, 1869, had still not been resolved by 8th December and the Deputy Chairman, General Manager and superintendent were instructed to liaise on the matter. The superintendent reported to the Traffic Committee on 22nd December that he did not think 'the business of the branch' could be 'properly conducted in the way suggested by Mr Blood' and the matter was dropped. In the same year it was noted the Aldborough Pier & Railway Co. had at last commenced preliminary work on the pier extension.

In early May 1870 a Mr Last of Aldeburgh requested the provision of a tramway to serve his proposed brickworks near Saxmundham Junction. The Engineer, having surveyed the site, estimated costs at £100 on Mr Last's land and £115 on GER land. The matter was raised at a meeting of the Way and Works Committee on 25th May when both the goods manager and superintendent objected to the scheme, as the provision of the siding would inconvenience traffic regulation with untold interference to train services, for little return of revenue. Last appealed but the scheme was again rejected on 6th July, 1870. In the meantime Richard Garrett had approached the GER with an offer to provide red bricks to the company at a cost of £1 6s. 0d. per 1,000 bricks from his Leiston brickworks. The offer was considered at the Way & Works Committee meeting on 20th July, 1870 when the members agreed that the district engineer could order supplies for local jobs but that a general contract would not be issued.

A decade after first conveying possibly the most unusual item of freight across the branch, the Secretary of the Royal National Lifeboat Institution wrote to the Directors on 11th October, 1870 stating that the Thorpeness lifeboat now required extensive repairs and had been ordered back to the builder's yard in London. He enquired if the GER would convey the boat to save the long journey along the coast mounted on another vessel. The Directors made it clear the following day that the railway company was 'most willing to accept the carriage of the vessel and for its safe return to Thorpeness', although there was no mention of the cost of conveyance.

The Directors, possibly concerned that some of Garrett's traffic was still being sent by sea from Slaughden Quay, asked the goods manager to provide details of traffic passing to and from the establishment at Leiston over the GER for the period 1st January to 30th September, 1870. The Board was evidently satisfied with the figures which showed reasonable returns:

| | Trucks | Miles | Earnings | Average per truck | Average per mile |
|---|---|---|---|---|---|
| | | | £  s.  d. | £  s.  d. | d. |
| To all GER stations except London | 825 | 35,517 | 794 9  2 | 19  3 | 5½ |
| To London | 478 | | 574 8  6 | 1  4  0¼ | 3 |

During 1870 the Privy Council raised the subject of water supplies for cattle in transit on railways and in August of that year the GER authorities requested a Dr Williams to advise on essential watering places. By 15th March, 1871 a number of sites had been earmarked and among these it was felt that the increase in traffic generated at Saxmundham, or interchanging to and from the Aldeburgh branch, necessitated a water supply for animals in transit at the junction. On 27th April, 1871 the Way & Works Committee sanctioned a sum of £27 for the provision of water supplies at Saxmundham. Further expenditure was agreed on 22nd May, 1871, after months of complaining by the station master at Aldeburgh, to carry out extensive alterations to the station house at a cost of £20. The work included the existing porters' room being converted into a kitchen, the cellar into the new porters' room and the existing kitchen into an additional bedroom.

Although some work on the extension of the 1½ mile line from Aldeburgh station to the pier authorized by the 1864 Act had been made, including the construction of an embankment, little else was achieved and alterations were required. On 19th January, 1871 the GER Board had been advised that Peter Bruff's revised Bill for Aldeburgh Harbour was to be presented to Parliament and, after due enquiries, a month later on 16th February the decision was made not to support the scheme. However, by 27th April, 1871 the Bill had been passed and the Aldborough Railway Act 1871 duly received the Royal Assent on 13th July, 1871 (35 Vict. cap. cxvii) authorizing the company to fully abandon the scheme authorized in the 1864 Act. The capital authorized in that Act was transferred to the new Act to finance the construction of

1. A railway or tramway, about six furlongs and five chains in length, commencing by a junction with the Aldborough branch of the Great Eastern Railway at the southern end of the passenger station at Aldborough and terminating at the southern end of the town of Aldborough, at the western side of the public road No 63, about 45 yards southwards of the southern extremity of the Ropery Yard, number 62 on the plan referred to in the Aldbrough Pier and Railway Act 1864.

2. A railway or tramway, three furlongs and about eight chains in length, commencing by a junction with the intended railway or tramway No. 1, at a or near a point on the driftway leading towards the River Alde, number 82 on the last mentioned plan, and about one hundred and sixty yards southwards of the junction of such driftway with the Town Marsh and Gasworks Road, and terminating at or near the southeastern corner of Hunt's Shipyard at Slaughden.

Three years were allowed for the compulsory purchase of land and five years for the completion of works. The statute authorized the company to cross on the level public roads Nos. 2, 3 and 4 in the parish of Aldborough on railway No 1 and road No. 99 in parish of Aldborough on railway No. 2. Within 150 yds southward of road No. 2 the company was to make and maintain an arch over a new road, the arch to be not less than 25 ft span and 13 ft in height. By clause 18 the company was empowered to enter into agreement with the GER on similar terms to those empowered in the 1864 Act.

In the meantime in the summer of 1871 considerable difficulty was experienced with the water supply to Leiston station and on 30th August the Way & Works Committee were advised a new water pump was required at a cost of £12. The matter was deferred until the meeting of 25th October when the General Manager was asked to arrange a replacement.

Mr Wentworth, the owner of considerable acreage of land bordering the line between Aldeburgh and Leiston made application in the autumn of 1871 to move an existing occupational crossing to assist with the improvement of drainage in the low lying land. The matter was discussed by the Way & Works Committee on 8th November and passed to the Land Agent for his comments. On 22nd November the agent reported the works would ultimately be advantageous to the GER and the scheme was approved, providing Wentworth financed all the works and completed the installation to the satisfaction of the railway engineer.

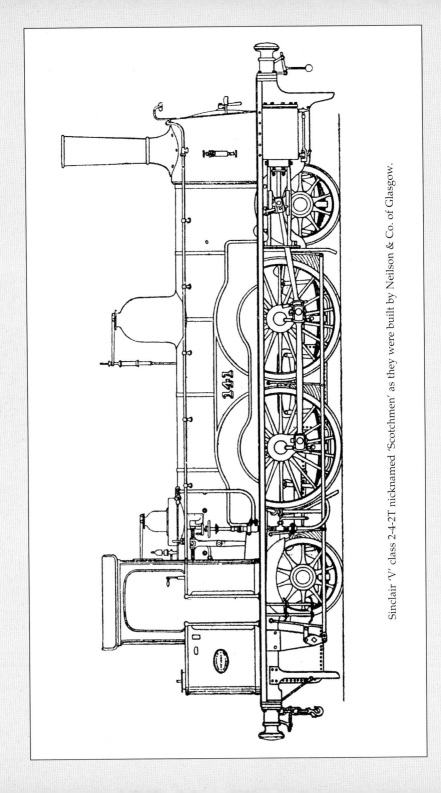

Sinclair 'V' class 2-4-2T nicknamed 'Scotchmen' as they were built by Neilson & Co. of Glasgow.

In the spring of 1871 Sinclair 'V' class 2-4-2T No. 146 working an up branch train collided with 'Y' class 2-4-0 goods locomotive No. 339 at Saxmundham causing temporary blockage of the line and damage to both engines. Fortunately the collision was at low speed and passengers were only shaken. Then in the autumn of 1871 the traffic superintendent urged the installation of the block telegraph on the East Suffolk line between Ipswich and Saxmundham to obviate pathing problems with express services, and branch trains especially to Aldeburgh, which were delayed by slower Parliamentary trains. The GER Traffic Committee raised the subject at their meeting on 12th March, 1872 when it was estimated that the cost of Tyer's telegraph, provision of new signal boxes and signals, including installations at Saxmundham and Saxmundham Junction, would be £3,800. The improved arrangements would involve additional costs of wages to signalmen, estimated at £8 per week or £400 per annum. The matter was placed in abeyance for further investigation.

Meanwhile at 7.45 pm on the evening of 3rd February, 1872 a special ballast train en route from Lowestoft to Stratford collided with the empty coaching stock of the Aldeburgh branch train, which was standing in the up platform at Saxmundham. As a result of the impact two passenger carriages and a brake van of the branch train and a coal wagon were derailed forcing a goods engine, standing on the adjacent down main line, off the rails. The branch train vehicles were considerably damaged, as were the level crossing gates which were demolished, the coaching stock being pushed through the barriers, as they were open for road traffic at the time. Fortunately no persons were injured and at the subsequent inquiry it was found that the ballast train was approaching the station at an excessive speed with the driver unable to stop his train before impact. Johnson, the locomotive superintendent, subsequently discharged the driver from GER employment. Then on 14th February, 1872, the GER law clerk was instructed to take all necessary steps to safeguard the rights of the GER when it was announced that the road from Saxmundham market place to the station was to be dedicated to parish use.

Passengers waiting the departure of the 6.35 am Aldeburgh to Saxmundham train on 18th March, 1872 became increasingly frustrated as the minutes passed and no locomotive appeared on the front of the coaching stock, despite clouds of dirty smoke wafting across the line from the direction of the engine shed. The train subsequently departed 1 hour and 40 minutes late, as the footplate crew had experienced difficulty raising steam on the engine! After an internal enquiry into the incident fireman Pheby was dismissed the service for gross negligence and the driver severely reprimanded. Pheby later sought reinstatement but on 7th May, 1872 the decision was upheld.

Many of the stations on the East Suffolk line were remote from the nearest habitation, although the same could not be said of Leiston, but following a spate of burglaries the GER Board on 4th June, 1872 authorized the provision of a new iron safe for Leiston booking office to obviate further possible incidents. Along the line at Saxmundham gas prices were increased again by 10d. per 1,000 cu. ft on 10th September, whilst prices increased from 6s. 8d. to 7s. 6d. per 1,000 cu. ft on 5th November. The price remained the same in March 1874 when the annual cost of gas supplies for the year 1873 was registered at £35 5s. 0d.

The Traffic Committee was advised on 5th November, 1872 that the revised figures for the installation of Tyer's train telegraph between Ipswich and Saxmundham, together with signal boxes, had reduced to £800. At the same meeting the superintendent was asked to report on wages cost and on 19th November advised that the cost of manpower would still amount to £400 per annum. The matter was then deferred pending further investigation but was finally sanctioned on 26th February, 1873.

Revenue protection on the branch left much to be desired for on 18th December 1872 the audit clerk presented a memorandum to the Traffic Committee to the effect that from mid-September until mid-November 1872 no less than 80 passengers had arrived at Aldeburgh station without valid tickets for travel, and were charged the fare from Saxmundham. It was suggested the tickets be examined before departure of the branch train from Saxmundham but the superintendent was of the opinion such action would lead to delay to branch services and result in passenger dissatisfaction. The superintendent was duly instructed to make arrangements for additional ticket checks to obviate loss of revenue, and subsequently a ticket platform was erected on the approach to Aldeburgh station so that guards and examining staff could examine and collect passenger tickets before the train pulled into the station platform. The ticket platform also proved to be an operational nuisance but remained *in situ*, little used, for over a decade before removal.

On 5th July, 1873, as the 11.50 am mixed train from Aldeburgh to Saxmundham was approaching Saxmundham Junction, the engine, wagons and two wheels of the brake van were derailed. The damage to the engine and wagons was slight but 40 yards of permanent way required relaying. The passenger vehicles at the rear of the train remained on the track and no passengers were injured. The inquiry found that the signalman had failed to lock certain points after the passing of the last down train and he was subsequently suspended from duty for his misdemeanour. The BOT, after being advised of the incident and studying the findings of the local inquiry, subsequently advised the Directors that the interlocking of the points and signals at the junction would have prevented the occurrence.

Gas prices at Leiston station were fixed at 8s. 4d. per 1,000 cu. ft on 25th March, 1874 with an estimated annual cost of £14 10s. 0d. On the following 24th April, Richard Garrett applied to plant a line of fir trees alongside the railway and the GER Directors agreed to this subject to a levy of 1s. 0d. per annum. Relationships, however, were not always amicable for on 22nd April it was reported that Garrett's granary at Saxmundham, built on GER land, had been sold. The law clerk was asked to review the outstanding rent and press for early payment and on 1st July it was agreed Garrett would be given six months' notice to remove all belongings from the site with effect from 1st May, 1875. Garrett was duly advised but the notice to quit was returned with complaints of incivility on the part of the railway company servants. The subject was raised at the Way & Works Committee meeting on 9th September, 1874 when the law clerk was instructed to serve another notice but with a GER Board apology for the method of service on the earlier notice. No doubt the apology was made because the railway company valued Garrett's trade.

As the formation of main line trains lengthened so services incurred considerable delay because of the short platforms at Saxmundham. Much time was spent allowing passengers in the front part of the train to alight before the train pulled up so that passengers in the rear part could also alight or join for their onward journey. The major difficulty was incurred by down trains where the platform was wedged between Albion Street and Chantry Road level crossings, which abutted to the north and south of the platform. The extended time spent at the station not only exasperated the operating authorities but annoyed road users when the crossing gates were closed across the thoroughfare for an excessive period of time. After investigation the GER authorities authorized the lengthening of the down side platform across and to the south of Chantry Road, together with alterations to the level crossing gates at a cost of £140 on 30th September, 1874; the work was completed in the spring of 1875, but without work on the gates.

On 6th January, 1875 Mr Balls of Friston was killed in a shunting accident at Saxmundham whilst unloading a railway truck, although the railway company was absolved from blame. By 24th February, 1875 the price of gas at Saxmundham was fixed at 6s. 8d. per 1,000 cu. ft whilst on the same day Garrett's agreed to provide gas to Leiston station at a reduced price of 7s. 6d. per 1,000 cu. ft and on 5th May it was reported that gas costs for 1874 were £14 14s. 0d.

The GER goods manager, on being notified that the Suffolk Agricultural Show was to be held at Saxmundham on 23rd and 24th June, 1876, and after consultation with the superintendent, agreed the sidings on the up side of the station were to be repaired and lengthened to handle the expected additional traffic. The matter was discussed at the Way & Works Committee meeting on 16th May, 1876 and the Engineer was instructed to finalize plans as a matter of urgency. The engineer reported back on 30th May that costs were estimated at £500 and the work was duly sanctioned, although on 14th June an additional £100 was authorized for additional sidings on the down side when it was realized that the original authority was inadequate.

After several years of inactivity at Aldeburgh, construction of a pier opposite the Moot Hall restarted in 1876 but was never to reach completion and was later demolished. In the same year an excursion for works people from Ipswich traversed the branch and terminated at Sizewell crossing where the 400 passengers detrained. How they alighted is not recorded for there was no platform at the crossing, so presumably steps were used and egress from the train must have been lengthy and time consuming. Then on Christmas Day 1876 a down train travelling between Saxmundham and Leiston ran through Saxmundham Road level crossing gates completely demolishing the barriers. The crossing keeper had failed to open the gates for the passage of the train but whether his oversight was due to too much festive food and ale is not recorded. He was, however, fined two days' pay for failing to properly attend to his duties. Aldeburgh pier was again the subject of discussion in the autumn of 1877 when on 3rd October G.W. Hutchinson wrote to the GER asking the company to guarantee interest on £5,000 debentures. The appeal was refused.

With the near completion of the installation of the block telegraph between Ipswich and Saxmundham, the Board on 22nd May, 1878 awarded a sum of

£500 for extension of the block telegraph from Saxmundham to Beccles. This sum was considered inadequate and on 19th June was increased to £520. During a tour of inspection later in the year, on 1st and 2nd October, 1878, the Directors visited the Snape branch and the Southwold Railway. They also halted their train at Saxmundham where they visited the warehouse and instructed the law clerk to obtain full possession of the building by evicting the tenant, as the building was owned by the GER.

By the beginning of 1879 increasing timber traffic brought problems in loading at Leiston. The goods manager reported the traffic was lucrative and further increase in tonnage and loadings were expected. The Way & Works Committee considered the matter on 11th February, 1879, and authorized £30 for the provision of a crane to assist with loading of the timber into wagons.

As far back as 25th March, 1874 it was reported that signals and points at the station and junction at Saxmundham were not interlocked. However, lack of finance meant such refinement was shelved until 26th February, 1879, when a sum of £340 was authorized for the provision of a new signal box and associated signalling at Saxmundham Aldeburgh [sic] Junction.

In December 1879 Alexander Ogilvie complained of the poor condition of Crown Farm (Sizewell) siding, which he used to load an average of 1,000 tons of manure traffic annually. The sleepers and rails in the siding had been deteriorating for some considerable time and he requested immediate repairs. The Way & Works Committee considered the application and sanctioned a sum of £44 to effect the remedial work. The superintendent endorsed the expenditure saying the manure traffic brought considerable revenue to the GER.

After the down platform at Saxmundham was extended complaints were made regarding the lack of suitable waiting accommodation especially in adverse weather, when many passengers had to stand in the open waiting for their train. Matters reached a head in December 1879 and on 16th March, 1880 the Directors agreed to the provision of a waiting room on the down platform, the £350 expenditure being approved on 4th May, 1880 and confirmed 15 days later. The winter of 1879/80 had brought with it the usual adverse weather conditions of snow, ice and rain which ultimately resulted in considerable complaints from farmers of the district who were forced to load cattle on and off trains at Leiston via cattle pens, deep in mud and excrement, which were difficult to clean because of the earthen surface. After an approach from the goods manager, authority was given on 6th April, 1880 for the paving of the cattle pens at a cost of £5. On the same day Garrett was seeking further improvements to the goods facilities at Saxmundham.

After an earlier inspection revealed deficiencies, Major General C.S. Hutchinson re-inspected the alterations at Saxmundham, Aldborough [sic] Junction on 26th April, 1880 and found that the resignalling work had been completed in compliance with BOT requirements. However, because of falling gradients between the junction and Saxmundham station the inspector required runaway catch points to be installed in the down main line to prevent vehicles running away towards the station. Having completed work at the junction and approved of the extension to the down platform, authority was given on 5th October, 1880 for the complete resignalling and interlocking at Saxmundham station, including the provision of a new siding, at a cost of £2,100 and confirmed 15 days later. Work commenced in December and was completed by March 1881.

Major General C.S. Hutchinson carried out the Board of Trade inspection of the new works at Saxmundham on 26th May, 1881. He found that the alterations comprised a new siding, junction and general arrangements at the station including the lengthening of the down platform. Points and signals were operated from a new signal box containing a 43-lever frame, which had been provided with block instruments. On inspecting the signalling, Hutchinson found numerous deficiencies which required rectification. Nos. 17 and 26 levers should not be interlocked with No. 18 lever pulled over but should be interlocked in other circumstances. Nos. 28 and 41 levers should not be interlocked. No. 5 disc signal should apply to Nos. 19, 20 and 21 points as well as No. 17. The up home signal required moving out to cover the outlet from No. 16 siding. The inspector was of the opinion that the siding should be brought nearer to the signal box. Hutchinson then turned his attention to other matters and noted that the fence at the back of the dock platform provided for Aldeburgh branch trains was too close to the line and required it to be moved back.

The Major General then inspected the lengthened down platform and was far from happy for he commented,

> The lengthening of a portion of the down platform has been made to the south of the southernmost of the two level crossings between which the old part of the down platform stood and there is consequently a gap between the old and the new platform at the southernmost crossing. This of course is objectionable but what is perhaps still more is that any long down train stopping at the station and using the new platform would of necessity stand over the southernmost crossing and obstruct it. For this reason I can never sanction the use of this additional piece of platform, though no doubt its use will only be occasional. The proper course would be to remove the down platform to the north of the northernmost level crossing when it will be opposite the up platform. [The inspector sanctioned the use of the other alterations but asked the GER representatives to consider amended plans for the down platform. Hutchison concluded his report:] Seeing that Saxmundham is an important station with a branch line service, I would strongly recommend the provision of a subway or overbridge for communication between the platforms.

After complaints were received from the Saxmundham station master on 17th May, 1881 regarding the lack of accommodation in the station house, the superintendent recommend improvements and on 7th June additions and alterations costing an estimated £150 were authorized. On the same day authority was given for the alterations to be made to the station in accordance with the BOT inspector's recommendations. However, on a visit to the station on 11th July the Directors and General Manager were informed that the extended platform had been in use for six years without any problems and the Chairman undertook to consult with the BOT inspector to see if he would alter his decision. The Chairman reported back to the Traffic Committee on 16th August, 1881 that the inspector was adamant the removal of the objectionable southward extension of the down main line platform should take place as a matter of urgency. The GER, however, later overcame the problem with the gap between the two sections of platform by incorporating a section of platform on to the down side level crossing gate so that when open for railway traffic it effectively formed an inter-connection between the two.

On 7th March, 1882 Mademoiselle Haldy, a 66-years-old governess, fell and broke her leg whilst crossing the railway at Saxmundham level crossing. Richard Garrett took up her case for compensation against the railway company for £100 medical expenses and £40 annuity.

As the 2.30 pm passenger train from Saxmundham to Aldeburgh was negotiating the 35 chains left-hand curve about three-quarters of a mile west of Leiston station on 30th August, 1882, the engine and four vehicles comprising the entire train derailed. Two passengers and the driver, fireman and guard of the train were all injured. The engine, which was running chimney first, ran for a distance of about 95 yards and stopped obliquely across the line just beyond Saxmundham Road level crossing, with its leading and middle wheels outside and to the right of both rails. The four-wheel bogie truck, under the trailing end of the engine, broke away from the bogie centre and stopped, still under the trailing end of the engine but turned to the right. The carriage next to the engine turned partly over on its left side, the window in the door of the left rear compartment falling upon one of the posts of the level crossing gates. The three rear passenger vehicles were all derailed but the whole train remained coupled together. In addition to the fractured bogie centre, the engine sustained slight damage as did the carriages and brake van. Several rails were bent by the impact, one being broken where the engine broke through, and 61 sleepers and 130 chairs required replacing.

Major General C.S. Hutchinson was delegated to hold the official BOT inquiry into the incident and found that the accident occurred on a 35 chains radius left-hand curve as approached from Saxmundham and on a falling gradient of 1 in 738. This after extending for 370 yards changed to a rising gradient of 1 in 79, which commenced at the level crossing and extended for 275 yards towards Aldeburgh. The permanent way at the point of derailment consisted of wrought-iron rails weighing 70 lb. per yard secured by outside keys to cast-iron chairs each weighing 21 lb.; there were seven sleepers partly half-rounded, partly rectangular under each length of rail, to which each chair was secured by two wrought-iron spikes passing through wooden bushes; the joints of the rails were staggered on the curve and ballast was of gravel. The cant of the outside rail was about three inches and the gauge about ¼ inch slack.

The engine, which was running chimney first, had commenced operating on the Aldeburgh branch on 1st July, 1882. It was an eight-wheeled engine with coupled leading and driving wheels and a four-wheeled trailing bogie, weighing altogether 42½ tons, of which 14½ tons were on the leading wheels, 13 tons on the driving wheels and 15 tons on the bogie wheels. The distance between the centres of the coupled wheels was 6 ft 10 in. and between the centre of the driving wheels and the bogie centre 10 ft 10 in. The bogie centre and some of the bearing surfaces were composed of cast iron, the thickness varying from ¾ in. to 1⅛ in. The method of working the single line was by Train Staff and Ticket [introduced in 1866].

First to give evidence to the inspector was Robert Bickerdike, who reported he had 37 years' service with the railway company, a driver for 29 years and seven years exclusively on the Aldeburgh branch. His engine on 30th August was No. 97, an eight-wheeled tank engine. A hand brake applied eight brake blocks to the four coupled wheels. The train departed Saxmundham at 2.30 pm with the engine, running chimney first, and four passenger vehicles including a brake van at the rear. He reported that the train was detained at Saxmundham Junction about three minutes awaiting an up fast train to pass and then proceeded on to the branch with the first stop at Leiston scheduled for 2.41 pm. Nothing unusual occurred until the train was approaching Kelsale or Saxmundham Road level crossing with steam on at a speed of between 25 and 30 mph, where a gang of platelayers were working. The platelayers made no signal that anything was wrong and the first intimation was the engine dropping to the left side at the trailing end. 'Then the engine seemed to burst the road until the right wheels crossed the right rail just on the level crossing, when it came to a stand in the oblique direction on the right side of the line.' Asked what action he had taken when the engine derailed, Bickerdike said he shut off steam and gave one sound on the brake whistle but did not reverse the engine. The firemen went to the hand brake directly the engine derailed and screwed it on as well as he could. Neither of the footplate crew jumped off the footplate. As a result of the incident the driver informed the inquiry he was badly shaken and was off duty for three days.

After the engine halted, the driver descended from the cab and found the bogie truck away from the centre on its wheels to the right of the engine but still partly underneath the locomotive. The carriage next to the engine was canted over on its left side with the left-hand gatepost on the Saxmundham side of the level crossing through the rear door. The couplings were still holding between the carriage and engine and the carriages behind it. The other three vehicles were derailed but were on their wheels and upright. To cross-examination the driver admitted he did not go back to see where the engine had derailed but was of the opinion it was near the second telegraph pole from the gates. He had seen no disturbance in the line as he approached the point of derailment but the platelayers appeared to be packing the sleepers. He had passed with an up train an hour before when the platelayers had also been at work. 'There was no notice of relaying operations at this part of the line, I had not observed when new sleepers had been last put in.' The engine had been running steadily before it derailed and the side tanks had been topped up with water at Saxmundham before the down run. The bunker had about a ton of coal, the full capacity being 1½ tons. Bickerdike concluded his evidence saying he did not need to increase the speed of the train to get up the bank on the Leiston side of the crossing. The day was fine, not very hot and the rails were dry.

Next to give evidence was Edward Howe, who had 14 years' service with the GER, 10½ years as fireman, certified as a driver for three years. He had been Bickerdike's regular fireman for about three years. The journey on the 30th was uneventful until the accident happened without any warning as the train was running at about 30 mph with steam on. The first sensation was of the engine dropping and it then ran on the ballast parallel with the rails before turning to the right at the level crossing. The engine stopped with the trailing end nearly opposite the Leiston side of the crossing gates. He confirmed that on feeling the engine drop the driver shut off steam but he did not hear him sound the brake whistle. Howe confirmed he had turned the hand brake lever two or three turns but the two men on the footplate were bumped against each other until the engine stopped. He had sustained injuries to the head and knee in the accident. Just as the locomotive halted the bogie truck separated from the engine, but remained partly underneath it. As it did so the bogie hoisted the engine up and threw both engine crew to the floor. The fireman initially walked to Saxmundham Junction with the Train Staff to protect the train and on returning to the engine inspected the line but could not make out why the locomotive had left the rails. To further questioning Howe stated that the engine had been running steadily before the derailment; he was on the left-hand side of the cab and had seen the platelayers at work as the train approached the crossing and believed they were lifting the road.

Guard Richard Spink, with 32 years' service with the GER and about 29 years as a guard, confirmed he was in charge of the 2.30 pm train from Saxmundham to Aldeburgh on the day of the accident. He was riding in the rear vehicle, which was a full van, with three passenger coaches making up the rest of train. The train departed Saxmundham at 2.33 pm, three minutes late waiting for a connecting down train to depart, and was subsequently detained at Saxmundham Junction for three minutes waiting for an up train to pass. Departure from the junction was between 2.36 and 2.37 pm, the first stop being Leiston. The run was uneventful and speed normal and the first intimation of trouble was when he realized the brake van was off the rails. The estimated speed was 30 mph when the vehicle was pulled off the rails bearing to the left. Spink stated he had tried to screw the hand brake on but only succeeded in getting hold of the handle before he was knocked off his feet by the sudden stop. He sustained slight injuries to his back but immediately went to the assistance of the passengers. None of the 15 or 16 passengers on the train complained of injuries at the time except for two ladies who were riding in the front carriage, which fell partly on its side against the level crossing gatepost. After attending to the passengers Spink advised the inspector that he had gone back to look at the line and found a mark on the inside of a left-hand rail with the right-hand rails bent outwards. He did not notice whether the spikes were in the chairs. To cross-examination he remarked he had not looked at his watch at the time of the incident but noted it at 2.49 pm some little time after the accident. He concluded his evidence saying the train was due to reach Aldeburgh at 2.52 pm and return to Saxmundham at 3.00 pm. 'The level crossing was about 3 miles from the junction' and he had 'not noticed an unusual speed just before the accident'.

William Griffiths was next to give evidence. He had been 23 years in the service of the GER, since the opening of the line to Leiston and a ganger for all that period. He explained that he was responsible for the length from Aldeburgh Junction [sic] to Leiston up distant signal, a distance of nearly four miles. He had two men in his gang of whom only one, Charles Smith, was with him at the time of the accident. The other man was engaged tightening bolts of the fishplates at a different section of the line. Griffiths explained that on 28th August he had been repairing from about the spot where the accident occurred, lifting the inside rail from ½ inch to 1½ inches, and putting in four new sleepers about 40 or 50 yds west of the point of derailment. The sleepers were all packed but the ballast was not all thrown back where the engine derailed. The cant was about three inches and the gauge about ¼ in. slack. All the chairs were fastened with two spikes each, passing through the wooden trenails with which the chair had originally been fastened, or through bushes which were now used instead of the trenails. The joints of the 21 ft rails were alternate or staggered. Griffiths explained that the rails had been turned before he took over the ganger's position, some six years earlier but were in fair order. On the day in question he was inserting two new sleepers 40 or 50 yards on the junction side of the site of the derailment. To do this it was not necessary to send a man back along the line and as the train approached he stepped to the left of the line and as he looked towards the engine, 'I thought it was oscillating more than usual, and the speed appeared to me to be rather fast'. He watched the engine as it passed and saw the trailing bogie drop off the track after it had travelled 40 or 50 yds. The derailing carriages blocked his view. After going to the train and providing assistance he returned and examined the road and noticed a distinct wheel mark some 5 ft in length along the top of the right-hand rail as well as a chair broken on the inside of the left-hand rail. The right-hand rails were all forced outwards in the centre next to the one on which there was a mark from 1¾ in. to 8¼ in., until the engine finally burst through the right rail close to the level crossing gates, which were partly smashed. The bogie of the engine was on part of the crossing with its wheels at right angles and trailing part of the engine resting on the bogie. To cross-examination Griffiths admitted that the line had not been touched since Monday 28th as he had not had time to replace the ballast, having had to remedy the gauge where a disturbance had occurred on two previous days. Asked as to whether he was of the opinion the locomotive was too heavy for the permanent way on the Aldeburgh branch, Griffiths replied that he had never complained of the engines being too heavy for the road. He concluded, 'This class of engine has been running on the road for some length of time. In my opinion, it was the dropping of the bogie end of the engine that caused the engine to mount'.

Charles Smith, seven years a platelayer between the junction and the Leiston up distant signal, said that, either on the day before the accident or the day before that, he and the ganger had been lifting low rails near where the accident occurred. When the incident occurred they were filling in ballast between sleepers about 40 to 50 yds from where the locomotive derailed. He reiterated they had put no new sleepers under the rails on the morning of the accident and where the accident occurred the 'road was properly boxed up'. To questioning Smith said he stepped aside to the left to allow the train to pass, the engine was 'swinging about, not perhaps more than usual nor was the speed faster than usual'. After the engine had passed the rear of the locomotive appeared to drop but kept a straight course until it reached the level crossing. The carriages appeared to go to the left. He concluded his evidence by saying he did not see the mark along the top of the high rail.

Benjamin Ayden the permanent way sub-inspector for the area from Wickham Market to Beccles including the branches, was next to give evidence. He had walked over the spot where the accident occurred the Saturday prior to the incident and had noticed nothing wrong with the line or given any instructions to the ganger. He did not notice that the low rail of the curve required special attention. He informed Hutchinson that he arrived at the scene of the accident at about 6 pm, by which time the bent rails had been removed but not the broken chairs. 'I could not see the mark along the top of the high rail spoken of by the ganger, though I looked for it and I saw nothing wrong either with this rail or the opposite one, or any marks on the chairs or sleepers supporting these rails'. The majority of chairs were broken on the high rail with fewer on the low rail, principally across the sole. The chairs all weighed 21 lb., fastened by spikes through hollow trenails; there were no chairs without two spikes in them, passing through either bushes or trenails. He continued that from the spot about two or three sleepers on the Saxmundham side of the mark, the ballast was opened out on the low rail for about 117 yds towards Saxmundham, but that part of the road was not disturbed in any way. The ganger was putting in new sleepers in this open part the same morning. Asked for his opinion on what caused the accident Ayden responded, 'I have come to no conclusion - we occasionally find the light chairs broken by these heavy bogie engines, and they tend to spread the gauge'.

Last to provide evidence was John Fisher, the permanent way inspector for the area from Manningtree to Beccles and branches. Fisher said he had not been across the Aldeburgh branch 'for a month of two'. He reached the site of the derailment at about 8 pm on 30th August, by which time the repairs were almost completed. 'I was shown the place where a wheel is supposed to have mounted the right rail, and saw a slight mark about a foot long near the Aldeburgh end of the rail and I then heard that a chair and fishplate bolt at the end of the next railhead been broken.' He had noticed the ballast was out from the low rail on the Saxmundham side of the incident. The cant of the rails the next morning was three inches. Concluding his evidence, Fisher thought that the right driving wheel kept inside the rail and the right leading wheel outside the rail up to the crossing. 'I have not come to any conclusion as to the cause of the accident. I do not think the line is suitable for a heavy engine exceeding a speed, of say, 25 mph.'

After hearing the relevant evidence Major General Hutchinson summed up from the information gleaned. The 2.30 pm train from Aldeburgh to Saxmundham, which actually departed at 2.33 pm, and formed of a tank engine and four vehicles was running round a 35 chains radius curve on a falling gradient on 1 in 738 at a speed stated to be between 25 and 30 mph when the engine and all vehicles left the rails at a spot close to where platelayers were working. The site was about 3 miles from Aldeburgh Junction [sic], where the train had been detained for three minutes to let an up main line train pass. The train departed the junction at 2.36 or 2.37 pm but there was unfortunately no record of the exact time of the derailment as when the guard looked at his watch at 2.49 pm, the accident had occurred some little time earlier. No estimate of the speed from the recorded time could therefore be judged. As the train was already 6 minutes late there was only a margin of two minutes between its arrival at Aldeburgh, if it had made up no time, and the time it was due to depart on the up journey. Just beyond the spot where the derailment occurred there was a sharp rise in gradient to 1 in 72 and the inspector was of the opinion that speed was in excess of that given in evidence. It also appeared that the ganger for the length of line and a platelayer were placing two new sleepers 40 or 50 yards on the junction side of the place where the derailment occurred, the inside rail of the curve having been lifted from ½ in. to 1½ in. and four new sleepers inserted near the spot two days prior to the accident. Though the sleepers were packed the ballast had not been thrown back. The ganger watching the approaching train had given evidence to the fact the locomotive was oscillating more than usual and speed was faster than normal. He continued to watch the engine and saw the trailing end drop about 40 to 50 yards after it had passed the point where he was standing; that on examining the road he found the distinct marks of a wheel five feet in length along the top of the outer or right-hand rail. A chair was broken along the outside of the right rail, other chairs were broken along the outside of the right rail and the inside of the left rail and in consequence the right rail was forced outwards from 2 to 8 inches until the engine broke through the right rail close to the level crossing gates and some 80 yards distant from the original mark. Hutchinson remarked of the considerable discrepancy between the evidence of the ganger and the platelayer. The sub-inspector having reached the site at about 6 pm was unable to detect a mark on top of the right-hand rail alluded to by the ganger, but the permanent way inspector arriving two hours later at 8 pm, saw a slight mark about a foot in length on the rail. Some of the sleepers had unfortunately been burnt by the time Hutchinson visited the site. 'This was a very wrong thing to have done, and necessarily leads to the conclusion that it was inexpedient to have their condition seen'.

Hutchinson concluded from the evidence, the nature of the engine and the character of the permanent way, the accident was probably caused by ,

> ... injudiciously high speed, considering the nature of the road, of a heavy tank engine weighing 42½ tons running on light permanent way weighing 70 lbs per yard, secured to chairs only weighing 21 lbs each at regular intervals of 3 feet, the condition of the some of the sleepers being probably defective, and the road being further weakened by the lack of ballast being thrown back after repairs. From these combined causes the engine appeared to have burst the road, and after running some 80 yards to have forced its way through the right rail, where the bogie centre was probably fractured and the bogie truck left its location before stopping in 15 yards. Considering the state of the road the driver should, I think have taken the means to slacken the speed of the train when it was approaching the spot where the ballast had not been replaced.

He was also critical of GER management and thought the light permanent way of the Aldeburgh branch was unsuitable for the heavier type of locomotive employed on the branch. His final criticism was aimed at the locomotive department:

> Although I am of the opinion the fracture of the bogie centre was not the cause of the accident, it will be observed that it was broken when the engine stopped after bursting through the right rail; the principal fracture occurred at the junction of the bogie centre with the cast iron plate which rests on the India rubber disc on which the bogie truck turns, the greatest thickness of the plate being 1⅝ inches and the least ⅞ inches. As these

cast iron plates are constantly found to break when an engine leaves the rails, I would strongly recommend their use being discontinued in the construction of future engines, and that wrought iron plates be substituted for them as the opportunity offers in existing engines.

After continuing complaints from the incumbent station master at Leiston regarding the lack of available space in the station house, authority was given on 5th September, 1882 for alterations to be made at a cost of £40. The goods manager had for some considerable time also been of the opinion that the goods yard at Leiston was too small to handle the ever-increasing interchange of traffic with Garrett's and outsorting wagons from Sizewell siding. An opportunity arose for the company to acquire land adjacent to the railway for additional sidings and on 6th February, 1883 the Directors sanctioned a sum of £518 towards purchase. The decision was confirmed when H.L. Carr approached the GER goods manager in March 1883 requesting the provision of a siding and wagon turntable to serve his brick and tile works at Leiston. After investigation, the matter was discussed at a meeting of the Way & Works Committee on 17th April, 1883 and the siding was sanctioned at a cost of £190, plus a £10 annual rental rising to £15 per annum on 1st May, 1883. As Garrett's traffic was growing rapidly with increased tonnage a new 5 tons capacity fixed crane was authorized at a cost of £100 on 19th June, 1883 to handle heavier commodities.

The Directors made a visit down the line from 4th to 6th September, 1883 and in the course of their itinerary visited Saxmundham, where it was agreed to shelve the provision of the awning over the up side platform until the following year. In the meantime Robertson, the traffic superintendent, was to make a renewed proposal. Along the branch at Leiston, Frank Garrett and some of his partners met the GER Chairman to discuss a proposed new road but were informed it could not be constructed unless a £100 contribution was made to the scheme. The use of a path beside the railway by passengers walking from the level crossing to the station was also to be stopped - many being Garrett's employees, but special agreement would be given to Garrett if he personally required such permission. Needless to say the £100 contribution was forthcoming.

As the 7.05 am train from Aldeburgh to Saxmundham was leaving Aldeburgh on 5th October, 1883, the engine derailed at a set of facing points leading to the engine shed and came to rest 17 yards beyond the point of the derailment. The train was formed of a 'K9' class 0-4-2 tank locomotive, two passenger coaches and a passenger full brake van. None of the carriages left the rails and no persons were injured. The only damage sustained to the rolling stock was a bent brake rod on the engine whilst the permanent way damage resulted in the fracturing of 10 chairs. Major F.A. Marindin was delegated to lead the resultant BOT inquiry into the accident and found that at Aldeburgh the signals and points were not interlocked. There were two sets of facing points to down trains approaching the station, some 230 and 220 yards from the end of the platform, and two sets of facing points facing up trains, both close to the end of platform. The first set of points, leading to the engine shed, was normally positioned for the main single line. All the points at the station were worked from the ground with ordinary weighted levers, and kept locked for the main line by means of a padlock and key, unless they were used for entry to the sidings. The locomotive had started its journey from a point about 33 yds from the facing points where it derailed and was running at a slow speed.

The first member of staff called to give evidence was Walter Hyam, porter at Aldeburgh, who had a little over two years' railway service. His duties were on the platform and to assist in the goods shed. He also attended to the points when the foreman porter was away. On the day of the accident he was on duty on the platform when the 7.05 am train departed. As the foreman porter was sick he had attended to the points, which were normally kept padlocked but were unlocked when shunting was necessary. Hyam admitted that he had unlocked the points leading out from the engine shed, which were facing points for up trains, at about 6.00 am for the engine and train to enter the platform. The train ran into the platform at about 6.55 am and no one was at the points when it ran out. He ought then have locked the points for the main single line but omitted to do so. He admitted he had totally forgotten to attend to the points. There had been an excursion train earlier that morning and he had been busy at work since 4.00 am. When the train shunted from the engine shed siding into the platform he was having breakfast but was on the platform for the departure and saw the engine derail at a slow speed. To cross-examination he reported that none of the carriages were off the rails and no one was hurt. To further questioning Hyam explained that when the foreman porter was away he had also to oil the points, a task usually carried out after the first train had departed. He oiled the points on 4th October but not on the morning of the 5th. After the accident he looked at the slide chairs and noted some grit on them. 'There had been a good deal of rain in the night, and water runs down that way. I tried the points after the accident, and I found there was sufficient grit to prevent the points going close back.'

Next to give evidence was driver James Hughes, who had been 12½ years with the GER and one year a driver. He told Marindin that he was the driver of the 7.05 am up departure from Aldeburgh on 5th October with locomotive No. 25 running chimney first. The train was the usual formation of two carriages and a guard's van. The guard had given the signal to start at the right time but he was unaware the facing points were unlocked until after the accident. The leading wheel of the engine 'got astride the switches, the right wheel going along the siding rail and the left wheel following the main line'. As the train was hardly moving he applied the brake and stopped in about 20 yards. The trailing wheels of the engine were on the main line rails but all other wheels had derailed. None of the carriages were off the line. Hughes explained to the inspector he had examined the points after the derailment and could see nothing wrong with them. 'There was no mark or any blow on the end of the switch.'

Last to be questioned was Robert Cadey, foreman platelayer in charge of the section of line, which included the yard at Aldeburgh. He reported that it was his duty to keep the points in order. The porter was responsible for oiling and he examined the points each morning. The points were in good order when he examined them on 4th October but he had not examined them on the day of the incident. After the accident he examined the points, which were in good order except the right-hand switch, which had been bent by the engine derailing. The gauge of the stock rail was correct and there was a little grit on the slide chair. He was of the opinion the points had not been oiled that morning.

Marindin concluded that the slight accident had been caused by the omission of the porter at Aldeburgh to lock the facing points for the main line, in accordance with instructions. Hyam had unlocked them an hour before to let the engine and train reverse into the station platform and completely overlooked the fact they had to be relocked again for the main line. The points had not been oiled and after a wet night there was sufficient dirt and gravel on the slide chairs to prevent the points from being properly closed by the falling back of the weighted lever. The inspector noted the derailment was caused by the right leading wheel of the engine running between the point of the switch and the stock rail on the right-hand side and so off the rails at the heel of the switches. The porter admitted he was solely to blame for the accident but Marindin noted with some sympathy that Hyam had been at work at an unusually early hour of 4.00 am to deal with the departure of the special excursion train. The inspector was, however, critical of the railway company. 'The best way of avoiding such accidents in future would be the concentration and interlocking of the levers working the points and signals, for the present arrangements at the station are antiquated and eminently unsatisfactory.'

On the afternoon of the following day, 6th October, 1883, station master John Taylor was standing near the engine shed at Aldeburgh when he was aghast to see the 5.22 pm train from Saxmundham approaching the station at a higher speed than was usual. His doubts were confirmed for the train consisting of a 'K9' class 0-4-2T, one third class carriage, one composite carriage, one passenger full brake van and another composite carriage overran the platform before colliding with a stationary coach standing close by the buffer stops at the end of the line. The empty carriage was forced over the shattered buffer stops before crossing the public road to come to a stand a few inches from the railings fronting a house on the far side of the road. All the wheels of the engine were derailed but the other vehicles in the formation remained on the track sustaining very little damage. Three passengers on the train reported being shaken by the impact but had no further injuries. The locomotive surprisingly was not damaged but the trailing headstock and buffers of the empty carriage were broken and the end panels damaged. The headstock of one of the carriages on the train also sustained damage. Of the infrastructure the buffer stops were completely destroyed, six chairs holding the permanent way were fractured and not surprisingly the fencing behind the buffer stops flattened.

Once again Major F.A. Marindin was delegated to conduct the inquiry into the incident. He noted that Aldeburgh, with a single platform on the east side of the line, was the terminus of the single line branch from Saxmundham. The approach to the station was protected by down distant and home signals but the points and signals were not interlocked. He was particularly concerned with and pointed out the various distances from the buffer stops which were pertinent to the accident.

| | |
|---|---|
| To the point where the engine should have stopped at the platform | 20 yds |
| To the west or outer end of the platform | 99 yds |
| To the home signal | 157 yds |
| To the engine shed | 206 yds |
| To the west end of the station yard | 330 yds |
| To the down distant signal | 962 yds |

The line approached on a 1 in 150 rising gradient to within 10 yards of the home signal from where it was practically level to the buffer stops.

The first to give evidence was station master John Taylor who advised the inspector that on the day of the accident he was standing at the back of the coke stage near the engine shed when the 5.22 pm train from Saxmundham, due at Aldeburgh at 5.45 pm, ran into the station. It had not stopped at the ticket platform and when he first heard it approaching he considered it was travelling faster than usual. When the train passed where he was standing it was running 'very fast'; he saw the driver on the engine but could not say what he was doing. To questioning Taylor admitted he could not say whether the steam was on or not or whether the brakes were applied. He was about 20 yards back from the single main line and heard no whistle sounding. Realising an accident was imminent the station master ran to the station and on arrival found the empty carriage which had been standing nearly against the buffer stops had been driven through it, and across the road to within a few inches of the railing in front of the house opposite. He noticed the buffers of the carriage were broken off; the buffer stops were smashed and the engine was off the rails but undamaged. The other vehicles in the train were on the rails and were 'scarcely damaged at all'. Of the 30 passengers on the train only three complained of slight injury and all were able to walk away from the vehicles. The station master confirmed to Marindin that it was a clear fine evening, the driver had been driving from Aldeburgh for some weeks and he believed him to be a steady man. 'I saw him about an hour after the accident; he was perfectly sober.' The driver considered it a 'bad job' but did not explain how the accident happened. Asked as to what speed the train was approaching the station, Taylor considered it was travelling at 15 mph when it passed the engine shed.

Porter Walter Hyam then gave evidence. On 6th October he was standing about midway along the platform when the 5.22 pm train from Saxmundham arrived at Aldeburgh. He had first noticed the train when it was nearly a mile away and watched as it approached. As it passed the distant signal he thought it was travelling '... too fast to stop. It was running faster than I could walk or run either when it passed me'. Questioned by the inspector, the porter noticed that steam had been shut off near the distant signal and did not see it applied after that. Although he did not see what the driver was doing when the train passed him he noticed the fireman had hold of the brake handle. He did not know whether the engine was reversed or not and heard no warning whistle. He also stated that the guard's brake was applied.

Richard Spink, 32 years in the company service and 30 years a guard, 9 years at Aldeburgh, confirmed that he was guard on the 5.22 pm train on the day in question. The train was formed of a tank engine running chimney first, a third class carriage, one composite carriage, one guard's brake van and another composite carriage. The rear vehicle was a spare empty carriage required for excursion work the following Monday. He confirmed there was no continuous brake on the formation. The train departed Saxmundham at 5.31 pm, nine minutes late, and Leiston at 5.43 pm, 10 minutes late, before arriving at Aldeburgh 6 minutes late at 5.51 pm. The train was due to depart Aldeburgh for Saxmundham at 7.00 pm. Spink was of the opinion the train was running too fast when passing the distant signal. 'Up to that time we had been running pretty fast, but nothing excessive.' He looked out for the signal and applied the brake when passing it and thought the driver had shut off steam at about the same time, 'I generally apply my brake at that place and release it again if necessary'. On this occasion he applied the brake and did not release it until after the accident. Cross-examined he thought the speed of the train was 20 mph passing the distant signal and about 10 mph when the engine struck the carriage and buffer stops. He was not knocked over as a result of the impact and books on his seat were not thrown off, as there was only a slight rebound. He examined the brake after the incident and it appeared in good order. It was a fine evening. Marindin asked the guard's opinion of the driver. Spink thought that he had been on the branch for about three months; he appeared a steady man but confessed that he did not speak to him during the day.

James Hughes, the driver of the train, advised Marindin that he had been driving on the Aldeburgh branch for three months during which time he had driven two engines, Nos. 20 and 25, both of the same class. He explained that they were six-wheeled tank locomotives, with leading and driving wheels coupled. A hand brake worked blocks on all six wheels. On 6th October he had signed on for work at Aldeburgh at 7.05 am and had six trips to make each way during his course of duty with the last trip due at Aldeburgh at 8.10 pm. He started the 5.22 pm train from Saxmundham nine minutes late, and departed Leiston 10 minutes late. To cross-examination Hughes was of the opinion he had not run the train any faster than usual after leaving Leiston. Asked as to his actions leading up to the collision he replied, 'I shut off steam at the usual place just before getting to the distant signal' and estimated his speed at 20mph. 'I thought I would stop all right until I got to the first points in the yard, and then I found I was going too fast.' The brake had been applied but the driver was unaware when the fireman had applied it. 'The place where it is usually applied depends upon the speed we are running at. I asked my fireman if the brake was tight on and he said it was.' Hughes then advised the inspector that he had immediately reversed the engine and applied steam as the locomotive passed the engine shed. He then opened the sand boxes at about the home signal. The train was still running at about 9 mph when the locomotive collided with the carriage and struck the remains of the buffer stop. He concluded his evidence stating that neither he nor his fireman had jumped off the engine and neither had received injuries. He could not account for the accident. 'The brake did not seem to have much effect, and speed did not lessen until I reversed.' He did not sound the whistle for the guard's brake but had no reason to believe it was not applied. He believed the brake to be in good order.

Fireman Charles Fryer, with eight years railway service and seven years as a fireman thought the train had not run any faster than usual from Leiston. 'Steam was shut off outside the distant signal when we were running at 10 or 12 mph.' He had applied the brake about midway between the distant signal and the engine shed but it appeared not to have much effect in retarding the train and he screwed the brake on as hard as he could. He corroborated the evidence of his driver that the engine was reversed passing the engine shed. To questioning Fryer told Marindin that the brake had been acting correctly throughout the day.

After hearing all the evidence Marindin made the obvious decision that the accident was solely due to the driver not getting his train under proper control when approaching the terminal station at Aldeburgh. 'The train was somewhat late; and as the evidence of the guard showed, the driver had made up three minutes in running the 4½ miles from Leiston to Aldeburgh.' It was clear that the speed must have been higher than the driver thought it was and owing to miscalculation he did not take steps to check the speed of the train soon enough. Although the driver was a steady and careful man it appeared he discovered he was running too fast when over 300 yards from the buffer stops. The inspector concluded that had the driver the benefit of continuous brake on the locomotive and rolling stock the accident might easily have been averted.

Yet another accident occurred, on 18th October, 1883, when the 4.35 pm mixed train from Aldeburgh to Saxmundham derailed between Leiston and Saxmundham. The train, consisting of a tank locomotive, four loaded goods trucks, brake van, one composite carriage and one third class carriage, was running at about 30 mph at a point a mile west of Leiston station when the trailing wheels of the rear truck left the rails and was immediately followed by the brake van. The train ran for 237 yards before it was brought to a stand, when it was found that all the vehicles behind the rear truck had also derailed, the brake van being turned towards the right side of the line and the passenger carriage standing nearly in line with the flanges of the left wheels in the hollow of the side of the left-hand rails, which had been turned over. One guard iron on the spring band on goods truck No. 12243 had fractured whilst brake van No. 137 sustained a broken spring plate. In the permanent way 300 chairs and 64 bolts were broken, 50 sleepers cut up and four rails bent so badly they had to be replaced. The guard of the train, who sustained severe shaking, was the only person injured by the derailment.

Major F.A. Marindin conducting the BOT inquiry into the accident found that when the Aldeburgh branch opened in 1859/60 (registered in the report as 1858), the permanent way consisted of 70 lb. per yard (quoted as 68 lb. per yard in the original inspection report) double-headed iron rails in 21 ft lengths, laid in 21 lb. cast-iron chairs, secured to half-rounded larch sleepers by means of two solid trenails to each chair. There were seven sleepers to each length of rail and the joints of the rails were connected by fishplates. In 1868 the solid trenails were bored and spikes inserted. The same rails and chairs were still in use but the rails had been turned from time-to-time and the line at the point of derailment was re-sleepered 14 months before the accident, after it was damaged by the accident on 30th August, 1882. Nine rectangular sleepers were now placed under each rail length and the chairs were secured by means of two hollow trenails with ⅝ inch iron spikes.

At the point of derailment the line was on a 35 chains right-hand curve, with a super elevation of the outer rail on the curve between 2¾ and 3 inches. The line was on a falling gradient on 1 in 79 towards Saxmundham and this gradient extended for about 100 yds westwards of the point the truck derailed and then altered to a rising gradient of 1 in 138 close to the level crossing. The truck which left the rails was one of a number used for the conveyance of heavy agricultural machinery. It entered into traffic on 15th December, 1876 and was last repaired at Ipswich in September 1883. The wagon weighed 5 tons, had elliptical springs and four wheels 2 ft 9 in. in diameter, a wheelbase of 9 ft and was 19 ft over buffers.

Robert Bickerdike was first to give evidence. He advised the inspector he had 38 years' service and 30 years as a driver. He was the driver of the 4.35 pm mixed train from Aldeburgh to Saxmundham on 18th October with the engine running chimney first. The train started from Aldeburgh 'right time' and at Leiston three loaded trucks were picked up. The revised formation, consisting of locomotive, four loaded trucks, brake van and two carriages, was travelling at about 25 mph a mile west of Leiston when he felt a sudden jerk and looking back noticed a vehicle was off the rails. His fireman also looking back called out and he shut off steam and whistled for the guard to apply his brake. His fireman also screwed on the hand brake and the train was stopped as soon as possible. On going back along the train Bickerdike saw that one truck was derailed but could not see where the brake van had jumped the track. On closer investigation he noticed the rear of the four trucks had its trailing wheels derailed, the brake van was off all wheels to the right-hand side and the two carriages were also off but standing in line. To questioning, Bickerdike advised he had not made any examination of the road behind the train. The road had been running well and he had not felt anything wrong with it on previous journeys. He was running the train steadily when the truck left the rails and had not checked speed suddenly, nor was the brake applied until after the derailment.

Thomas Bell, 8½ years' service with the GER including 7½ years as a fireman, advised the inspector he was fireman to Bickerdike on 18th October. Just before reaching the level crossing after leaving Leiston he was looking back and saw the right trailing wheel of the rear truck drop into the 'four foot'. He shouted to his driver that the truck was off the road and immediately applied the hand brake He had not noticed anything amiss before the incident. As soon as the truck derailed he saw the leading edge of the brake van turn to the right. To questioning, Bell said he could not see when the passenger carriages left the rails and after stopping did not inspect the road behind the train.

The next to provide evidence was Charles Fennell, an order clerk employed by Messrs Garrett & Son. He advised the inspector that he superintended the loading of the portable steam engine on the truck, which was first to derail. The engine was destined for Vienna and weighed 8 tons 8 cwt but the fly wheel, funnel, pole and pulley were loaded in another truck, so that the load on the derailed truck was down to 7 tons 13 cwt. The load was 9 ft above the truck and just cleared the loading gauge. The engine was on its wheels and Fennel was of the opinion the centre of the weight would be about 4½ ft above the bed of the truck. The portable steam engine was properly secured and had not moved a ¼ in. after the accident. It was undamaged and after the accident was returned to Leiston for reloading. To questioning the order clerk said that Garrett's sent away numbers of similar engines, which were not as heavy as traction engines. It was the practice to block up the back of the trucks on which the engines were loaded, so that the weight did not come on to the wagon springs until the load was in position. When the portable steam engine was loaded the truck appeared to be in good order, the springs were not examined and nothing appeared wrong with them when the truck was transferred to the railway company for onwards transit.

Richard Spink, who was involved in the accident on 5th October, was next to give evidence to Marindin. He confirmed he was the guard on the 4.35 pm mixed train from Aldeburgh to Saxmundham. The train departing Leiston was formed of tank locomotive, four loaded trucks, brake van, a composite carriage and a third class carriage. He remarked, 'we don't have a rear van on the up journeys'. The train departed three minutes late from Leiston at 4.49 pm and the 'road was running well with speed between 25 and 30 mph', when he heard a jerk from the truck in front of the brake van. Spink then related that he immediately felt the brake van jump and derail and went to apply the hand brake. When the train finally stopped he found that the two carriages behind his van were off the rails, but in line, with the flanges of the left wheels being on the sides of the rails, which had turned on their sides. He did not think the trailing wheels of his brake van or the carriages had derailed until the road burst just before the train stopped. To questioning Spink advised there were about 10 passengers on the train and none were hurt. His van was running 'very roughly' and he was badly shaken by the event. The only vehicle on the train to sustain damage was the derailed truck, which was missing a spring off the right trailing wheel. Spink advised the inspector the train did not always run as a mixed formation. The guard then informed the inquiry that as he went back to protect the train he examined the road and found the place where one wheel on the left had mounted and run along the top of the rail for some distance before dropping off. There was no sign of any damage to the rails on the Leiston side of the point of derailment and no low point that he could detect. He concluded his evidence saying that he was unable to find the missing spring on the line.

Ganger William Griffiths was next to be called and stated he was in charge of maintenance for four miles of the Aldeburgh branch commencing near Leiston up distant signal. He walked the length every morning and had done so on the day of the accident and everything was in good order. He had gauged the line where the incident occurred two or three days previously and nothing had been done since to the road on the Leiston side of where the accident occurred. He was working at Leiston with his gang and after hearing whistling from the locomotive thought something was wrong, left immediately, and arrived at the scene of the derailment soon after 5 pm. He met someone between the train and Leiston but as it was getting dark did not recognize the person, although he thought it might have been the guard. As soon as he arrived at the scene he set to work to get the road repaired. After about 30 minutes he examined the line behind the train and about 240 yds back found a mark where a wheel on the left-hand side had mounted and perhaps run 18 ft along the top of the rail before it dropped off outside the left side. The first chair on that side after the wheel dropped was chipped and the next broken. The first mark on the right side was a chipped chair on the same sleeper as the first broken one of the left side. A number of other chairs and sleepers were broken on both sides all the way back to where the train was standing. The road, however, had not burst out of gauge until four rail lengths behind the rear of the train. Judging from the mark, he was of the opinion that no more than two pairs of wheels had derailed all the way to where the road had burst out. The carriages were standing with the left wheels in the hollow of the sides of the rails, which were turned over. The chairs on the other side were barely damaged and most other wheels were on the rails. To cross-examination Griffiths admitted he had lifted the rails at about the place where the truck ran off the line about three to four weeks before the incident. The line was re-sleepered about 14 months earlier, and there was nothing wrong with the road and it was true to gauge.

Carriage examiner William Ellis of Saxmundham told the inquiry that on 17th October, the day before the incident, he had examined all the trucks going on to the Aldeburgh branch. He had tapped the wheels and examined the grease boxes and springs in the usual way and all appeared correct.

Charles Arthur Robinson, locomotive foreman for the Ipswich district of the GER, was last to give evidence and stated that he arrived at the scene of the accident at 8.40 pm. The rear truck on the train, No. 12243, was one of a pattern made especially for carrying agricultural machinery and was rather lower and stronger than ordinary wagon stock. It had spring buffers and was equipped with elliptical springs. Robinson was not able to say when the vehicle was built or last in shops for overhaul but he examined it the morning after the accident and subsequently. He found one guard iron and the right trailing axle-guard broken off evidently as a result of the accident. The trailing wheels were underneath the truck 'but not much out of place'. He later found the right trailing spring on the outside of the right rail, halfway between the train and the gatehouse of the level crossing. It was lying with the plates apart and unbroken but close together and not scattered. The top band was missing and this, minus one side and half the bottom, was later found in the 'four foot'. At the time of the inquiry the other portion was still missing. Robinson questioned persons likely to know whether the spring had been picked up and placed where he found it, but of those questioned none had any knowledge. The locomotive foreman then explained the outcome of his examination of the spring. There was an old fracture where the band joined the shoe, and that only ⅛ in. of the thickness of metal was a fresh fracture. The band was 3 inches wide and 2½ in. deep and the metal ⁵⁄₁₆ inch thick. It was Robinson's opinion the band and shoe were forged in one piece and the band drawn down to proper thickness and turned back. He concluded his evidence by saying that the wheels and axles were in good order and true to gauge whilst all the vehicles in the train were in good order.

Marindin concluded from the evidence and from an examination of the line that although some rails were greatly worn there was nothing in the condition of the permanent way to account for the accident. The line had been put in order and strengthened after the accident at almost the same spot in August 1882. It was clear the first pair of wheels to derail were the trailing pair of truck No. 12243, loaded with heavy machinery weighing 7 tons 13 cwt. The left trailing wheel had mounted and then run along the top of the left-hand rail for a distance of about 21 ft before dropping off on the outside of the rail. After the accident the right trailing spring of the truck was missing and although the plates and bands were found about 100 yds behind the rear of the train the top band was broken at an old fracture. One side and half the bottom of the band were still missing. The Major had no doubt the missing part fell off further back along the line towards Leiston, causing the weight of the 'somewhat top heavy load' to fall unduly on the right trailing wheel of the truck and the left wheel then to mount the rail and run off outside it. Marindin was of the opinion it was fortunate the road did not burst its gauge until 40 yards before the train came to a stand so the passenger carriages only derailed when the speed of the train was much reduced. He concluded that the cause of the accident was the breaking of the top band of the right trailing spring of the truck and, judging from its appearance, the old fracture in the band was in existence when the truck was in the shops a few weeks prior to the accident. If such was the case a more careful examination of the spring might have detected the flaw. Major Marindin, however, was not finished for there was a final sting in the tail for the GER over the operation of mixed trains. 'Passengers ought not to be exposed to the risk of such an accident as this, due to the objectionable practice of running mixed trains with goods wagons in front of the passenger carriages.'

As Aldeburgh became more popular as a watering place for the gentry and middle classes so the number of passengers travelling on the branch trains increased, especially in the spring and summer months. With increasing passenger numbers the usual two- or three-coach branch trains required strengthening with additional stock. Although the existing platform was capable of accommodating trains of this length the GER authorities sanctioned the extension of the platform on 1st April, 1884 at a cost of £40. Along the line at Leiston the goods manager had requested the provision of a crossover road to facilitate the working of freight services and on 5th August the work was authorized and confirmed on 19th August at an estimated cost of £90. Nearly a month later on 17th September, 1884 carriage examiner William Ellis, who had given evidence at the 1883 accident inquiry, received fatal injuries at Saxmundham as a result of a shunting accident.

By 1884 the East Suffolk main line was open continuously to handle the increasing number of goods and fish trains which ran during the night. When the timetabled service was running to schedule there were few problems but the late docking of fishing boats at Lowestoft and Yarmouth, and to a lesser extent Aldeburgh, seriously affected the pathing of trains and last minute alterations were often made to get services away as quickly as possible. Here the GER local officers experienced difficulties for any rescheduling of trains had to be advised to intermediate signal boxes along the route and in most instances the 'speaking telegraph' instruments (i.e. telephones) were located in station booking offices, which were closed for about 11 hours from early evening to early the following morning. During the hours of closure considerable delays occurred as signalmen had no idea what trains were coming and which should take priority. Having received considerable complaints from farmers, traders and the fishing industry, the General Manager reported to the Way & Works Committee on 30th December, 1884 that the solution was the provision of a separate telephone circuit in signal boxes between Ipswich and Beccles. The Signal & Telegraph Engineer estimated the cost of the circuit at £350 and due authority was given for the work to be completed as a matter of urgency.

From the opening of the railway in 1859 the up platform at Saxmundham had been devoid of a canopy. Over the years there had been many complaints in the local press and to the railway authorities that, as there was limited waiting accommodation, many passengers had to wait in the open for the train to arrive, a decidedly unenviable occupation in adverse weather conditions. Provision was mooted in 1883 but deferred until the following year. However, authority only finally relented on 2nd February, 1886 when the canopy was sanctioned at a cost of £150. Further improvements were authorized on 6th July, 1886 when the Way & Works Committee agreed to a further extension of the down platform at a cost of £46.

Aldeburgh's popularity led to the development of land on The Terrace and during the summer of 1886 a special train brought approximately 500 from London to attend an auction for the sale of property.

The increasing tonnage of coal handled at Leiston often meant the fuel was dumped away from the designated coal storage area as merchants experienced difficulty unloading wagons in the existing restricted area. The delay resulted in increased demurrage payments, to which the merchants objected. To obviate the problem authority was granted on 17th May, 1887 for a new coal storage area at a cost of £60.

An accident marred the smooth operation of the branch on 25th July, 1887 when railway porter Knights was seriously injured after he was run over by a truck during a shunting movement at Aldeburgh.

To permit trains to depart from Leiston goods loop line in the up direction without having to back into the station platform an up advance starting signal was authorized at Leiston at a cost of £95 on 5th February, 1889. Later in the year Row & Sons applied for a siding to serve their premises at Saxmundham. The Way & Works Committee considered the application on 6th August, 1889 and, after the superintendent advised that the firm gave considerable traffic to the company, sanctioned the provision of the siding at cost of £53, subject to the usual rental charges. The increase in cattle grazing in the area around Sizewell also resulted in a greater flow of traffic to and from the siding, which had lain almost disused for several years and where the facilities were wholly inadequate. After representation from the goods manager, authority was given on 5th November, 1889 for a complete refurbishment of the siding and provision of a cattle loading dock and pens at a cost of £490.

The Regulation of Railways Act 1889 amongst other things enforced major railway companies to adopt block working on all single lines except where the Train Staff without Ticket and One Engine in Steam systems existed. As the Aldeburgh branch was worked on the Train Staff and Ticket method of operation it was thus evident that the branch would have to be fully upgraded. In accordance with the procedures the company was required to confirm to the BOT within two years the method to be adopted for working the branch. On 3rd December, 1889 the Traffic Committee discussed the future working of the Aldeburgh, Snape, Framlingham, Brightlingsea, Eye and Hadleigh branches at length, and required the operating officers to confirm if the existing methods were satisfactory and to be continued. It was subsequently agreed that Train Staff and Ticket working was to be maintained on the Aldeburgh branch.

# Chapter Four

# Consolidation

The 1889 Regulation of Railways Act, as well as requiring block working on most lines and interlocking of points and signals, also stipulated the compulsory provision and use of continuous brakes on passenger trains, and the correct marshalling of mixed trains, the absence of which had contributed to the accidents of 5th and 18th October, 1883 on the Aldeburgh branch. Increasing speeds and traffic growth, combined with ineffective braking systems, inevitably led to accidents and as a result the Railway Inspectorate had campaigned long and hard for passenger vehicles on mixed trains to be coupled to the locomotive with goods wagons marshalled behind the passenger stock with a goods brake van at the rear of the formation.

Burdened with considerable legislation, the GER requested an extension of time to comply with all the regulations but in the meantime day-to-day problems continued to occur. The water storage tank used for locomotive replenishment at Saxmundham was deteriorating and the engineer reported increasing leaks necessitating an early replacement. On 4th February, 1890 the Way & Works Committee authorized a sum of £250 for work to be carried out. Then minor signalling alterations at Saxmundham involving the re-siting of a signal, costing £30, was authorized on 5th April, 1890. Another problem was remedied when on 17th June authority was given for the installation of trap points in the Aldeburgh branch back platform at Saxmundham at a cost of £40. On several previous occasions during a rough shunt or as a result of brakes not being properly applied, a number of runaway vehicles had passed out on to the main line. The increasing dispatch of commodities from Garrett's manufactory was often held up waiting use of the company weighbridge. To obviate delays a separate weighbridge for the sole use of Garrett's traffic was authorized on 3rd February, 1891 at a cost of £142.

After what seemed an inordinate length of time Dutton & Co. of Worcester was awarded the contract for the provision of new signal boxes and the interlocking of the signals and points at Leiston and Aldeburgh on 21st April 1891, although curiously block working was not authorized until 22nd December, 1891 at a cost of £250. However, when the work, including the rearrangement of sidings and trackwork, was completed in the autumn 1892, the contract was by Stevens.

Major General C.S. Hutchison duly visited the branch on 14th February, 1893 to conduct the official BOT inspection of the alterations at Leiston and Aldeburgh. At Leiston he found that the sidings had been rearranged and extended and the signalling remodelled. Points and signals were controlled from a new signal box containing a 35-lever frame with 29 working and six spare levers. Hutchinson found the new arrangements satisfactory save that some adjustment was required in the interlocking between Nos. 11, 14 and 26 levers. Along the line at Aldeburgh the sidings had been rearranged and the whole layout resignalled with points and signals controlled from a new signal box containing a 21-lever frame with 16 working and five spare levers. The inspector found the work to his satisfaction and recommended the new facilities be brought into use.

In the late summer of 1892 the passenger manager had reported cramped conditions in the booking office at Saxmundham and that increasing volumes of traffic had necessitated the employment of an additional clerk, which exacerbated the problem. After due discussion the Way & Works Committee on 4th October agreed to alterations at a cost of £95 and work was completed in the spring of 1893.

The lack of a footbridge at Saxmundham was a constant source of complaint from the general public as the level crossing gates were invariably closed for considerable periods for the passage of trains, especially during shunting movements. Matters came to a head early in 1893 when the demand for the structure intensified and a memorandum was sent to the GER Directors seeking immediate action. At the meeting of the Way & Works Committee on 7th February the Directors finally conceded to pressure and authorized the installation of the footbridge provided costs did not exceed £300. However, when the engineer sought tenders from the usual contractors no such price could be found and when the contract was awarded to Head Wrightson on 2nd May, 1893 the cost was £408 4s. 7d. without covered canopy over the stairs and span.

As the years progressed so the engineering output from Garrett's at Leiston continued to increase not only in volume but also in weight, as boilers became larger and farming machinery more complex. The inadequacy of the crane power to handle such items seriously hindered the future use of railway transportation and the firm advised the goods manager that they seriously considered sending larger items by sea. The mild threat concentrated the minds of the GER Directors, who on 6th June, 1893 gave authority for the urgent provision of a new 15 ton capacity crane at a cost of £480.

On 15th August, 1893 the General Manager reported that Saxmundham Voluntary School, a parochial establishment supported almost wholly by the Long family of Hurst Hall, Saxmundham, was experiencing a shortage of funds. It had been recently reported that the present squire was averse to carrying on with the donation without support and a subscription was being solicited to obviate the calling of the school board and possible closure. The parish assessment was £5,862 per annum with the GER contributing £813. The immediate deficiency was £80 of which the GER rateable share was £11. After due discussion by the Traffic Committee and fearing an escalation of similar applications William Birt suggested, and the Board agreed, to assist the subscription by donating a one-off sum of £6 6s. 0d.

The initial bridges provided when the Aldeburgh branch was first opened to traffic were wholly unsuitable for the heavier locomotives and rolling stock, which were being introduced on passenger and goods services. The Engineer recommended the replacement of three bridges between Leiston and Aldeburgh. The contract for the replacement of ironwork on Valley underbridge No. 1110 at 95 miles 37 chains was awarded to Braithwaite & Kirk on 5th September, 1893 after they tendered at £110 12s. 6d. The contract for work on Aldringham underbridge, No. 1111 at 97 miles 03 chains, and Pettitt's underbridge, No. 1113 at 97 miles 75 chains, was awarded to Horseley of Tipton, Staffordshire on 15th May, 1894 after the firm tendered a price of £55 16s. 0d. for each structure. On 16th October, 1894 the railway company contracted a local firm Cutting & Sons of Saxmundham to provide new waiting rooms on the down side platform at Saxmundham at a cost of £275.

Continuous heavy rain combined with a high tide, which washed over the flat land of the Meare, caused flooding of the railway between Leiston and Aldeburgh on 1st January, 1895. The ballast was washed from under the track and 300 yards of fencing was damaged so that train services were suspended between the two stations and a horse bus service substituted. Remedial work commenced as soon as the water subsided and the train service was reinstated the following day with a severe 5 mph speed restriction over the site of the breach. In the same year Saxmundham was again chosen as the selected site for the Suffolk Agricultural Show but, despite the previous enhancements to the goods yard made in 1876, the goods manager requested several unspecified improvements to handle the impending traffic. On 5th June, 1895 a sum of £27 was allocated to the project. Much of the smaller items of freight traffic arriving or departing Saxmundham was handled in the granary, which by the summer of 1895 was showing signs of neglect and disrepair, and on 15th October, an allocation of £90 was sanctioned to make the building watertight in time for winter weather.

At the end of 1895 a decision was made to transfer coaching stock equipped with gas lighting to various branches and cross-country routes to replace oil-lit carriages. On 4th February, 1896 the General Manager announced that 10 sites were to receive gas storage holders, which were to be regularly refilled from travelling gas wagons, so that coaching stock could be replenished as required. Saxmundham was included in the proposal, costed at £1,200 for the complete scheme. By 28th July it was established that five new gas wagons were also required also at a cost of £1,200 and that the cost of fixing the static gas holders at stations with the necessary piping and one filling point was £200.

The Directors made a periodic visit along the line between 11th and 13th June 1896 and on the first day halted at Saxmundham to view the infrastructure. During the visit a deputation from Saxmundham parish council presented a petition seeking the paving of the level crossing alongside the footbridge, the removal of the steps in front of the GER cottages and paving of the footpath near the entrance to the goods yard. The Directors noted the application but declined the request.

By the mid-1890s Aldeburgh was a popular holiday resort attracting many visitors on day and weekend trips. Many travelled from local stations as well as Ipswich and Norwich but an increasing number came from the capital as excursion and cheap tickets were made available. A traffic count was maintained to assess the popularity of the various offers and at the beginning of November 1896 the Directors were advised that passenger receipts for traffic from London and suburban district stations to Aldeburgh totalled £4,000 between March and October 1896, a reduction of £44 over the previous year.

The Directors made a further visit to Saxmundham during a tour of inspection on 26th March, 1897. After visiting Maldon the special train continued to Saxmundham where it was decided on the recommendation of the superintendent to provide a booking office at the London end of the north section of the down platform. This would be convenient for passengers travelling on the down line for stations to Lowestoft and Yarmouth as well as Aldeburgh. After second thoughts and undisclosed costs the facility was considered a luxury and was not provided.

After many complaints from the travelling public and staff regarding the condition of some of the company stations, the GER authorities arranged to put into effect a regular repair and repainting programme. As part of the scheme Joslin & Co. were awarded the contract for the decoration and repairs to Saxmundham station on 6th April, 1897 after the firm tendered a price of £90, later increased to £92 10s. 0d.

By the summer of 1897 the increasing weights and lengths of special trains taking excursionists to Aldeburgh taxed the existing classes of locomotives working the services. The superintendent and locomotive engineer were of the opinion that larger and longer locomotives could be utilized by the slight easing of the alignment of the curve on to the branch at Saxmundham Junction. Authority was given on 2nd November for the work to be carried out at an estimated cost of £29. Later in the month a strong north-easterly gale combining with an abnormally high tide on Sunday 28th and Monday 29th November resulted in flooding of the line between Thorpeness and Aldeburgh. Train services were suspended beyond Leiston until Tuesday 30th November with a horse bus service operating between Leiston and Aldeburgh.

When the Directors made their annual visit down the line on 10th June, 1898 they again visited Saxmundham and by prior arrangement met with a deputation consisting of Mr Collins, Mr Flick and the Reverend Brown to discuss improvements at the station. As a result of the meeting it was agreed to provide a paved crossing on the Ipswich side of the road level crossing gate, with paving sufficiently wide to serve also for foot passengers passing over the railway between the road crossing gates when open to the public. The footbridge was to be provided with a canopy over its entire length. The question of obtaining parliamentary powers to widen the North Entrance underbridge No. 449 at the Yarmouth end of the station to allow the platform to be lengthened in that direction and the subsequent relocation of the water crane was to be investigated. The crossing at Mill Lane/Chantry Road was also to be part paved for foot pedestrians. Along the line at Aldeburgh the station received the benefit of the repair and painting programme on 4th October, 1898 when a contract was awarded to C. Stearn after he tendered at £230. Then after a series of complaints from the Leiston station master regarding cramped accommodation in the station house, authority was given on 15th November, 1898 for improvements at a cost of £95. The Directors made yet another line visit on 27th, 28th and 29th November, 1898 when they visited such diverse places as Saffron Walden, Hunstanton, Brightlingsea and Braintree. The Aldeburgh branch was also traversed on the second day when during a brief halt at Saxmundham the Engineer was instructed to arrange for the footbridge canopy to be provided as a matter of urgency.

The GER authorities regularly monitored earnings from London and suburban stations booking to east coast resorts and it was announced in January 1899 that passenger traffic receipts to Aldeburgh from March to October 1898 registered £3,855 against £5,809 registered for Southwold via Halesworth and the Southwold Railway. For the same period in 1899 the total to Aldeburgh showed a welcome increase to £4,558.

Six years after the signalling alterations at Leiston and Aldeburgh, it was realized the changes made at Saxmundham required enhancing to improve the pathing of trains on the East Suffolk main line. On 7th February, 1899 a new up main advance starting signal was authorized at a cost of £30, whilst further minor signalling improvements were sanctioned on 4th July, 1899 at cost of £50.

Yet another fatality occurred at Saxmundham on 10th April, 1900 when lad porter G. Wells was killed in a shunting accident. Later in the spring the goods manager reported that increasing traffic handled at Leiston had required the employment of additional staff and the existing goods office was totally inadequate for the necessary book keeping and invoicing. As Garrett's were an important customer, the Directors readily sanctioned the provision of a new goods office on 19th June, 1900 at a cost of £185, and the building was completed and fitted out in January 1901 at the increased cost of £203. Leiston passenger station also received the benefit of the repair and painting programme when S. Brock was awarded the contract on 17th July, 1900 after tendering at £275.

Gas prices which had stabilized for some time were increased at Saxmundham by 6d. per 1,000 cu. ft and at Aldeburgh by 10d. per 1,000 cu. ft on 18th September, 1900, but reduced at Saxmundham by the same amount on 19th November, 1901. Aldeburgh had to wait until February 1902 before prices were reduced by 10d. per 1,000 cu. ft.

Following complaints from the station master at Saxmundham regarding the poor condition of the station house, a contract for minor repairs was awarded to W.H. Gibbs on 7th October, 1902 at a cost of £53 10s. 0d.

For some time the inhabitants of Southwold had been dissatisfied with the main line train services to Halesworth and the connections with the 3 feet gauge Southwold Railway. After due representation, arrangements were made for the Town Clerk of Southwold and others to meet the GER Directors on Tuesday 2nd October, 1900 regarding improvements to the services. The following day the GER Board included in their agenda the continuing request by the Southwold Railway for their undertaking to be purchased, when it was revealed the line was valued at £27,322. At the meeting the Board members were advised that the capital of the Southwold Railway at 31st December, 1899 was £76,626 and the operating profit for the year £2,128, which at 3 per cent represented a capital of £70,933. It was considered a sum of £60,000 was not an exorbitant sum to pay for the purchase provided the stations, rolling stock and permanent way were in fair condition. The GER Engineer was requested to carry out a re-examination of the line and report on the cost of converting the railway from Halesworth to Southwold to standard gauge with sufficient land to enable the line to be doubled at a later date. He was also instructed to report on the cost of constructing an alternative single-track standard gauge railway between Saxmundham or Leiston and Southwold, again with provision for future widening.

The survey was completed in time for the following Board meeting on 7th November, 1900. At that meeting the General Manager reported that Arthur Pain, the Southwold Railway Engineer and Director, whilst initially accepting the £60,000 offer, had advised that his fellow Directors were willing to sell the line at a fair and reasonable price to be agreed, or in the event of disagreement to settle by arbitration. The GER Engineer then reported on the alternative line, the route proposed penetrating more sparsely populated tracts of Suffolk than the Blyth valley followed by the Southwold Railway. It commenced 27 chains north of Saxmundham Junction signal box and ran mostly on gradients of 1 in 100 for just over 10 miles to a terminal at Southwold. Stations were proposed at Westleton, Dunwich and Walberswick before the River Blyth was crossed on a swing bridge. Alternative approaches and sites for the terminus were proposed at Southwold, one running close to Walberswick parallel to Salt Creek, along the base of Skilman's Hill then through Strickland Place to terminate near the Post Office. The second proposed route ran to a point between the Southwold Railway swing bridge over the Blyth and Blackshore to terminate about 3½ chains south of the existing Southwold station. The cost of the new line was estimated at £145,445 against £158,887 for the purchase and rebuilding of the Southwold line (£98,887 for re-gauging and £60,000 purchase), which would not be an 'express' line. The GER Board, after debating the dubious merits of the viability of the new line, resolved that no further steps would be taken at present to purchase the Southwold Railway. The Southwold management was duly advised and thus had to pursue a different course for possible extension of their system. Nothing came of the ambitious scheme for extension or takeover and within three decades the narrow gauge Southwold Railway was closed.

Back on the Aldeburgh branch train drivers and guards regularly reported that services had been delayed on the approach to Crown Lands level crossing No. 15 between Leiston and Aldeburgh, and after investigation the traffic superintendent reported that the problem was the late opening of the gates for the passage of trains. The barriers were operated by a gate lad who earned 10s. 0d. per week and who was accommodated in a makeshift hut besides the crossing. The position was difficult to fill as the location was isolated and on several occasions the lad had fallen asleep and had to be aroused by the crew of an approaching train. Supervision of the crossing by the station master at Leiston was difficult due to its isolated position. It was suggested to the Way & Works Committee on 17th February, 1903 that the solution was to provide a cottage for a platelayer at the location, whose wife could supervise the opening and closing of the gates. The cost of land for the cottage was estimated at £20 and the building £300. The annual maintenance charges were estimated at £16 and after due consideration the Traffic Committee authorized the provision of the gatehouse; the structure was ultimately completed at a cost of £339 in November 1905.

From the summer of 1904 when the seaside summer holidays were firmly established, express services were provided from Liverpool Street to both Yarmouth and Lowestoft and return. Passengers travelling from Aldeburgh and Leiston received the benefit of an additional connection at Saxmundham when on 8th March, 1905 it was announced that an up, formerly non-stop, train from Lowestoft to London in the summer months would stop at Saxmundham with a connection to and from Aldeburgh and be decelerated by eight minutes. At Ipswich it then combined with a portion from Felixstowe. From 1906 the Felixstowe portion was discontinued and through coaches from Aldeburgh were attached to the Lowestoft train at Saxmundham.

Garrett & Sons wrote to the GER Directors on 11th July, 1905 advising that they had devoted their best energies in the last 12 months to the development of a steam tractor for use by railway companies and other large and important carriers. A photograph was included with the correspondence and having produced the machine, which they believed to be superior to any on the market, they considered that if desirable they would send an engine for trial on the GER. The company Directors were somewhat taken aback when the General Manager replied the following day that no facilities could be afforded; the GER was building its own motor buses and if any other vehicle was required it would be built in their own workshops. On 13th July Garrett's expressed disappointment as they hoped to have found a means of increasing the valued account of the company. It was felt sure that the supply of steam tractors to the GER would be advantageous; they were already negotiating with other railway companies as they were unable to produce them in small quantities. The matter was brought before the Traffic Committee on 18th July when the General Manager was instructed to inform Garrett's that if the company required any product they would invite quotations.

Over the years the branch railway was often used by local people taking a short cut from town or village to their intended destination, fortunately without serious consequences, but on 24th January, 1906 a young lad called Brook was run down by the branch train while trespassing on the railway between Leiston and Aldebugh receiving fatal injuries. The GER authorities were forced to reiterate to the public in the local press the folly of such actions.

A heavy gale with winds driving off the German Ocean (North Sea) on 22nd February, 1908, caused considerable damage across Norfolk and Suffolk. Many GER stations reported minor damage to infrastructure but Leiston and Aldeburgh, adjacent to the coast, sustained greater damage and train services were suspended so that debris could be removed from the line. Later on 1st August W. Madle, employed by a local contractor, received fatal injuries when hit by a branch train at Saxmundham.

At about 7.30 am on 11th August, 1908, 19-year-old Edward Thurkettle, employed as a horse chain youth by Thomas Durrant & Son, local horse shunting agents for the GER, received injuries in an accident at Saxmundham. On the morning in question two loaded cattle wagons were being shunted by horses from No. 2 cattle dock siding to the down main line ready to be attached to an up cattle train. The two horses under the charge of horse driver J. Clarry, who was also in the service of the shunting agents, were unnecessarily attached to the draw bar of the first vehicle and consequently the horses and Thurkettle, who held the rein of the leading horse, had to walk between the rails in the 'four foot'. On reaching a crossing Thurkettle, to keep close to the horses, unwisely stepped on the crossing and trapped his right foot between the wing rails. Before his foot could be released or the wagons stopped, his foot was run over incurring injuries, which necessitated amputation. The inspecting officer Amos

Excursionists waiting on the platform at Leiston in the early 1900s as an 'M15' class 2-4-2T approaches the platform with empty coaching stock. Note the down home signal and up advance starting signal on the tall post in the background and the ornate yard lamp in the foreground. *Author's Collection*

Leiston station built by the East Suffolk Railway for the opening of the line in 1859 with small ornate canopy fronting the main station building. This view with station staff on the platform was taken before the goods shed to the left was extended in 1911. The station master's living accommodation was on the first floor. *Author's Collection*

Moss, conducting the investigation for the BOT, found that not only were the horses attached to the draw bar, contrary to railway company regulations, but instead of walking close to the brake lever, the horse driver unwisely walked close to the draw bar from which position he was unable to see Thurkettle until the wagon was near to him. Before he could get to the brake and stop the vehicles the first wheel had passed over Thurkettle's foot. The accident was caused solely by the rash action of horse driver J. Clarry, who was well acquainted with the railway company's shunting instruction but chose to ignore them with unfortunate results.

In January 1910 Garrett's approached the GER for additional goods facilities including extra sidings and passenger facilities at Leiston. After meetings between the goods manager and the representatives of the company it was revealed that for some time the existing accommodation for traffic had been unsatisfactory and the company was asking for the complete site to be remodelled. The matter was discussed at the meeting of the Traffic Committee on 3rd February when sanction for the improved facilities was sought. The provision of additional siding accommodation and increased capacity weighbridge (from 20 to 25 tons) was estimated at £744. The extension to the existing goods shed, a new coal shed, the conversion of the granary into a stable block, provision of a 2 ton capacity cart weighbridge and alterations to the passenger booking hall and associated telegraph charges was estimated at £752. It was also decided to provide an awning over the platform fronting the goods shed to protect waiting passengers from inclement weather at a cost of £110. The additional sidings required 0.269 acres of land belonging to Garrett and the firm was willing to release this at a cost price of £67 5s. 0d. The Traffic Committee was advised that Garrett's provided 80 per cent of the total tonnage handled at Leiston, which had been steadily increasing over the past decade.

| Year | Tonnage |
|------|---------|
| 1899 | 26,139 |
| 1900 | 23,971 |
| 1901 | 22,505 |
| 1902 | 25,315 |
| 1903 | 28,645 |
| 1904 | 29,102 |
| 1905 | 31,263 |
| 1906 | 32,049 |
| 1907 | 35,052 |
| 1908 | 34,693 |

After hearing that Garrett's practically provided the whole of the manpower for dealing with their traffic and employed two shunting horses, which worked almost continually in the yard, the Directors authorized the £1,673 5s. 0d. expenditure for the improvements. As part of the overall scheme the contract for the alteration to station buildings and awnings at Leiston was awarded to Alfred Coe of Ipswich on 3rd November, 1910 at a cost of £580. The entire scheme costs were later reduced to £1,594 and the work was completed by 21st December, 1911 at an actual cost of £1,233.

A 'Y14' class 0-6-0 stands on the main single line at Leiston station whilst shunting the branch freight train. A selection of GER open wagons stand on the loop road; the small canopy fronting the station building and newer canopy fronting the goods shed can be seen to good effect.

*Author's Collection*

For many years the considerable tonnage of goods traffic handled at Leiston justified the employment of horsepower for shunting and certainly before the introduction of the shunting locomotive *Sirapite*, Garrett's employed horses. Here two shunting horses are shown on the main single line accompanied by a horse driver and shunter around the turn of the century and before the extension of the goods shed. Note the down starting signal on the down side of the line at the east end of the station platform.

*Author's Collection*

The decision to hold the 1910 Suffolk Show at Saxmundham stirred the GER management into action after it was revealed that by careful programming the holding of the show in the town in 1895 had caused only little inconvenience. However, traffic in the intervening 15 years had increased and the existing accommodation was now considered totally inadequate. To meet the requirements for the temporary loading and unloading of livestock there was the necessity to raise the down platform at the London end from the existing height of 1 ft 10 in. to the standard height of 3 ft. It was also agreed to extend the same platform at the south end and the Traffic Committee authorized the work, costing an estimated £350, on 17th March, 1910. The new works, which were deemed to be permanent, were completed at a cost of £238. To spruce up the passenger station for the occasion the Directors authorized a contract for the repairs and painting at Saxmundham and this was awarded to G. Allen on 7th April, 1910 at cost of £344 17s. 0d. From 1910 first class branch passengers were afforded the luxury of footwarmers during the winter months after facilities were provided at Aldeburgh for filling and emptying the containers.

At 11.07 am on 19th January, 1911, 34-year-old shunter John Henry Pheby was fatally injured in a shunting accident at Saxmundham. He had been on duty for 3 hours 7 minutes in a 12 hours shift. Amos Ford conducted the BOT inquiry into the accident and found the accident had occurred when a down goods train was being shunted from the down main line into a siding to allow a passenger train to pass. Whilst Pheby was standing on some point rodding in the 6 ft space between the up and down main line, giving hand signals to the driver of the goods train, five empty coaches which had been standing in the up platform were set back over the cross-over to the down platform. Almost as soon as the carriages had been set in motion the footstep of the leading vehicle struck Pheby, causing him to fall and strike his head against the axlebox of one of the wagons moving on the down main line. As he fell he sustained a fractured skull and died from the injury. Ford was of the opinion that the mishap was purely accidental but for future safety he required the GER to issued instructions forbidding men to stand in the 'six foot' between two main lines during shunting operations, unless some form of protection was provided to warn of trains approaching on the adjacent line.

In 1911 a limited company with Frank Garrett, junior as Chairman was formed for the purpose of supplying gas to Leiston and district. Works were to be established by the side of the Aldeburgh branch railway and application was duly made for the provision of a siding to serve the new gas works, which subsequently opened later the same year. The goods manager was asked to investigate and reported to the Traffic Committee that tonnage was not likely to be heavy for some time but with a view to encouraging trade the GER agreed to accept 5 per cent rental on the railway outlay, instead of the usual 10 per cent, with a 5 per cent rebate if tonnage increased. The Traffic Committee duly authorized the installation of the siding on 5th October, 1911 at an estimated cost of £589. The figure was later amended to £575 and the work was completed in May 1912 at the much-reduced price of £473.

Aldeburgh station was again repaired and repainted in 1912 after Andrews Ltd was awarded the contract on 18th April, tendering at £426 16s. 0d. A month later the cost of gas supplies to the station was reduced by 5d. to 4s. 7d. per 1,000 cu. ft.

View facing south in 1911 from the down goods reception siding at Saxmundham showing Albion Street level crossing with the up platform to the left and Saxmundham Station signal box to the centre. Note the intricate pointwork in the foreground leading from the up main/down main crossover to the down reception siding and shed roads. There was no facing access from the down main line to the goods yard and all down trains were required to run past the goods yard and reverse into the various sidings. The wagons being sheeted are standing on the shed road headshunt, which served the premises of T. Durrant & Son, corn and coal merchants.

*Windwood Collection*

The Aldeburgh branch train shunting on the up main line at Saxmundham before traversing the crossover to the down side in the early 1900s. Note the GER practice of placing the signal box name on the front of the building rather than at the ends of the structure as later adopted by the LNER.

*Author's Collection*

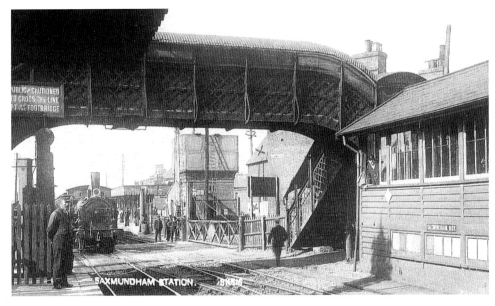

By the Great Eastern Railway Act 1912 (2 and 3 Geo. 5 cap. xxxvii), which received the Royal Assent on 7th August, 1912, the company was empowered to acquire a strip of land in the parish and urban district of Leiston-cum-Sizewell on and adjoining the south side of Leiston station for future development. On 17th August, 1912 Lieutenant Colonel P.G. Von Donop inspected the alterations completed in May at Leiston, and found that a new connection facing down trains leading to the gas works had been installed on the down side of the single line east of the station. The associated points and ground signals were worked from a 6-lever ground frame which was locked by the key on the Train Staff for the section of line. The interlocking was correctly carried out and Von Donop authorized use of the siding connection.

In 1913 the GER Directors were concerned that Garrett's were contemplating removing their works from Leiston away from the GER system, as the existing works were incompetitively [sic] located. Considerable discussion took place between the GER goods manager and Garrett's Directors, after which the firm agreed to remain provided the railway company increased accommodation and installed additional sidings on Garrett's land. The matter was discussed at the Traffic Committee meeting on 14th February, 1914 when it was revealed that goods and coal tonnages handled at Leiston had increased from 28,645 tons in 1903 to 44,978 tons in 1912, a 57 per cent increase in 10 years. The tonnage was practically all for Garrett's and the year-by-year breakdown was:

| Year | Goods | Coal | Total |
|------|-------|------|-------|
|      | tons  | tons | tons  |
| 1903 | 18,559 | 10,086 | 28,645 |
| 1904 | 18,824 | 10,278 | 29,102 |
| 1905 | 19,934 | 11,329 | 31,263 |
| 1906 | 20,218 | 11,831 | 32,049 |
| 1907 | 23,099 | 11,953 | 35,052 |
| 1908 | 22,881 | 11,812 | 34,693 |
| 1909 | 26,763 | 12,305 | 39,068 |
| 1910 | 32,588 | 13,614 | 46,202 |
| 1911 | 34,058 | 14,632 | 48,690 |
| 1912 | 31,522 | 13,456 | 44,978 |

The Traffic Committee duly agreed the total cost of £6,308 was to be borne by the GER with Garrett's providing the necessary land free of charge. The expenditure included the provision of a 30 tons capacity electric crane in place of the existing 15 tons capacity hand crane, with the firm agreeing to supply the electric power and labour free of charge. The cost was later reduced to £5,298 and the works were finally completed in May 1916 at a cost of £4,559.

Further reductions in gas prices for supply to branch stations was welcomed by the GER authorities when on 6th February, 1913 the tariff at Saxmundham was reduced by 3d. per 1,000 cu. ft to 4s. 9d. to be followed by a reduction at Aldeburgh by 1d. to 4s. 6d. per 1,000 cu. ft in May 1914.

A syndicate under the title of Bungalows Ltd led by Stuart Ogilvie, the owner of a considerable acreage of land at Sizewell, had from 1912 developed the Bury estate for housing at Thorpeness, his father having made a fortune as a result of a partnership with Thomas Brassey, the railway contractor. An approach was

From a postcard entitled 'Tea Time', the entrance to Garrett's Bottom Works is shown in 1912 with the tramway connection from the station interchange siding on the lower right before crossing the Saxmundham Road, later Main Street. The Long Shop which now contains an excellent museum in just visible to the right. *Long Shop Museum*

It was originally intended to terminate and start Aldeburgh branch services from the up side bay platform at Saxmundham but as this 1911 view shows the site was restrictive and a train standing in the platform effectively blocked the entrance to the up side goods yard. The scene looking towards the buffer stops shows two GER horse boxes and a cattle wagon standing on the dock road headshunt whilst other cattle wagons occupy the 210 ft cattle dock road and open wagons occupy the dock road. The down bay starting signal can be seen over the top of the wagons. Note the trap points in the platform line, interlocked by the starting signal, and re-railing ramps by the buffer stops. *Author's Collection*

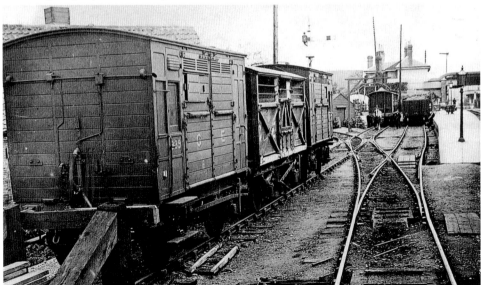

The rural approach to Thorpeness Halt soon after the opening of the station. Beside the level crossing is the crossing keeper's cottage. *Author's Collection*

Aldeburgh station viewed from the entrance in Victoria Road. The pine trees were planted when the line opened for traffic to enhance the approach. The overall train shed is prominent but W.H. Smith's bookstall has yet to be erected. *Author's Collection*

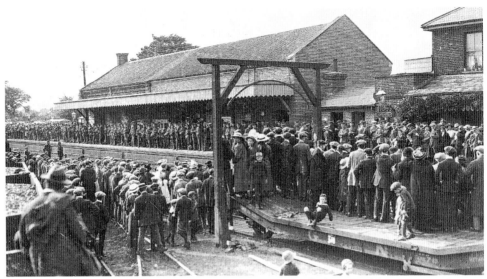

Leiston station on 5th August, 1914, the day following the declaration of Britain's entry into World War I. Crowds gather to offer 'Good Luck' to Leiston H Company of the Territorial Army en route to military service. Many of the men in cloth caps would follow in due course to also serve their country - many never to return. A Great Northern Railway implement wagon in the foreground provided a grandstand view, probably before being used for the conveyance of machinery from Garrett's works. The loading gauge with double posts is of interest whilst the goods shed shows evidence of the original structure to the left and the later extension with newer brickwork to the right. *Author's Collection*

As with many towns, Leiston not only provided for the war effort in World War I with Garrett's making armaments and military equipment, but many young men volunteered to fight for King and Country - some never returning from the battlefield. Here hundreds wait on the platform for a troop train as Frank Garrett on the extreme right surveys the scene; he is standing by a flat wagon conveying a timber load. *Long Shop Museum*

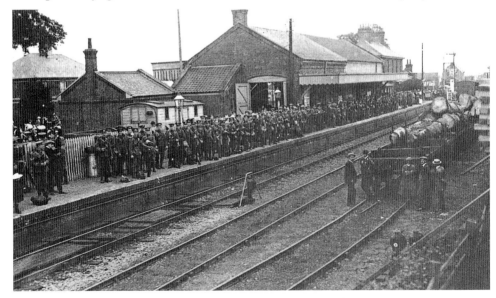

made to the GER for a small station to serve the development and the company enthused in the July 1913 house magazine,

Thorpeness – yet another sea coast resort has been added to the twenty served by the GER – a hamlet one mile or so north of Aldeburgh but at present more conveniently reached from Leiston, passengers being carried to and fro by motor conveyance known as the *Vitesse*, a combination of an open carriage and omnibus, the two being run together or as an open vehicle according to requirements. It was capable of accommodating 30 passengers, whilst the front part of the chassis was adapted to convey heavy luggage. The place is in its infancy, a 'kursaal' has been erected as part of the bungalow town and there are hard tennis courts and a croquet and bowling green. Thirty to forty bungalows have been erected so far of wood with a tile roof.

The outcome was evident for after learning that Aldeburgh branch traffic for 1913 had shown considerable signs of expansion the GER Traffic Committee on 16th July, 1914, ever keen to consolidate their position against a possible rival road competitor, agreed to the provision of a small halt to assist the development of the estate, at a cost of £270. The small piece of land required for the halt was to be donated by Bury Limited at a nominal rent of 1s. 0d. per annum as long as the halt existed. The station, known as Thorpeness Halt, located on the down side of the single line was completed in a surprisingly short time for it opened to traffic on 29th July, 1914.

On the outbreak of World War I just a few days later in August 1914 the GER, with other British railway companies, came under Government control but at the outset the Aldeburgh branch services continue to run to pre-war timetables. Soon after the outbreak of hostilities Lieutenant Colonel P.G. Von Donop conducted the BOT inspection of Thorpeness Halt on 23rd October, 1914. He found that the new halt consisting of a single platform, 300 ft in length by 12 ft wide and 3 ft in height, was located on the down side of the single line. It was provided with a shelter for passengers, lamps, a nameboard and a booking office with a suitable public approach from the adjacent road. The inspector was satisfied the halt could be used for trains, provided their length was accommodated within the length of the platform and noted that the only item requiring attention was the addition of station names on the cases of the oil lamps. The GER official attending the inspection agreed to the remedial work being undertaken as a matter of urgency. Unfortunately within days of the opening of the halt the intended holidaymakers had departed and the army now occupied the village.

The provision of new sidings at Leiston coincided with the opening of Garrett's Station, or Top Works, in 1914, which almost immediately turned to production for the war effort with increased imports of raw material and exports of armaments and machinery for the armed forces. The increased productivity resulted in the employment of additional skilled artisans and workers who, living in the town, used the footpath to the west of Leiston station to access the works. However, for some years pressure had been mounting for the abolition of the footpath, as it crossed the tracks of the single branch line and sidings of the goods yard and exchange sidings for Garrett's premises. Train crews and goods yard staff had complained of the danger to the public and especially Garrett's workers crossing the line during shunting operations or during the hours of darkness. With increased patronage because of the war effort the GER Directors decided on 5th November, 1914 to seek powers for the diversion of footpath and replacement by a footbridge.

The diversion of the footpath was subsequently authorized by the Great Eastern Railway Act 1915 (5 and 6 Geo. 5 cap. xvi) which received the Royal Assent on 9th June, 1915. Clause 22e of the statute granted the company powers to divert so much of the footpath in the parish and urban district of Leiston-cum-Sizewell in the county of Suffolk (Eastern Division) leading from Saxmundham Road to Buckleswood Road as crossed the company's Aldeburgh Branch Railway; such diverted footpath to be carried over the said railway by means of a footbridge. The contract for the provision of the footbridge spanning the yard and main single line and associated sidings at Leiston was duly awarded to Eastwood Swingler at a cost of £622 0s. 3d. on 7th October, 1915, and work was completed early in 1916.

Tragically later in the same year on 4th December, 1915, district relief signalman H.C. Moore was killed whilst going on duty at Saxmundham. Walking along the line in the darkness towards the Junction signal box he was run down by a train.

The railway saw the departure of many men who volunteered to serve with the armed forces and on occasions the platforms at Aldeburgh, Leiston, Saxmundham, and to a lesser extent Thorpeness Halt, were crowded as loved ones watched their departure and hoped for an early return. Several railwaymen also joined the colours and older men continuing in service or the recruitment of women ensured the temporary vacancies were covered. Sadly not all who departed returned to their native Suffolk. The opening of airfields at Leiston and to a lesser extent Orfordness brought an influx of aircrew and ground staff to serve at the establishments, many travelling by rail to and from Leiston before onward conveyance by road.

The war also brought an increase in goods traffic as additional produce from local farms was sent to towns and cities to make up for the loss of imported goods. Training sessions were also arranged for troops in the coastal area around Thorpeness and Aldeburgh involving the running of special trains to convey men and horses to and from manoeuvres. During this period Garrett and Sons Limited continued manufacturing steam tractors, shells and government wagons for the war effort. Despite the hostilities, the programme of repairs and painting of stations was maintained and on 1st June, 1916 W. Staines was awarded the contract for work at Leiston station after tendering at £236.

By December 1916 the strain of the war effort was taxing the resources of all British railways to such an extent that the Railway Executive Committee issued an ultimatum that they could only continue if drastic reductions were made to ordinary services. The Lloyd George Coalition agreed to a reduction of passenger services from January 1917, but with the economic measures the Aldeburgh branch lost only one passenger train in each direction. It was also deemed the branch was of military importance as it served the East Anglian coast, which was bearing the brunt of enemy hostilities. So concerned were the military and railway authorities of possible invasion that the Aldeburgh branch was considered a front defensive line for the conveyance of troops and civilian personnel, if the Germans managed to land their troops. For many months during this period the Aldeburgh branch engine was kept in steam continuously 24 hours a day, seven days a week, ready for instant action should the necessity arise, with a second locomotive allocated to the branch at times as cover.

The war affected servicemen in many ways, not only those serving at the front but for those subsequently experiencing physical and mental torment as result of injury and emotional stress. On 9th May, 1917 Corporal C.J. Reeves of the King's Service Corps stepped in front of a train at Saxmundham and was killed outright. A verdict of suicide was reached at the subsequent inquest into the fatality. The war came ever nearer to Aldeburgh when on the night of 16th/17th June a German Zeppelin airship No. L48 was attacked and shot down over the Sizewell Gap before drifting ablaze until it crashed at Theberton. The railway later became involved when the scrap metal recovered from the wreckage was dispatched by train from Leiston.

Despite dangers of aerial bombardment the station repair and painting programme continued when a contract for work at Saxmundham was awarded to Mr Hayward on 4th October, 1917 after he tendered at £345. Unfortunately not all casualties of the war were servicemen for on 27th November, 1917 a train travelling between Leiston and Aldeburgh struck and killed a man. At a later inquest the deceased was named as driver A. Green and a verdict of suicide recorded.

The end of hostilities in November 1918 was greeted with great relief and the branch stations were decorated with flags to celebrate the armistice. The year was tinged with sadness for Frank Garrett senior, who had done much to develop the Leiston works and engender a close working relationship with the GER, passed away.

The branch settled to renewed peacetime operation, which was rudely shattered when from 26th September to 5th October, 1919 there was a general railway strike and services on the Aldeburgh branch were initially suspended. Garrett's workers had other ideas and with the full agreement of railway management they worked some of the services using GER locomotives. The strike had, however, undermined the patronage enjoyed by the railway as prospective passengers readily turned to alternative modes of transport. Railwaymen were also critical of the strikebreakers and for many years afterwards tensions existed between the company servants and Garrett's employees.

Early in 1920 Garrett's announced they were again extending their premises at Leiston and required yet more siding accommodation. After due negotiation the railway company agreed to install the sidings at a cost of £4,515 and the Traffic Committee on 5th February, 1920 authorized the work to proceed on property belonging to the firm provided the land was given free of charge. The committee further discussed the matter on 11th March, 1920 endorsing the urgent implementation of the scheme in view of the considerable payments made by R. Garrett & Sons for the previous three years: 1917, £5,190; 1918, £4,811 and 1919 £10,600 and noting the proposed reception sidings for the marshalling of the

"Carrying on" during the Railway Strike.
Leiston Oct.2.19.

During the short strike by railwaymen in October 1919 Garrett's provided volunteer labour to ensure traffic movements were maintained during the stoppage. Here a group of strike breakers are shown at Leiston on the footplate of 'Y14' class 0-6-0 No. 569, later LNER No. 7569 then 5467 and BR No. 65467, which had a long association with the Aldeburgh branch.                                        *Long Shop Museum*

firm's traffic were to be installed on land conveyed free of charge to the GER. After further surveys the proposed accommodation was reduced and the work was subsequently completed in November 1922 at a cost of £2,238.

In August 1920 Stuart Ogilvie applied for the provision of siding accommodation at Thorpeness and the matter was brought to the attention of the Traffic Committee on 30th September. The goods manager reported that the siding would generate the delivery of building and construction materials in connection with the further development of the area, whilst a small amount of agricultural traffic would be sent away. The Traffic Committee approved of the siding, which was estimated to cost £1,261. On the same day authority was given for additional water supplies for station and locomotive use at Saxmundham at a cost of £1,600. On a sadder note the members learned of the death of gate lad B.J. Cracknell at Saxmundham East Green crossing, the coroner recording a verdict of death by misadventure.

The programme of station repainting and repairs continued and on 9th November, 1922 Mr Greenwood received the contract for work at Saxmundham after he tendered at £181 14s. 0d. In the final throes of the GER ownership the installation of the siding at Thorpeness was completed in December 1922 at a cost of £1,121, a saving of £140 on estimate. The Aldeburgh branch had survived relatively unscathed through the recent hostilities and it was hoped the impending Grouping of the railways would engender an increase in receipts as more people travelled to the east coast of East Anglia for their leisure.

# Chapter Five

# Grouping

As a result of the 1921 Railways Act, from 1st January, 1923 the GER amalgamated with the Great Northern, Great Central, North Eastern and North British, and several smaller railways to form the London & North Eastern Railway. In the initial months little changed but gradually the identity on the locomotives and rolling stock working the branch services altered, with the legend 'LNER' on the tank and tender sides, whilst coaching and wagon stock also showed the ownership of the new company. Major G.L. Hall made the BOT inspection of the new works at Thorpeness Halt on 9th May, 1923, and found that an intermediate siding connection facing traffic from Aldeburgh had been made in the Leiston to Aldeburgh single line Train Staff section. The points were laid on the section of line where the gradient was falling at 1 in 164 towards Aldeburgh and was to be worked by an engine at the lower end of the train to prevent a runaway. Independent disc signals were provided for entry to and exit from the siding, which was worked by a 5-lever ground frame controlled by the Annett's key on the Train Staff. One of the levers was the release lever, the second operated the bolt lock, the third the points whilst the remaining two levers operated the disc signals. Hall found that the facing point bar originally shown in the plan submitted by the railway company had not been installed. The inspector reminded the engineer attending the inspection that disc signals in such a situation were not now a requirement and the official said he was aware of the ruling. Hall was of the opinion an economy could be made in the working levers by dispensing with the release lever and substituting an economical type of facing point bolt. Despite his observations the inspector found the interlocking correct and the arrangements 'generally satisfactory'.

Before all items of rolling stock received the LNER livery, industrial action affected affairs and a seven-day railway strike from 20th January, 1924 brought a decline in traffic. The deteriorating relationship between trades unions and the railway company only served to encourage competition and gradually bus services offering almost door-to-door services appeared on local roads. However, the branch stations received the benefit of the repair and painting programme in 1924 when on 31st July a contract was awarded to A. Bagnell & Son for work at Leiston and Aldeburgh costing £205 10s. 0d. and £275 14s. 6d. respectively.

The London and North Eastern Railway Act of 1924 (14 and 15 Geo. 5 cap. liii), which received the Royal Assent on 1st August, 1924, granted the company powers to acquire by compulsory purchase lands in the urban district of Saxmundham on the north side of and adjoining Albion Street and west of and adjoining Saxmundham station, and lands in parish of Aldringham with Thorpe on the west side of and adjoining the company's Aldeburgh branch and south of and adjoining Thorpeness crossing for future possible development.

The affairs of the branch were again disrupted by the General Strike in early May 1926. Railway union members withdrew their labour in support of the miners and subsequently train services could not be guaranteed. On several days the Aldeburgh branch services were suspended. Fortunately within a week regular railwaymen returned to duty and services resumed. The impact of the continuing miners strike meant reduced coal stocks available to the railway companies and the LNER authorities decided on the only course of action available to conserve stocks by reducing train services. Thus from 31st May, 1926 a much reduced service was operated until the situation improved some weeks later.

As a result of the lessons learnt from World War I, Territorial Army units regularly conducted exercises to maintain a backup for regular troops in the event of armed conflict. On one such occasion the 4th Suffolks attended a weekend of exercises on the North Norfolk coast and organized a special train from Ipswich to West Runton on Saturday 16th July, 1927. The service picked up Territorials at Ipswich as well as Woodbridge, Wickham Market, Saxmundham, Halesworth and Reedham. The branch train provided a connection from Aldeburgh and Leiston for participants attending the event.

The last few days of 1927 brought the first serious wintry weather to affect the Aldeburgh branch for some years. The blizzard came at a most inconvenient time as local railwaymen settled down with their families on the evening of Christmas day. The rising wind and driving snow found that by Boxing Day morning the branch was blocked in several places by snowdrifts. Train services were abandoned until the Ipswich snowplough, which had initially been used to keep the main lines clear, could concentrate on clearing the East Suffolk line branches. It was 27th December before services were resumed from Aldeburgh despite permanent way staff assisting with clearance of snow by hand.

The problems encountered by the LNER management during the early years of Grouping saw the branch passenger and parcel receipts fluctuate dramatically as the figures below show.

| | Passengers | Passenger receipts £ | Parcel receipts £ | Season tickets receipts £ | Total £ |
|---|---|---|---|---|---|
| **1923** | | | | | |
| Saxmundham | 50,551 | 7,549 | 2,386 | 326 | 10,261 |
| Leiston | 41,157 | 4,248 | 1,268 | 572 | 6,088 |
| Thorpeness Halt | 11,968 | 848 | 136 | 1 | 985 |
| Aldeburgh | 26,679 | 4,865 | 783 | 314 | 5,962 |
| *Total** | *79,804* | *9,961* | *2,187* | *887* | *13,035* |
| *Total†* | *130,355* | *17,510* | *4,573* | *1,213* | *23,296* |
| | | | | | |
| **1924** | | | | | |
| Saxmundham | 51,356 | 8,200 | 2,207 | 317 | 10,724 |
| Leiston | 36,901 | 4,048 | 1,299 | 197 | 5,544 |
| Thorpeness Halt | 11,504 | 789 | 135 | 12 | 936 |
| Aldeburgh | 23,293 | 4,692 | 973 | 347 | 6,012 |
| *Total** | *71,698* | *9,529* | *2,407* | *556* | *12,492* |
| *Total†* | *123,054* | *17,729* | *4,614* | *873* | *23,216* |

\* Total branch stations only.
† Total branch stations and Saxmundham.

|  | Passengers | Passenger receipts £ | Parcel receipts £ | Season tickets receipts £ | Total £ |
|---|---|---|---|---|---|
| **1925** | | | | | |
| Saxmundham | 49,314 | 8,397 | 3,011 | 284 | 11,692 |
| Leiston | 42,058 | 4,036 | 1,376 | 81 | 5,493 |
| Thorpeness Halt | 10,000 | 738 | 120 | – | 858 |
| Aldeburgh | 20,957 | 4,431 | 983 | 453 | 5,867 |
| *Total** | *73,015* | *9,205* | *2,479* | *534* | *12,218* |
| *Total†* | *122,329* | *17,602* | *5,490* | *818* | *23,910* |
| **1926** | | | | | |
| Saxmundham | 41,334 | 7,528 | 4,559 | 418 | 12,505 |
| Leiston | 38,546 | 3,535 | 1,210 | 59 | 4,804 |
| Thorpeness Halt | 8,110 | 636 | 117 | – | 753 |
| Aldeburgh | 16,470 | 4,104 | 1,148 | 339 | 5,591 |
| *Total** | *63,126* | *8,275* | *2,475* | *398* | *11,148* |
| *Total†* | *104,460* | *15,803* | *7,034* | *816* | *23,653* |
| **1927** | | | | | |
| Saxmundham | 44,578 | 8,274 | 4,424 | 202 | 12,900 |
| Leiston | 39,669 | 3,506 | 1,035 | 17 | 4,558 |
| Thorpeness Halt | 10,938 | 807 | 128 | – | 935 |
| Aldeburgh | 17,462 | 4,153 | 1,044 | 300 | 5,497 |
| *Total** | *68,069* | *8,466* | *2,207* | *317* | *10,990* |
| *Total+* | *112,647* | *16,740* | *6,631* | *519* | *23,890* |
| **1928** | | | | | |
| Saxmundham | 48,850 | 7,976 | 3,620 | 295 | 11,891 |
| Leiston | 43,111 | 3,468 | 1,141 | 41 | 4,650 |
| Thorpeness Halt | 12,125 | 847 | 125 | – | 972 |
| Aldeburgh | 20,431 | 3,887 | 1,087 | 424 | 5,398 |
| *Total** | *75,667* | *8,202* | *2,353* | *465* | *11,020* |
| *Total+* | *124,517* | *16,178* | *5,973* | *760* | *22,911* |

The average daily number of passengers using the branch stations totalling 219 in 1923 reduced to 173 in 1926 before recovering to 208 by 1928. Receipts, however, declined considerably for the daily £27 7s. 2d. in 1923 had dwindled to £22 10s. 7d. by 1928 giving further evidence of the inroads made by the competitive bus services.

On 30th January, 1930 the Divisional General Manager (Southern Area) reported that the Aldeburgh branch, 7 miles 72 chains in length, was at present maintained by three permanent way gangs comprising a total of 11 men. He recommended that by introducing a motor trolley the branch could be maintained by one gang comprising eight men with a net annual saving of £296. He considered the provision of a motor trolley was necessary to reduce maintenance costs. The matter was brought to the attention of the Works Committee at their meeting on 8th January, 1931 and after due consideration they agreed the estimated expenditure of £535. This included the cost of the trolley and telephone token apparatus to enable the trolley to be removed from the line when it was necessary to allow the passage of a train.

The 1930s saw increased usage of the branch especially at weekends and bank holidays when holidays and rambles in the country were fashionable. Often groups

'F3' class 2-4-2T No. 8070 shunting the Aldeburgh branch train to the down main line before setting back into the down platform to form a down departure. The locomotive is carrying the correct stopping passenger train headcode of one white disc under the chimney.

*Author's Collection*

'F4' class 2-4-2T No. 7146 makes for Aldeburgh with a branch train formed of 6-wheel coaching stock in the 1930s. The train is approaching Thorpeness Halt.          *Author's Collection*

of ramblers would join the branch train at Saxmundham, alight at one of the stations and walk to another before catching a late evening return train. Others took advantage of their days off to travel to Thorpeness or Aldeburgh, either returning the same day or, if travelling outward on Saturday, returning on Monday.

The railway company was always keen to keep wagons on the move to ensure greater utilization and usually demurrage was charged on vehicles detained by traders reluctant to offload or load within a specified period. In the spring of 1932 an exception was made when a pair of thrushes built a nest containing five eggs between the handbrake and body planking of an LNER coal wagon standing in Leiston yard. With great compassion local railway staff refused to allow the wagon to be moved until the five chicks had hatched and fledged. Only then did normal traffic resume in the sidings.

During the 1930s collections were regularly made, with the full agreement of railway management, at stations in Suffolk for the East Suffolk and Ipswich Hospital Contributory Fund. As an example, collections for the year ending 31st December, 1934, included Saxmundham £13 15s. 0d. and Leiston and Aldeburgh £14 15s. 0d.

Just before the Grouping in 1922 the Pullman Car Co. assembled a set of first and third class vehicles nominally for use in connection with race meetings and the GER operated some of these between St Pancras and Newmarket via Cambridge, using first class stock from the South Eastern & Chatham Railway allocation painted in crimson livery. From 1924 the LNER altered the London terminal to Kings Cross and the train ran via Hitchin and Cambridge. The GER also ventured into operating a Sundays-only Clacton Pullman from Liverpool Street from 16th July, 1922 and these trains continued with the LNER during the summer months each year until 1928. From 1924 the GN section provided the Pullman vehicles but the operation of one train to one destination on one day of the week meant the set was underutilized and a wider use for the stock was suggested. Thus from 1929 the LNER developed the idea of the 'Eastern Belle Pullman Limited' offering a series of high speed de-luxe excursion facilities on selected days from Liverpool Street to a group of East Coast seaside resorts nearest to London, with passengers travelling in Pullman cars. Destinations for the 'Eastern Belle', as it was usually called, were published in advance enabling travellers to select the days for visiting the resorts of their choice. Passengers with ordinary tickets were allowed to travel provided they paid the Pullman supplements, the greatest attraction being the cheapness of round-trip day tickets, and the combined rail and Pullman supplement fare was priced at 10s. 6d., later 11s. 3d., first class and 6s. 6d., later 7s. 9d., third class.

The first excursion ran on Monday 3rd June serving Felixstowe and the pattern thereon was for the train to travel to Felixstowe on Mondays, Clacton on Tuesdays, Frinton and Walton on Wednesdays, Dovercourt and Harwich on Thursdays and Thorpeness and Aldeburgh on Fridays. Holders of season tickets could also travel on payment of a supplement of 2s. 2d. first class and 1s. 6d. third class. Table d'Hote lunch and supper was available on board, provided by Pullman catering staff at a cost of 3s. 0d. first class and 2s. 6d. third class, as well as an à la carte menu for other meals and refreshments served at every seat. The original timing from Liverpool Street to Aldeburgh was 2 hours 50 minutes for the 99½ mile journey. Dovercourt and Harwich were only served in the first year and in 1930 had been replaced by a half-day excursion to Clacton. Certain difficulties were experienced in handling

Thorpeness Halt in LNER days with the bodies of the coaching stock used as station
accommodation painted in cream and green livery.                    *Author's Collection*

Road frontage of Saxmundham station up side buildings, which were similar to other structures
erected on the East Suffolk main line but with additional adornments. The station master's
accommodation was located on the first floor and station offices on the ground floor.
                                                                    *Author's Collection*

the 'Eastern Belle' on the Aldeburgh branch, not least on the severe 1 in 58 gradient as the branch swung east from Saxmundham Junction, and the lack of a turntable and restricted layout at Aldeburgh. A correspondent on a trip in the early 1930s reported the train being hauled by a 'D16/3' class 4-4-0 locomotive from London to Saxmundham where the train was then double-headed by having another 'D16/3' class locomotive working tender first piloting the train between Saxmundham and Aldeburgh. This proved an expensive operation but the alternative was equally costly for a single locomotive hauling the train, which after arrival at Aldeburgh, ran light tender first to Ipswich to turn and for the tender to be replenished with coal, before returning light engine tender first to Aldeburgh to pick up the return working. 'B12/3' class 4-6-0s took over the working of the seven- or eight-coach train when the 'Eastern Belle' ran to Aldeburgh. The engine ran round the train and then shunted the stock into the run-round loop where it stood until after the arrival and departure of the ordinary branch train which was only achieved by further shunting to release the branch engine. The 'Eastern Belle' stock then ran empty to Leiston where it was kept until the evening - the engine going to Ipswich. On return from Ipswich the engine ran tender-first, collected the stock at Leiston, and carried on to Aldeburgh where it ran round the stock and, after loading, hauled the train to Liverpool Street.

In 1933 the 'Eastern Belle' was accelerated in timing and Aldeburgh was reached in 2 hours 15 minutes. By this time destinations had expanded including Felixstowe, Lowestoft, Yarmouth, Cromer, Sheringham, Clacton, Hunstanton and Skegness as well as Aldeburgh. By 1935 the Aldeburgh trip was on Tuesdays departing Liverpool Street at 11.00 am returning from Aldeburgh at 7.15 pm and reaching Liverpool Street at 9.37 pm. In that year the train also ran to Cromer on Mondays, Clacton on Wednesdays, Sheringham on Thursdays and Hunstanton on Fridays. By the summer of 1938 there were only three visits to the Aldeburgh branch, reduced to one in 1939 when on 17th August, 1939 the 'Eastern Belle' hauled by 'B12/3' class locomotive No. 8577 failed soon after running on to the branch at Saxmundham Junction. Having made a fast trip between Liverpool Street and Saxmundham the seven-coach train was detained for 20 minutes waiting for the branch train to clear the single line. On restarting No. 8577 was soon in trouble and was brought to a stand. After setting back to the main line the second attempt was successful. On the outbreak of war the 'Eastern Belle' services were curtailed.

The LNER management ever keen to encourage station staff in good housekeeping arranged 'Best Kept Station and Station Garden' competitions. Saxmundham achieved third class prizes in 1923, 1927 and 1930 with the station master the recipient of a cheque for £3 to share with his staff. Aldeburgh fared better and regularly achieved special class category between 1923 and 1939 with a £10 prize. To the credit of the staff the money was usually spent purchasing garden ornaments or plants for the next year's competition!

Just prior to the outbreak of World War II the LNER with all other railway companies came under the control of the Railway Executive Committee. Within weeks of the commencement of hostilities local bus services were reduced and some were removed from the roads by petrol rationing. In May 1940 some improvements were made when the last of the six-wheel coaches, which had formed the branch train for almost three decades, were withdrawn from service

From 1929 the LNER operated a Pullman train from Liverpool Street to various East Anglian seaside resorts each weekday during the summer months including Aldeburgh. Initially 'D16/3' class 4-4-0s hauled the train but problems were soon encountered on the Suffolk branch, which necessitated the substitution by the more powerful 'B12/3' class 4-6-0s. However, occasionally the train encountered difficulties such as on 17th August, 1939 when No. 8577 having made a fast run to Saxmundham was forced to wait at Saxmundham Junction for the Aldeburgh branch train to come off the single line. On restarting No. 8577 quickly ran into trouble with the heavy seven-coach train on the 1 in 58 gradient, ran short of steam and came to a stand. After a short while permission was given to set back and with a rebuilt fire and fresh head of steam the 'B12/3' locomotive topped the rise without difficulty and continued to Aldeburgh.   *The late Dr I.C. Allen*

Aldeburgh station showing the overall roof protecting part of the platform with smoke-blackened awning in the 1930s. The usual formation of six-wheel coaching stock at the south end of the platform is augmented by the through bogie coach from Liverpool Street nearest the camera and carrying the destination board denoting 'Thorpeness and Aldeburgh'. Through coaches to and from Liverpool Street were regularly operated from introduction in 1906 until withdrawal on the outbreak of World War II.   *Stations UK*

Aldeburgh engine shed on 17th May, 1937 with 'F3' class 2-4-2T No. 8073 awaiting its next turn of duty. The shed was a through structure with a short siding to the rear and the shed siding could accommodate one engine in the shed and one outside at the rear, although usually a coal wagon occupied the latter. *The late W.A. Camwell*

For many years 'F3' class 2-4-2Ts were the mainstay of Aldeburgh branch motive power. No. 8043 spins along a straight section of line near Thorpeness Halt with a down train in 1938. Short rail sections are conspicuous in the cess denoting that the bullhead track is shortly to be renewed. *The late Dr I.C. Allen*

and replaced by corridor bogie vehicles. Then in 1941 first class facilities were withdrawn from the branch trains and remained so for a decade, whilst cheap day tickets were withdrawn. In order to safeguard against air raids especially at night when station lamps remained dimmed, staff utilized shielded hand lamps to attend to train or shunting duties. Other precautions against enemy ground attacks included the removal of the station nameboards, which were stored in lamp rooms or signal boxes but were later reinstated. The agricultural nature of the branch was of the utmost importance as vital provisions of home-grown food, grain and vegetables were dispatched and conveyed to markets at Ipswich, Norwich and London. In addition to the outflow of traffic, the war years brought an influx of tinned foods and dried milk for distribution in the area under the auspices of the Ministry of Food. Over 6,000 evacuees were sent to Saxmundham from the London area soon after the outbreak of hostilities but were sent back when local invasion was considered likely despite the beaches being wired off. By the end of 1939, the military were well established in the area when the 2/4th Battalion Essex Regiment set up headquarters at Aldeburgh Lodge School, to be joined in April 1940 by the 9th Battalion The King's Regiment with their headquarters at Belstead School. By April 1942 a battle school was also established at Belstead School and trainees travelled to and from the course by rail.

As the Aldeburgh branch served a Suffolk coastal area considered vulnerable to enemy attack, coastal defence armoured trains patrolled the line as well as serving the neighbouring Framlingham and Snape branches between June 1940 and July 1943. The train was initially manned by British soldiers but later Polish soldiers joined the crew, and when not on patrol the train was usually stabled in the former Row siding at Saxmundham., the soldiers being billeted at Fairfield Road School. Train 'D' initially covered the branch, and then train 'C', which made its last recorded run on the line on the afternoon of 26th March, 1943, although it was not officially disbanded until June. After returning from patrols in Cornwall train 'D', now based at Mistley, resumed its activities on Essex and Suffolk branches until disbanded in July 1943. The LNER authorities were not over-enthusiastic trying to accommodate these trains, which were equipped with a 6 pounder Hotchkiss gun dating from 1917, as siding accommodation was at a premium. Conflict arose in February 1941 when the local corps commander wanted to transfer armoured train 'C' from Saxmundham to Ipswich for operational purposes. He was advised the transfer could only be achieved if one of the 'Warflat' trains stabled at Ipswich was transferred to Saxmundham and that the armoured train would be stabled in a siding alongside the goods sorting yards at Ipswich, where delays might occur if the train was required in an emergency. The 'Warflat' train was left undisturbed but the corps commander was adamant the move from Saxmundham was necessary. Armoured train 'C' duly transferred to Westerfield, which had no watering facilities for 'F4' class 2-4-2T No. 7214 allocated to the train. At Saxmundham water was available for the locomotive as well as coal and water at Aldeburgh and at its new base the engine therefore had to go to and from Ipswich shed for replenishment of coal and water, a routine which often caused operating problems. To obviate some of the unnecessary movements the Director of Transportation asked that an armoured locomotive tender be allocated to armoured train 'C' but it is believed the tender was not supplied until May 1942.

Situated on the vulnerable East Coast and liable to air bombardment the branch was fortunate that only two major incidents affected services. In April 1941 a bomb exploded near Sheepwash crossing, severely damaging the cottage and destroying about a hundred yards of track. No trains were in the vicinity and a substitute bus service was operated until track repairs were completed. Then at about 9.30 am on 4th October, 1943 four unexploded anti-personnel bombs were discovered beside the branch between Leiston and Aldeburgh. The line was immediately closed between the two points and a bus service substituted. The bombs were subsequently rendered harmless and normal working was resumed at 4.00 pm.

From 1943 rubble from blitzed buildings was sent down from London to Leiston and initially used for construction of an airfield at Theberton for the

During World War II armoured trains operated on coastal branches between June 1940 and July 1943. This view purported to have been take on the Aldeburgh branch shows a flat wagon suitably camouflaged being propelled by an 'F4' class 2-4-2T which is partially protected by armour plating.                                     *Imperial War Museum*

United States 8th Airforce, serving principally as a fighter escort base. The wagons were shunted into the back road siding for the rubble to be transferred to road vehicles for onwards transit. The operation was not without incident for on one occasion a train left in the holding sidings was moved without permission by USAF personnel who were impatient with the shunter who was absent taking his lunch. The wagons were subsequently moved by gravity and gaining speed were too fast for staff to pin down the brakes when it was realized the points were incorrectly set. The outcome resulted in a derailment, which blocked the yard for the rest of the day. The moral being more haste - less speed. The 358th Fighter Group was the first to be based at the new airfield becoming operational in December 1943, their place soon being superseded by the 357th Group flying 'P51' 'Mustang' fighters. The USAF left the base in July 1945 and from October Royal Air Force No. 18 Recruit Centre, Technical Training Command was established for some years, the recruits often travelling by rail.

The increasing attacks by 'V1' and later 'V2' rockets from 1944 necessitated the urgent movement of London's anti-aircraft batteries from the southern to the Eastern Counties. Guns and tanks were transported hurriedly to new destinations by road but when heavy rains came in October it was realized huts were required for the protection of army personnel manning the batteries. A programme known as the 'Winterisation' of anti-aircraft sites required offloading points for huts and concrete for the bases. Sizewell was established as one of the 18 chosen sites in East Anglia and part of a field adjacent to the railway was commandeered so that a siding, long enough to accommodate 12 wagons, could be established to enable all vehicles to be unloaded at one time. A shuttle service ran to and from the sidings from Leiston and as no run-round facilities existed at Sizewell special dispensation and temporary local instructions were authorized to enable an engine to propel the train in one direction. The siding handled a total of 1,383 wagons and in one period of 24 hours, 127 wagons were received and offloaded. The operation went smoothly except for one slight delay when a wagon derailed but the offending vehicle was soon re-railed using a portable jack and sleepers. The lack of water column at Sizewell inspired a member of the footplate staff working one of the trains to draw a caption above the inscription 'Wot no water!' Beach batteries of the Coastal Artillery consisting of 2.6 inch guns in protected pits were also established at Aldeburgh.

After the war the railways resumed peacetime activities with rundown and life-expired rolling stock and equipment in need of maintenance. Questions were raised in Parliament regarding the deteriorating services offered by the LNER and the Aldeburgh branch was no exception. The severe weather in early 1947 brought problems, initially with drifting snow blocking the shallow cuttings along the line and then rapidly thawing snow causing minor flooding on sections of the branch. Damage between Leiston and Thorpeness was so severe that permanent way staff had to substitute new sleepers for many that were waterlogged and replace clinker ballast washed away by the excess water. As petrol rationing eased so the Eastern Counties Omnibus Co. improved the frequency of its services in East Suffolk. However, the decline in passenger traffic finances was not as severe as the neighbouring Framlingham and Waveney Valley branches and it was hoped the impending nationalization of the railways and increasing free time for holidays by the sea might bring improvements and a brighter future to the Aldeburgh branch.

# Chapter Six

# Nationalization and Closure

The nationalization of the railways from 1st January, 1948 brought few immediate changes to the Saxmundham to Aldeburgh branch, which retained its GER/LNER atmosphere until the withdrawal of steam traction from the line. Most stocks of LNER tickets initially remained but those in constant demand to popular destinations were soon replaced with tickets bearing the legend 'Railway Executive' or 'British Railways'. Locomotives working the line soon lost their NE or LNER identity in lieu of the austere BRITISH RAILWAYS on side tanks or tenders, and although varnished teak or brown remained on the older branch coaching stock some ex-LNER suburban coaches soon appeared in the new corporate crimson livery.

British Railways made few alterations to the timetable in which trains were inconveniently timed for people wishing to travel to Ipswich to work, or make a day return trip to London. Market day travel to Ipswich was a shadow of pre-war years but an encouraging sign was the return of day and weekly travellers to Thorpeness and Aldeburgh for a relaxing time by the sea. As petrol rationing eased so the new management, whilst keeping a constant survey on passenger traffic, were concerned that freight traffic was showing a steady decline as farmers and growers increasingly preferred to dispatch their produce and goods by motor lorry. Livestock traffic especially to and from Ipswich and other local markets in the surrounding area was sent by road, a method obviating the double handling of animals at both forwarding and receiving stations.

The 'F3' class 2-4-2Ts, which had served the branch over a period of almost two decades were finally drafted away or condemned, an action hastened after one of the class failed on a down train in the early summer of 1949, as it climbed the 1 in 58 gradient from Saxmundham Junction. After considerable delay the train was finally assisted by a light engine sent from Ipswich but unfortunately with brakes dragging the pair made heavy weather of the onward journey to Aldeburgh; and on passing Thorpeness golf course, the pyrotechnics resulted in much of the undergrowth and hedges being set ablaze. Unfortunately a prominent member of the British Transport Commission was engrossed in a competitive game when the cavalcade passed. With undue haste telegrams and telephone calls to Eastern Region headquarters at Liverpool Street and Marylebone demanded the ancient steeds with 'long chimneys' be withdrawn forthwith and alternative motive power sought. The 'F6' class 2-4-2Ts released from duties in the London suburban area were the planned substitute but they looked almost as ancient as the existing motive power and as matters came to a head, former London Midland & Scottish Railway 2-6-2T No. 41200 of more modern lineage was transferred from Bangor shed to operate the branch services for the rest of the summer, a task she also performed in 1950 before returning to Bangor.

On a lighter note Saxmundham station received second class certificates for the best kept station garden competition in the Norwich district in 1949, to be

With safety valves lifting 'F6' class 2-4-2T No. 67220 begins the 1 in 58 climb away from Saxmundham Junction with an Aldeburgh branch train formed of GER clerestory composite to diagram 212 or 231 (arranged luggage/2 x first class compartments/pair of lavatories/4 x third class compartments), dating from 1900 to 1906, then LNER diagram 340 brake/third with four compartments. The third carriage is LNER lavatory composite to diagram 215 comprising 4 x third class compartments/lavatory and 2 x first class compartments. The final vehicle is an LNER non-corridor 8-compartment third.                    *The late Dr I.C. Allen*

'F6' class 2-4-2T No. 67220 departs from Thorpeness Halt and makes for Aldeburgh with the 6.08 pm Saxmundham to Aldeburgh train on 27th July, 1954.                    *G.R. Mortimer*

followed by first class certificates in 1950, 1951 and 1955 whilst Aldeburgh station achieved first class in 1947, 1949, 1950, 1951, 1952 and 1955 to 1958 inclusive.

The cost-conscious Railway Executive constantly seeking to reduce costs had directed the railway Regions to investigate unremunerative lines and by the autumn of 1951 it became all too evident that services on the neighbouring Mid-Suffolk Light Railway from Haughley to Laxfield were totally unviable in the new national railway network. The rumours of impending closure were confirmed in November when railway management informed members of staff and National Union of Railwaymen (NUR) and Associated Society of Locomotive Engineers and Firemen (ASLEF) trades unions that such proposals were actively in hand. The public was informed in December and an Eastern Area Transport Users' Consultative Committee (TUCC) meeting was held in February to consider the arguments for the retention of the passenger and goods services. All was to no avail for complete closure of the Mid-Suffolk line was advocated on and from 28th July, 1952, but as no Sunday trains operated the last trains ran on Saturday 26th July, 1952. The publicity associated with the closure of the 'Middy' completely overshadowed the announcement of the intention of withdrawing passenger services from another near neighbour, the Wickham Market to Framlingham branch. The same procedures followed, the local staff and trades unions were advised, followed by the public announcements. Once again representations were made against closure to the TUCC and after due consideration the announcement was made that, subject to adequate alternative bus services being provided, no case could be found for the retention of passenger trains. British Railways, Eastern Region (BR/ER) duly advised that passenger services would be withdrawn on and from Monday 3rd November, 1952, and in the absence of Sunday services the last train ran on 1st November, 1952. Two months later the Waveney Valley line passenger service on the Norfolk/Suffolk border between Beccles and Tivetshall succumbed when trains were withdrawn on and from 3rd January, 1953 after 97 years' service to the community, hauled by a 'J15' class 0-6-0.

On 2nd December, 1953, 'L1' class 2-6-4T No. 67705 worked across the Aldeburgh branch as far as Leiston with an officer's special formed of one 6-wheel inspection saloon, although the class was officially banned from the line. At the time it was rumoured the visit was in connection with the possible withdrawal of passenger traffic but in truth it was a permanent way and infrastructure inspection, which was only half completed.

Despite the closures, the Aldeburgh branch continued in the hope that the combination of seasonal seaside traffic and the imports and exports from Garrett's at Leiston would ensure a stable future in the changing railway scene. Rolling stock had improved slightly with the introduction of LNER Gresley and Thompson suburban coaches replacing the ageing former GER corridor stock and ex-North Eastern Railway vehicles, in which the first class compartments especially displayed an aroma of mustiness and clouds of dust if the moquette was disturbed. The third class was little better.

The steam services continued to make a heavy losses until the Aldeburgh branch received the benefit of the BR modernization programme when diesel

A busy time at Saxmundham with an East Suffolk main line train hauled by 'B17' class 4-6-0 No. 61658 *The Essex Regiment* standing at the down platform, whilst the connecting Aldeburgh train hauled by 'J15' class 0-6-0 No. 65459 stands on the up main line ready to shunt across to the down side once the main line train had departed. Saxmundham Station down starting signal and Saxmundham Junction down distant are cleared for the main line train.          *The late Dr I.C. Allen*

On a very wet day in June 1956 'K3' class 2-6-0 No. 61970 departs Saxmundham with a Liverpool Street to Yarmouth South Town/Lowestoft train whilst 'J15' class 0-6-0 No. 65447 waits in the down reception road with the connecting service to Aldeburgh. In the absence of a connection with the down main line near the signal box the branch train will reverse over the connection to the up main line then use the crossover between the up main and down main before reversing into the down platform prior to departing for the coast. Diesel-multiple-units took over the branch services the following week.          *The late Dr I.C. Allen*

'F6' class 2-4-2T No. 67230 on a Saxmundham to Aldeburgh working pulling into Leiston station with her three-coach train as Garrett's Aveling & Porter 0-4-0 *Sirapite* stands astride the points on the loop line leading to the Top Works ready to collect a 16 ton all-steel mineral open wagon.
*The late Dr I.C. Allen*

Aveling & Porter 0-4-0 *Sirapite* standing on the curve of Garrett's tramway just to the south of Leiston station, with regular driver Peter Newstead on the left and shunter 'Jumbo' Brightwell on the right. Note the bullhead track. The tramway continued on a falling gradient of 1 in 38 between houses in Station Road and Dinsdale Road before levelling out over Main Street and then rising into the Bottom Works yard.
*The late Dr I.C. Allen*

'E4' class 2-4-0s were regularly employed on the Aldeburgh branch in the 1920s and 1930s but with the demise of most of the class after World War II their visits were rare. Here No. 62789 works an officers' special between Thorpeness and Aldeburgh with the train formed of GER saloon No. 48 to diagram 20 accompanied by an LNER Gresley gangwayed brake/third.

*The late Dr I.C. Allen*

'B12/3' class 4-6-0 No. 61564 approaching Saxmundham Junction with a Sunday excursion train from Aldeburgh where the fireman is ready to hand over the hoop containing the short section of the split Train Staff to the signalman. The coaches include a Gresley corridor brake/third and a two-coach articulated set dating from the 1930s. The train has been given a clear road for Saxmundham Station up branch distant signal is lowered.           *The late Dr I.C. Allen*

'J15' class 0-6-0 No. 65467 running on the loop road in the process of running round her train at Aldeburgh and passing 'J17' class 0-6-0 No. 65513 waiting to depart with the up branch goods train to Ipswich. No. 65513 is fitted with the smaller 2,640 gallon tender.    *The late Dr I.C .Allen*

'J17' class 0-6-0 No. 65560 fitted with an 3,500 gallon capacity tender makes for Leiston with the branch 'bonus' freight from Aldeburgh and is passing over Aldringham underbridge No. 1111 at 97 miles and 03 chains.    *The late Dr I.C. Allen*

'J15' class 0-6-0 No. 65447 departing Thorpeness Halt with a Saxmundham to Aldeburgh train.
The trailing connection to the single 280 ft-long goods siding can be seen diverging from the
main single line.                                                    *The late Dr I.C. Allen*

Two-car Metropolitan-Cammell dmu No. E79047/E79263, working from Aldeburgh to
Saxmundham, passing Saxmundham Junction up branch fixed distant signal, complete with
decorative finial.                                                   *The late Dr I.C. Allen*

multiple units replaced steam traction on passenger services from 10th June, 1956. The last steam-hauled passenger train ran across the branch on 9th June, 1956 hauled by 'J15' class 0-6-0 No. 65447, the locomotive which had hauled the last passenger train on the Mid-Suffolk Light Railway from Haughley to Laxfield and return on 26th July, 1952. The new traction brought with it the optimistic forecast that passenger services were assured and a bonus of the new operation was that some trains formed through workings to and from Ipswich. Aldeburgh engine shed was closed with the withdrawal of steam traction and the footplate and shed staff transferred to Ipswich. Initially the two-car railcars used on the line were of Metropolitan-Cammell build but these were often replaced on the cyclic workings by Derby lightweight or Craven units. When diesel services were introduced the booking offices at Thorpeness and Aldeburgh were closed and the conductor-guard issued tickets from these stations on the train. Further rationalization came when the Saxmundham station master took charge of the three branch stations. It was also expected some of the level crossings would become trainman operated to save further costs

The diesel trains were popular with travelling public but the inconvenient siting of the stations proved a severe handicap to effectively counter the increasing competition from local buses and ever growing menace of the private car. It was hoped the combination of conveniently timed through trains to Ipswich plus attractive cheap fares would give the railway the advantage and initially the cheap day return fares to Ipswich were popular. The reliability of the railcars was generally good but the failure of an up diesel-multiple-unit from Aldeburgh approaching Saxmundham Junction on 1st October, 1958 involved an unusual rescue. The connecting up train from Yarmouth and Lowestoft hauled by 'B17' class 4-6-0 No. 61611 *Raynham Hall* was stopped at the main line up home signal so that the locomotive could be detached and run on to the branch to rescue the stricken unit and haul it into Saxmundham station. After much shunting the engine then returned to its main line train to haul it forward to Saxmundham station and thence to Ipswich and Liverpool Street.

The introduction of the diesel units had resulted in some operating savings but further economies were made when on 5th January, 1959 the weekday and Sunday diesel unit diagrams for the Aldeburgh branch were reduced to be accommodated within a 12-hour shift and the train service subsequently reduced. The further benefit of the modernization programme came with the allocation of diesel-electric locomotives when BTH/Paxman type '1' (later BR class '15'), North British type '2' (later BR class '21'), BR/Sulzer type '2' (later BR classes '24' and '25') and Brush type '2' (later BR class '31') replaced steam traction on the branch freight services.

On 2nd March, 1959, BR, ER closed almost the entire former Midland & Great Northern line from Yarmouth Beach to South Lynn, Spalding and Bourne (with connections to the Midland at Leicester) to passenger traffic leaving only short stub-end sections available for local passenger traffic and freight. It was always the fear that other cross-country routes including the East Suffolk main line and surviving branches would follow. The omen came to fruition when the commencement of the run-down of East Suffolk main line services commenced on and from Monday 2nd November, 1959. Through services to Yarmouth South Town were withdrawn and the Beccles to Yarmouth South Town section closed, the last trains actually running on 1st November. Road transport had by now removed all but general goods and coal traffic from Saxmundham and Leiston and the continuing ailing receipts finally forced BR, ER authorities to effect local economies when freight facilities were withdrawn from Aldeburgh and Thorpeness siding on and from 30th November, 1959. In the same year Parliamentary powers were obtained for the reduction in status of Sheepwash level crossing No. 20 to that of a public footpath as sanctioned by the British Transport Commission Act 1958.

In 1960 the impending construction of a nuclear power station on the shores of the North Sea at Sizewell earned the Aldeburgh branch a five year reprieve when it was announced that some of the materials would be delivered by rail. However, another close neighbour of the Aldeburgh branch, the goods only line to Snape maltings, closed to traffic on and from 7th March, 1960, with the last train running on Friday 4th March hauled by 'J15' class 0-6-0 No. 65389. The 'J15' class locomotives had been retained at Ipswich shed to work the branch because of the weak timber bridges as no substitute type of main line diesel locomotive could be found, but traffic had declined and closure was inevitable.

After the withdrawal of freight facilities at Aldeburgh the goods yard sidings were removed but the run-round loop was retained should a locomotive-hauled special visit the branch. The loop came in useful in August 1962 when three covered vans were used to convey light fittings to the town in connection with a street lighting programme, thus providing the last goods revenue at the terminal station.

Thereafter the East Suffolk line continued to operate with the threat of possible closure on the horizon. Three years of silence led to mistaken optimism the branch would survive but in 1963 the infamous Beeching Report was published showing the Aldeburgh branch conveyed 0 to 5,000 passengers a week, with Aldeburgh and Thorpeness Halt passenger traffic receipts in the £0 to £5,000 per annum bracket, Leiston £5,000 to £25,000 per annum and Saxmundham station over £25,000 per annum. Whilst specifically referring to passenger traffic, the maps included with the report also showed average freight tonnages and receipts for the branch as 0 to 5,000 tons per week with Sizewell siding handling 0 to 5,000 tons per annum and Leiston and Saxmundham 5,000 to 25,000 tons per annum. The outcome was the intended withdrawal of all remaining passenger services on the East Suffolk main line, the Aldeburgh branch and the Lowestoft to Yarmouth direct line. Little maintenance had been carried out and a 45 mph speed limit was imposed over the entire length of the East Suffolk system. Traffic was not encouraged for on 18th September, 1963 planning permission for a proposed caravan site adjacent to Thorpeness Halt was refused, even after the planners argued that many staying at the site would have travelled by train.

The decision to close was met with a combination of outright disbelief and fury by local MPs, some of whom had supported the Beeching Report and its findings, together with the county councils, local district and parish councils, individual local people and not the least the railwaymen and women serving on the line. An action plan to oppose closure was gradually formulated. In the meantime BR introduced a revised timetable for the line on 2nd March, 1964 including two through trains from Lowestoft to London, a basic two-hourly service serving all stations supplemented by additional journeys each end including some of the Aldeburgh branch trains running from and to Ipswich.

Against all the intended rationalization plans, on 24th April, 1964, BR purchased a portion of land approximately 0.45 of an acre adjacent to Sizewell goods yard for £140 from A.G. Ogilvie to permit the enlargement of the siding facilities in connection with the increase in traffic destined for the Magnox Sizewell A nuclear power station. This was the only encouraging action, for with effect from 30th April, 1964 the British Railways Board (BRB) was released from liability to maintain attendance at the crossing keeper's lodge at Leiston level crossing. As a foretaste of things to come the disposal of surplus land and property commenced on 18th June, 1964 with the sale of Thorpeness Halt crossing cottage, together with an area of approximately 40 sq. yds, to S.B. Bent for £2,275.

Freight facilities were withdrawn from Marlesford and Parham on the neighbouring Framlingham branch on and from 13th July, 1964, and further cost cutting came in the same year with the removal of staff from all but the more important East Suffolk line stations. However, costs still exceeded income and plans for the closure of the entire line between Ipswich and Lowestoft were accelerated.

Passenger counts from the detailed analysis of East Suffolk line stations on Tuesday 3rd November, 1964, included 53 travelling from Saxmundham to Liverpool Street and 12 from the Aldeburgh branch stations. Despite favourable numbers travelling from other East Suffolk line stations British Railways were adamant further savings were to be made and proposed conductor-guard working on trains, a feature which was already in operation on the Aldeburgh branch. There was considerable criticism of the proposed replacement bus services, which as well as incurring additional running time were unable to accommodate parcels traffic, prams and bicycles. The bus timetable based on existing George Ewer/Grey-Green company schedules also required an additional 10 minutes to cater for railway requirements. The Liberal Parliamentary candidate for Eye, Donald Newby even went to the length of hiring three buses to follow the route of the proposed replacement service. The test run conveying two Mayors and other civic leaders demonstrated it was impossible to expect the bus to maintain railway schedules, for the vehicles arrived at Ipswich station 23 minutes after the connecting train to Liverpool Street had departed.

Yet further cuts came when freight facilities were withdrawn from Saxmundham and all stations to Beccles on and from 19th April, 1965, the same day as the freight traffic finished on the Framlingham branch. As this was Easter Bank Holiday Monday, the last trains ran on Maundy Thursday 15th April. Then on 20th August, 1965 Crown Lands crossing cottage on the Aldeburgh branch, together with an area of 375 sq. yds of land, was sold to D.J. Munt for £1,300. Cutbacks began in earnest when contractors removed the overall roof at Aldeburgh station in August and September 1965 leaving the

Brush type '2', later class '31', 1,365 hp diesel-electric No. D5662 standing at Leiston station with the up branch freight train. To the right Garrett's Electromobile electric shunting locomotive pulls round the curve from the Top Works connecting siding with a pair of plate wagons and an open wagon. The former up loop line, now reduced in status to a siding with access to Garrett's is parallel to the main single line.                          *The late Dr I.C. Allen*

BR/Sulzer 1,160hp, later class '24', diesel-electric locomotive No. D5048 standing on the former main single line with a train of open wagons alongside Sizewell siding where the 48 tons atomic flask is about to be loaded to the 50 ton capacity vehicle in the siding by the CEGB gantry crane.
*The late Dr I.C. Allen*

platform totally exposed to the elements; the structure being considered unsafe through lack of maintenance and costing too much to renovate and retain.

Train services continued through the uneasy truce and the two-day public inquiry into the withdrawal of services from the East Suffolk line was held at Saxmundham on 28th and 29th September, 1965. The TUCC for East Anglia were presented with 1,916 written objections from 75 local authorities and other bodies, whilst over 150 individuals also protested. Because of the large numbers of objections, many of the arguments went unheeded but the Chairman L.A. Carey indicated he and the committee were willing to set a date for a further hearing. However, he was of the opinion that the TUCC members, having heard the vehement strength of opposition, had sufficient evidence on which to recommend to the Minister of Transport that the closure be opposed. The chief grounds for objecting to closure of the main line were the longer journey times and the inability of replacement bus services to convey heavy luggage. Buses had little or no toilet facilities and would be less comfortable and colder in winter, when they would also be prone to disruption in bad weather. It was evident severe hardship would be experienced by the withdrawal of rail services from the East Suffolk main line but no such hardship would be experienced by the withdrawal of services on the Aldeburgh branch.

The run-down of the branch services affected the numbers travelling to the Suffolk coast and in 1965 only 16,008 tickets were collected at Aldeburgh. Yet further retraction came when Sizewell siding was closed for general traffic on and from 7th March, 1966 although facilities were retained to cater for the atomic flask and other materials destined for Sizewell nuclear power station, which was now dominant on the skyline to the east. Other cost savings required the guard to open and close the gates at Thorpeness crossing.

With the large number of lines and stations throughout Britain awaiting decisions on closure it was not until 29th June, 1966 that Barbara Castle, the Minister of Transport, announced her decision to reprieve the East Suffolk main line and the Lowestoft to Yarmouth via Gorleston link, whilst permitting the withdrawal of the Aldeburgh branch passenger services.

BR Eastern Region took little time to announce the withdrawal of passenger services on and from Monday 12th September, 1966, but as no Sunday service operated the last day of operation was Saturday 10th September and notices were posted on local stations and in the Suffolk local newspapers. Within days of the announcement passenger numbers increased as railway enthusiasts and local people took advantage of a last ride across the branch. Holidaymakers from further afield also travelled to Aldeburgh on day trips or weekend breaks to savour their last journey to and from the resort by train. On the night before the final closure local residents held a champagne party at Thorpeness Halt to reflect on the sad occasion.

The last regular passenger trains ran across the branch on Saturday 10th September, 1966 when 2-car Metropolitan-Cammell dmu No. E79066/E79282 formed the final down departure to Aldeburgh and return with driver E.A. Skeels of Ipswich in charge. Crowds thronged the platform at Saxmundham well before departure time and when the train departed the two-car unit was crowded to full and standing. The stations, houses and level crossings along the

Aldeburgh station with two-car Metropolitan-Cammell dmu stopped well short of the buffer stops by the presence of a red flag in the 'four foot'. A few passengers alight as two railway enthusiasts, including G. Wright, the then Hon. Secretary of the Norfolk Railway Society, survey the scene.                                                                          *The late G. Pember*

By September 1966 considerable rationalization had taken place at Aldeburgh. Viewed from the buffer stops which had already been moved further north, the overall roof had been removed leaving the back wall and beyond that the main station building. The signal box and goods shed had been abolished following the withdrawal of freight traffic on and from 30th November, 1959 and the associated sidings have been lifted leaving only the run round loop *in situ. Robert Powell*

The rather spartan platform at Aldeburgh is crowded with prospective passengers and well-wishers as the two-car Metropolitan-Cammell dmu arrives with the last down passenger train, the 18.55 from Saxmundham, on 10th September, 1966. *G.R. Mortimer*

The final passenger train, formed of a two-car Metropolitan-Cammell diesel-multiple-unit departing from Aldeburgh on Saturday 10th September, 1966 to the cheers of the spectators on the platform. The departure was accompanied by exploding detonators. *G.R. Mortimer*

BR/Sulzer, class '24', 1,160 hp diesel-electric locomotive No. D5048 has left her train on the down reception siding at Leiston as she reverses to collect wagons to add to the formation. Back or coal road is to the left alongside the road called Westward Ho whilst the main single line is in the near foreground. To the right is Garrett's No. 2 reception siding, No. 1 reception siding, occupying the space between the main single line and No. 2 reception siding, had already been lifted.                                                                        *The late Dr I.C. Allen*

Brush type '2', 1,365 hp diesel-electric locomotive No. 5632 hauls a lengthy train of open wagons and one van along the Aldeburgh branch on the 1 in 58 climb near Saxmundham Junction.
*The late Dr I.C. Allen*

route were all lined with local people paying their last respects. Apart from passengers shouting from the windows of the train and the returned waves from those by the lineside, the down journey was uneventful. The return journey of the last up train 19.22 hours ex-Aldeburgh was, however, not entirely without incident. The porter at Aldeburgh, suitably attired wearing a GER cap, waved the train away and the unit departed over exploding detonators as the driver repeatedly sounded the two-tone horn, adding to the noisy occasion. Aldeburgh was left in gathering dusk with a sad knot of people watching the red tail light disappear into the distance towards Thorpeness for the last time. The train lights were switched on before the approach to Thorpeness Halt, where the platform was bedecked with bunting borrowed from Aldeburgh Borough Council and with a banner erected alongside the track bearing the inscription 'Give Us Back Our Train'. The waiting room still showed evidence of the previous night's champagne party. Departure from Thorpeness was delayed as someone had prematurely padlocked the level crossing gates across the railway. The key was soon found and the gates were opened as to more exploding detonators the train departed in darkness across the flat lands to Leiston, where more crowds gathered on the platform to see the train away. Few exploding detonators marked the departure from the town as cheers resounded but on the approach to Saxmundham Junction a cacophony of bangs pierced the night air as the train swung past the signal box and on to the up main line to terminate at Saxmundham, thus ending 107 years of service to the community.

Five days after the running of the last passenger train the sale of Sheepwash level crossing cottage together with an area of 832 sq. yds of land to G.A. Keen was concluded for a price of £650. As a result of the inquiry the disputed annual costs of £250,000 for operating the East Suffolk line quoted to TUCC with revenue of £120,000 were revised to £178,000 direct costs and £155,000 direct earnings. Gerard Fiennes, the Eastern Region General Manager, aggrieved at the implications of the closure proposal, estimated costs could be reduced yet further to £84,000 by the introduction of paytrain facilities.

British Railways subsequently announced it was planned to convert the Ipswich to Lowestoft line into a basic railway of single track with passing loops at Woodbridge, Saxmundham, Halesworth and Beccles, together with unstaffed stations and automatic level crossings. On 11th November, 1966 revised passenger services were introduced on the surviving main line, formed of nine dmu-operated trains calling at all stations in each direction, augmented by a daily Liverpool Street to Lowestoft diesel locomotive-hauled through train each way. Conductor-guard working was introduced from 10th March, 1967, postponed from 2nd January after considerable opposition from the NUR, when all stations became unstaffed with tickets issued on the train. The major part of the scheme, however, was not initially implemented and the line remained double track with nine signal boxes and 44 manually-operated level crossings.

Following application from BR, the Ministry of Transport issued an order dated 18th May, 1967 authorizing a change of status for Leiston Station level crossing at 95 miles 05 chains: 'The gates at the above public level crossing shall be kept constantly closed across the railway instead of across the road except when engines or vehicles passing along the railway have occasion to use the

BTH/Paxman type '1' 800 hp diesel-electric locomotive No. D8223 standing on the branch on the approach to Sizewell siding with a train of recovered permanent way removed from the section of line north of Thorpeness in August 1967.                    *The late Dr I.C. Allen*

In August 1967 the track between Aldeburgh and Sizewell siding was lifted using the Ipswich steam crane. One of the problems encountered was the limited water capacity of the crane. Here BTH/Paxman 800 hp diesel-electric locomotive No. D8236 stands at Leiston platform having taken the crane to the station to enable it to be replenished with water from the gentlemen's lavatory, a time consuming exercise. The crane has its jib raised to facilitate the replenishment whilst on the left is Garrett's electric shunting locomotive standing alongside the loading gauge.
*The late Dr I.C. Allen*

road.' Then on 14th July, 1967 BR was absolved from maintaining lodges and authorized to withdraw the attendance of crossing keepers at Knodishall level crossing No. 3 at 92 miles 49 chains, West House level crossing No. 5 at 93 miles 32 chains, Saxmundham Road level crossing No. 8 at 94 miles 02 chains and Sizewell level crossing No. 13 at 95 miles 71 chains. The disposal of assets then followed with the sale of Knodishall crossing cottage and an area of land equal to 871 sq. yds to E.E. and P.V. Powline on 17th January, 1968 for £650, followed by West House crossing cottage and 850 square yards of land to F.W. Fitches for £550 on 2nd February, 1968. Two weeks later the sale of Saxmundham Road crossing cottage and 774 sq. yds of land was made to W.H. Redhead for £1,725, followed by Sizewell crossing cottage and 375 sq. yds of land to G.G. and E.M. Kitching for £500.

The contract for the removal of the permanent way from Sizewell siding to Aldeburgh was awarded early in 1968 and the lifting of the track commenced in the spring, starting at Aldeburgh. The rails were cut into short lengths and loaded with other materials on to flat wagons, which had been propelled to the work site usually by one or two BTH/Paxman 800 hp diesel-electric locomotives, depending on the weight of the returning load. Once a convenient number of wagons were loaded the locomotive hauled the vehicles back to Leiston yard where much of the scrap was offloaded on to road vehicles for dispersal. Concurrent with the track removal the tramway connection and tramway at Leiston was lifted by A. King & Sons of Norwich.

After the lifting of the permanent way between Sizewell and Aldeburgh further assets were sold commencing with an area of 7 acres 443 sq. yds of the disused branch near Aldeburgh to J.R. Somerville on 20th June, 1969 for £480. Aldeburgh Borough Council then purchased 4,452 square yards at a cost of £750 on 14th July. Later in the year on 25th November S.B. Bent purchased an area of 435 sq. yds of land at Thorpeness for £50. Thorpeness station and yard totalling 1 acre 920 sq. yds in area was sold to Blythe Rural District Council for £300 on 19th March, 1970. At about this time the coal traffic to Charringtons fuel depot on the site of the former Leiston gas works ceased and with only the occasional freight train proceeding on to the branch to Leiston or Sizewell siding, Saxmundham Junction signal box became an expensive luxury. On 11th July, 1971 the box was abolished and replaced by a 3-lever ground frame released from Saxmundham Station signal box to operate the points to the branch to Sizewell.

The sale of Aldeburgh station buildings and 2 acres 2,905 sq. yds of land to Stonebanner Ltd for £46,650 was finalized on 25th April, 1973, but later the property passed to Drayson Properties for redevelopment. The following year on 20th June, 1974, 14 acres 1,854 sq. yds of the disused branch line at Thorpeness was sold to C.S. Ogilvie for £375, whilst 1¾ chains of trackbed equal to 727 sq. yds of land at Aldeburgh was sold to the executors of J.R. Somerville for £100 on 15th December, 1977. An area of 51 sq. yds of land adjacent to Leiston level crossing was dedicated to Suffolk County Council on 24th July, 1979 in consideration of £150 to facilitate road widening and improvements.

After a period of almost 11 years a railway enthusiasts' dmu special train organized by the East Suffolk Travellers' Association conveyed passengers en

After the withdrawal of the three 5-car 'Brighton Belle' electric-multiple-units from the Southern Region in 1972, *Vera*, the former first class Pullman car, was purchased privately and subsequently delivered to its final resting place at Westleton - a small Suffolk village. Here Brush type '2', 1,365 hp diesel-electric locomotive No. 5550 propels the coach and attendant open wagon along the branch from Leiston to Sizewell siding. With the help of the Central Electricity Generating Board gantry crane the vehicle was offloaded and transferred on to a road vehicle for the final few miles to its destination. *Vera* was subsequently acquired in 1985 and joined the British Venice-Simplon Orient Express operational fleet in 1990.          *The late Dr I.C. Allen*

A sad reflection of Aldeburgh station with the track removed and before demolition of the site to make way for housing development.                              *Author's Collection*

route from Felixstowe to Lowestoft across the branch to Leiston and Sizewell on 25th June, 1977, and participants walked around Leiston station before the train returned to the main line. Another special train organized by the Railway Correspondence & Travel Society and formed of two 2-car dmus ran from Ipswich to Felixstowe Dock and then to Leiston and return to Ipswich on 1st November, 1980, although passengers were not permitted to alight at Leiston.

In the meantime during 1976 the Suffolk Preservation Society had called a meeting of parties interested in the future use of the remains of the Bottom Works of Richard Garrett's Engineering at Leiston and especially the Long Shop, which was considered unique as an engineering shed in Britain. As a result a group was established to consider the feasibility of converting the building into an industrial museum. In May 1978 Richard Garrett generously offered to make the site available for the group led by Lord Cranbrook and by March 1979 the first major exhibit arrived at the museum, a 1923 Garrett steam roller, which had spent its entire working life in Spain and which had been returned to England by the Transport Trust and offered to the museum on permanent loan.

The inconvenience of staggered platforms at Saxmundham was finally removed and with the lifting of the down side goods yard opportunity was taken to re-site the down platform. The new timber structure was erected north of Albion Street level crossing opposite the up platform and was opened on 23rd March, 1981. In the meantime the canopy over the up platform had been replaced in 1980.

The *East Anglian Daily Times* of 25th April, 1981 optimistically reported that BR was considering reopening the entire Aldeburgh branch line for passenger traffic; the argument in favour being the increase in population of Leiston from 3,000 in 1961 to 5,000 by 1978 and even larger numbers with the construction of Sizewell B power station. The Central Electricity Generating Board (CEGB) had announced that they would consider using the line for the delivery of materials to Sizewell to build the new power station. A spur was installed to Sizewell B with the CEGB applying to the Government for a grant to pay for rail facilities to keep heavy traffic off the roads, after local people had vehemently opposed the estimated 400 lorries running daily to Sizewell conveying construction material.

It was also announced in 1981 that the East Suffolk line incurred annual direct costs of £1,200,000 against revenue of £400,000, although the divisional manager at Norwich estimated that if all possible rationalization measures, including radio signalling and automatic half-barriers at level crossings, were adopted then direct expenses could be reduced to match the income. On 26th October, 1981 flask trains were working to Sizewell and on 21st December class '37' diesel-electric locomotive No. 37173 was noted hauling a train conveying four flasks. On the same date the station sidings and coal concentration depot at Leiston stood forlorn and disused.

The movement of atomic flasks to and from the Sizewell power stations was unpopular with certain factions and on 12th August, 1982 a group of protestors held up the Sizewell to Sellafield flask train hauled by class '37' diesel-electric locomotive No. 37091 by staging a 'sit in' at Leiston station. Nine protestors

Brush type '2', 1,365 hp diesel-electric shunting locomotive No. D5635 eases a freight train through Leiston station. Note the up loop road, rail connections to Garrett's siding, and signal box have all been abolished and the platform fence dismantled to reveal the derelict weighbridge office and goods shed office. The leading vehicle in the train conveys atomic flasks from Sizewell siding.                                                                    *The late Dr I.C. Allen*

An unidentified Brush type '2', 1,365 hp diesel-electric locomotive wends its way along the Aldeburgh branch near Westhouse crossing with the annual weed killing train.
                                                                                *The late Dr I.C. Allen*

were arrested and from the next working in September the trains carried a British Transport Police guard complete with guard dog. In the spring of 1983 BR announced that they were keen to extend the branch beyond Leiston and Sizewell siding to the proposed site of Sizewell B nuclear power station but the CEGB countered saying that they now had no intentions to extend the line.

The Serpell Report of 1983 again fuelled rumours of possible closure of the East Suffolk line, for amongst the options was the closure of all routes except the main line from Ipswich to Norwich. Fortunately the forecast was inaccurate and after some years of planning BR in August 1983 received the necessary authority for the £1.6m low cost radio signalling scheme on the East Suffolk line. The plans included the singling of 34 of the 48 miles of line between Westerfield Junction and Lowestoft, whilst 22 level crossings were to be equipped with remotely-controlled automatic half-barriers replacing conventional level crossings. The dmus required to work across the line were to be fitted with mini computers for electronic tokens block working with the radio-controlled signalling system, with Saxmundham signal box becoming the control centre for the line. The East Suffolk line then had 45 level crossings, 30 of which were staffed and the new scheme, with expected completion by 1986, would result in the saving of 42 staff. Revised figures showed the line earned £470,000 per annum but incurred operating costs of £650,000, with track and signalling costs at £900,000. The track would be singled from Woodbridge to Saxmundham and from Halesworth to Oulton Broad South with double line retained between Saxmundham and Halesworth. Nine manned signal boxes were to be replaced by one radio centre at Saxmundham with the signalman controlling all train movements and with the facility to talk directly to the drivers. A display in the cabs of the refurbished dmus and the locomotives used on the Sizewell flask trains would confirm instructions from the signalman to enter and exit single line sections. The section to Saxmundham was scheduled for completion by mid-1984 and the remainder of the line by early 1985. As a prelude to improvements in September 1983 contractors began demolishing the former station buildings and south of Albion Street crossing at Saxmundham.

The work to convert the East Suffolk main line to Radio Electronic Token Block with automatic level crossings replacing the conventional road crossings commenced in earnest when single line working with Electric Token block was introduced over the up line between Melton and Saxmundham from 10th July. This permitted the down line to be re-laid as the permanent single line and trains were retimed from 11th July. On and from 2nd September, 1984 working switched to the former down line.

In the meantime on the former Aldeburgh branch by December 1983 the platform at Leiston was still extant as was the goods shed which was in use as a DIY warehouse. West of the station the loop and siding were rusted and overgrown whilst east of the station the coal depot siding was out of use with the six-lever ground frame rusting. In the entrance road to Garrett's premises the rails were set in tarmac; Garrett's had ceased trading in 1981. The branch leading to Sizewell and the single siding east of the gated level crossing displayed signs of irregular use as traffic had not operated for many months and the overhead gantry crane, used to transfer the nuclear waste containers from Sizewell A power station from road to rail, sat stark against the skyline.

Traffic on the branch soon resumed and on 12th April, 1984 the Sizewell to Sellafield train conveying a flask containing fuel rods from Sizewell power station, and hauled by class '31' diesel-electric locomotive No. 31221, was halted on the approach to Saxmundham after the flask was reported leaking. Checks were made and the leakage proved to be rainwater. The following month a Leiston councillor suggested the reopening of the branch to passengers to allow unemployed young people to take up places outside Leiston under the Youth Training Scheme. However, without ceremony Leiston public delivery siding was closed to goods traffic on and from 7th May, 1984.

The last regular locomotive-hauled passenger trains ran across the East Suffolk main line on 12th May, 1984. Class '37' 1,750 hp diesel-electric locomotive No. 37094, carrying an 'East Suffolk Broadsman' headboard, worked from Lowestoft to Liverpool Street whilst the last down working was hauled by sister locomotive No. 37115 carrying two headboards. At this period Saxmundham station level crossing was still equipped with manned barriers and the station signalled for bi-directional working. The 125th anniversary of the opening of the ESR was celebrated on 4th June, 1984 when the 11.20 Colchester to Saxmundham and 14.10 Saxmundham to Colchester trains were formed of a class '101' dmu equipped with public address system and conveying local councillors and representatives of travellers' associations.

On 16th September, 1984 the connection 280 yards south of Saxmundham signal box was brought into use and normal double line working resumed through the station. The trailing crossover on the Halesworth side of the station, which formed the connection from the single line to the down main, was abolished whilst the connection to the up sidings became ground frame operated. At the same time alterations were made to the signalling and Albion Street level crossing gates were replaced by manually-controlled lifting barriers controlled from the signal box, whilst the catch points in the down main line at 91 miles 21 chains were removed and replaced by plain track. Then on 7th October, 1984 Chantry Road level crossing at 91 miles 02 chains was converted to remotely-controlled lifting barrier operation controlled from Saxmundham signal box.

Structural alterations made to Saxmundham signal box during February 1985 and completed on the 23rd, including the provision of large windows at each end of the building and removal of the door and steps to the opposite end adjoining the down platform. The lever frame was reduced to four working levers and all distant signals were fixed at caution. In the meantime BR awarded the contract for Radio Controlled Electronic Token signalling to GEC-General Signals Ltd and an individual functional switch panel replaced the 43-lever Saxby & Farmer frame later in the year. Radio signalling trials took place on Tuesdays and Thursdays between 15th October and 7th November, 1985 using 3-car class '105' dmu No. 53315/59418/53330. Thereafter train timings were extended by three minutes in the down direction and six minutes in the up direction to allow for radio test exchanges as all trains had to stop at radio token exchange points. Radio Electronic Token Block (RETB) working was due to be introduced on the Sizewell branch on 24th November, 1985 but was postponed due to technical problems until 8th December, then 5th January, 1986, before final introduction on 16th February, 1986. A distant board was provided 476 yards before reaching the stop board at the branch exit points. The junction remained controlled by the existing ground frame. By then the loop and siding at Leiston were out of use. Because of further teething troubles RETB on the main line and branch was also not fully operative until 16th February, 1986. As well as Metropolitan-Cammell class '101' dmus Norwich sets Nos. 92, 94, 96, 100, 101, 102, 103 and 104 being initially equipped with the radio equipment, class '37' diesel-electric locomotives Nos. 37138, 37140, 37144, 37216 and 37219 were also provided with equipment to operate East Suffolk services including the Sizewell branch. From 16th February, 1986 conventional signalling was abolished and the route between Woodbridge and Saxmundham and Halesworth and Oulton Broad North operated as a single track leaving the section from Saxmundham to Halesworth as double line. The Sizewell branch serving the nuclear power station was operated under the 'one train' principle.

Because of increasing traffic the track layout at Sizewell was enlarged and extended in 1988 to facilitate the three-year contract to supply cement and steel for construction of Sizewell B nuclear power station. The construction traffic comprising cement and steel was conveyed by 7T75 22.00 hours Ipswich to Sizewell train. Such was the flow of traffic that the *East Anglian Daily Times* on 16th September, 1989 reported local residents had complained of the excessive noise and calls were made for the siding to close, the large gantry crane spanning the tracks being used to load the atomic waste flasks on to 'Flatrol' wagons, the waste coming from the nearby Sizewell A and future B atomic power stations. It was also rumoured that a third power station Sizewell C would be constructed. BR pressed for an extension of the line to the construction site but the CEGB scotched any progress by advising that the rail extension would cost £1.5 million more than the construction of a road. Sizewell B pressurized water nuclear power station was constructed between 1988 and early 1995. Generating commenced on 14th February, 1995, with estimated decommissioning in 2035.

The transportation of nuclear flasks did not always go to plan for on 2nd March, 1995, a loaded flask containing spent fuel rods was left suspended from a broken down crane jib at Sizewell for over 12 hours. The predicament was the immediate focus of attention and lengthy discussions between representatives of Railtrack, Nuclear Electric Mainline and Freight and Transrail resulted in the flask being finally removed at 2.15 am the following day.

Few physical alterations were made until the last remaining refuge at Saxmundham, Hay siding on the up side of the main line between the station and junction, was reduced in length by 7 chains in September 1995, because of deteriorating track at the north end. At the same time the former loop at Leiston was noted clamped out of use and the associated siding overgrown.

Flask traffic to Sizewell from Wembley Yard, originating as 7Z58 18.15 ex-Sellafield, resumed on 27th August, 1998 with the train being topped and tailed by class '37s' Nos. 37431 and 37684. English Electric class '20/3' diesel-electric locomotives later worked the trains, Nos. 20307 and 20309 being noted on 26th November and Nos. 20306 and 20314 on 2nd December.

Restoration of passenger services on the branch were again mooted late in 2003 when the *East Anglian Daily Times* for 5th December reported, 'Sizewell power stations could eventually pave the way towards reviving passenger services to

English Electric type '3' class '37' No. 37023 crosses Valley underbridge No. 1110 at 95 miles 37 chains, spanning Valley Road to the east of Leiston, with a train of ballast hoppers en route to Saxmundham on 2nd March, 1994.                    *David Pearce*

Leiston. Network Rail [Railtrack's successor] has announced it is investing in the Sizewell branch as part of its on-going maintenance and renewal programme for rebuilding Britain's railways. During a 12-day, £30,000 scheme, 1,500 wooden sleepers will be renewed between Saxmundham and Sizewell using the latest railway technology.' Frank Huxley, chairman of Leiston town council, hoped the improvements would help passenger trains become a realistic possibility in the future. Although 'delighted to hear they are doing the work', he was of the opinion the return of passenger trains to Leiston 'may be a long way away.' Huxley thought such a service would bring benefits augmenting the hourly bus service operated to Ipswich. The idea of a passenger train link had been placed on the 'wish list' at the recent meeting on the new local plan. A possible site for a new Leiston station was earmarked near the town's old gas works, as the former station had been converted into housing. Huxley also hoped the improvements might alleviate some concerns raised about the state of the line by anti-nuclear campaigners. A spokesman for Network Rail had confirmed that as freight trains were heavier, the lines would be able to take passenger trains. The town council had also recently raised concerns about the condition of the sleepers at the town's crossings and Leiston town council clerk hoped particular attention would be paid to these crossings. The sleeper renewal programme commenced on Monday 1st December, 2003 was completed by Friday 12th December.

The atomic flask workings to and from Sizewell continued on an, 'as and when required' basis, with the branch often mothballed for months at a time before resumption of traffic. The branch was closed in March 2005 for about three months until on 4th June Direct Rail Services (DRS) class '47' diesel-electric locomotive No. 47802, outbased at Stowmarket, ran light to Norwich and then Lowestoft for RETB testing before continuing to Sizewell on 6th June. Whilst on the branch opportunity was taken to inspect the infrastructure and permanent way in readiness for a resumption of flask traffic the following day. All was found correct and DRS class '20' diesel-electric locomotives Nos. 20306 and 20309 worked the first train on 7th June. By this time the Nuclear Decommissioning Authority owned the nuclear flasks as well as owning DRS.

After the much publicized shut down of Sizewell 'A' reactor on 31st December, 2006, it was anticipated that trains conveying contaminated material would continue to run for several years while the plant was decommissioned. The trains, hauled by two class '20s' or a class '20' and a class '37' and operating at irregular intervals, commenced on 29th December, 2006 and then ran in 2007 on 5th, 12th, 16th and 23rd January. The 04.46 Willesden to Sizewell and 15.34 return working continued on 30th January and again on 16th February and increased in frequency during March with trips made on 2nd, 9th, 13th and 20th. A further run on 26th March was delayed by about seven hours when class '20' No. 20304 failed with brake trouble at Willesden. DRS class '47' No 47501 was dispatched post haste to Willesden via Cambridge and Hitchin and then departed at 11.18 dragging class '20' No 20302 and one flask reaching Ipswich at 13.50. The pair continued to Sizewell and returned to Ipswich by 18.00, the class '47' working the train throughout to Crewe. A brief run down of services continued until July when three services ran across the branch on 5th, 12th and 16th hauled on each occasion by the same pair of class '20s', Nos. 20304 and 20307. Five flask trains ran during August 2007 on 2nd, 9th, 16th, 23rd and 30th each hauled by a pair of class '20s'. The programme continued into September when trains ran on the 6th, 11th and 20th but what was believed to have been the final Sizewell flask train for at least two years ran on 3rd October, 2007 hauled by Nos. 20313 and 20314. An interloper during the year was the Pathfinder Tours 'East Anglia on a Mission' railtour train, 05.30 Crewe to Leiston and Sizewell, which traversed the branch on 10th March, 2007 hauled by class '47' No. 47501 with English Electric class '20s' Nos. 20313, 20314 and 20315 at the opposite end of the 13-coach formation, the longest passenger train ever seen on the branch.

With regular flask traffic continuing to and from Sizewell the former Aldeburgh branch is thus an operational railway through Leiston, where all traces of the station platform have been demolished and the goods shed converted to apartments. Garrett's Old Works except for the Long Shop, which is a museum, has been demolished and the land used for building. Some of the company offices were converted to flats whilst a portion of the New Works was retained as small industrial units; the offices being converted to apartments. Beyond Sizewell siding the trackbed can be followed in places with part being reserved as a footpath through the Royal Society for the Protection of Birds estate and beyond but much of the land has reverted to farming or an extension of Thorpeness golf course. At Aldeburgh the station site has been redeveloped and is now a small housing estate. This account therefore must be regarded as the 'Old Testament', for the continuing use of the branch to Sizewell is much dependent on the development of nuclear energy in Britain. Thus it is for future historians to record the 'New Testament' of the former railway to Aldeburgh.

# Saxmundham

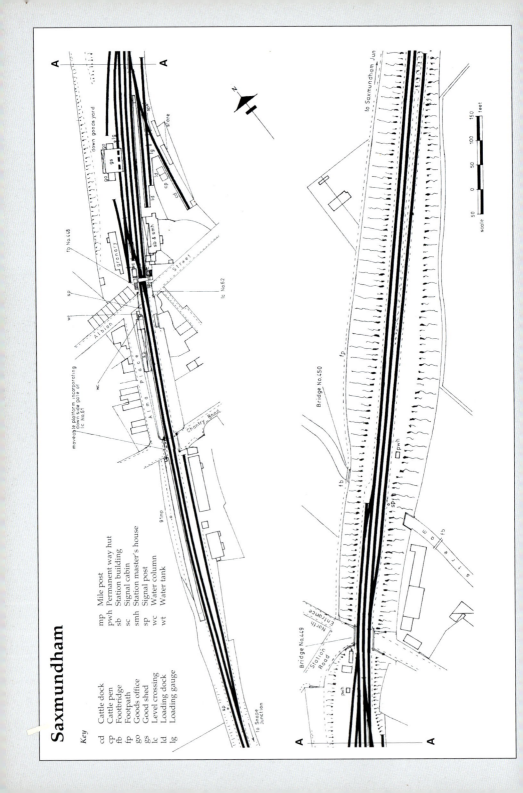

## Key

| | |
|---|---|
| cd | Cattle dock |
| cp | Cattle pen |
| fb | Footbridge |
| fp | Footpath |
| go | Goods office |
| gs | Good shed |
| lc | Level crossing |
| ld | Loading dock |
| lg | Loading gauge |

| | |
|---|---|
| mp | Mile post |
| pwh | Permanent way hut |
| sb | Station building |
| sc | Signal cabin |
| smh | Station master's house |
| sp | Signal post |
| wc | Water column |
| wt | Water tank |

to Saxmundham Jun

Bridge No.450

Bridge No.449

North Entrance

Station Road

down goods yard

fb No.448

lc No.62

Chantry Road

Albion Place

Alma Place

Street

moveable platform incorporating down side gate of lc No.61

To Snape Junction

scale
50  0  50  100  150  feet

# Chapter Seven

# The Route Described

Saxmundham station, 91 miles 06 chains from Liverpool Street, was the junction for the Aldeburgh branch and was conveniently positioned for the centre of population which generally lay to the east of the East Suffolk main line. The station was an operational nightmare for the platforms were staggered with the down side south of the gates of Albion Street level crossing and the up platform to the north. Behind the up platform was a bay platform initially provided for Aldeburgh branch services but little used by them as trains invariably departed from the down main platform, there being no connection from the up main line to the up bay platform. The procedure for starting trains from the up bay was convoluted, for up branch trains could not terminate in the bay and so terminated in the up main platform. The engine then ran round the stock using the two crossovers before re-coupling to the vehicles and hauling them via the north crossover to the down main line prior to propelling into the back platform.

The up platform, 410 ft in length, could accommodate five and a half 63 ft 6 in. coaching vehicles whilst the up bay, 270 ft long, could hold 3¾ vehicles. The up platform was host to the main station buildings constructed of white brick including booking office and booking hall, waiting rooms, parcels office, station master's office and porters room. The station master's living accommodation was located on the first floor. The frontage to the platform was relatively short because of the restricted layout but was balanced by extensions on the road approach side, the centre being of two storeys with hipped roof, and single floor additions on either side. A small canopy was provided on the road approach to the booking hall whilst an ornate canopy was provided for passenger protection over the platform in 1886. In 1893 a footbridge, No. 448, was provided at the south end of the platform immediately to the north of the level crossing to enable passengers to cross the railway to the down platform and as a public right of way. Initially it was open to the elements but in 1900 a covering was placed over the entire bridge. The provision of the bridge hindered the sighting of the signalman in the adjacent signal box, located on the down side, as the structure somewhat overshadowed the building.

The down main platform was originally 280 ft in length, limited by its location between Albion Street level crossing to the north and Chantry Row, later Chantry Road level crossing, No. 61 at 91 miles 02 chains, to the south. To the west of the line Chantry Road crossing led to Mill Lane. A much needed extension was built south of Chantry Road crossing in the 1870s but the absence of a platform bridge over the level crossing went undetected by the Board of Trade for six or seven years. A section of moveable platform was authorized on 30th September, 1874 but nothing was completed until after the further lengthening of the platform at the south end in 1881. The new structure 640 feet in length could then accommodate seven of the 63 ft 6 in. coaches. The moveable platform formed part of the level crossing gates and was swung across the

Aerial view of Saxmundham station looking north in July 1920, with Saxmundham Junction to the top of the picture. In the foreground Chantry Road bisects the down platform and to the south of the crossing on the up side of the line is Row siding serving a coal shed and corn store. The siding was taken over by the Stowmarket Creamery Co. in the 1930s and milk traffic was dispatched in tank wagons; only to be superseded in World War II when the coastal defence train was stabled in the siding between runs on the Aldeburgh and Snape branches. *Aerofilms*

View facing towards Saxmundham station from the north in 1911 with the trailing points from Hay siding to the up main line in the foreground. Two open wagons and a flat truck are standing on the down reception road immediately by the girders of Saxmundham North Entrance underbridge No. 449 at 91 miles 14 chains from Liverpool Street. In the background is the down side goods yard. *Windwood Collection*

Albion Street level crossing Saxmundham in 1911 facing north with the Station signal box just beyond the footbridge and the up platform to the right. The view shows clearly the trailing crossover from the up main line to the down main line leading to the down reception siding, occupied by an assortment of open wagons and covered vans, and the shed roads. The crossover was used extensively by the Aldeburgh branch trains after terminating on the up side and crossing to the down line to form the return working, an operation not popular with local people who continuously complained of the incessant delays to road users. *Windwood Collection*

The up bay platform at Saxmundham in 1911 occupied by Sherwood Colliery and GNR open wagons loaded with coal. The view is taken from the dock road with the loading dock to the right. Ahead is the access points to the up side yard protected by a stop signal for down departures, access from this yard only being available to the down main line. To the far left the down side goods yard is occupied by an assortment of GER and other company wagons.

*Windwood Collection*

View from Saxmundham Station signal box in 1911 looking north with the up platform to the right and the former Aldeburgh bay platform occupied by Sherwood colliery and GNR open wagons loaded with coal. In the foreground the crossover from the up and down main lines connects with the down reception line, occupied by covered vans, and the shed road leading to the goods shed occupied by open wagons. To the left is the dock road, which terminated short of the goods office.

*Windwood Collection*

View facing north from the up main line at Saxmundham in 1911 with the up goods yard to the right. This yard could only be shunted from the down main line, as there was no facing access from the up main line. It was for this reason that Aldeburgh branch trains terminated in the up platform and then shunted to the down side for the return journey. To the left is the down side goods yard showing the reception line, shed road and back road occupied by wagons.

*Windwood Collection*

View facing north from wagons standing in the down reception road at Saxmundham showing the down and up main lines curving away over Saxmundham North Entrance underbridge No. 449 to Saxmundham Junction. The trailing points from the up main line lead to the 1,070 ft-long Hay siding.

*Windwood Collection*

The down platform at Saxmundham viewed from Albion Street level crossing with a lorry crossing the railway at Chantry Road crossing halfway along the very low and substandard platform. The water crane at the north end of the platform was fed from the tank raised aloft the adjacent tank house. *Author's Collection*

View of the down platform at Saxmundham across Albion Street level crossing from the up side. Note the gap in the platform where Chantry Road level crossing bisected the line. In the foreground is the trailing crossover from the up main line to the down main line and the down goods reception siding. The building in the right background in Alma Place was the former police station. *D. Clayton*

Saxmundham station after the lifting of the connection to the goods yard and removal of the footbridge. The down platform is still located south of Albion Street level crossing whilst the signal box controls the crossover between the up and down main lines and the shortened up starting signal at the south end of the up platform. *Author's Collection*

Saxmundham station looking south from the down reception siding in the 1950s. The up platform, still showing signs of whitewash on the platform edge from the war years, is host to the main station buildings fronted by an ornate canopy. To the right is the Station signal box and beyond Albion Street level crossing the down platform. The gates are open for the railway although both up starting and down starting signals are at danger. *Author's Collection*

Looking south from the down platform at Saxmundham with Chantry Road level crossing gates No. 61 bisecting the up and down East Suffolk main lines, showing the down platform extension beyond the crossing.                                                    *Author's Collection*

View of Chantry Road level crossing from the down platform extension and facing north. The gates were operated by a porter and latterly by a lad porter, who was accommodated in the hut on the platform. The barriers were only closed across the road for an approaching train and staff were advised to open the gates for rail traffic by the signalman in the Station signal box giving one long ring on an electronic bell. After the passing of a train the bell was repeated to advise it was safe to reopen the gates for road traffic. The gates were demolished in the late 1950s by an engineer's train when the brakes failed, and thereafter the moveable platform was replaced by conventional level crossing gates resulting in the south end extension of the down platform being taken out of use. Down trains were then required to pull up twice to enable passengers in the rear of the train to alight, although instructions were given for passengers requiring Saxmundham to ride in the front part of the train.                    *Author's Collection*

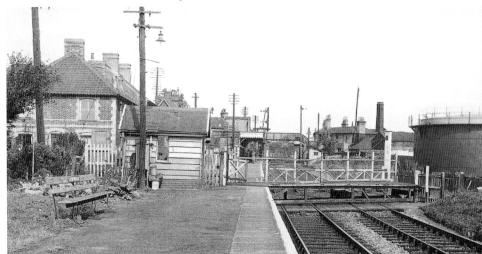

roadway for the passage of a train and then back across the railway after the rail service had passed. Together with the similar facility provided at Halesworth, the crossings were possibly unique in the country. It was possible to run-round seven coaches between the crossovers and 10 coaches in the down goods siding. New brick-built waiting facilities were provided on the down platform in 1880, fronted for almost its entire length by a canopy with cantilevered supports. The accommodation consisted from the south end, gentlemen's toilet, lock-up store, general waiting room, parcels lock-up and ladies waiting room and toilets. A white brick wall along the entire length of the back of the platform formed the boundary of railway property with the parallel Alma Place. A water tank on a brick base was provided at the north end of the down platform to supply locomotive water cranes located at the north end of the down platform and south end of the up platform. At Saxmundham a loud gong worked from the Station signal box was fixed outside the down sidings at the Yarmouth end of the station. The gong was used to warn goods guards and shunters that shunting was to cease and the main line kept clear to allow for the passage of a down train.

The main goods yard at Saxmundham was located on the down or west side of the line north of the level crossing with road access from Albion Street and later from Station Road. Trailing points from the down main line led to the goods loop road, 770 ft in length, with a 30 ft headshunt at the south end and a 30 feet headshunt at the north end. There was also a trailing connection from the up main line direct to the goods loop road but curiously no direct facing access from the down main line. From the loop road connections led to the 370 ft shed road serving the brick-built goods shed and 310 ft back road serving coal storage facilities used by local fuel merchants. At the south end of the shed road a 170 ft-long connection led to a 80 ft siding serving a loading dock. Further goods facilities were provided on the up side of the line with connection off the 330 ft-long back platform road leading to a 300 ft-long dock road which was bisected by another connection serving the 210 ft cattle dock road. Two trailing reception sidings leading from the up main line were provided, that at the north end of the station with connection to the north of North Entrance underbridge No. 449 extending almost to Saxmundham Junction signal box, known as Hay siding and 1,070 ft in length whilst that at the south end, located south of Chantry Road crossing, on the up side was Row siding later serving Stowmarket Creamery, 660 ft in length. The goods yard to the north of Albion Street level crossing was closed with the withdrawal of freight facilities on and from 19th April, 1965 and after removal of the track a new down side platform was erected north of the level crossing and signal box and opened on 23rd March, 1981. Conventional gates replaced the gated part of the original Chantry Road crossing after an accident and they were later again replaced by controlled full barriers.

Saxmundham Station signal box, dating from 1881, which controlled all points and signals at the station was located on the down or western side of the down main line immediately north of Albion Street level crossing and opposite the south end of the up platform. It was of timber construction but later had concrete block inserts as replacement for the lower six boards and contained a 43-lever frame. It is still in existence as the control point for Radio Electronic

Saxmundham station 91 miles 06 chains from Liverpool Street looking north from the down platform in the 1930s. The up platform is beyond Albion Street level crossing and covered footbridge No. 448 at 91 miles 08 chains.                    *Author's Collection*

Saxmundham down platform facing towards Yarmouth in 1957. By this date the footbridge No. 448 adjacent to Albion Street level crossing had been removed, as had the store on the up side of the line near the gates.                    *Author's Collection*

Saxmundham station from the north with the up platform to the left. The 770 ft down goods reception line with connection to the up main line is in the foreground and the 370 ft shed road serving the goods shed is to the right. The open wagons are stabled on the 170 ft connection to the loading dock road.                              *Author's Collection*

Saxmundham goods shed located in the down side goods yard to the west of the main line and north of Albion Street level crossing. The brick structure, with goods office to the right, was served by the 370 ft-long shed road, and had capacity for storage of 25 quarters of grain.
                              *Author's Collection*

# Saxmundham Junction

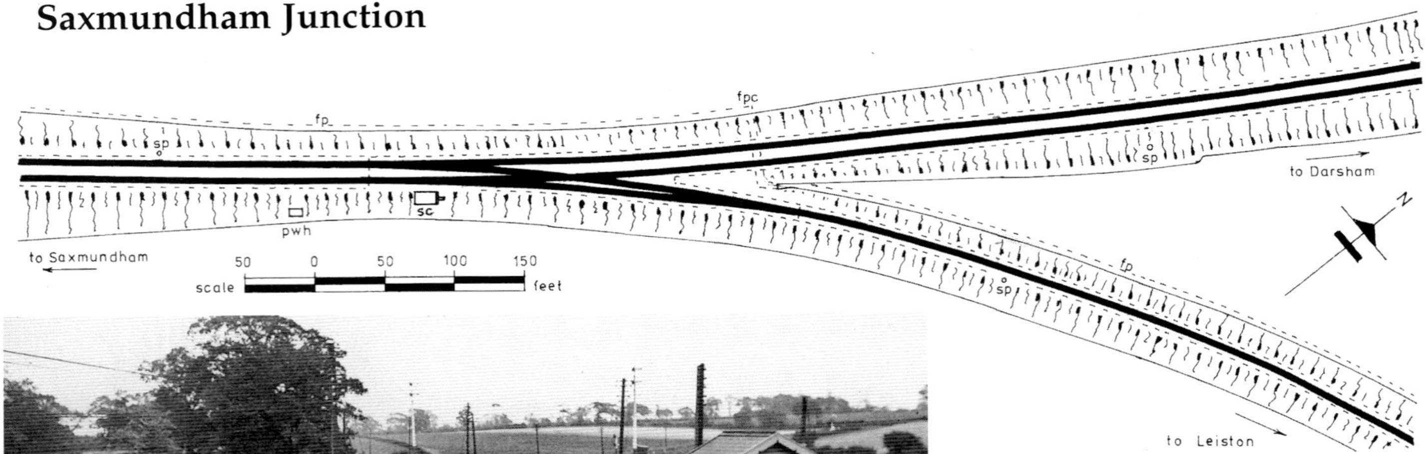

to Darsham

N

to Leiston

fpc

fp

sp

sp

fp

sp

sp

pwh

sc

to Saxmundham

scale

50    0    50    100    150    feet

*Left:* Saxmundham Junction and signal box in 1911 facing north, and showing the down and up main line to the left and the Aldeburgh branch curving away to the right.

*Windwood Collection*

Token Block Working of the East Suffolk Line and an individual function switch panel replaced the lever frame in 1985 to enable RETB to be introduced on 16th February, 1986. At the same time the conventional level crossing gates of Albion Street were replaced with manually-controlled barriers.

Aldeburgh trains usually departed from the down platform passing over Albion Street level crossing No. 62 at 91 miles 07 chains and under station footbridge No. 448 at 91 miles 08 chains before following the down main line northward. If in rare circumstances the branch train departed from the up back platform the bay platform starting signal authorized the movement. If the locomotive was beyond the starting signal because of the length of train, and later after the removal of the fixed signal, the signalman gave the driver authority to depart by displaying a green flag. The down main line initially fell at 1 in 587 and then climbed at 1 in 100 over North Entrance underbridge No. 449 at 91 miles 14 chains, which carried the railway over the main A12 road. Because of the rising gradient runaway catch points were placed in the down main line some 300 yards from the station. Initially this ran off plain line but after the turn of the century ran off into the goods loop line. A ground disc signal was provided to advise drivers of the position of the points.

The Aldeburgh branch junction was originally referred to as such in 1879 when signalling was approved but then became known as Saxmundham Junction. The branch diverged at a double junction, 34 chains from Saxmundham at 91 miles 40½ chains from Liverpool Street, and swung away from the East Suffolk main line heading east and climbing at 1 in 58. Saxmundham Junction signal box, located on the up or eastern side of the main line 91 miles 40 chains from Liverpool Street, was built of timber and placed on timber piling because of the instability of the embankment. This location proved an inconvenience for the signalman in the later years, as the wood at the back of the building rotted and the signal box was supported by baulks of the timber. It subsequently developed a decided list so that even a cup of tea was difficult to pour. There was never any electricity supply and lighting was by oil lamp and the glow from the fire in the stove. Later a tilley lamp provided night-time illumination. Coal was distributed to the box by bucket loads being offloaded from passing trains, which were stopped especially and the only toilet available was a bucket, with the contents swilled and then thrown over the bank at the back of the box. Drinking water was supplied in 4 gallon cans from Saxmundham station. In the final years a toilet was provided in a detached hut.

The line continued climbing at 1 in 58 initially on a low embankment for about half a mile to the 92 mile post before falling for a short distance at 1 in 158. The branch then passed Saxmundham Junction up branch distant signal located on the up side of the line and followed a 1 in 121 falling gradient passing farm and fields for almost a mile. There were no further earthworks of note before the line passed Clayhills, later Knodishall, level crossing at 92 miles 49 chains, where a minor road leading from Knodishall Green to East Green bisected the railway. The branch started to curve to the south-east just before the 93 mile post and then climbed at 1 in 203 to the 93¼ milepost before falling again at 1 in 454 passing Westhouse crossing No. 5 at 93 miles 32 chains, where the lane leading to Westhouse Farm crossed the line. Tyrell's occupational crossing No. 6 at 93 miles

Metropolitan-Cammell two-car dmu forming the 10.05 Ipswich to Aldeburgh service negotiates the points at Saxmundham Junction and heads up the 1 in 58 gradient. In the far left background is Saxmundham goods shed whilst the 1,070 Hay siding also on the left was on the level as the main lines climbed at 1 in 100 towards the junction.                                     *G.R. Mortimer*

The Saxmundham Junction signalman holds the single line Train Staff for the crew of Brush type '2' diesel-electric locomotive No. D5682 to collect whilst working the 11.20 Ipswich to Leiston freight train on 7th September, 1966.                                                           *G.R. Mortimer*

39 chains was passed before a falling gradient of 1 in 83 was followed by a short rise at 1 in 127 from the 93¾ milepost. The railway then descended again at 1 in 1 in 130 over Snowson's occupational crossing No. 7 at 93 miles 68 chains to the 94 milepost before bisected the Saxmundham Road public level crossing No. 8 at 94 miles 02 chains, which had been a crossroads before it the coming of the railway. Now running in an easterly direction, and climbing initially at 1 in 80 and then 1 in 808 past Leiston down distant signal on the down side, the line passed over Coxwell's footpath crossing No. 10 at 94 miles 33 chains and Harper's occupation crossing No. 11 at 94 miles 39 chains in quick succession. The railway reached a minor summit at the 94½ milepost as Buckleswood Road accompanying the railway on the down or north side of the line heralded the approach to Leiston. From the summit the line fell at 1 in 186 passing three reception sidings on the down side (replacing the single original siding 260 ft in length), and the tall down home signal on the up side of the line before passing under the elegant lattice footbridge No. 1110A at 94 miles 67 chains. The branch single line then passed the Leiston up advance starting signal located east of the bridge, the goods yard and the up starting signal on the down side before entering Leiston station with a single platform on the down side of the railway. The 95 mile post stood on the platform and officially 3 miles 75 chains from Saxmundham and 95 miles 01 chains from Liverpool Street.

The 360 ft-long platform was long enough to accommodate a five-coach train of 63 ft 6 in. coach vehicles whilst it was possible to run-round nine coaches by using the sidings in the yard. The wall of the large goods shed located at the back of the platform supported an awning over the platform; the goods shed extension and awning over the platform was authorized in 1910 and completed the following year. The station building located east of the goods shed supported a smaller canopy over the platform. The ramp at the end of the platform leading to the booking hall was a relic of earlier times before the platform was raised in height. The station house was a typical ESR building in red brick, unlike Melton and Wickham Market, which were in Suffolk White brick, and contained accommodation for the station master on the first floor. The ground floor contained the usual booking hall and booking office, general waiting room and ladies waiting room. The valencing of the canopy over the platform was removed in later years.

On the down side of the main single line, west of the station, was Leiston goods yard with the 720 ft-long back or coal road located alongside the road called Westward Ho with its short 80 ft-long headshunt at the east end. This was originally a short 270 ft siding with a 65 ft headshunt. The cattle dock and associated pens was located in the middle of the yard close to the 1 ton 10 cwt capacity (later increased to 2 x 1 ton 10 cwt) fixed hand cranes, and was served by the 100 ft-long dock road, where 30 ft into the siding a connection led across the goods loop and main single line to connect with the up side loop close to the points leading to Garrett's siding. At the west end of the dock road was a 380 ft connection to the down goods reception sidings and a 280 ft connection to the back road. A connection at the east end of dock road led to the back road headshunt whilst a straight section, 230 ft in length, running parallel with the goods shed road ended in a 35 ft-long headshunt. Here there was a set of points

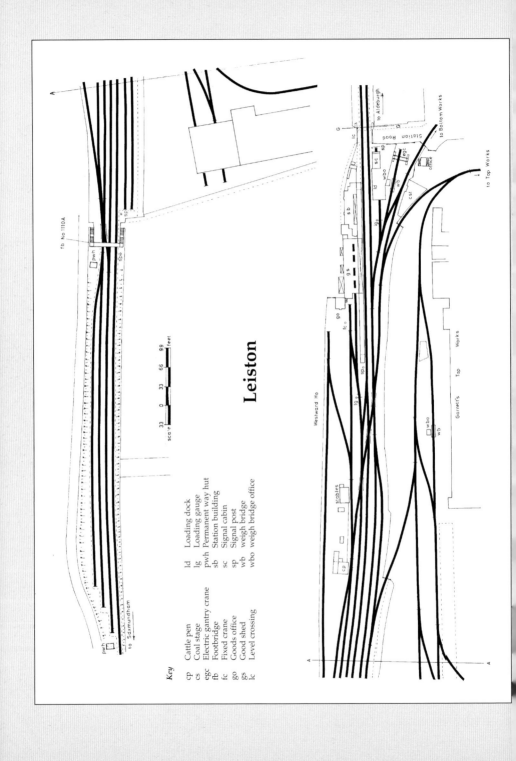

# Leiston

Key

| | | | |
|---|---|---|---|
| cp | Cattle pen | ld | Loading dock |
| cs | Coal stage | lg | Loading gauge |
| egc | Electric gantry crane | pwh | Permanent way hut |
| fb | Footbridge | sb | Station building |
| fc | Fixed crane | sc | Signal cabin |
| go | Goods office | sp | Signal post |
| gs | Good shed | wb | weigh bridge |
| lc | Level crossing | wbo | weigh bridge office |

scale 33 0 33 66 99 feet

to Saxmundham

fb No 1110A

to Aldeburgh

to Bottom Works

to Top Works

Station Road

Westward Ho

Garrett's Top Works

stables

leading to the down goods reception siding at its connection with goods shed road. The 280 ft-long shed road served the goods shed located at the back of the station platform. The shed was lengthened in GER days but was always separated from the adjacent station building. At the west end of the layout were the three down reception holding sidings, No. 1 road nearest the main single line 610 ft in length, No. 2 road 590 ft and the shorter No. 3 road 520 ft in length, which were used extensively to marshal stock requiring forwarding or dispatch from the brickworks siding, the gas works siding or Garrett's various sidings. Originally only two shorter sidings were provided. Footbridge No. 1110A, at 94 miles 67 chains, spanned the main single line and the throat to the three reception sidings and was the replacement for an inconveniently located public footpath crossing.

The 540 ft-long loop line located to the south or up side of the main single line could not be used to pass passenger trains only a passenger train standing at the platform and a goods train in the loop, or two goods trains. At the east end of the loop east of the level crossing was a 115 ft-long headshunt. West of the level crossing at the east end of the loop was an end- and side-loading dock surmounted in the latter years by an electric 30 tons capacity gantry crane served by two short sidings, 80 ft and 200 ft in length. Behind the crane a siding curved away from the loop to serve Garrett's, the upper part known as the 'Old' 'Town', or 'Bottom' Works, which was located 600 yards south of the railway and the 'New' or 'Station' Works adjacent to the line. Two exchange sidings known as up holding No. 1 and No. 2 were located between the main line and the works boundary. No. 1 was 750 ft in length and No. 2 620 ft. On the latter a connection 280 ft from the buffer stops formed a trailing access to Richard Garrett's 'Station' Works opened in 1914. Two sidings ran in front of the main engineering shop, the 1,110 ft-long outer road divided into a 260 ft-long headshunt at the west end and 390 feet outer loop with the remainder curving round to meet the connection from the down side goods yard. The inner road nearest the engineering works was 950 ft-long with a 260 ft-long siding curving away to the south alongside one of the shops and ending in a 150 ft-long headshunt parallel with the outer road headshunt.

Garrett's 'Town' Works was served via a private tramway which was paved in granite setts and curved across Station Road by an open crossing to the south of the Aldeburgh branch level crossing. Just beyond the crossing a connection was made with Carr's brickworks tramway, which bisected the Aldeburgh branch at right angles, by level crossing. Garrett's tramway then swung southwards down a 1 in 38 gradient for 12 chains to the rear of dwelling houses in Station Road and Dinsdale Road (formerly Foundry Lane), after which it passed the post office and council offices and crossed Saxmundham Road (later Main Street) on another level crossing, which was originally protected by gates, but these were later removed. The tramway then entered the main 'Town' Works by the main gate on a cable-worked incline and ran up the works yard to the foundry and boiler shop, whilst a branch ran off to the gas works. Incoming wagons were drawn out of the station interchange sidings or goods yard by Suffolk Punch horses to the commencement of the south curve and released individually to reach the works by gravity until halted by the adverse

The west end of Leiston goods yard viewed from the footbridge with from left to right, the main single line, and No. 1 reception siding 610 ft in length, No. 2 reception siding 590 ft in length and No. 3 reception siding 520 ft in length, the latter occupied by covered vans. Westward Ho siding is beyond the boundary fence. The shed beyond the buffer stops of No. 1 road accommodated the permanent way trolley. *The late B.D.J. Walsh*

By 1915 it was deemed dangerous for Garrett's employees to cross the goods yard and main single branch line by occupational crossing and so a footbridge No. 1110A at 94 miles 67 chains was erected across the railway to obviate accidents. In this view facing towards the station the down home signal is to the right protecting the main single line with the points leading to Nos. 1, 2 and 3 reception holding sidings left to centre foreground. The continuation of No. 1 holding siding leads to the down siding and next that are dock road and shed road with back or coal road alongside the road called Westward Ho. *Author's Collection*

View looking west from Leiston platform towards Saxmundham, with the 95 mile post from Liverpool Street prominent by the back fence. The up starting signal (larger arm) shares the same post as the calling-on arm authorizing entry to the down side goods yard loop road. The up goods loop line is parallel with the main single line with the up side reception sidings to the left used for the receipt and dispatch of Garrett's traffic.                    *The late B.D.J. Walsh*

The east end of Leiston goods yard viewed from an up train with the down loop road in the foreground leading to the goods shed. The covered van and open wagon are standing on the 280 ft-long shed road whilst the back or coal road to the left on the boundary of railway property is occupied by an open wagon. The lean-to shed by the goods shed housed the weighbridge. The goods office can be seen behind the 1 ton 10 cwt capacity goods yard fixed crane.    *D. Clayton*

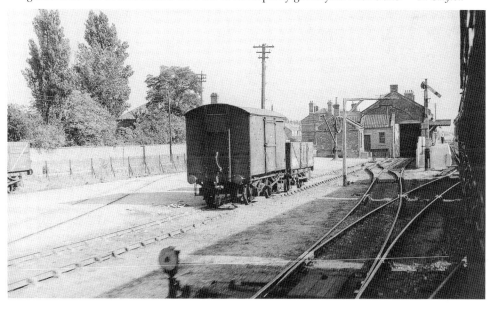

Leiston station looking east towards Aldeburgh with the two-storey hipped-roof structure similar to buildings provided at Aldeburgh and Saxmundham. The station master's accommodation was located on the first floor and station offices and staff rooms on the ground floor. When the goods shed was extended in 1911 the opportunity arose to provide a more substantial canopy for intending passengers to shelter from inclement weather. The goods loop runs parallel to the single main branch line with the loading dock and signal box in the background. The down starting signal has been cleared for a train.          *The late B.D.J. Walsh*

The 360 ft-long platform at Leiston viewed from the signal box with, from the right, the main station building fronted by a small canopy, which had been altered from earlier years, the goods shed extension fronted by a larger ornate canopy and the original goods shed. The up side goods loop is in the foreground with connections leading to Garrett's works          *Author's Collection*

The road approach to Leiston goods shed with the yard entrance gate to the right. The shed was extended at the station or east end in 1911 when two additional bays were added. A fixed crane of 1 ton 10 cwt capacity was located on the shed internal platform to assist with loading and unloading of goods to and from wagons and supplemented the 1 ton 10 cwt crane in the down yard. The road approach to Leiston station is to the left. *The late B.D.J. Walsh*

The road approach to Leiston station with the level crossing beyond the buildings. The station master's accommodation, later occupied by a member of the traffic staff, was on the first floor and station offices and staff rooms on the ground floor. The goods shed casts a shadow on the right. *Author's Collection*

General view of the loading dock alongside the up loop line at Leiston with the signal box wedged between the dock and Station Road level crossing, seen on 5th June, 1954. The lower quadrant down starting signal protects the barriers and in the background is the 30 tons capacity gantry crane used by Garrett's to load and unload heavy engineering items into and out of railway wagons. *Author's Collection*

Leiston signal box provided in 1892 together with the up side level crossing gate and down starting signal. Cyclists approach Station Road level crossing whilst there is a good view of the 30 ton capacity gantry crane. In the background are the buildings of Garrett's Top Works. *Author's Collection*

rising gradient. The wagons continued their journey to the foundry hauled by rope worked from a capstan powered by the foundry 48 in. steam winding engine. Coal for the winding engine was stored in bins below track level but all traces of the coal drops disappeared many years before the demise of the factory and branch line. Outgoing wagons were also released individually with horses completing the haulage to the station interchange sidings. In 1929 a pair of outgoing wagons were derailed demolishing part of a house and involving Garrett's in settling claims for compensation. As a result of this Garrett's purchased the steam locomotive *Sirapite* to haul the wagons up and down the 1 in 38 gradient to and from the interchange sidings and later replaced between 1962 and 1968 by a small battery locomotive. At the far side of the 'Town' Works stood the powerhouse with a tall ornate chimney, a landmark for miles. On one of the gables of the building was affixed a steam siren known locally as 'the Bull' because of its deep bellowing sound.

Back on the Aldeburgh branch opposite the east end of the station platform adjacent to and west of the level crossing gates was Leiston signal box, which controlled the signals and most of the points at the station. The timber structure was opened in late autumn 1892 when a new siding connection for Carr's brickworks traffic eliminated the turntable in the main single line, which itself had earlier replaced Carr and Garrett's joint tramway flat crossing east of Station Road level crossing. Specific instructions were in operation before the elimination of the turntable crossing. A turntable, provided with a single set of rails, was laid down in the tramway crossing the main single line on the Aldeburgh side of Leiston station. The turntable when not in use was to be kept locked and set for the siding parallel to the main single line. The key was in possession of the Leiston station master, who, before allowing the turntable to be used was required to see that the up and down home and distant signals were at danger. When the branch engine or other engine in steam was at the Aldeburgh end of the line the station master was required to send a man back 800 yds towards Aldeburgh with hand and detonator signals to protect the line during the time the turntable was in use. After work was completed the turntable was to be relocked in its proper position, and the key returned to the station master. Catch points were also laid in the tramway line north of the main single line and were normally set for the catch siding and padlocked in that position. When it was necessary to open the points for the purpose of passing trucks across the main single line, the station master was required to take the same precautions for protecting the line. As there was then only one station signal provided at Leiston, with arms mounted on the same post for each direction of travel and located at the country end of the station platform, the turntable being kept set for the siding parallel to the main line provided protection against an up train running through the level crossing gates in the event of such a train failing to stop.

From Leiston the single branch line and up side loop line continued falling at 1 in 186 past the protective down starting signal before bisecting Station Road, later B1122 level crossing No. 12 at 95 miles 05 chains, where the gates were hand operated and opened and closed by the signalman. The single line then passed Leiston up home signal on the up side and the connection to the 360 ft-long brick works siding on the down side of the line, served by facing points in

Leiston station facing east with Brush type '2' diesel-electric No. D5554 waiting to depart with the 14.05 freight to Ipswich on 6th September, 1966. The goods yard to the left is host to a rake of 16 ton all-steel mineral wagons occupying the shed road. The loop line to the right gave access to Garrett's sidings.                                                                *G.R. Mortimer*

Leiston station with Brush type '2' diesel-electric No. D5554 departing for Ipswich with the 14.05 branch freight to Ipswich on 6th September, 1966.                                          *G.R. Mortimer*

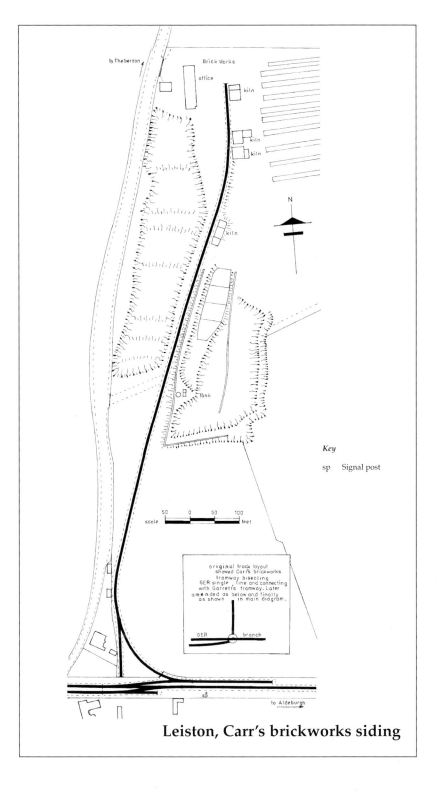

to Theberton

Brick Works

office

kiln

kiln

kiln

kiln

N

*Key*

sp   Signal post

50    0    50    100

scale ———————— feet

Tank

original track layout
showed Carr's brickworks
tramway bisecting
GER single line and connecting
with Garrett's tramway. Later
amended as below and finally
as shown in main diagram.

GER ———○——— branch

sp

to Aldeburgh

## Leiston, Carr's brickworks siding

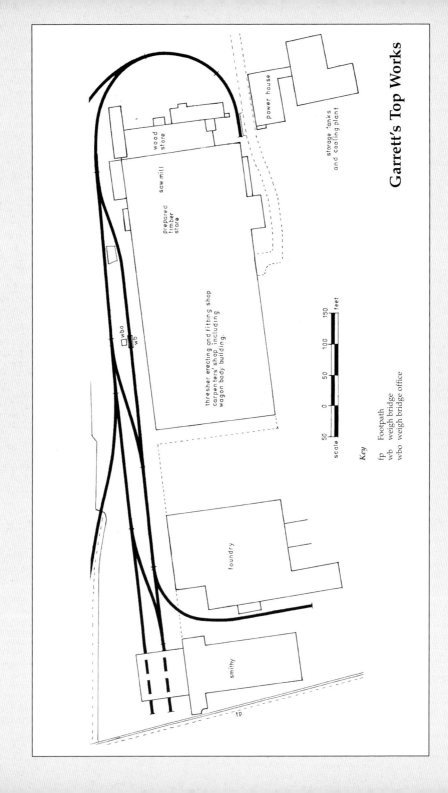

Garrett's Top Works

power house

storage tanks
and cooling plant

wood
store

saw mill

prepared
timber
store

wbo

wb

thresher erecting and fitting shop
carpenters' shop including
wagon body building.

foundry

smithy

fp

Key

fp   Footpath
wb   weigh bridge
wbo  weigh bridge office

50   0   50   100   150   feet

scale

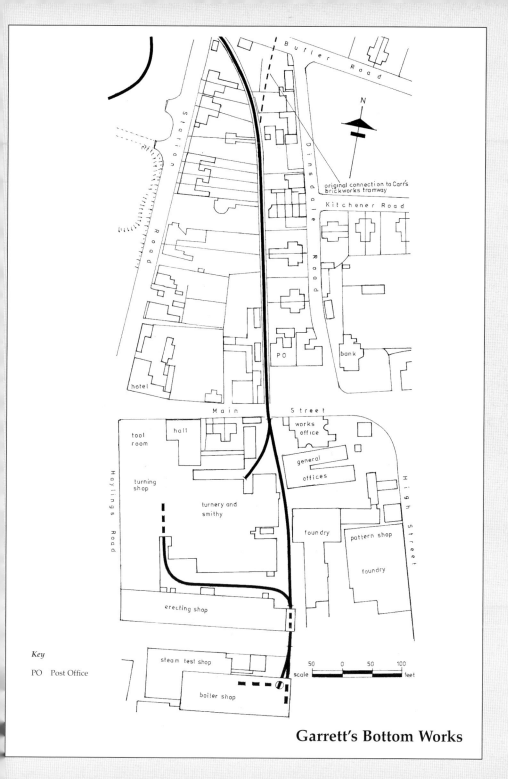

Butler Road

Station Road

Dinsdale Road

original connection to Carr's brickworks tramway

N

Kitchener Road

PO

bank

hotel

Main Street

works office

Haylings Road

tool room

hall

general offices

turning shop

turnery and smithy

foundry

pattern shop

High Street

foundry

erecting shop

steam test shop

50    0    50    100

scale                    feet

boiler shop

Key

PO    Post Office

**Garrett's Bottom Works**

Garrett's Electromobile battery electric locomotive built in 1927 for Metropolitan-Vickers of Eaglescliffe, and purchased in April 1962 as a replacement for the steam locomotive *Sirapite*. Here it is in charge of driver Peter Newstead approaching the main line interchange siding after crossing Station Road at Leiston hauling a plate wagon from the Bottom works.

*The late Dr I.C. Allen*

The 30 tons capacity gantry crane at Leiston viewed from Station Road with the rear of Leiston signal box to the right and the ornate station building in the background.    *Author's Collection*

Garrett's Electromobile battery locomotive approaches Main Street level crossing on its way to the Bottom Works. The driver of the Ford 'Cortina' has obviously underestimated the clearance and no doubt had to reverse his vehicle to allow the locomotive to pass.     *Long Shop Museum*

A flagman halts traffic on Stowmarket Road, formerly Main Road, at Leiston as Garrett's battery electric locomotive departs from the Bottom Works with a plate wagon.     *The late Dr I.C. Allen*

Aveling & Porter single cylinder 0-4-0 geared locomotive *Sirapite* at Garrett's Bottom Works having climbed the steep incline from the main line yard.                    *Long Shop Museum*

Electromobile battery-electric shunting locomotive, Works No. W247, dating from 1927 and purchased by Garrett's in April 1952, awaits its next duties at Bottom Works.     *Robert Powell*

the down direction. A connection in this siding, 210 ft from the buffer stops, led to an 8 chains radius curve which continued to form the 1,550 ft-long siding leading north at right angles to the main single line ultimately serving Carr's brick kilns. From the north end of the curve a trailing connection led to a small truncated siding which until 1892 bisected the main single Aldeburgh branch. Continuing towards Aldeburgh another connection on the down side led to the 660 ft-long gas works siding opened in 1912 for Leiston Gas Co. on the north side of the line at 95 miles 19 chains where the points were operated by a 6-lever ground frame released by a key on the single line Train Staff. In later years the points were repositioned and the siding was reduced to a length of 430 feet. Beyond the siding and at the 95¼ milepost the line began climbing at 1 in 97 for a quarter of a mile curving to the right to cross Valley Arch underbridge No. 1110 at 95 miles 37 chains, where the line crossed Valley Road.

Beyond the structure the line continued curving to the right past Leiston up distant signal located on the down side of the railway, falling at 1 in 284 through a shallow cutting before swinging on a 50 chains radius curve to the south. The railway then bisected Sizewell Road level crossing at 95 miles 71 chains with its attendant gatehouse on the down side of the line south-east of the crossing and the adjacent Crown Farm siding, later known as Sizewell siding, with points facing down trains travelling towards Aldeburgh. The siding was originally 300 ft, later 540 ft in length. Much coal traffic for Leiston was handled here and it was also used for loading cattle, which had grazed on the adjacent marshes before being sent to market. The siding connection was worked by a 5-lever ground frame accommodated in a hut opposite the cottage, the frame being released by the Annett's key on the single line Train Staff which continued until the introduction of RETB. Prior to World War I a 30 ft headshunt was located at the west end of the layout but was later removed and replaced by trap points. In the late 1890s the siding was nearly doubled in length to 540 ft. It is here that the siding for the atomic power station at Sizewell is located with the original coal siding removed and a new siding repositioned further back from the former main single line to accommodate the gantry crane to lift the atomic flasks into and out of the flask carrying wagons.

In GER, LNER and early BR days special instructions were issued for the operation of Sizewell siding. With the points facing down trains all trucks for the siding had to be worked through to Aldeburgh and then brought back so that they could be shunted into the siding. Once shunting was completed, the man in charge of the siding was responsible for seeing that the trucks were placed inside the catch point and clear of the main single line and that the points were replaced and locked for the main single line before handing the Train Staff back to the driver. The Leiston station master was responsible for the siding and was required to satisfy himself that the instructions were duly carried out. To accommodate the flask trains and ensure smooth operation certain track alterations were made at Sizewell. A holding siding with points facing down trains was provided west of the level crossing, whilst a run-round loop was provided south of the siding spanned by the gantry so that the locomotive or locomotives could run round the stock and reverse the flask wagons under the gantry before returning with the up working.

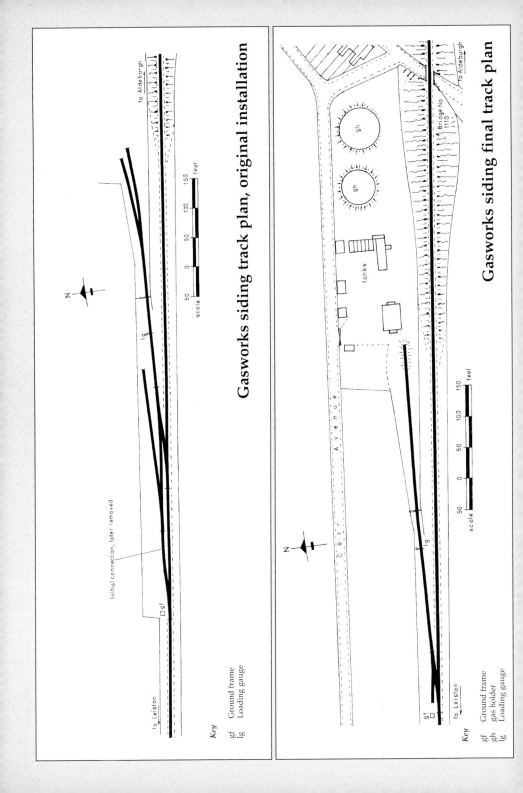

Gasworks siding track plan, original installation

to Aldeburgh

to Leiston

Initial connection, later removed

lg

gf

N

scale

50  0  50  100  150
feet

**Key**

gf  Ground frame
lg  Loading gauge

Gasworks siding final track plan

to Aldeburgh

Bridge No 1110

gh

gh

tanks

C a r r   A v e n u e

lg

to Leiston

gf

N

scale

50  0  50  100  150
feet

**Key**

gf  Ground frame
gh  gas holder
lg  Loading gauge

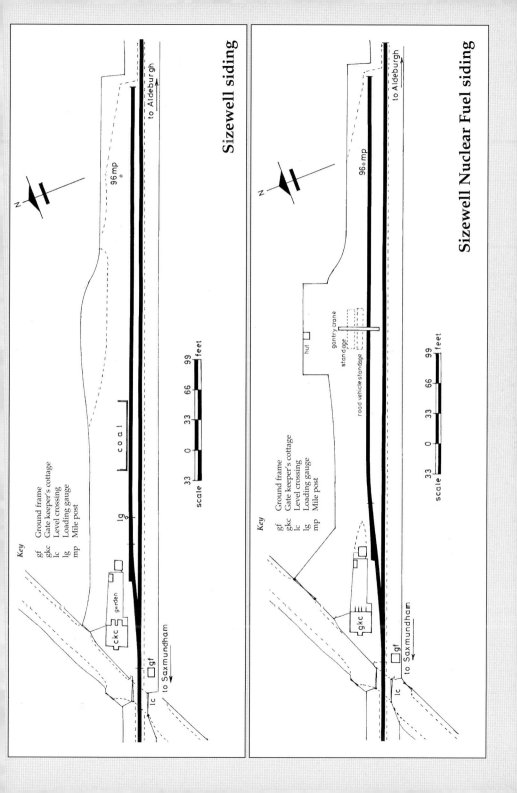

Sizewell siding

Key

gf    Ground frame
gkc   Gate keeper's cottage
lc    Level crossing
lg    Loading gauge
mp    Mile post

N

96 mp

coal

lg

gkc

garden

gf

lc

to Aldeburgh

to Saxmundham

scale    33    0    33    66    99

feet

Sizewell Nuclear Fuel siding

Key

gf    Ground frame
gkc   Gate keeper's cottage
lc    Level crossing
lg    Loading gauge
mp    Mile post

N

96 mp

hut

gantry crane

standage

road vehicle standage

gkc

gf

lc

to Aldeburgh

to Saxmundham

scale    33    0    33    66    99

feet

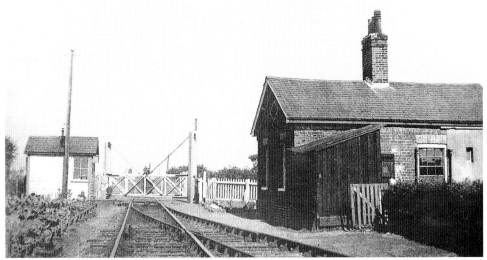

Sizewell level crossing No. 13 at 95 miles 71 chains from Liverpool Street looking towards Saxmundham with the attendant crossing keeper's cottage on the down side of the line. The timber hut on the up side contained a 5-lever frame controlling the points to Sizewell siding diverging to the right from the main single line. *Author's Collection*

Sizewell siding and level crossing facing towards Aldeburgh soon after the installation of the overhead gantry crane. The provision of the crane required the repositioning of the siding further back from the main single line. The ground frame is contained within the wooden hut to the right whilst the gatekeeper's cottage is to the left. *R. Kennell*

Sizewell siding with crossing keeper's cottage to the left and ground frame hut to the right; view facing towards Aldeburgh in the 1950s when the siding was still used for offloading coal traffic for Leiston. *Author's Collection*

Sizewell siding 540 ft in length viewed from a passing train with the crossing keeper's cottage beyond the wagons on the down side of the line. The siding was initially used for cattle traffic and later for the receipt of coal and coke traffic, latterly by the Leiston Co-operative Society, before conversion for atomic flask traffic. *The late B.D.J. Walsh*

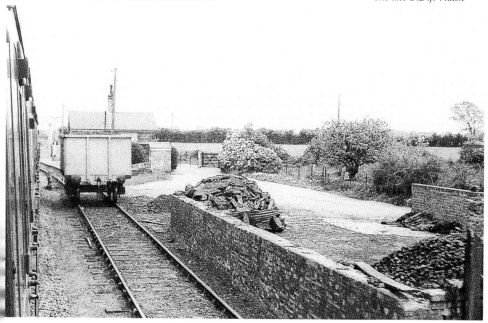

Sizewell siding with the CEGB gantry crane lowering an atomic flask on to a flask wagon. Brush type '2', 1,365 hp diesel-electric locomotive No. D5699 stands with the train on the siding while in the foreground the former main single branch line to Aldeburgh terminates in buffer stops.
*The late Dr I.C. Allen*

Sizewell siding facing towards Saxmundham with the former single branch line occupied by a goods brake van to the left and the CEGB siding occupied by 50 ton flask wagons. The siding spanned by the gantry crane, was specifically installed for the atomic flask traffic emanating from Sizewell A and B nuclear power stations.
*The late Dr I.C. Allen*

From the siding the single line branch continued on the 1 in 284 falling gradient to cross Crown Farm occupational crossing No. 14 at 96 miles 06 chains and the little used track from Leiston to Sizewell Common by Crown Lands crossing No. 15 at 96 miles 16 chains with its adjacent crossing keeper's cottage on the down side of the line south of the crossing. From Crown Lands crossing the railway bisected the vast expanse of heather and gorse, stretching east to the coast and forming part of the locally known walks and Aldringham Common. This was typical of the Suffolk Sandlings with open heathland supporting a large population of rabbits and other wildlife. A line of trees concealed the neighbouring Sizewell Hall. Local people often picknicked in the area conveniently near to the Crown Lands crossing cottage where the crossing keeper would provide water for tea or coffee to be brewed on a gorse fire or a primus stove.

Beyond Crown Lands crossing the line climbed a short section of 1 in 308 over occupational crossing No. 16 at 96 miles 23 chains before falling at 1 in 179 with heathland to right and left on low embankments or shallow cuttings interspersed by two footpath crossings, Nos. 17 at 96 miles 58 chains and Stone Cottages crossing No. 18 at 96 miles 62 chains, in quick succession. After passing Stone Cottages crossing the greens of Thorpeness golf club adjoined the line on the up or west side of the railway and beyond the 97 milepost the branch continued on the 1 in 179 falling gradient before bisecting the Thorpeness Road, later B1353, by crossing No. 19 at 97 miles 25 chains. Immediately beyond the level crossing was Thorpeness Halt, with its single 300ft, later 350 ft-long, platform on the down or east side of the railway, 97 miles 28 chains from Liverpool Street and 6 miles 22 chains from Saxmundham. The term 'Halt' was dropped from the public timetables from 1st May, 1933 but remained in the working timetables until closure. The platform could accommodate a train of six 63 ft 6 in. coaches. When the railway first opened to traffic there was but the tiny hamlet of Thorpe sheltering by the dunes, but just before World War I the area was developed into the garden village of Thorpeness, a creation of Glencairn Stuart Ogilvie, a dramatist and author who owned a considerable estate in the area.

When neighbouring Dunwich was a flourishing town, principal port and Episcopal centre of East Anglia between the 7th and 14th century, Thorpe Haven was a harbour into which flowed the Little Hundred River and which supported a small fishing fleet as well as providing shelter for the Aldeburgh fishing vessels. Coastal erosion resulted in Dunwich disappearing under the waves of the German Ocean and the mouth of the Little Hundred River silting up. The Haven became a marsh with the tiny hamlet of a few flint cottages built on a shingle bank above the beach. When the marshy area was first developed it was considered a good example of artistic town planning with the houses built in attractive styles of the Jacobean and other periods. The work included the excavation of a man-made lake known as the Meare, a shallow island-dotted stretch of water on former marshy ground often liable to flooding as the Hundred River still flowed through the area, the 60 acres containing facilities for rowing, sailing and punting. The development also included a dance hall, a country club, concert hall and theatre, tennis court and an 18 hole golf course. In the village the several striking buildings included the Dolphin Inn and a riding establishment together with a unique building called 'The House in the

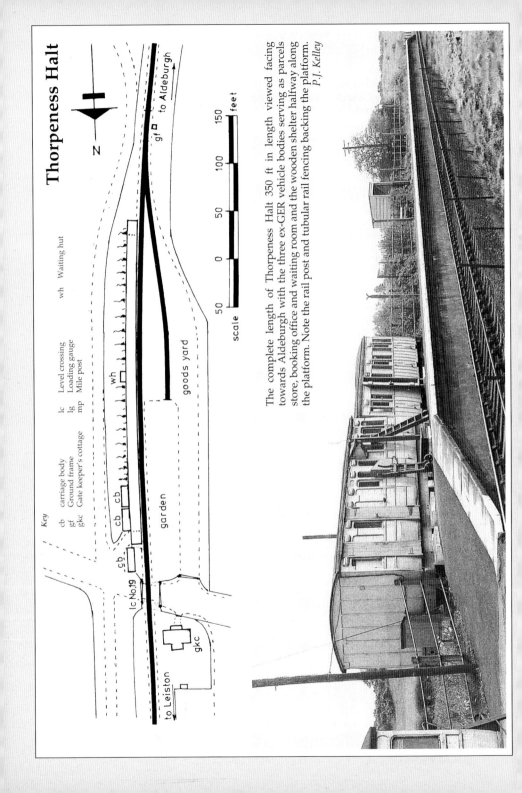

# Thorpeness Halt

**Key**

| | | | |
|---|---|---|---|
| cb | carriage body | lc | Level crossing |
| gf | Ground frame | lg | Loading gauge |
| gkc | Gate keeper's cottage | mp | Mile post |
| | | wh | Waiting hut |

scale — feet

The complete length of Thorpeness Halt 350 ft in length viewed facing towards Aldeburgh with the three ex-GER vehicle bodies serving as parcels store, booking office and waiting room and the wooden shelter halfway along the platform. Note the rail post and tubular rail fencing backing the platform.

*P.J. Kelley*

Clouds' where the false top windows disguised the water tower serving the village. The lower windows were provided for the associated living accommodation. An old post-windmill was removed from its original site and set up to serve as a pump mill supplying the village water tower.

After sufficient petitioning the GER opened Thorpeness Halt on 29th July, 1914 to serve the locality. Initially the gates of the level crossing were opened by a resident crossing keeper who lived in the adjacent crossing cottage located on the up side of the line north of the crossing. The cottage was provided with four rooms and had a cess toilet at the bottom of the garden and for most of its life had domestic water being drawn from a well. With the opening of the Halt the gates were opened by station staff but in the final few months of passenger train operation when the station became unstaffed and after the sale of the cottage, the conductor-guard was responsible for opening and closing the gates for the passage of each train. Three second-hand coach bodies provided station accommodation on the platform located on the east side of the single line. The first, standing at the foot of the ramp at the north end of the platform near the crossing and serving as a store shed, had been a 5-compartment 1883 second class coach. The other bodies stood at the back of the platform: that serving as a booking office was a former 5-compartment third dating from 1880, whilst the waiting room had been an 1897 first class saloon. Further along the platform was a small open-fronted waiting hut.For many years the coach bodies were painted in an ochre livery. A tubular rail fence backed the platform and oil lamps in ornate cases, later tilley lamps provided illumination during the hours of darkness. When the Halt was manned by regular staff the gardens on the up side of the line between the buffer stops of the siding and the level crossing were regularly tended, but usually fenced and protected from rabbits or foxes which would destroy the crops within minutes.

Interior of the waiting room of the first class carriage at Thorpeness. The coach had been one of many suburban vehicles widened from 8 ft to 9 ft to provide additional accommodation. The additional inset portion can be seen under the notice regarding conductor-guard working.                                              *The late Dr I.C. Allen*

Thorpeness Halt looking towards Saxmundham on 14th May, 1956 showing the station garden on the up side of the single line and the small crossing keeper's cottage beyond. The road entrance to the goods yard was by the gate opposite the cottage.     *The late H.C. Casserley*

Thorpeness Halt on 6th September, 1966.                              *G.R. Mortimer*

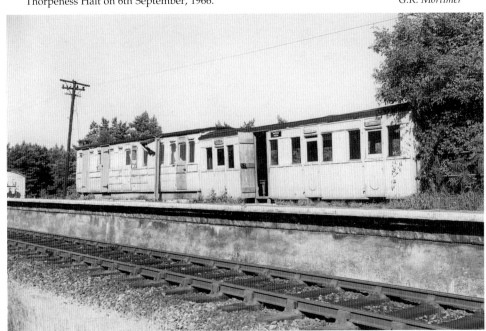

An agreement was reached on 31st December, 1921 for the installation of a 280 ft-long siding with the connection facing for up trains at the Aldeburgh end of the station on the up side of the line opposite the platform. The points were originally operated by a 5-lever ground frame but after the inspecting officer reported that the siding connection was 'over signalled' the points were operated by a single lever released by the key on the Train Staff. The access road for the siding was on the west side of the line from the adjacent road. The siding was little used in the later days of the line and freight facilities were withdrawn on and from 30th November, 1959, although the siding was not removed until April 1965.

Away from Thorpeness Halt the branch fell for a short distance at 1 in 164/1 in 440 before short sections of 1 in 220 climbing and 1 in 122 falling took the railway past the reeds and willows encircling the Meare on the down side of the line. The gradient eased to 1 in 1813 falling past Ward Hill as the railway bisected Sheepwash crossing No. 20 at 97 miles 56 chains, with its attendant crossing keeper's cottage on the up side of the railway north of the crossing, where a minor track crossed the line. When the branch was under construction a ballast siding, with points facing down trains, diverged a few yards north of the crossing to cross Thorpe Common, which later became part of the Meare, to terminate on the shore just south of Seaview Cottages. The points were removed soon after the opening of the railway although the siding, minus connecting points, was shown in the 1882 Ordnance Survey map of the locality.

South of Sheepwash crossing the line climbed at 1 in 1496 before encountering short 1 in 300 falling and 1 in 335 rising gradients across open country and grazing land, passing through a shallow cutting. To the east of the railway the narrow road linking Thorpeness to Aldeburgh ran parallel to the line and just beyond the road could be seen the shingle ridge lining the top of the beach, though the water's edge was out of sight. After another mile the branch passed Aldeburgh down distant signal on the down side of the line before reaching Brick Kiln Cottage and bisecting the adjacent Brick Kiln occupational crossing No. 23 at 98 miles 48 chains with Crag Pit farm to the west of the railway. The branch then negotiated short sections of 1 in 308 falling, 1 in 273 rising and 1in 880 falling to the 99 mile post. The railway then climbed at 1 in 152 over Northfield Covert footpath crossing No. 25 at 99 miles 13 chains before approaching Aldeburgh on a 1 in 880 rising gradient passing the up advance starting signal and down home signal with the parish church of St Peter and St Paul, an unusually wide perpendicular building, dominating the skyline at the top of West Hill. Houses also came into view as the branch passed the engine shed and Aldeburgh signal box and up starting signal on the down side of the line before entering the single platform of the station, 430 ft in length also located on the down side to terminate under a timber overall roof at 8 miles 26 chains from Saxmundham and 99 miles 32 chains from Liverpool Street. The rails and platform stretched beyond the overall roof to the buffer stops 99 miles 36 chains from Liverpool Street. The station, known as Aldborough until 1st June, 1875, originally to be sited south of Victoria Road until wiser counsels adopted the position north of the thoroughfare, was inconveniently located about half a mile inland from the main part of the town.

The station buildings were constructed of white brick in typical ESR style, with the overall roof over the single platform and the main single line, a clerestory being provided over the running rail to assist with smoke emission. This substantial train

Aerial view of Aldeburgh station and adjacent windmill in June 1920 with Victoria Avenue running from top left to bottom right. It was originally planned to site the terminus to the south of this road but wiser counsels decided against this action to obviate a level crossing. The outskirts of the town are to the top of the photograph and the Station Hotel is set back near the entrance to the goods yard.

*Aerofilms*

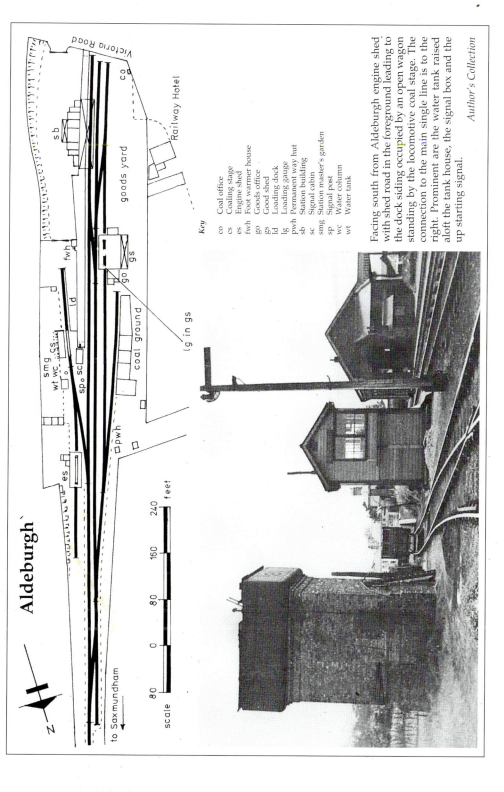

# Aldeburgh

Victoria Road

Railway Hotel

goods yard

co

s b

fwh

gs

go

ld

lg in gs

coal ground

smg

wt wc cs

sp sc

pwh

es

to Saxmundham

scale
feet
80   0   80   160   240

N

*Key*

co   Coal office
cs   Coaling stage
es   Engine shed
fwh  Foot warmer house
go   Goods office
gs   Good shed
ld   Loading dock
lg   Loading gauge
pwh  Permanent way hut
sb   Station building
sc   Signal cabin
smg  Station master's garden
sp   Signal post
wc   Water column
wt   Water tank

Facing south from Aldeburgh engine shed with shed road in the foreground leading to the dock siding occupied by an open wagon standing by the locomotive coal stage. The connection to the main single line is to the right. Prominent are the water tank raised aloft the tank house, the signal box and the up starting signal.

*Author's Collection*

The flat terrain of the coastal region of East Suffolk is evident from this view of Aldeburgh engine shed, up starting signal and signal box in 1956.                    *Author's Collection*

Aldeburgh engine shed located on the down or east side of the main single line was 60 ft in length and similar in design to the shed provided at Framlingham. It was served by the 260 ft-long shed road and was a through structure to enable wagons or a locomotive to be stabled north of the building by the buffer stops.                    *Author's Collection*

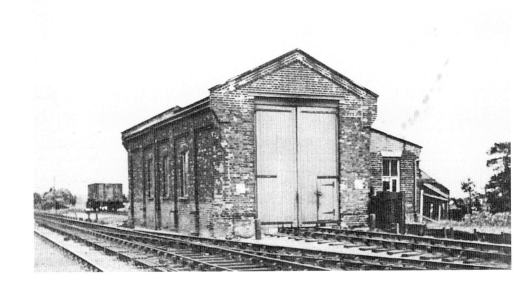

The 150 ft-long dock road at Aldeburgh with loading dock at the back of the station platform, used in the latter years for storage of excess supplies of locomotive coal, not accommodated on the coal stage to the right. Beyond the coal stage is the locomotive water tank and then the shed siding leading to the engine shed. *Author's Collection*

An up train hauled by a 'J15' class 0-6-0 prepares to depart from Aldeburgh in 1952. The 500 ft loop road is parallel to the main single line, whilst the 640 ft-long shed road occupied by a wagon served the goods shed. *Author's Collection*

Aldeburgh goods shed, constructed of brick, had a gabled roof on raised parapets at each end of the structure. It was equipped with a 1 ton 10 cwt capacity fixed crane on the internal loading platform, whilst a projecting canopy to the rear provided protection for traders loading and unloading wares in inclement weather. The building was served by the goods shed road, which at the south end was used for unloading coal and coke traffic. *Author's Collection*

Aldeburgh goods shed from the approach road with an ornate canopy over the loading platform door. In this view taken in latter days of freight working the sign on the end wall advises customers that the goods office was at the passenger station. *Author's Collection*

shed covering much of the south end of the platform was originally quite short but was extended to 140 ft in length in 1893 to accommodate longer trains, the extension being built to the north and the south of the original structure with arches at intervals, whilst doors in the wall led to various railway offices and staff rooms. The overall roof fronting on to the station buildings was supported on the west side of the main single line by a brick wall extending from ground level with blank arcading and supporting the other end of the roof trusses. The station stood adjacent to Victoria Road and contained the usual offices: from north to south, gentlemen's toilet, booking hall and office, lamp room, and station master's office, with a W.H. Smith bookstall attached to the south end of the building. The station master's living accommodation was originally on the first floor but before World War II the station master had been provided with housing in Fawcett Road and the occupancy was taken over by traffic staff, latterly Edgar Bird, the motor driver, and his family. A small brick building provided halfway along the platform was originally a waiting room, then a facility for filling and disposing of footwarmers (in the heyday of the line the charge to passengers was 2$d$. per footwarmer), and was later converted to a staff room and material store. The single platform, extended in 1884 to 430 ft, could accommodate a train of six coaches, each 63 ft 6 in. in length, but it was possible to run-round eight coaches using the crossover in the middle of the platform road and the crossover at the Saxmundham end of the station. This run-round loop was 500 ft in length with a 170 ft headshunt at the north end and a 350 ft headshunt at the south end.

The goods yard lay to the west of the station on the up side of the main single line and was served by two sidings leading from the loop road. The 640 ft shed road running parallel with the loop road served the commodious goods shed constructed of red brick with offices at each end. The shed had a protective canopy over the carting road and contained a 1 ton 10 cwt capacity fixed crane. In the latter years most coal traffic was concentrated at the south end of the shed road nearest the road entrance to the goods yard. From shed road siding a connection at the north end led to the short 240 ft-long cattle dock road serving the cattle pens. At the north end of the yard a local builder, William C. Reade, rented grounds and a small timber building, and had access from the Leiston Road. Goods facilities were completed by a loading dock served by a 150 ft-long siding provided in 1893, which ran behind the signal box and behind the station platform. At the north end the connection served the 260 ft-long engine shed siding which contained the red brick double-ended structure similar to the shed provided at Framlingham, which could accommodate one locomotive, the siding projecting 115 ft beyond the north end of the building. A water tank and coal stage was located to the south of the building east of the shed road, although often coal was unloaded on to the loading dock if the coal stage was full. In the latter years of steam working, coal was unloaded direct from wagon into the locomotive tender or bunker to save double handling.

Points and signals at the station were operated from Aldeburgh signal box, dating from 1892, and containing a 21-lever Stevens frame with 16 working and five spare levers. The timber structure, located on down side of the line at the north end of the platform, was abolished on 17th July, 1961. After closure the crossovers between the single line and the run-round loop were locked at each end by Hodgson's lock with the key retained in Leiston signal box, when not required.

Aldeburgh station, 99 miles 32 chains from Liverpool Street and 8 miles 26 chains from Saxmundham, view facing towards the buffer stops. *Author's Collection*

View from the buffer stops at Aldeburgh with the ornate overall roof spanning the platform and single branch line. To the right is the station bookstall, whilst the 350 ft run-round loop headshunt and 640 ft shed road are to the left. *Author's Collection*

Aldeburgh goods yard from the road entrance with the station roof retaining wall to the right and alongside the loop road headshunt, occupied by a selection of open wagons and covered vans. The goods shed and goods office are in the background and served by the shed road. A lorry and tractor and trailer were in use to load and unload traffic into and out of railway vehicles. *Author's Collection*

Aldeburgh station from the approach yard with station staff lined up for the photograph. The covered train shed over the platform fronts the fine station building, with station master's accommodation on the first floor. Note the variation in the colour scheme in the awning over the station entrance and the end awning on the train shed. The engine shed, signal box and water tower are in the far distance. *Author's Collection*

Aldeburgh station from the Victoria Avenue approach on 19th July, 1952 with the train shed prominent in the background and the steam exhaust ventilators open. Hot sunny weather has forced the W.H. Smith bookstall manager to pull the sun blinds down to protect the books and papers from fading in the bright light.            *J.H. Meredith*

The station was some distance from the centre of poulation and from the opening of the line carriers met all trains to convey goods to commercial premises while many of the important hotels employed a horse-drawn bus to take passengers and luggage. In the latter years as rationalization took effect Aldeburgh station was a miserable shadow of its former glory for the overall roof was removed in August and September 1965. The engine shed and goods shed had been demolished by this time and all sidings removed apart from the loop line. The forlorn station buildings were subsequently demolished in June and July 1975 and the site cleared for housing development.

In early GER days all up and down goods trains were to stop at Saxmundham station before proceeding whether the signal was clear or not. Passenger trains and light engines were restricted to a speed limit of 10 mph when passing through the station, later raised to 30 mph. At Saxmundham Junction all up Aldeburgh branch trains and light engines were to be brought to a stand at the junction clear of the main line, whilst at Leiston station all up and down trains and light engines were to stop before proceeding. Later the speed limit for Aldeburgh branch trains was restricted to 10 mph when passing over the points at Saxmundham Junction, later raised to 15 mph and then to 20 mph by the LNER. On the branch the speed limit was 30 mph, later raised to 40 mph, although this was often exceeded when dmus took over the service. After the withdrawal of passenger services the speed limit was reduced to 25 mph with trains stopping at Knodishall, West House, Saxmundham Road, Leiston station and Sizewell level crossing for the trainmen to open and close the gates. Mileposts were generally on the down side of the line and gradient posts on the up side.*

In GER days station staff rang a platform bell at Aldeburgh five minutes before a train was due to depart and again at starting time to warn passengers of the imminent departure. At Saxmundham the platform bell was sounded two minutes before starting time.

---

* Note that the mileages shown are from GER, LNER and early BR documents – later some surveys by LNER and BR showed differences of between + 9 and + 10½ chains.

# Chapter Eight

# Permanent Way, Signalling and Staff

*Permanent Way*

The original permanent way of the Leiston branch was of two types. The first, similar to that used on the ESR main line, was formed of double-headed rails measuring 18 and 21 ft in length weighing 70 lb. per yard (incorrectly quoted in the original inspection report as 68 lb.), fished at the joints with wrought-iron fish plates and screw bolts, secured in cast-iron chairs weighing 21 lb. each by ordinary wooden keys. The chairs were fixed to creosoted sleepers by wooden trenails, the sleepers being spaced on average 3 ft apart. The remainder of the track was formed of bridge rails, weighing 60 lb. per yard and fastened by dog spikes to sleepers laid on average 2 ft 4 in. apart. The ballast was formed of a mixture of gravel and sand. On inspecting the railway, Captain H.W. Tyler stated he would have preferred to see a proportion of iron bolts employed to attach the bridge rails to the sleepers and iron spikes in place of wooden trenails on the curves, where the latter were employed, to secure the chairs to the sleepers. The company engineer advised the inspector that care had been taken to select cast chairs without sharp edges in the lower part of the trenails, in order to safeguard against a shearing action that would otherwise occur on the curves. Tyler pointed out that it was still important during maintenance of the line to keep a careful watch and that iron spikes be inserted as and when the trenails aged or showed symptoms of failure.

The extension from Leiston to Aldeburgh was laid with double-headed rails measuring 18 and 21 ft in length weighing 70 lb. per yard. The joints were fished with wrought-iron fishplates and fixed by ¾ in. bolts. The half-rounded sleepers were placed 3 feet apart and the chairs were secured to the sleepers by means of oak trenails. Captain H.W. Tyler duly reminded the ESR officials attending the inspection of his earlier comments made when the Saxmundham to Leiston section was inspected and still required additional security for the permanent way by the insertion of iron spikes in place of the oak trenails on the curved sections of line.

By the mid-1880s the whole branch had been relaid with 80 lb. per yard bullhead rails in 24 ft lengths laid in chairs weighing 38 lb., fastened by iron spikes and wooden trenails to creosoted sleepers measuring 8 ft 6 in. by 10 in. by 5 in. Fishplates weighing 40 lb. per pair connected the rails. Around the turn of the century bullhead rails weighing 85, 90 and 95 lb. per yard laid on sleepers measuring 8 ft 11 in. by 10 in. by 5 in. gradually replaced the lighter track and these sufficed with the replacement of worn-out rails until just before Grouping. From 1923 the LNER commenced replacing the 24 ft length rails with 30 and 45 ft rails, initially weighing 85 to 97 lb. per yard, but in the mid-1930s the weight was increased to 90 and 95 lb. per yard track. Much of the equipment on the branch was second-hand after use on the main line. Bullhead track remained in use until closure of the branch beyond Sizewell siding, when latterly some 95 lb. per yard rail was introduced. To accommodate the heavier diesel-electric

Section of line near the 93 mile post west of West House level crossing No. 5 and 93 miles 32 chains on an undulating section of the branch with the dip falling at 1 in 121 and then rising at 1 in 203. This view from an up train shows clearly the permanent way trolley run-off point beside the telegraph pole to the left.                         *The late B.D.J. Walsh*

Saxmundham Junction facing south towards Saxmundham and Ipswich, with the Aldeburgh branch to the left and the East Suffolk main lines to the right. The signal box dating from 1880 has developed a decided list away from the line, whilst the gradient post is evidence of the 1 in 58 climb encountered by branch trains away from the junction.          *Author's Collection*

locomotives on the flask trains the truncated branch has been relaid with flat-bottom rails weighing up to 109 lb. per yard.

The original ballast formed of a mixture of gravel and sand was soon found inadequate for it rotted the sleepers and was unsuitable for the weight of the rolling stock used at that period. Ballast was also obtained from the shingle beach north of Aldeburgh, where a siding was installed, but the connection was removed soon after the opening of the line. As axle loading increased the GER introduced ashes and clinker, having found that ashes were adequate for ballasting secondary routes and branch lines, and that supplies were readily available from the company's locomotive depots. When such supplies were not available, wagon loads of ashes were obtained from Tate & Lyle's sugar refinery at Silvertown and after the mid-1920s from the British Sugar Corporation factories at Cantley, Bury St Edmunds and Ipswich.

The branch was originally maintained by three permanent way gangs, one covering Saxmundham station area and a section of the East Suffolk main line, which also included the section of the branch to Saxmundham Junction up distant signal. The Leiston gang then covered the section from Saxmundham Junction distant signal to Leiston up distant signal inclusive with the Aldeburgh gang maintaining the section thence to the terminus. After the LNER took over, the use of three gangs was considered an expensive luxury and in 1931 the permanent way maintenance arrangements on the branch were rationalized with the provision of a permanent way trolley when the three gangs of men with a complement of 11 men was reduced to one gang comprising eight men. Telephone token apparatus with plug points was provided and the annual saving was estimated at £296 per annum. This maintenance arrangement continued until after the withdrawal of the passenger service in 1966 when initially a gang covering maintenance of the main line took over the branch to Sizewell. Although routine inspection is still carried out regularly, the maintenance is now covered by a team travelling to site to work on the line on an as and when required basis.

In the 1880s Robert Cadey was foreman platelayer in the Aldeburgh gang and others serving on the branch at the time included William Griffiths, ganger, William Spink, ganger and Charles Smith, platelayer. Benjamin Ayden was permanent way inspector for the section Wickham Market to Beccles and branches at this time. Henry Godfrey had an illustrious career in the civil engineering department after entering the service at Chappel in 1891. After serving at Braintree, March and Bury St Edmunds Yard he was appointed permanent way sub-inspector at Woodham Ferrers in June 1909 before transferring to Saxmundham in the same capacity in December 1911. His tenure there was short, however, and he was promoted to Ipswich in August 1913. Harry Hart was foreman platelayer in the Leiston gang, which won an award for the best kept section of permanent way between Leiston and Aldeburgh in 1915. He resided rent free in Sheepwash Crossing cottage, the gratis accommodation being provided in return for either he, when not on permanent way duties, or his family opening and closing the level crossing gates for the passage of all trains. Other permanent way staff living rent free at crossing cottages for similar duties in 1913 included Alfred Coates at Aldringham-cum-Thorpeness, Henry Philpot at Crown Lands, Horace Butler at Knodishall, Robert Brown at West House and Robert

Bridges at Saxmundham Road. William Smith of the Saxmundham gang residing in the cottage at Albion Street crossing, however, had to pay an annual rental of £13, as he was not required to attend to the gates.

World War I took its toll of several of those permanent way staff that volunteered for military service including William Abbott, who died of his wounds on 13th October, 1917 aged 24 years. He entered service with the GER in December 1914 as a permanent way labourer with the Saxmundham gang as an extra hand before enlisting with the East Surrey Regiment on 24th April, 1917. Of the other permanent way staff employed on the branch William Wells, for many years a platelayer at Saxmundham, passed away aged 83 years in November 1928. In the same month A. Coates, an underman in the Leiston gang, died aged 69 years. On 24th January, 1932 W.H. Brightwell, a ganger based at Leiston, retired after 30 years' service. He commenced his railway service in March 1882 at Wickham Market before going to Ipswich then back to Wickham Market before serving with the Aldeburgh branch gang at Leiston. On 21st December, 1932 R. Edmunds, a ganger based at Saxmundham, passed away. R. Newby a Saxmundham ganger retired on 30th January, 1937 after 41 years' service and at a gathering of local staff was presented with a gift by station master R.A. Roe. A.J. Flatman, a lengthman in the Saxmundham gang, retired on 23rd December, 1939, whilst sub-ganger C. Saunders in the same gang retired on 30th June, 1941. Clifford Beamish was a ganger at Leiston. Of the supervisory staff, permanent way inspector A.G. Blowers at Saxmundham was promoted to Yarmouth in November 1946.

After World War II maintenance continued under the District Engineer, Ipswich. Charles Wright, based at Saxmundham was the inspector responsible for the line from Bealings (inclusive) and Beccles (exclusive) and branches. Permanent way gangs for the Aldeburgh line were based at Saxmundham and Leiston, the Saxmundham gang being formed of seven men with ganger William Newsome in charge of sub-ganger John Self and lengthmen Sidney Beamish, William Burr, James Leveritt, Chris Stannard, Robert Greene and Reginald Coxage. The 'Aldeburgh' gang based at Leiston was formed of ganger 'Whip' Thompson, later replaced by Cliff Beamish and lengthmen John Smith, Robert 'Velvet' Brightwell, 'Chicken' Fitch and Edward Hart. The gangs had the benefit of a petrol driven trolley and when in operation the ganger used his 'occupational key' which was inserted into plug points at various locations on the branch to advise signalmen of the presence of the maintenance team and to prevent them withdrawing the single line Train Staff.

As well as attending to the day-to-day track maintenance, the permanent way gangs on the Aldeburgh branch were responsible for cleaning the toilets at stations where no mains sewerage existed and on hot summer days, especially during harvest time, they acted as beaters to extinguish any small fires caused by stray sparks emitted by passing locomotives. They also cut the grass on the side of embankments and cuttings and this was used as fodder for railway horses, or in World War I was sent to London and other East Anglian towns for feeding military horses.

Except for the last few years the Aldeburgh branch always came under the control of the district engineer based at Ipswich, which in GER days was No. 6 district, later district civil engineer Ipswich.

*Signalling*

The initial signalling on the branch was formed of semaphore signals with coloured aspect glasses rotating by the action of a connecting rod attached to bell crank levers and operated from the station platforms. Leiston station originally had a stop signal for each direction of travel mounted on the same post on the platform and an auxiliary signal for the down direction located 800 yds in the rear of the stop signal. After the extension of the line to Aldeburgh, Leiston retained the stop signal for each direction of travel mounted on the same post on the platform but then had auxiliary or distant signals for each direction of travel, located 800 yards in the rear of the stop signals. Aldeburgh station was provided with stop signals for each direction of travel mounted on the same post on the platform but only needed an auxiliary signal for the down direction, 800 yds in the rear of the stop signal. Saxmundham Junction was protected by stop signals for each direction of travel mounted on separate posts, with associated auxiliary or distant signals 800 yds in the rear on the up main line and branch but at a lesser distance on the down main line. Specific instructions were issued in the event of an auxiliary signal being at danger. The driver of the approaching train having brought the train to a stand wasimmediately to move his train forward with great care making sure the line ahead was clear, so as to bring his train well within the protection of the signal. Drivers were especially cautioned that their failure to carry out this regulation could cause an accident, which would otherwise have been avoided. If it was not practicable to draw the train far enough within the signal to afford sufficient protection from a following train, the guard was required to go back at once with hand and percussion [*sic*] signals to protect his train.

As a result of the Regulation of Railways Act 1889, the GER authorities were required to renew most of the signalling equipment on the branch and by 1892 the old style semaphore signals were replaced by lower quadrant home and distant signals with pitch pine posts, cedar arms and cast- and wrought-iron fittings. The Act also required the interlocking of points and signals and the new signals were provided to GER design. In common with GER practice, each signal arm was stamped on the reverse with the name of the controlling signal box. Around the turn of the century modifications were made to the operating distant signals on the branch. At that time the GER distant signals were painted the same red as stop signals and showed the same red and green aspects to drivers at night. To avoid confusion with home and starting signals, the distant signals were fitted with Coligny-Welch lamps which displayed an additional white > at night beside the signal aspect. With the advent of the LNER the distant signals were gradually repainted the familiar yellow with black > and the Coligny-Welch lamps removed or modified to serve as ordinary lamps. After World War II some of the remaining signal posts were found to be rotten and were replaced by those of tubular steel. Lower quadrant arms were replaced by LNER or BR upper quadrant arms on the same posts, including Saxmundham up starter and down starter (the latter with Saxmundham Junction distant) Saxmundham Junction down home signals and up branch home with Saxmundham station distant and Leiston down home. Interestingly Saxmundham Junction up branch distant was a slotted signal where the arm initially slotted into the post when in the clear position but later was fixed at caution.

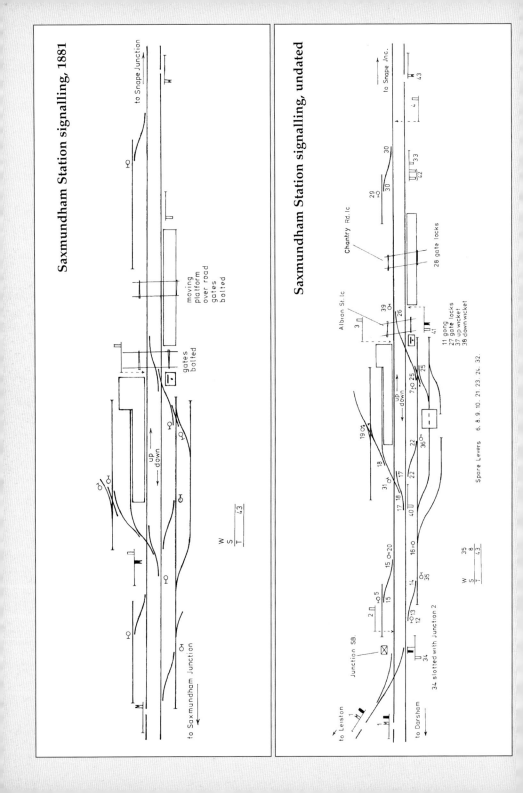

Saxmundham Station signalling, 1881

to Snape Junction

moving
platform
over road
gates
bolted

gates
bolted

up
down

W
S
T    43

to Saxmundham Junction

Saxmundham Station signalling, undated

to Snape Jnc.

43

Chantry Rd. lc

30

29
30

33
42

28 gate locks

Albion St. lc

39

3

26

41

11 gong
27 gate locks
37 up wicket
38 down wicket

19

18

up
down

7   25

25

31

17

22

36

17 18

22

40

Spare Levers    6. 8. 9. 10. 21 23 24. 32.

15   20

16

35

2

15

W    35
S    8
T    43

14
35

13
12

to Leiston

Junction SB.

34

34 slotted with Junction 2

1

to Darsham

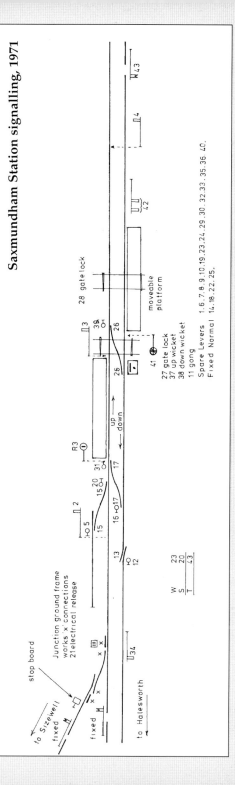

Saxmundham Station signalling, 1969

to Wickham Market Junc.

28 gate locks

41 RY Station
(1 YG Junction

11 gong
27 gate locks
37 up wicket
38 down wicket

Spare Levers   6. 7. 8. 9. 10. 14. 16. 19. 21. 22. 23. 24. 25. 29   30. 32. 35. 36. 40.,

up
down

34 slotted with Junction 2

Junction SB

| W | 24 |
| S | 19 |
| T | 43 |

to Leiston

to Darsham

Saxmundham Station signalling, 1971

moveable
platform

28 gate lock

27 gate lock
37 up wicket
38 down wicket
11 gong

Spare Levers   1. 6. 7. 8. 9. 10. 19. 23. 24. 29. 30. 32. 33. 35. 36. 40.
Fixed Normal  14. 18. 22. 25.

up
down

stop board

Junction ground frame
works 'x' connections
21 electrical release

fixed

fixed

| W | 23 |
| S | 20 |
| T | 43 |

to Sizewell

to Halesworth

Saxmundham Station signal box provided in 1881 was equipped with a 43-lever Saxby & Farmer 5 in. relock frame controlling points and signals at the station. *Author's Collection*

Saxmundham Station signal box was provided originally with 40 working and three spare levers. The box survives in much altered form from that originally constructed. In the first decade of the 20th century the locking room windows were altered and concrete blocks and brick replaced the lower layers of the timber cladding. Further structural alterations were made in February 1985 with the provision of large windows at each end of the building and removal of the door and steps to the opposite end of the building. The lever frame was reduced to four working levers with all distant signals fixed. Later a GEC-General Signals Ltd individual function switch panel replaced the frame in connection with the introduction of Radio Electronic Token Block workingon the East Suffolk line. *Author's Collection*

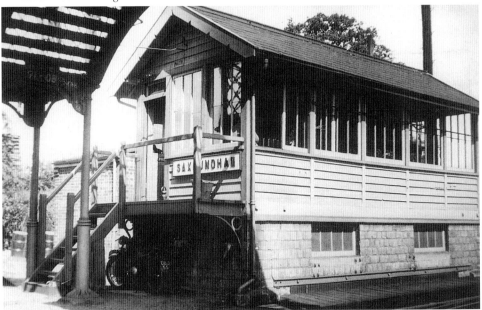

Looking south from Saxmundham Junction signal box on 7th September, 1966 as Brush type '2' diesel-electric locomotive No. D5682 working the 11.20 Ipswich to Leiston freight train waits at the splitting down home signal for the 12.08 Aldeburgh to Ipswich dmu to clear the branch.

*G.R. Mortimer*

The driver of the Metropolitan-Cammell two-car dmu forming the 12.23 Aldeburgh to Saxmundham train leans out of the cab to surrender the single line Train Staff to the signalman at Saxmundham Junction on 20th August, 1966.

*G.R. Mortimer*

*Left:* The Saxmundham Junction signalman collects the Leiston-Saxmundham Junction single line train staff from the driver of an up branch train. The staff was in two sections, the train staff section and metal ticket section which were normally bolted together and in this view the large protrusion through which the padlock passed can be seen. If two trains required to work through the single line section the staff was unpadlocked and split - the driver of the first train being shown the train staff section before being handed the ticket section as his authority to pass over the single line. The driver of the second train then conveyed the staff section to the other end of the single line where either the signalman at Leiston or Saxmundham Junction reunited the two sections and padlocked then together. Because of the relative short length of each short section a hoop was made bespoke to carry the staff for ease of exchange between signalman and driver.

*R. Kennell*

*Below:* Saxmundham Junction up branch distant signal mounted on a post suitable for a slotted signal stands gaunt against the Suffolk skyline. By the date this photograph was taken the arm was fixed at caution and the green glass removed from the spectacle. *The late Dr I.C. Allen*

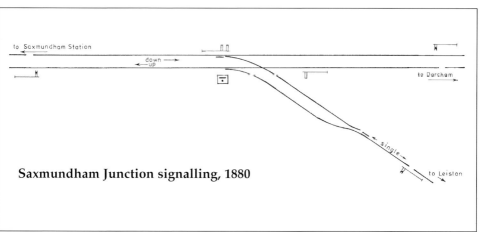

**Saxmundham Junction signalling, 1880**

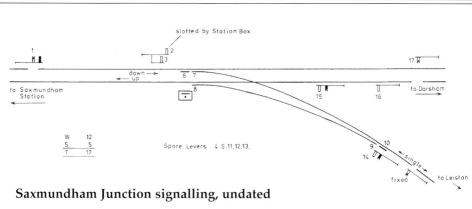

**Saxmundham Junction signalling, undated**

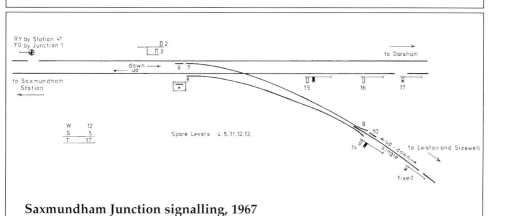

**Saxmundham Junction signalling, 1967**

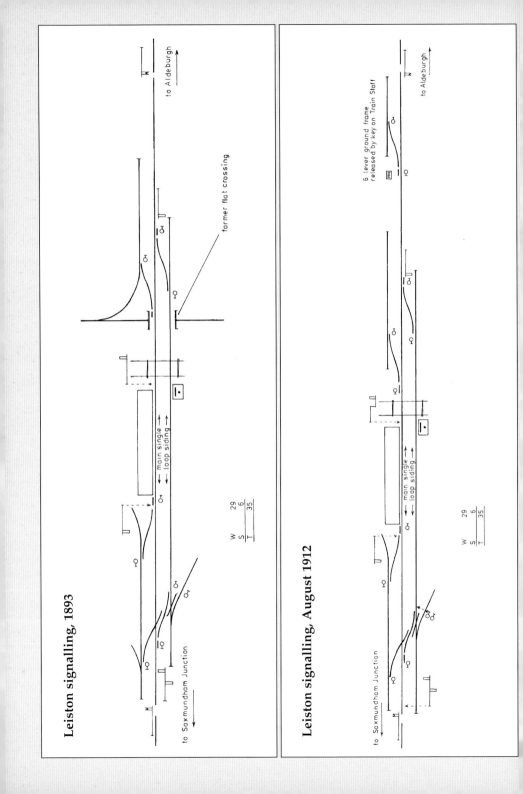

**Leiston signalling, 1893**

to Aldeburgh

former flat crossing

main single
loop siding

W 29
S 6
T 35

to Saxmundham Junction

**Leiston signalling, August 1912**

to Aldeburgh

6 lever ground frame
released by key on Train Staff

main single
loop siding

W 29
S 6
T 35

to Saxmundham Junction

Saxmundham Station signal box was provided with distant, home, starting and advance signals in the down direction and distant, home, starting and advance starting signals on the up road. In the early years a down starting signal was provided for the up side bay platform for Aldeburgh branch trains. Saxmundham Junction signal box was provided with distant and home signals for the down main line and for the branch, the latter being on a bracket signal south of the junction, the left-hand arm denoting the down main line and the right hand arm denoting the branch. In the up direction, distant, outer and inner home signals were provided on the up main line and a distant and home signal on the branch protecting the junction. Leiston station was provided with distant, home and starting signals for each direction of travel with an advance starting signal also provided in the up direction, whilst Aldeburgh was provided with distant and home signals in the down direction and a starter for up road departures. After the withdrawal of passenger services all remaining operating distant signals were fixed at caution.

The Leiston branch and subsequent extension to Aldeburgh was initially worked on the 'One Engine in Steam or two or more coupled together' principle utilizing the Train Staff only. The Train Staff stations were Saxmundham Junction, and initially Leiston, but after the line was extended, Aldeburgh. The Train Staff was round in shape, coloured green and lettered Saxmundham and Aldborough. By special order No. 1224 dated 1st October, 1866 the working was converted to Train Staff and Ticket using the same Train Staff whilst the paper tickets were also green in colour. By 1906 the Train Staff was lettered Saxmundham and Aldeburgh and by 1914 Leiston had been made a Train Staff station with the Saxmundham Junction to Leiston Train Staff round in shape and green in colour and the Leiston to Aldeburgh Train Staff square shaped and coloured red. The paper tickets corresponded with the colour of the Train Staff.

As passenger trains could not pass one another at Leiston specific instructions were issued regarding the pathing and acceptance of services through the station. A ballast or goods train was allowed to leave Saxmundham Junction or Aldeburgh for Leiston and there be shunted clear into the down siding next to the main single line until it was required to leave Leiston. After the ballast or goods train had arrived and been shunted clear of the main single line a down train or up train could be accepted by the Leiston signalman, if he was in a position to do so. After the Leiston signalman had accepted a down train from Saxmundham Junction he was not allowed to accept a train from Aldeburgh. In a like manner after the Leiston signalman had accepted an up train from Aldeburgh he was not permitted to accept a down train from Saxmundham Junction.

At some time in the late 1930s the Split Train Staff was introduced on the branch thus eliminating the issue of paper tickets. Each section Saxmundham Junction to Leiston and Leiston to Aldeburgh was equipped with a Split Train Staff, so necessary to ease the working of additional armaments traffic to and from Garrett's and for maintaining coastal defence traffic in World War II. Each train staff was padlocked at a bracket at the centre unless required to split into staff and ticket sections to permit two trains to pass through the respective single line section in the same direction. Because of the difficulty experienced by footplate staff and signalmen exchanging the short staff or ticket section when split, especially at Saxmundham Junction, a hoop was fabricated similar to a train

*Above:* Leiston signal box containing a 35-lever Stevens tappet frame with 4⅛ in. centres, with 29 working and six spare levers on 19th May, 1966. The down starting signal protects the gates of Station Road level crossing.

*G.R. Mortimer*

*Right:* Part of the lever frame in Leiston signal box with levers Nos. 6 and 14 exhibiting lever collars. No. 8 lever pulled over with the obligatory cloth was the locking bar for No. 24 points. No. 16 facing points were locked by No. 17 lever.

*The late B.D.J. Walsh*

Internal fitments above the signalman's desk in Leiston signal box with the Train Register in the foreground. From left to right are the telephone used for ganger's trolley occupation of the Leiston to Aldeburgh section of single line, clock, general circuit phone linking Saxmundham Junction, Leiston and Aldeburgh signal boxes, communication phone to the goods yard and ganger's trolley phone for the Leiston to Saxmundham Junction section. The phone bell code list is to the left of the clock. *The late B.D.J. Walsh*

Signalman Arthur Goddard stands askance in Leiston signal box. He served at Leiston from 1919 until retirement in 1961. After this date he continued to cover for annual leave and sickness during the summer months until the withdrawal of passenger services in September 1966. Harry Sawyer served for many years at Leiston on the opposite shift to Arthur Goddard. *The late B.D.J. Walsh*

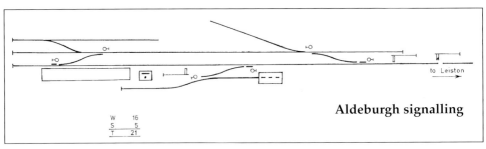

**Aldeburgh signalling**

to Leiston

W  16
S   5
T   21

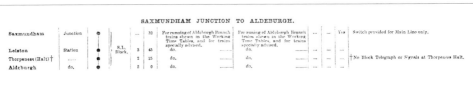

| Saxmundham | Junction | | | ... | 32 | For running of Aldeburgh Branch trains shewn in the Working Time Tables, and for trains specially advised. | For running of Aldeburgh Branch trains shewn in the Working Time Tables, and for trains specially advised. | ... | ... | Yes | Switch provided for Main Line only. |
| Leiston | Station | | S.L. Block. | 3 | 45 | do. | do. | | ... | ... | |
| Thorpeness (Halt)† | ...... | | | 2 | 25 | do. | do. | ......... | ... | ... | †No Block Telegraph or Signals at Thorpeness Halt. |
| Aldeburgh | do. | | | 2 | 0 | do. | do. | ......... | ... | ... | |

Opening and closing of signal boxes  1924.

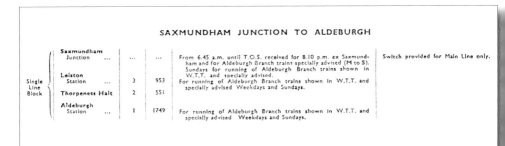

**SAXMUNDHAM JUNCTION TO ALDEBURGH**

| Single Line Block | Saxmundham Junction ... | ... | ... | From 6.45 a.m. until T.O.S. received for 8.10 p.m. ex Saxmundham and for Aldeburgh Branch trains specially advised (M to S). Sundays for running of Aldeburgh Branch trains shown in W.T.T. and specially advised. | Switch provided for Main Line only. |
| | Leiston Station ... | 3 | 953 | For running of Aldeburgh Branch trains shown in W.T.T. and specially advised Weekdays and Sundays. | |
| | Thorpeness Halt | 2 | 551 | | |
| | Aldeburgh Station ... | 1 | 1749 | For running of Aldeburgh Branch trains shown in W.T.T. and specially advised Weekdays and Sundays. | |

Opening and closing of signal boxes  1947.

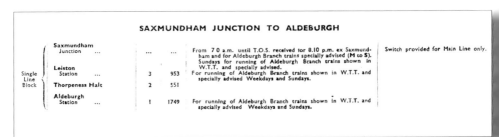

**SAXMUNDHAM JUNCTION TO ALDEBURGH**

| Single Line Block | Saxmundham Junction ... | ... | ... | From 7 0 a.m. until T.O.S. received for 8.10 p.m. ex Saxmundham and for Aldeburgh Branch trains specially advised (M to S). Sundays for running of AldeBurgh Branch trains shown in W.T.T. and specially advised. | Switch provided for Main Line only. |
| | Leiston Station ... | 3 | 953 | For running of Aldeburgh Branch trains shown in W.T.T. and specially advised Weekdays and Sundays. | |
| | Thorpeness Halt | 2 | 551 | | |
| | Aldeburgh Station ... | 1 | 1749 | For running of Aldeburgh Branch trains shown in W.T.T. and specially advised Weekdays and Sundays. | |

Opening and closing of signal boxes  1950.

tablet hoop for the Saxmundham Junction to Leiston section but with the staff or ticket section attached by straps to the base of the hoop. With the drop in traffic between Leiston and Aldeburgh and the introduction of dmus on passenger services and withdrawal of freight facilities at Thorpeness and Aldeburgh it was found unnecessary to retain this method of working as most additional freight traffic only ran as far as Leiston. By 1959 the Split Train Staff method of operation was altered to Split Train Staff from Saxmundham Junction to Leiston and then 'One Engine in Steam' thence to Aldeburgh. The Split Train Staff for the Leiston to Aldeburgh section, still padlocked together, was ulitized for the 'One Engine in Steam' working but when the abolition of Aldeburgh signal box was in hand the Train Staff was taken to Garrett's for the two sections to be welded together to form one Train Staff. The work cost the princely sum of 2s. 6d. but Garrett's would not release the Train Staff until the requisite money had been paid by signal & telecommunications personnel. From 1st December, 1967 'one engine in steam' working was introduced between Saxmundham Junction and Sizewell siding for the nuclear flask traffic using the former Saxmundham Junction to Leiston Train Staff, until replaced by Radio Electronic Token Block.

Double line block working was in operation on the East Suffolk main line between Saxmundham Station and Saxmundham Junction signal boxes using Tyers two-position block instruments. Block working on the branch in connection with the Train Staff and Ticket working was not introduced until 1893 with Tyers one wire single needle instruments in use between Saxmundham Junction and Leiston signal boxes and between Leiston and Aldeburgh signal boxes.

Saxmundham Station signal box dating from 1881, originally of timber construction, measured 26 ft in length by 11 ft wide with its operating floor 5 ft 6 in. above rail level and was provided with a Saxby & Farmer 43-lever, 5 in. relock frame. In the first decade of the 20th century the locking room windows were altered and concrete blocks and brick replaced the lower layers of the timber cladding. In 1921 the box had 40 working and three spare levers. Structural alterations were again made in February 1985 when large windows were installed at each end of the building and the door and steps were removed from the south to the north end of the structure. The lever frame was reduced to four working levers and all distant signals were fixed at caution. Radio Controlled Electronic Token Block signalling came when a GEC-General Signals Ltd individual functional switch panel replaced the 43-lever frame later in 1985.

Saxmundham Junction signal box dating from 1880, and originally titled Aldborough Junction, was of timber construction on piling to the rear, as it was perched on the up side embankment, and was provided with a Saxby & Farmer 17-lever, 5 in. relock frame. The structure measured 17 ft 6 in. in length by 11 ft wide with the operating floor 5 feet 3 inches above rail level. A block switch was provided for the main line only so that the box could be switched out of use for periods when the Aldeburgh branch was closed. For most of its existence the box had 12 working and five spare levers. The signal box was abolished on 11th July, 1971 and replaced by a 3-lever ground frame to work the points for the Sizewell branch. The ground frame worked the trailing connection from the up main to the branch line and associated trap points and was electrically released by Saxmundham Station signal box No. 21 lever but from 1986 was released by the RETB.

Aldeburgh signal box located on the down side of the line to the north of the station was erected in 1893 and provided with a 21-lever Stevens tappet frame with 4⅛ in. centres, which for most of its career had 16 working and five spare levers and later 17 working and four spare levers controlling all points and signals at the terminus.                                                                *Author*

A two-car Metropolitan-Cammell dmu approaching Aldeburgh in September 1962. The signal box had been abolished on 17th July, 1961 and the post for the former up starting signal is devoid of an arm. Although the sidings in the goods yard have been lifted the run-round loop is still in position and is occupied by three covered vans, which were believed to have brought light fittings to the town in connection with a street lighting programme and thus providing the final goods traffic revenue at Aldeburgh. By this time the points to the run-round loop were released and locked by Hodgson's lock with the key, one coloured red and the other coloured blue, retained in Leiston signal box.                                                                *R. Kennell*

Leiston signal box provided in 1892 had a Stevens 35-lever tappet frame with 4¼ in. centres. The structure, constructed of timber, measured 26 ft in length by 11 ft 6 in. in width with the operating floor 10 ft above rail level and initially boasted 29 working and six spare levers. The signal box was abolished on 1st December, 1967 when the associated level crossing was converted to 'Train Crew Operation'. By 20th August, 1912 a 6-lever ground frame was provided 400 yards east of Leiston station level crossing to control the points leading to Leiston Gas Co. sidings, the ground frame being released and locked by the Annett's key on the single line Train Staff. The siding was still in use in August 1972 but was closed soon after.

When a siding was provided on the east side of the line south of Sizewell crossing in 1879 a 5-lever ground frame was provided to work the points and associated ground signals. After some years the siding was taken out of use but was then reinstated with the ground frame enclosed within a small timber hut and the frame released and locked by a key on the single line Train Staff. From 1st December, 1967 when 'One Engine in Steam' working was introduced the frame was released by Annett's key on the Train Staff. These sidings were enhanced with the construction of Sizewell 'B' power station and were then used for the associated flask traffic.

In an agreement dated 31st December, 1921, a siding connection was authorized at Thorpeness located on the up side of the line opposite the platform with points facing up trains. Initially a 5-lever ground frame was installed operating the release lever, bolt lock, points and two disc signals. The inspecting officer considered the connection was 'over signalled' and after rationalization a single lever, released by key on the single line Train Staff, operated the points. Goods facilities were withdrawn from 30th November, 1959 but the siding was not taken out of use until April 1965. In the very early years of operation the ESR obtained shingle ballast from the beach north of Aldeburgh and a long siding was provided on the down side of the line with points facing down trains. The connection was released and locked by Annett's key on the Train Staff. Once ample supplies of ballast had been obtained the siding was removed.

Aldeburgh signal box provided in 1892 had a 21-lever Stevens Tappet frame with 4¼ inch centres located within the timber structure, measuring 20 ft in length by 11 ft 6 in. wide with the operating floor 7 ft 6 in. above rail level. Initially it had 16 working and five spare levers but this was later amended to 17 working and four spares. The box was abolished on 17th July, 1961 and after closure the crossovers between the single line and the run-round loop were locked at each end by Hodgson's lock with the keys, one coloured red and the other blue, retained in Leiston signal box. After the abolition of Aldeburgh signal box special instructions were issued regarding the departure of trains. Immediately prior to departure from Aldeburgh the guard was required to give two beats on the plunger provided on the platform to the signalman at Leiston, which would then be acknowledged by repetition. In the event of the two beats not being acknowledged it was assumed a failure had occurred and the guard informed the driver to proceed cautiously being prepared to stop short of the intermediate level crossing gates. On arrival of the train at Leiston the guard was required to advise the signalman that the plunger had failed so that repairs could be effected. All signal boxes displayed a white diamond sign on the side of the structure to denote that equipment was operating satisfactorily. If the diamond was reversed to exhibit a black surface, equipment was not working and required the attention of the signal fitter.

In 1891 Saxmundham Station signal box was open day and night, on weekdays but was only open for the running of trains on Sunday and closed in the intermediate periods. Saxmundham Junction signal box on weekdays was closed and switched out from 15 minutes after the last branch train of the day had departed until 7.00 am the next morning. On summer Sundays the box only opened for Aldeburgh branch trains and closed in the intermediate periods. From 1st October until 30th June the same weekday timings were relevant but on Saturdays the box closed and switched out after the last Aldeburgh train had left until 7.00 am on Monday morning as no trains ran on the Aldeburgh branch. Leiston and Aldeburgh signal boxes were closed at night and also closed on Sundays between the running of booked trains in the working timetable. These timings remained in operation in 1897. By 1906 there were only slight amendments brought about by signalling alterations. Whilst Saxmundham Station signal box was open day and night, Saxmundham Junction signal box was switched out after the last branch train had left on weekdays until 7.00 am the following morning. On Saturdays the box closed after the last branch train had departed until 20 minutes before the first up branch train was due on Sunday morning and then 15 minutes after the last down branch train had left until 7.00 am on Monday. When Saxmundham Junction signal box was switched out the Junction down main home signal was slotted with the Station signal box and became the Station down advance starting signal. Leiston and Aldeburgh signal boxes were closed at night and also on Sundays between the running of booked trains in the working timetable.

By 1919 Saxmundham Station signal box was open continuously from 10.00 pm on Sunday until 6.00 am the following Sunday and then opened for the running of trains shown in the working timetable and for trains specially advised. Saxmundham Junction, Leiston and Aldeburgh signal boxes were open for the running of Aldeburgh branch trains shown in the working timetable and for branch trains specially advised. In 1926 Saxmundham Station signal box was open continuously from 1.30 am on Mondays until after the passage of the 1.05 am mail and goods train from Ipswich on Sunday and then for the running of trains shown in the working timetable and for trains specially advised. Saxmundham Junction, Leiston and Aldeburgh signal boxes were open under the same arrangements as in 1919. These timings continued until the outbreak of World War II, save that in 1937 Saxmundham Station box was open continuously from 4.50 am on Mondays until after the passage of the 4.50 am newspaper train ex-Ipswich the following Sunday and then for the running of trains shown in the working timetable or for trains specially advised. In 1940 Saxmundham Station box was open continuously from 2.50 am on Mondays until 'train out of section' was received for the 4.45 am ex-Ipswich the following Sunday or for trains shown in the working timetable or trains specially advised. The other signal box opening times were unchanged. Despite the increased war traffic these times remained unaltered save for a variance of a few minutes at Saxmundham Station box. In 1949 Saxmundham Station box was open from 6.00 am on Monday until 10.00 pm on Sunday or until 'train out of section' was received for the last booked train or trains specially advised on Sundays. Saxmundham Junction signal box was open on weekdays from 7.00 am until 'train out of section' was received for the 8.10 pm train ex-Saxmundham and then for Aldeburgh branch trains specially advised and on

Sundays for the running of Aldeburgh branch trains shown in the working timetable. Leiston and Aldeburgh were both open for the running of branch trains and for those specially advised. By 1961 Saxmundham Station signal box was open from 5.00 am until 10.25 pm on weekdays and 8.45 am until 11.10 pm on Sundays whilst Saxmundham Junction was open from 6.25 am to 9.50 pm Saturdays-excepted (SX) and 10.05 pm Saturdays-only (SO) and 9.10 am until 2.45 pm and then again from 6.05 pm until 10.05 pm on Sundays. Leiston box was open from 6.30 am until 9.10 pm SX and 10.00 pm SO whilst on Sundays it was open from 9.00 am until 2.45 pm and then again from 6.00 pm until 9.45pm. Winter opening times varied slightly. By this date Aldeburgh signal box had been abolished and Leiston box was abolished on 1st December, 1967.

A 3-lever ground frame replaced Saxmundham Junction signal box on 11th July, 1971 to enable the flask traffic to proceed to Sizewell siding and return. Trains arriving at Saxmundham station on the down main line destined for the Sizewell branch had, after the driver obtained possession of the single line Train Staff, to cross on to the up main line via the crossover and then proceed along the up main line towards the points giving access onto the Sizewell branch, upon the appropriate signal being lowered. Drivers then had to bring their train to a stand on the approach side of these points to enable the guard to operate the ground frame. When the guard was satisfied the route for the branch was correctly set he signalled to the driver to proceed until it was clear of the points before resetting all levers to normal for the up main line. Similarly a train from Sizewell stopped at the stop board and, after the guard had correctly set the connection from the branch, hand-signalled the train through the points. The train would be brought to a stand clear of the trailing points in the up main line to allow the guard to restore the levers in the ground frame to normal, before allowing the train to continue its journey. The gates of the intermediate level crossings at Knodishall, West House, Saxmundham Road, Leiston Station and Sizewell were opened and closed by trainmen whilst it was permissible for a locomotive to propel not exceeding 14 wagons between Leiston and Sizewell siding in daylight and clear weather only. By 1990 this had been amended to 13 fitted 'single length units' with a brake van in which the guard or shunter was riding as the leading vehicle.

RETB replaced one train working between Saxmundham Junction and Sizewell on 16th February, 1986. The existing semaphore signals at Saxmundham were abolished together with the 'limit of shunt' indicator on the up main and 'stop' board at the Sizewell branch ground frame. The telephone at the down colour light signal SM4 was removed and a down direction distant board provided 684 yards before reaching signal SM4. A 'station limits' board for up movements was provided 300 yds on the Ipswich side of signal SM4 and a notice board for up movements worded 'stop, obtain token' was provided at the up direction colour light signals SM1 and SM2. Distant boards were provided for both lines, 821 yards before reaching signals SM1 and SM2. Notice boards for down movements worded 'stop, obtain token and permission to proceed' were provided at the Lowestoft end of the down platform and for the up line 170 yards on the Lowestoft side of signal SM2. Station limit boards for down movements were provided for the down and up lines, 320 yards on the Lowestoft side of signals SM1 and SM2. A miniature distant board and station limits board were provided for up branch

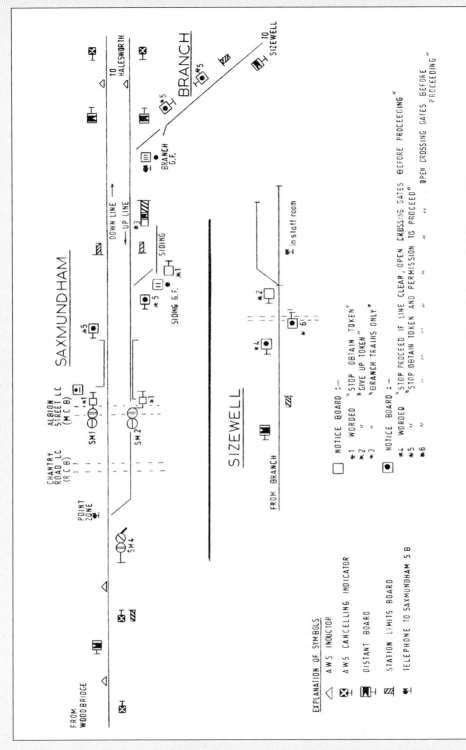

RETB signalling diagram Saxmundham to Sizewell branch from 16th February, 1986.

line trains 170 yards on the Saxmundham side of the branch ground frame points. A notice board worded 'stop, obtain token' was provided at the exit points to Saxmundham siding, which ground frame could only be operated when the driver of a train was in possession of the 'Saxmundham to Siding' or 'Siding to Saxmundham' token or the Saxmundham shunting token. The ground frame was locked with the key held in the signal box.

Access to the branch continued to be via the existing ground frame connection, which could only be operated when the driver was in possession of the 'Saxmundham to Branch' or 'Branch to Saxmundham' Token. Notice boards worded 'Stop, obtain token and permission to proceed' were provided for up movements at the branch exit trap points and for down movements, 170 yds on the Sizewell side of the trap points. A station limits board for down movements was provided 150 yds on the Sizewell side of the down stop board. A distant board was provided for up movements 476 yds before reaching the up direction 'stop' board. At Sizewell a notice board for down movements worded 'stop, proceed if line clear, open crossing gates before proceeding' was provided 25 yds before reaching Sizewell level crossing and just beyond the level crossing a board worded 'Give up token' was erected. A distant board was also provided 404 yds before reaching the 'stop' board. A notice board for up movements and shunting worded 'Stop, obtain token and permission to proceed, open crossing gates before proceeding' was provided immediately before reaching Sizewell level crossing. In the event of the failure of radio communication a telephone communicating with Saxmundham signal box was provided in Sizewell staff room. Driver's special authority cards were also available in a locked box in the room.

Some problems occurred not long after introduction of the RETB, band II frequencies were withdrawn and the system engineered to operate band III, formerly used by ITV monochrome TV transmissions. Occasional problems still occurred with localized poor reception and 'lost' tokens, but the system generally worked satisfactorily. RETB now over 25 years old, life expired and obsolete with spare parts difficult or impossible to maintain required replacement and Network Rail gave thought to the European Rail Traffic Management System (ERTMS) as ideal, providing a platform for a modern version of RETB on the East Suffolk line. However when OFCOM gave notice in 2011 that band III radio frequencies used by RETB were to be withdrawn at the end of 2012, continuing problems with the commissioning of the first installation of ERTMS on the Cambrian lines meant that timescales for conversion and reluctance to embark on a second ERTMS installation without operational experience, required an alternative means of signalling. Thus from October 2012 RETB on the East Suffolk line will be replaced by conventional colour light signalling with, according to Network Rail, a new kit allowing trains to run from signal to signal rather than use continuous signalling. As part of the work a new passing loop was installed at Beccles so that an increased frequency of trains can operate. Saxmundham signal box will remain the control centre for the line, with RETB equipment removed and new interlocking installed. Track circuit block will monitor train positioning and Token Stop boards will be replaced by LED colour light signals. The ground frame at Saxmundham will be released by the signalman allowing access to the short siding and the Sizewell branch, the single line being 'one train only' with track circuit block and the driver must be in possession of the single line Train Staff.

It is not always remembered that the railways first brought standard time throughout the country. Before its coming, each town or village varied in time from minutes to hours. The standard scheme finally adopted by the GER before the advent of the public telegraph and radio was, like other companies, of giving a 10.00 am time signal to each station and signal box on the system. By the time the headquarters at Liverpool Street had telegraphed down the line and the message had been manually passed on, it was three minutes past the hour before the stations and signal boxes on the Aldeburgh branch received their time check. The gap in time was generally accepted and adjustments made, as this was a far better system of ensuring standard time throughout the land than was possible by any other method. Once standard time was set, clocks and watches in the villages and towns served by the line were invariably aligned with station time.

The maintenance of signalling and telegraph equipment on the Aldeburgh branch was always under the control of the district signalling and telecommunications engineer at Ipswich but for many years signalling maintenance staff were retained at Saxmundham to carry out routine remedial work and minor installations. W.B. Mulley was employed as a signal fitter based at Saxmundham for several years before retiring in 1928 whilst S.W. Burden, a signal & telegraph fitter's mate, retired from Saxmundham on 22nd October, 1941. In later years mechanical maintenance was handled by Frederick Hammond assisted by Mark Pratt and electrical and telephonic equpment by Harold Holley assisted by a reliefman from Ipswich. As well as covering the Aldeburgh branch the men were also responsible for equipment on the Framlingham and Snape branches and the main line from Bealings (inclusive) to Saxmundham.

### Station Masters

From the opening of the line Mr Doggett was station master at Saxmundham but was dismissed in June 1860 for misappropriating ESR funds. John Grover, who was transferred on promotion from Needham Market, replaced Doggett and remained at the junction station until early 1869. In that year William Henry Carr was appointed and served in the post for over a decade until 1880. Thomas Woods Wooltorton was then appointed at Saxmundham and remained in charge until February 1894. From 5th February, 1894 Horace George Wright was the next incumbent, gaining promotion from Leiston and serving at the station until 19th December, 1908. William Henry Bailey was promoted from Mistley to station master Saxmundham on 27th December, 1908, paying rental of £24 per annum for the station house in 1913, later increased to £26. After serving nearly 20 years at the junction station he subsequently gained further promotion to Maldon East including Maldon West on 30th November, 1918, before later transferring to take charge of Yarmouth South Town and Vauxhall stations in January 1922. Bailey retired from Yarmouth on 3rd July, 1927, after nearly 50 years' service, having started his career as clerk at Witham in 1877. Bailey was awarded £5 in 1918 in appreciation of a suggestion made to effect economies in station administration including stores and stationery. One of his suggestions was the 'address code' for telegrams adopted by the GER in 1916, which was of great benefit to the working.

Ernest George Turner was appointed to the vacancy at Saxmundham on 1st December, 1918 and served at the station until retirement on 10th August, 1929. He commenced his railway career at Bishopsgate in 1884, was appointed to Blake Hall on the Ongar line as station master in January 1890 before transferring to Forty Hill on the Churchbury loop line in 1902. He then progressed to Seven Kings in 1905 and on to Saxmundham in December 1918. He received a retirement gift of barometer from the station staff and local tradesmen. On 16th December, 1929 R.A. Roe, a relief clerk in the Norwich District superintendent's office, gained promotion as station master at Saxmundham serving for almost 16 years including the difficult times in World War II, before retiring on 8th September, 1945 after 50 years' service with the GER and LNER; although for a short period in 1933 E. Devereux covered the post before he gained promotion to Battlesbridge on the Wickford to Southminster line. At a reception held at the Bell Hotel Saxmundham, Roe was presented with a cheque for a sum of £45 8s. 0d. collected by his colleagues. Unfortunately he did not enjoy a long retirement for he passed away on 21st January, 1946. L.W. Bass was then promoted from Aldeburgh to take charge at the junction station but passed away whilst in the post on 3rd June, 1952.

Next to take charge at the junction station was F.A. Spurgeon who for the three years whilst at Saxmundham served as a Justice of the Peace. When Spurgeon

Saxmundham station staff in the 1950s with, *from left to right*: porter Henry Watson, motor driver 'Waffy' Fryer, station master Charles Wilson, goods foreman Geoffrey Cadman, porter Richard Pearce, porter Monty Baskett and porter Tony Spatchet.            *M. Baskett Collection*

departed for pastures new in March 1955 he was not immediately replaced and three months elapsed before Frederick Chadwick was appointed. He served at the station until October 1958 but the vacancy was not filled until March 1959 when H.C. Burningham was appointed, relief staff covering in the interim. Burningham's tenure was short and he departed within six months to be replaced by Charles C. Wilson from January 1960. Wilson served at the station during the running down of the East Suffolk line and retired in June 1966 when the post was abolished.

In 1883 David W. Skuffham was recorded as station master at Leiston, whilst as mentioned earlier Horace George Wright, who had been station master at Eye, was in charge of Leiston until 5th February, 1894 when he gained promotion to Saxmundham. Frank Robert Lilley was station master at Leiston in 1913 paying annual rental of £20 for accommodation in the station house. C. Wilby the next incumbent at Leiston retired in 1924, having previously served in similar positions at Holme Hale, Thurston, Wendling, Narborough and Worstead before transferring to Leiston. He subsequently passed away on 2nd October, 1931. John Cater was duly promoted to Leiston but then transferred to Histon on the Cambridge to St Ives line in January 1929. Cater was succeeded by A.J. Morgan who was promoted from Trimley on the Felixstowe branch but his stay was short for in September 1930 he was again promoted, to take charge of Wickham Market including Marlesford. On 5th June, 1935 Frank Robert Lilley the retired station master from Leiston passed away. After World War II Dennis J. Eastaugh, a relief clerk from the district superintendent's office at Norwich for over 40 years, was appointed station master at Leiston in September 1945. As part of a rationalization programme Easthaugh took over the administration of Aldeburgh station before he retired and was followed by Peter Girling.

In 1883 John Taylor was station master at Aldeburgh, whilst in 1913 Walter Isaac Allen was in charge at the terminus paying annual rental of £22 for the station house. On 7th February, 1938, W.I. Allen the retired station master from Aldeburgh passed away to be followed by another former incumbent, W.R. Orford who passed away on 24th August, 1939. L.W. Bass station master at Lea Bridge was transferred to take charge of Aldeburgh including Leiston and Thorpeness in January 1940 at an annual salary of £283 10s. 0d.; here he served throughout the years of hostility. Bass was followed for a short period by E.R. Wright but in March 1946 E.E. Lee, station master at Bures, was appointed to take charge at Aldeburgh. He stayed for just over three years and in June 1949 B..L Reeve was transferred from station master Finningham to the vacancy at Aldeburgh. J. Carter served as the final station master at Aldeburgh.

### Traffic Staff

The names of many traffic staff serving on the Aldeburgh branch have faded with the mists of time and only a few can be mentioned. George Maskell, goods clerk at Leiston in 1872, was appointed station master at Snape in 1877, later finishing his career as station master at Walton on Naze in June 1917. P.J. Riley, the chief goods clerk at Saxmundham, retired from the railway service on 31st December, 1934 and at a small reception held to celebrate his retirement, Riley

Porter William (Billy) Botterill served from 1921 until 1966 as porter at Aldeburgh station and was responsible for enthusiastic work on the station gardens, which resulted in best kept station garden awards.                                                                   *Author's Collection*

was presented with a case of pipes and tobacco by station master Roe on behalf of Saxmundham and Aldeburgh branch staff. Clifford Lilley, goods clerk at Leiston, retired after 45 years' service in November 1949. He commenced his railway career at Saxmundham in 1905, and moved to Leiston in 1909 continuing there until retirement. Succeeding chief goods clerks included Albert Denney and Sidney Beales. Other goods office clerical staff at Leiston in the latter years included Peter Blowers, Ivan Watling and Pamela Strowger, the latter two also serving at Aldeburgh. Clerical staff serving in the booking office at Leiston after World War II included Joan Meadows, George Woolnough, Rex Debenham, John White, Horace Parker and Geoffrey Smith, whilst those at Aldeburgh included Sidney Beales, who later served at Leiston, Thelma Block, Marie Block, Pamela Strowger, Ivan Watling and Basil Barlow, the latter the last serving clerk before the booking offices were abolished and conductor-guard working introduced.

Of the platform staff, porters serving at Leiston included Annie Taylor and Daisy Sharland during the years of World War II, Owen Allcock, Percy Cooper, Leslie Ashford, Robert Cross and district relief Sidney Skippings. Porter/ shunters at Leiston included 'Punch' Goodwin and Harry Sawyer, known to some as 'Mr Yardmaster'. Walter Hyam served as porter at Aldeburgh station for many years whilst Percy Tweed started at Aldeburgh in 1881 as a porter and was noted for maintaining immaculate station gardens. William (Billy) Botterill worked at Aldeburgh for over 40 years from 1921 until 1966, starting his railway career at the terminal as a lad porter when the station had a station master, eight porters, four clerks and two signalmen on the payroll. Other porters included Pat Barley, Thomas Churchyard, George Ward, Theodore 'Skinny' White, and Oswald Everitt. During World War II several staff joined the Local Defence Volunteers, from August 1940 called the Home Guard, including station master Bass, Billy Botterill, Jimmy Gilbert, Edgar Bird and the two signalmen, James Knights and Frank Partridge. George Ayden retired as station inspector at Bury St Edmunds on 30th

Porter William 'Bill' Noy issuing tickets to prospective passengers at Thorpeness Halt. Nearby is the sack truck provided for parcels traffic and the stepladder to enable the Tilley lamps to be illuminated.                                                              *Barbara and May Noy*

Porter William 'Bill' Noy cleaning the Tilley lamps used for illumination during the hours of darkness at Thorpeness Halt.                                                    *Barbara and May Noy*

The interior of former GER coach body No. 1480 at Thorpeness Halt, which served as a booking office until the introduction of conductor-guards on trains. Arthur Cant, the motor driver from Leiston, is covering duties as rest day relief in place of the usual incumbent. *The late B.D.J. Walsh*

September, 1930, having started his career as a gate lad at Saxmundham station. Staff at Saxmundham included booking clerks Edward Allerton, Dennis Eastaugh, Edward Cockerill, Peter Girling, James Warey, Pat Brady, Ivan Watling and Helen Brown. Chief goods clerk was George Pryke, and later Cecil Barlow. Goods shed foreman was Geoffrey Cadman with goods porters Albert Adams, Bert Boland and Walter Watson. On the platform were porters Henry Watson, Richard Pearce, Frank Warren and William Penock.

H.W. Crosby, a carman at Leiston, retired in April 1912 after spending 30 years at the station. He joined the GER in 1882 as a horseman and then became a porter before being promoted to carman and horseman. Arthur Cant was employed as motor driver at Leiston before retirement, when William Noy took over. Edgar Bird was motor driver at Aldeburgh before the work was transferred to Leiston.

Charles Samuel Codd was crossing keeper at Sizewell crossing in 1913 where he and his family lived rent free in return for opening and closing the gates for all trains. Permanent way staff or their wives manned the other crossings but in the latter years Frederick Ginger was employed as relief crossing keeper covering for rest days and annual leave.

Several railwaymen working on the Aldeburgh branch enlisted in the armed forces in World War I but unfortunately some never returned from the conflict. These included George Henry Southgate, porter at Aldeburgh, serving in the Suffolk Regiment who was killed in action in September 1916 aged 22 years; Frank Edward Thurston, parcels delivery porter at Leiston, who joined the Royal Fusiliers also killed in action in 1916 at the age of 22 and Arthur Harold Baldrey, gate lad at Saxmundham, who after volunteering with the South Wales Infantry was killed in France during an air raid on 7th July, 1917, aged 21 years. Others Saxmundham staff who sacrificed their lives included gate lad William Leeder, gate lad Eric Edmunds and lad porter Samuel Copping. Edmund's father, also employed as a gate keeper at the station, was so distraught at the loss of his son that he devoted his spare time to charity work collecting on behalf of prisoners-of-war and the East Suffolk and Ipswich Hospital.

Henry (Harry) Rice, porter-in-charge grade 1, retired on 19th January, 1946, after 47 years' service, including almost 32 years as the sole member of staff at Thorpeness Halt, having kept the station and gardens immaculate over that span of time. He started his railway career at Diss on 27th November, 1899 and was appointed goods foreman at Leiston on 22nd August, 1910. On the opening of Thorpeness Halt he moved to take charge on 29th July, 1914, and remained there until retirement. The next appointee at Thorpeness was William (Bill) Noy, who had joined the GER in October 1918, and was recorded as a porter at Leiston in 1921. Later in the 1920s he worked at Stratford as a carriage cleaner before returning to Suffolk in the 1930s where he was employed as a horse driver at Ipswich. After passing out as a lorry driver in 1935 he regularly covered the Framlingham and Saxmundham district and when the vacancy arose at Thorpeness in 1946 he took charge of the station, living with his family in the adjacent crossing cottage. When Thorpeness was reduced to the status of an unmanned halt, Noy became a guard based at Aldeburgh and later covered as relief crossing keeper at Saxmundham Road level crossing. Finally he took a motor driving refresher course in March 1963 and took over the Aldeburgh road delivery work from Edgar Bird who had retired, the work then being concentrated on Leiston before being transferred to Ipswich. Noy left the railway service in October 1966 after a very versatile career.

An early member of the signalling staff at Leiston was James Simmons, who commenced his railway career in 1866 as a porter/signalman before transferring to Braintree in 1869. George Howard, signalman at Woodbridge, who retired in March 1915 and died on 20th May, 1919, commenced his railway career as a goods porter at Saxmundham in October 1872 before being promoted to signalman at Saxmundham in November 1874. The following month he transferred to Woodbridge. J. Firman, a retired signalman at Saxmundham having serving at both the Station and Junction signal boxes died on 31st March, 1935. W. Ward who also served as signalman at both the Station and Junction boxes at Saxmundham retired on 31st October, 1942. Other signalmen at Saxmundham Junction included Peter Punchard, Monty Baskett and Gordon Wigg, whilst at Saxmundham Station box were Fred Felgate, Arthur Green, Charles Todd and William Boreham. Signalmen at Leiston in the latter years included Arthur Goddard, William Boreham, who subsequently transferred to Saxmundham, Peter Spall and Brian Ginger, whilst at Aldeburgh signalmen were James Knights, Frank Partridge, Michael Beamish, Henry Vale and Hubert Havers. Ipswich district relief signalmen Monty Baskett and Tony Spatchett also served at the branch signal boxes.

Some of the passenger guards based at Aldeburgh can also be mentioned: Richard Spink, W.H. Branch who retired on 13th February, 1937, and a colleague F.H. Wilmon, who had retired earlier, died on 20th July, 1938. Others serving at the terminus in the latter years included William Wright, Walter Barnes and William Noy, although when the diesel-multiple-unit services commenced, Ipswich guards covered the duties.

For many years Saxmundham station staff held an annual supper where those off duty and their partners could enjoy a social gathering, staff from Leiston and Aldeburgh also being invited. On one such occasion the event was held on 26th January, 1912 at the Market Hall presided over by station master W.H. Bailey.

# Chapter Nine

# Timetables and Traffic

The Aldeburgh branch was initially built to serve Richard Garrett's engineering works at Leiston; the entrepreneur, by becoming a Director of the ESR, ensured that such a connection made with the East Suffolk main line would maintain trading association with the outside world, hitherto only available by a poor road network or by sea via Slaughden Quay, the latter subject not least to the vagaries of the German Ocean. The possibility of lucrative passenger traffic from Leiston alone was questionable and so when ambitious developments at Aldeburgh were mooted, including the provision of a pier, the extension of the branch railway to the coastal town was of natural consequence. The extension to Aldeburgh was completed within one year of the opening of the line to Leiston but unfortunately the planned improvements at Aldeburgh failed to materialize. Aldeburgh thus remained a minor port subservient to the likes of Lowestoft and Yarmouth but the arrival of the railway engendered upper class families to establish the town as a holiday resort. The GER and LNER played their part by fostering this area of the east Suffolk coast with cheap return tickets and excursion fares and, from 1906 until 11th September, 1939, one or two through coaches ran weekdays only to and from Liverpool Street. The whole area, however, was too isolated from the major commercial centres of Suffolk and Norfolk whilst the terminal station was inconveniently situated to attract day-trippers and later holiday trade was limited.

The fishing industry at Aldeburgh, and to a lesser extent Thorpeness, initially profited from the line and often consignments of sprats and other fish were dispatched daily to local markets and Billingsgate. By 1914 shingle banks had decimated fishing as well as the surviving coastal trade and with little other development at Aldeburgh and the reliance of Garrett's to provide the majority of trade at Leiston, the population served by the branch remained under 10,000 souls (*see below*). Thus during the 107 years' existence a service of between five and nine passenger services on weekdays and two to four each way on Sundays sufficed, latterly with some through workings to and from Ipswich by diesel multiple unit. These were augmented by a weekday goods service to and from Ipswich together with 'as and when' required 'Q' local services to clear any important traffic.

|  | 1851 | 1861 | 1871 | 1881 | 1891 | 1901 | 1911 | 1921 | 1931 | 1951 | 1961 | 1971 |
|---|---|---|---|---|---|---|---|---|---|---|---|---|
| Aldeburgh | 1,627 | 1,721 | 1,990 | 2,106 | 2,159 | 2,405 | 2,374 | 2,889 | 2,479 | 2,689 | 3,007 | 2,555 |
| Aldringham | 467 | 471 | 485 | 524 | 577 | 573 | 642 | 901 | 855 | 805 | 954 | 708 |
| Leiston | 1,580 | 2,227 | 2,252 | 2,439 | 2,616 | 3,259 | 4,359 | 4,632 | 4,184 | 4,056 | 4,121 | 4,855 |
| Saxmundham | 1,180 | 1,222 | 1,292 | 1,318 | 1,371 | 1,452 | 1,404 | 1,366 | 1,260 | 1,438 | 1,543 | 1,695 |
| Total* | 3,674 | 4,419 | 4,727 | 5,069 | 5,352 | 6,237 | 7,375 | 8,422 | 7,518 | 7,550 | 8,082 | 8,118 |
| Total+ | 4,854 | 5,641 | 6,019 | 6,387 | 6,723 | 7,689 | 8,779 | 9,788 | 8,778 | 8,988 | 9,625 | 9,813 |

* Total excluding Saxmundham. + Total including Saxmundham.

The initial train service on the Leiston branch from 1st June, 1859, consisted of four trains in each direction with two each way on Sundays, with connections to and from Ipswich and London as follows:

| Up | | Weekdays | | | | Sundays | |
|---|---|---|---|---|---|---|---|
| | | *am* | *am* | *pm* | *pm* | *am* | *pm* |
| Leiston* | dep. | 6.40 | 11.45 | 4.25 | 7.00 | 7.10 | 7.20 |
| Saxmundham | arr. | 6.50 | 11.55 | 4.37 | 7.12 | 7.20 | 7.30 |
| | dep. | 6.55 | 11.59 | 4.41 | 7.18 | 7.25 | 7.33 |
| Ipswich | arr. | 8.05 | 12.55 | 5.40 | 8.30 | 8.35 | 8.45 |
| London | arr. | 10.30† | 4.10 | 9.00 | | 12.15 | |

* For Aldborough. † Also arrive 12.15 pm by Parliamentary train.

| Down | | Weekdays | | | | Sundays | |
|---|---|---|---|---|---|---|---|
| | | *am* | *am* | *am* | *pm* | *am* | *pm* |
| London | dep. | | 9.15† | 11.27 | 4.25 | | 4.30 |
| Ipswich | dep. | 6.50 | 12.00 | 2.35 | 6.41 | 8.00 | 7.47 |
| Saxmundham | arr. | 8.00 | 1.10 | 3.26 | 7.52 | 9.10 | 8.58 |
| | dep. | 8.05 | 1.15 | 3.30 | 7.55 | 9.15 | 9.03 |
| Leiston* | arr. | 8.15 | 1.25 | 3.40 | 8.05 | 9.25 | 9.15 |

† Also depart 7.25 am by Parliamentary train. * For Aldborough.

The 4.25 and 7.00 pm ex-Leiston on weekdays and the 9.03 pm ex-Saxmundham on Sundays ran as mixed trains but all services conveyed goods traffic when required. On weekdays the branch locomotive worked goods traffic in the up direction after arriving at 1.25 pm in order to work the 3.30 pm down service and worked goods traffic in the down direction after arriving at Saxmundham at 4.37 pm before working the 7.00 pm up train.

After the opening of the extension to Aldeburgh the following service was operated from May 1860 with goods traffic handled by the passenger services.

| Up<br>Class | | Weekdays | | | | | Sundays | |
|---|---|---|---|---|---|---|---|---|
| | | 1,2,3,P | 1,2,3 | 1,2 | 1,2,3 | 1,2,3 | 1,2,3,P | 1,2,3 |
| | | *am* | *am* | *pm* | *pm* | *pm* | *am* | *pm* |
| Aldborough | dep. | 6.20 | 11.15 | 3.00 | 4.10 | 6.45 | 6.55 | 7.00 |
| Leiston | dep. | 6.35 | 11.30 | 3.15 | 4.25 | 7.00 | 7.10 | 7.15 |
| Saxmundham | arr. | 6.45 | 11.40 | 3.25 | 4.35 | 7.10 | 7.20 | 7.25 |
| Ipswich | arr. | 8.05 | 12.50 | | 5.45 | 8.30 | 8.35 | 8.45 |

| Down<br>Class | | Weekdays | | | | | Sundays | |
|---|---|---|---|---|---|---|---|---|
| | | 1,2,3 | 1,2,3,P | 1,2 | 1,2 | 1,2 | 1,2,3 | 1,2,3 |
| | | *am* | *am* | *pm* | *pm* | *pm* | *am* | *pm* |
| Ipswich | dep. | 6.50 | 11.55 | 2.35 | | 6.50 | 8.00 | 7.47 |
| Saxmundham | dep. | 8.05 | 1.10 | 3.35 | 4.45 | 8.00 | 9.15 | 9.05 |
| Leiston | dep. | 8.15 | 1.20 | 3.45 | 4.55 | 8.10 | 9.25 | 9.15 |
| Aldborough | arr. | 8.30 | 1.35 | 4.00 | 5.10 | 8.25 | 9.40 | 9.30 |

The working timetable for 1862 showed a weekdays service of four passenger, one Parliamentary (P), one empty coaching stock Mondays-only (MO) and one goods train in the down direction balanced by four passenger, one Parliamentary, one excursion MO and one goods train on the up road. The 6.35 am up Parliamentary from Aldeburgh was balanced by the 12.50 pm down working from Saxmundham, whilst the goods traffic was worked by the 5.25 pm ex-Aldeburgh train returning from Saxmundham at 6.05 pm. The load of the branch engine was not to exceed 10 trucks and the load of ordinary goods trains was limited to 15 trucks. The MO excursion train departed Aldeburgh at 10.30 am running non-stop to the junction with the stock returning as empty coaching stock (ECS) at 11.00 am. Despite the fact that the 11.50 am and 2.50 pm train from Aldeburgh and the 3.25 and 4.55 pm ex-Saxmundham were shown conveying first and second class accommodation only, third class passengers were conveyed locally by all trains between Saxmundham and Aldeburgh. When required the branch engine was permitted to make a special trip between 8.15 am and 11.00 am between Aldeburgh and Saxmundham for any goods traffic. On Sundays a passenger train service ran from Aldeburgh departing at 7.05 am returning from Saxmundham at 9.02 am whilst a Parliamentary train operated in each direction in the evening. The working timetable for January 1863 showed an identical service, save that the excursion from Aldeburgh and return ECS from Saxmundham were withdrawn.

The working timetable for 1865 showed six passenger and one goods train in each direction on weekdays, with all passenger trains conveying first, second and third class passengers. The 6.35 am ex-Aldeburgh and the 1.05 pm from Saxmundham also conveyed Parliamentary class passengers and services were allowed between 22 and 27 minutes for the 8 miles 26 chains journey. Freight traffic was conveyed by the 5.25 pm goods train from Aldeburgh and the 6.05 pm return from Saxmundham, the up train being allowed 30 minutes and the down train 27 minutes for the journey. Ordinary passenger trains could convey goods traffic when necessary, whilst the Aldeburgh branch engine was permitted to make a special trip between 7.00 and 8.15 am and between 8.40 and 10.00 am between Aldeburgh and Saxmundham or vice versa to clear outstanding or urgent goods traffic. The tail load for the branch engine was not to exceed 10 trucks, whilst the goods trains were not to exceed a load of 15 trucks. On Sundays two passenger trains ran in each direction, with the evening services also conveying Parliamentary fare-paying passengers.

The working timetable for the following year 1866 continued to show six passenger and one goods train in each direction on weekdays, although not all passenger services conveyed first, second and third class passengers, the 10.25 am ex-Aldeburgh only conveying first and second class clientele. Parliamentary fare-paying passengers were conveyed by the 6.35 am ex-Aldeburgh and 1.10 pm ex-Saxmundham services. The goods train timings were unaltered and ordinary passenger trains were permitted to convey goods traffic when necessary. When required the Aldeburgh branch engine could make a special trip across the branch between 7.00 and 8.15 am and again between 8.40 and 11.00 am to clear urgent goods traffic. On Sundays two passenger trains ran in each direction, with the evening services conveying Parliamentary fare-paying passengers.

By 1870 the working timetable showed a reduced service of five passenger trains in each direction on weekdays only. All trains with the exception of the 10.15 am ex-Aldeburgh conveying first, second and third class passengers, the exception not conveying third class. Parliamentary fare-paying passengers were conveyed by the 6.40 am ex-Aldeburgh and 1.08 pm ex-Saxmundham trains. Running times for the 8 miles 26 chains journey varied between 22, 25 and 27 minutes and

# Aldborough Branch.—(Single Line.)

## Down.

### Week Days. / Sundays.

| Milestrom Saxmundm | FROM | 1 Pass 1 2 3 | 2 Parl 1 2 3 | 3 Pass 1 2 | 4 Pass 1 2 | 5 Gds 1 2 3 | 6 Pass 1 2 3 | 7 | 8 | 9 | 10 | 11 | 12 | 13 | 14 | 15 | 16 | 17 | 18 | 19 | 20 | 21 | 22 Pass 1 2 3 | 23 Parl 1 2 3 | 24 | 25 |
|---|---|---|---|---|---|---|---|---|---|---|---|---|---|---|---|---|---|---|---|---|---|---|---|---|---|---|
| | | a.m. | p.m. | p.m. | p.m. | p.m. | p.m. | | | | | | | | | | | | | | | | a.m. | p.m. | | |
| | Saxmundham | 7 50 | 12 50 | 3 25 | 4 55 | 6 5 | 7 47 | … | … | … | … | … | … | … | … | … | … | … | … | … | … | … | 9 2 | 8 50 | … | … |
| 4½ | Leiston | 8 2 | 1 2 | 3 37 | 5 5 | 6 29 | 7 57 | … | … | … | … | … | … | … | … | … | … | … | … | … | … | … | 9 15 | 9 0 | … | … |
| 6½ | Aldborough | 8 15 | 1 15 | 3 50 | 5 15 | 6 32 | 8 10 | … | … | … | … | … | … | … | … | … | … | … | … | … | … | … | 9 25 | 9 10 | … | … |

On this Branch the load of the Branch Engine is not to exceed 10 Trucks, & the load of the regular Goods Trains is not to exceed 15 Trucks.

## Up.

### Week Days. / Sundays.

| Milestrom Aldboro' | FROM | 1 Parl 1 2 3 | 2 Pass 1 2 | 3 Pass 1 2 3 | 4 Pass 1 2 | 5 Gds 1 2 3 | 6 Pass 1 2 3 | 7 | 8 | 9 | 10 | 11 | 12 | 13 | 14 | 15 | 16 | 17 | 18 | 19 | 20 | 21 | 22 Pass 1 2 3 | 23 Parl 1 2 3 | 24 | 25 |
|---|---|---|---|---|---|---|---|---|---|---|---|---|---|---|---|---|---|---|---|---|---|---|---|---|---|---|
| | | a.m. | a.m. | p.m. | p.m. | p.m. | p.m. | | | | | | | | | | | | | | | | a.m. | p.m. | | |
| | Aldborough | 6 35 | 11 5 | 2 50 | 4 15 | 5 25 | 6 50 | … | … | … | … | … | … | … | … | … | … | … | … | … | … | … | 7 5 | 7 5 | … | … |
| 4½ | Leiston | 6 47 | 12 2 | 2 58 | 4 28 | 5 43 | 7 2 | … | … | … | … | … | … | … | … | … | … | … | … | … | … | … | 7 15 | 7 1 | … | … |
| 8½ | Saxmundham | 7 0 | 12 15 | 3 15 | 4 42 | 5 55 | 7 15 | … | … | … | … | … | … | … | … | … | … | … | … | … | … | … | 7 27 | 7 27 | … | … |

Third Class locally by all Trains between Aldborough and Saxmundham.

When required the Aldborough Branch Engine is to perform a Special Trip, between 8.15 a.m. and 11.0 a.m., between Aldborough and Saxmundham, for the service of the Goods Traffic.

GER working timetable 1863.

rationalization had taken place with goods traffic being worked by any of the passenger services when necessary. The Aldeburgh branch engine was also permitted to work a special trip between 7.00 and 8.00 am and between 8.40 and 10.00 am from Aldeburgh and Saxmundham and return to clear any goods traffic.

The working timetable for 1875 showed a weekdays-only service of four passenger trains in each direction commencing with the 6.35 am ex-Aldeburgh and finishing with the 7.58 pm down service from Saxmundham. The first up service from Aldeburgh and the 12.30 pm ex-Saxmundham ran as Parliamentary trains and when necessary, goods traffic was worked by the ordinary passenger trains. the arrangements for special goods trips were as before. Running times varied between 25, 27 and 30 minutes.

The timetable for 1877 showed an increased passenger service on the branch of five Saturdays excepted and six Saturdays only trains in each direction, weekdays only. As before, goods traffic was conveyed by the passenger services when required with the 9.30 am (SO) ex-Saxmundham running as a mixed train.

| Up | | | Weekdays | | | | | |
| | | | | SO | | | | |
| | | | am | am | am | pm | pm | pm |
| Aldeburgh | dep. | | 6.35 | 8.59 | 11.45 | 2.40 | 4.20 | 6.50 |
| Leiston | dep. | | 6.47 | 9.02 | 11.57 | 2.53 | 4.33 | 7.07 |
| Saxmundham | arr. | | 7.00 | 9.15 | 12.09 | 3.05 | 4.45 | 7.20 |
| Ipswich | arr. | | 8.12 | | 1.15* | | 5.59 | 8.35 |

| Down | | | Weekdays | | | | | |
| | | | | SO, M | | | | |
| | | | am | am | am | pm | pm | pm |
| Ipswich | dep. | | 7.10 | | 11.25 | 2.20 | 4.35 | 6.49† |
| Saxmundham | dep. | | 8.15 | 9.30 | 12.55 | 3.18 | 5.25 | 7.58 |
| Leiston | dep. | | 8.27 | 9.47 | 1.07 | 3.31 | 5.37 | 8.11 |
| Aldeburgh | arr. | | 8.40 | 9.55 | 1.20 | 3.45 | 5.50 | 8.25 |

* Arrive 1.25 pm SO.  † Depart 6.52 pm SX.  M Mixed.

The working timetable for 1883 showed a service of seven passenger and one goods train in the up direction, weekdays only, the first departure from Aldeburgh at 7.05 am running as a Parliamentary train and on Tuesdays conveying not more than four trucks of cattle from Aldeburgh and Leiston for Ipswich market. The 6.55 pm up passenger was permitted to work not exceeding six trucks of important goods whilst the 10.28 am goods train ex-Aldeburgh worked Crown Lands siding at Sizewell and was allowed 38 minutes for the journey. In the down direction an equal number of passenger and goods trains ran with the 8.05 am passenger ex-Saxmundham permitted to work, when required, not exceeding six trucks of important goods to Leiston and Aldeburgh and the 1.10 pm from the junction running as a Parliamentary. The goods train departed Saxmundham at 9.40 am with a 33 minutes timing to Aldeburgh. The branch engine worked all the passenger and goods services.

The weekdays-only passenger timetable for the branch and connections to and from Liverpool Street in November 1889 is shown on page 206.

# ALDEBURGH BRANCH.

*Junction with East Suffolk Main Line at Saxmundham.*

## DOWN TRAINS.

WEEK DAYS.

| Miles from Saxmundham | FROM | morn | morn | morn | morn | morn | noon | noon | even | even | even | even |
|---|---|---|---|---|---|---|---|---|---|---|---|---|
| | LONDON (L'pool St.) dep. | 5 10 | 7 20 | 9 10 | 10 42 | 11 19 | 12 0 | 1 25 | 2 30 | 3 35 | 5 0 | |
| | Colchester " | 6 34 | 9 28 | | 11 19 | | | | 3 58 | 5 39 | ... | |
| | | Parl. | | | | | | | | | | |
| | Ipswich | 7 12 | 10 30 | | 11 57 | | 2 6 | | 4 38 | | 6 40 | |
| | Saxmundham arr. | 8 11 | 11 21 | | 12 37 | | 2 57 | | 5 18 | | 7 41 | |
| | Yarmouth dep. | 6 15 | ... | | 11 10 | | ... | | 4 0 | | 6 10 | |
| | Lowestoft " | 6 30 | ... | | 11 15 | | ... | | 4 4 | | 6 28 | |
| | Beccles " | 6 43 | ... | | 11 47 | | ... | | 4 31 | | 6 57 | |
| | Saxmundham arr. | 7 34 | ... | | 12 29 | | ... | | 5 4 | | 7 36 | |
| 44 | Saxmundham dep. | 8 10 | 11 30 | | 12 44 | | 3 5 | | 5 33 | | 7 42 | |
| | Leiston " | 8 23 | 11 41 | | 12 56 | | 3 17 | | 5 53 | | 7 57 | |
| 8½ | Aldeburgh arr. | 8 35 | 11 52 | | 1 10 | | 3 30 | | 5 30 | | 8 10 | |

## UP TRAINS.

WEEK DAYS.

| Miles from Aldeburgh | FROM | morn | morn | morn | noon | even | even | even |
|---|---|---|---|---|---|---|---|---|
| | Aldeburgh dep. | 7 2 | 8 55 | | 12 0 | 2 25 | 4 25 | 6 55 |
| | Leiston " | 7 14 | 9 7 | | 12 11 | 2 38 | 4 40 | 7 12 |
| 44 | Saxmundham arr. | 7 25 | 9 20 | | 12 22 | 2 50 | 4 55 | 7 25 |
| | Saxmundham dep. | 8 5 | ... | | 12 40 | 3 0 | 5 22 | 7 40 |
| 29½ | Beccles " | 8 44 | ... | | 1 15 | 3 30 | 5 56 | 8 20 |
| 34½ | Lowestoft arr. | 9 25 | ... | | 1 40 | 4 0 | 6 23 | 8 50 |
| 38½ | Yarmouth " | 9 58 | ... | | 1 45 | 4 18 | 6 27 | 9 0 |
| | Saxmundham dep. | 7 67 | 9 29 | | 12 32 | 4 27 | 5 10 | 7 45 |
| | Ipswich " | 8 35 | 10 14 | | 1 27 | 4 10 | 5 54 | 8 20 |
| 48 | Colchester " | 9 13 | 10 48 | | 2 7 | 4 47 | 6 42 | |
| 99½ | LONDON (L'pool St.) " | 10 30 | 0 13 | 1 15 | 3 25 | 6 0 | 9 0 | ... |

GER public timetable 1882.

The Trains on this Single Line are worked by Train Staff and Train Staff Ticket, according to the "Train Staff Regulations" contained in the "Appendix" to this Working Time Book.

No Engine or Train is to be run on this Branch without a Train Staff or Train Staff Ticket. The Train Staff Stations are Saxmundham and Aldeburgh.

# ALDEBURGH BRANCH.—Single Line.

## Down Trains—Week Days.

| Miles from Saxmundhm. | FROM | 1 A Pass. | 2 Gds. | 3 Pass. | 4 B Pass. | 5 Pass. | 6 Pass. | 7 Pass. | 8 | 9 | 10 | 11 | 12 | 13 |
|---|---|---|---|---|---|---|---|---|---|---|---|---|---|---|
| — | Saxmundham ...dep. | a.m. 8 5 | a.m. 9 35 | a.m. 11 20 | p.m. 1 10 | p.m. 2 57 | p.m. 5 53 | p.m. 7 48 | ... | ... | ... | | | ... |
| 4¼ | Leiston ............ | 8 18 | 9 55 | 11 31 | 1 21 | 3 8 | 6 4 | 7 59 | ... | ... | ... | | | ... |
| 8¼ | Aldeburgh ......arr. | 8 30 | 10 8 | 11 42 | 1 32 | 3 20 | 6 15 | 8 10 | ... | ... | ... | | | ... |

A   No. 1 Down may not work exceeding 6 important Trucks.

B   No. 4 Down may work not exceeding 3 Trucks of important Goods when too late for No. 2 Down Goods Train.

## Up Trains—Week Days.

| Miles from Aldeburgh. | FROM | 1 D Pass. | 2 Pass. | 3 E Gds. | 4 Pass. | 5 Pass. | 6 Pass. | 7 F Pass. | 8 | 9 | 10 | 11 | 12 | 13 |
|---|---|---|---|---|---|---|---|---|---|---|---|---|---|---|
| — | Aldeburgh ......dep. | a.m. 7 5 | a.m. 8 50 | a.m. 10 23 | p.m. 12 30 | p.m. 2 20 | p.m. 4 30 | p.m. 6 55 | ... | ... | ... | | | ... |
| 4 | Leiston ............ | 7 18 | 9 1 | 10 47 | 12 41 | 2 31 | 4 44 | 7 12 | ... | ... | ... | | | ... |
| 8¼ | Saxmundham ...arr. | 7 27 | 9 12 | 11 0 | 12 52 | 2 42 | 4 55 | 7 25 | ... | ... | ... | | | ... |

D   No. 1.  May work not exceeding 4 Trucks of Cattle in all from Aldeburgh and Leiston.

E   No. 3.  To work the Crown Lands Siding at Sizewell Crossing near Leiston.  For working regulations see "Appendix" to the Working Time Tables.

F   No. 7 Up may work not exceeding 6 important Trucks.

GER working timetable 1885.

| *Up* | | | | | WO | M | M |
|---|---|---|---|---|---|---|---|
| | | *am* | *am* | *noon* | *pm* | *pm* | *pm* |
| Aldeburgh | *dep.* | 7.03 | 8.50 | 12.00 | 3.30 | 4.30 | 6.53 |
| Leiston | *dep.* | 7.14 | 9.01 | 12.11 | 3.41 | 4.44 | 7.04 |
| Saxmundham | *arr.* | 7.25 | 9.12 | 12.22 | 3.52 | 4.55 | 7.20 |
| | *dep.* | 7.35 | 9.22 | 12.32 | | 5.06 | 7.39 |
| Ipswich | *arr.* | 8.35 | 10.05 | 1.28 | | 5.56 | 8.30 |
| Liverpool St | *arr.* | 10.30 | 12.15 | 3.25 | | 8.00 | |

| Down | | M | | | WO | | |
|---|---|---|---|---|---|---|---|
| | | *am* | *am* | *am* | *noon* | *pm* | *pm* |
| Liverpool St | *dep.* | 5.10 | 7.08 | 10.00 | 12.00 | 3.30 | 5.00 |
| Ipswich | *dep.* | 7.08 | 10.15 | 11.57 | 2.07 | 5.00 | 6.45 |
| Saxmundham | *arr.* | 7.57 | 11.05 | 12.38 | 2.56 | 5.47 | 7.33 |
| | *dep.* | 8.05 | 11.15 | 12.45 | 3.02 | 5.53 | 7.44 |
| Leiston | *dep.* | 8.18 | 11.26 | 12.56 | 3.13 | 6.04 | 7.55 |
| Aldeburgh | *arr.* | 8.30 | 11.37 | 1.07 | 3.25 | 6.15 | 8.06 |

M  Mixed on branch.  WO  Wednesdays only on branch.

By 1897 the branch weekday service consisted of three passenger trains, Wednesdays and Saturdays excepted, four passenger trains Wednesdays and Saturdays only, two mixed and two goods trains in each direction. The two mixed trains in the up direction, 7.05 am and 7.00 pm ex-Aldeburgh were permitted to work through goods traffic to Saxmundham, whilst the 10.25 am goods train ex-Aldeburgh worked traffic from Sizewell siding when required. If traffic was not cleared from Garrett and Sons works at Leiston a special goods train was to run from Aldeburgh to Saxmundham after the arrival of the 11.18 am ex-Saxmundham passenger train, the engine and brake van returning light Saxmundham to Aldeburgh to take up the next working, with Leiston and Aldeburgh station masters making the necessary arrangements. The 4.35 pm passenger train from Aldeburgh worked 'brake goods' for up road stations either in the guard's van or in a fitted goods van. In the down direction the 8.06 am and 7.44 pm mixed trains ex-Saxmundham were permitted to work goods traffic to Aldeburgh, whilst the 5.05 pm goods train from the junction was a short working to Leiston returning at 5.25 pm, the driver being required to be in possession of the Saxmundham to Aldeburgh single line Train Staff. The Wednesdays and Saturdays only passenger trains departed Aldeburgh at 2.20 pm and returned from Saxmundham at 2.55 pm. On Sundays, only one passenger service ran in each direction, 6.20 pm from Aldeburgh and 7.05 pm ex-Saxmundham. Passenger trains were allowed 20 minutes running time and mixed trains 23 minutes for the journey across the branch. Goods services were permitted 30 and 35 minutes to allow for yard shunting.

    The passenger timetable for 1905 showed the following services, with times accelerated to 19 minutes for most trains in the up direction:

| Up | | Weekdays | | | | | | | Sundays |
|---|---|---|---|---|---|---|---|---|---|
| | | M | | | WSO | SX | SO | | |
| | | am | am | am | pm | pm | pm | pm | pm |
| Aldeburgh | dep. | 6.57 | 8.50 | 11.53 | 2.23 | 4.25 | 4.37 | 6.53 | 6.32 |
| Leiston | dep. | 7.09 | 9.00 | 12.03 | 2.33 | 4.35 | 4.47 | 7.03 | 6.42 |
| Saxmundham | arr. | 7.20 | 9.09 | 12.12 | 2.42 | 4.44 | 4.56 | 7.12 | 6.51 |
| | dep. | 7.30 | 9.23 | 12.25 | 3.32 | 4.57 | 5.09 | 7.46 | 7.02 |
| Ipswich | arr. | 8.28 | 9.54 | 1.22 | 4.15 | 5.54 | 6.04 | 8.40 | 7.56 |
| Liverpool St | arr. | 10.33 | 11.35 | 3.30 | 6.00 | 8.05 | 8.15 | | 10.03 |

| Down | | Weekdays | | | | | | | Sundays |
|---|---|---|---|---|---|---|---|---|---|
| | | M | | | WSO | | | M | |
| | | am | am | am | am | pm | pm | pm | pm |
| Liverpool St | dep. | 5.08 | 8.33 | 10.00 | 11.45 | 3.25 | 5.00 | 5.00 | 4.15 |
| Ipswich | dep. | 7.04 | 10.30 | 12.05 | 2.00 | 5.10 | 6.38 | 6.56 | 6.07 |
| Saxmundham | arr. | 7.51 | 11.18 | 12.45 | 2.49 | 5.57 | 7.18 | 7.43 | 6.58 |
| | dep. | 8.00 | 11.25 | 12.53 | 2.58 | 6.06 | 7.25 | 8.16 | 7.06 |
| Leiston | dep. | 8.11 | 11.35 | 1.03 | 3.08 | 6.16 | 7.35 | 8.28 | 7.16 |
| Aldeburgh | arr. | 8.23 | 11.45 | 1.13 | 3.18 | 6.26 | 7.45 | 8.40 | 7.26 |

M  Mixed on branch.  WSO  Wednesdays and Saturdays only on branch.

In 1904, when the seaside holiday was firmly established for the middle class clientele, the GER had provided a weekdays-only train which ran non-stop from Liverpool Street for both Yarmouth and Lowestoft. The latter was often lightly loaded and in 1905 was combined with a Felixstowe portion, which was altered with through coaches to and from Aldeburgh in 1906.

The 1907 working timetable showed the weekday branch service had increased to one mixed, six passenger, two goods and a light engine working on the up road and two mixed, six passenger and two goods trains in the down direction. The 6.57 am mixed train from Aldeburgh was permitted to work through goods traffic from the terminus to Saxmundham, whilst the 4.25 pm up passenger train could convey brake goods for up road stations either in the guard's van or in a wagon fitted with Westinghouse brake pipes. The light engine working, 7.52 pm ex-Aldeburgh to work the 8.16 pm down mixed train could, when necessary, work one or two trucks of fish or important goods traffic to Saxmundham, Aldeburgh advising Saxmundham when a goods brake was required. In the down direction the two mixed trains, 8.00 am and 8.16 pm from Saxmundham, could work through goods traffic only from the junction station to Aldeburgh. Of the goods services the main train worked through from Ipswich departing 6.10 am and from Saxmundham at 9.55 am serving Leiston, where 10 minutes was allowed for shunting, and arriving at Aldeburgh at 10.25 am. The train returned at 11.57 am and, with 13 minutes allowed at Leiston, arrived at Saxmundham at 12.35 pm before continuing to Ipswich arriving at 3.55 pm. The other goods train, a short trip from Saxmundham to Leiston and return worked by the branch engine between passenger turns, required the driver to be in possession of the single line Train Staff. If the up working, 5.25 pm ex-Leiston, had not cleared all traffic from Garrett & Sons works, a special goods train was run after the arrival of the last down passenger train at Aldeburgh with the engine and brake returning light to Aldeburgh. When required this special was to work traffic to and from Sizewell

# ALDEBURGH BRANCH.—Single Line.

The Trains on this Single Line are worked by Train Staff and Train Staff Ticket, according to the "Train Staff Regulations" contained in the "Appendix" to this Working Time Book.

No Engines or Trains to be run on this Branch without a Train Staff or Train Staff Ticket. The Train Staff Stations are Saxmundham Junction and Aldeburgh.

## DOWN TRAINS—Week Days.  SUNDAYS.

| Miles from Saxmundham | FROM | 1 A Mxd a.m. | 2 B Pass a.m. | 3 C Gds a.m. | 4 Pass a.m. | 5 Pass p.m. | 6 D Pass p.m. (Weds & Sats) | 7 R Gds p.m. (Nob Sats) | 8 R Gds p.m. (Sats only) | 9 Pass p.m. | 10 Pass p.m. | 11 E Mxd p.m. | 12 Pass p.m. | 13 Pass p.m. |
|---|---|---|---|---|---|---|---|---|---|---|---|---|---|---|
| | Ipswich ............dep. | | | 6 0 | | | | | | | | | | |
| | Saxmundham ,, | 8 0 | 9 45 | 6 45 | 10 15 | 12 56 | 2 58 | 3 7 | 4 55 | 5 17 | 7 25 | 8 25 | 7 12 | |
| .33 | Saxmundham Junc. {arr. / dep.} | 8 1 | 9 44 | 10 18 | 12 57 | 2 59 | 3 7 | | 6 13 | 7 28 | 8 26 | 7 13 | | |
| 3.75 | Leiston {arr. / dep.} | 8 10 | 9 52 | 10 28 | 1 5 | 3 7 | 5 7 | 6 31 | 7 34 | 8 35 | 7 21 | | | |
| | | 8 11 | | 11 35 | 1 6 | 3 8 | | 6 23 | 7 35 | 8 35 | 7 22 | | | |
| 8.27 | Aldeburgh ............arr. | 8 23 | 11 18 | 11 43 | 1 14 | 3 16 | | 6 31 | 7 43 | 8 49 | 7 30 | | | |

See page 168.

**A** No. 1. May work Trucks of London Goods for Leiston and Aldeburgh, the total number for both places not to exceed 10.

**B** Nos. 2, 7 and 8 Down and Nos. 8 and 9 Up. The Driver to be in possession of the Saxmundham and Aldeburgh Train Staff.

**C** No. 3. To perform Station shunting at Leiston when necessary.

**D** No. 10 may work Through Traffic only from Saxmundham to Aldeburgh.

**F** No. 5. To work Sizewell Siding, near Leiston, and also Gas Works Siding, but both Sidings are to be worked same day. Aldeburgh to make necessary arrangements.

## UP TRAINS—Week Days.  SUNDAYS.

| Miles from Aldeburgh | FROM | 1 Pass a.m. | 2 B Mxd a.m. | 3 Pass a.m. | 4 Pass a.m. | 5 F Gds p.m. | 6 H Pass p.m. (Weds & Sats) | 7 H Pass p.m. (Not Sats) | 8 H Pass p.m. (Sats only) | 9 B Gds p.m. | 10 Pass p.m. | 11 Mxd p.m. | 12 J Pass p.m. | 13 J Pass p.m. |
|---|---|---|---|---|---|---|---|---|---|---|---|---|---|---|
| | Aldeburgh ............dep. | 7 9 | 8 50 | | 11 53 | 12 5 | 4 25 | 4 25 | 4 37 | 9 23 | 6 45 | 7 53 | 5 52 | 6 32 |
| 4.52 | Leiston {arr. / dep.} | 7 18 | 8 59 | 9 8 | 12 | 12 16 | 4 33 | 4 34 | 4 47 | 9 32 | 6 54 | 8 1 | 6 1 | 6 41 |
| | | 7 18 | 9 | 8 10 | 7 13 | 12 30 | 4 33 | 4 41 | 4 47 | 9 33 | 6 55 | 8 3 | 6 6 | 6 42 |
| 7.74 | Saxmundham Junc. {dep.} | 7 19 | 9 10 | 10 18 | 12 43 | 4 43 | 4 44 | 4 56 | 5 40 | 7 5 | 8 10 | 6 10 | 6 50 | |
| 8.27 | Saxmundham ...........arr. | | | 3 35 | 5 42 | 7 8 | 8 15 | 6 11 | 6 51 | | | | | |
| | Ipswich ............arr. | | | | | | | | | | | | | |

See p. 161.

**H** Nos. 7 and 8. Break Goods from Aldeburgh for Up Road Stations may be forwarded by this Train either in the Guards Van or in a Truck fitted with a Westinghouse Brake pipe.

**J** No. 13. *Will not run after 27th October.* No. 18. *Commences running 3rd November.* Nos. 12 and 13 may work not exceeding 2 Westinghouse piped wagons containing spares from Aldeburgh to Saxmundham, the Traffic to be worked forward from the latter Station by the 8.31 p.m. Lowestoft to Ipswich Mail Goods Train.

**N.B.**—In the event of No. 9 Up Goods Train not clearing all Traffic from Messrs. Garrett & Sons' Works, a Special Goods Train is to be run from Aldeburgh to Saxmundham after arrival of the last Down Passenger Train, returning Engine and Brake to Aldeburgh. Leiston and Aldeburgh to arrange and advise all concerned.

**The Load of a First Class Goods Engine over this Branch, to be as shown in Appendix to Working Time Tables.**

GER working timetable 1912.

siding, the traffic having been worked down to Aldeburgh by the 2.43 pm ex-Saxmundham passenger train, down rated to a mixed service if required. On Sundays the branch locomotive worked all passenger services with three trains in the up direction and two on the down road, the engine returning light from Saxmundham to work the last round trip from Aldeburgh to Saxmundham in the evening.

The working timetable for 1913 showed six passenger, two mixed and two goods trains in each direction on weekdays and three passenger trains each way on Sundays. The 6.57 am ex-Aldeburgh mixed train was permitted to work through traffic only from Aldeburgh to Saxmundham whilst the return mixed train, 8.00 am ex-Saxmundham, could work trucks from the goods service from London for Leiston and Aldeburgh, provided the total loading for both places did not exceed 10 wagons. The final down mixed train of the day, 8.25 pm from Saxmundham, was permitted to work through traffic only from Saxmundham to Aldeburgh, whilst the 4.25 pm passenger train ex-Aldeburgh could work brake goods from the terminal for up road stations either in the guard's van or in a truck equipped with the Westinghouse brake. Of the two goods services the first down working was a through train from Ipswich and worked by an Ipswich engine and crew, serving all yards on the branch and arriving at Aldeburgh at 10.25 am. The up working departed Aldeburgh at 12.00 noon as a through working to Ipswich arriving there at 3.55 pm. The second goods working of the day was a short trip from Saxmundham, departing 5.05 pm to Leiston and returning at 5.30 pm worked by the branch engine, with the driver in possession of the Saxmundham to Aldeburgh Train Staff. If this train was unable to clear all traffic from Garrett's sidings a special goods train ran from Aldeburgh to Saxmundham after the arrival of the 6.07 pm down passenger service from Saxmundham at Aldeburgh. If the special was operated the station masters at Aldeburgh and Leiston made the necessary local arrangements. This special could work traffic to or from Sizewell siding, which had been worked down by the 2.45 pm passenger train ex-Saxmundham. The branch engine worked the three Sunday trains.

The branch passenger timetable for 1917 showed a slight reduction of services with only one mixed train in each direction and an unbalanced working when the branch locomotive hauled a freight service from Aldeburgh to Saxmundham to resume passenger working with the 12.47pm down train. On Sundays two trains ran in the up direction with only one down working, the engine returning to Aldeburgh with ECS and any urgent goods traffic. After the opening of Thorpeness Halt passenger trains were now allowed 22 minutes running time across the branch.

| Up | | Weekdays | | | | | | | Sundays | |
| --- | --- | --- | --- | --- | --- | --- | --- | --- | --- | --- |
| | | M | | | | | | | | |
| | | am | am | am | pm | pm | pm | pm | am | pm |
| Aldeburgh | dep. | 7.05 | 8.50 | 10.43 | 12.09 | 1.42 | 4.18 | 7.06 | 6.28 | 8.36 |
| Thorpeness Halt | dep. | 7.11 | 8.56 | 10.49 | 12.15 | 1.48 | 4.24 | 7.12 | 6.34 | 8.42 |
| Leiston | dep. | 7.24 | 9.03 | 10.56 | 12.22 | 1.55 | 4.31 | 7.19 | 6.41 | 8.49 |
| Saxmundham | arr. | 7.35 | 9.12 | 11.05 | 12.31 | 2.04 | 4.40 | 7.28 | 6.50 | 8.58 |
| Liverpool Street | arr. | 10.28 | 11.38 | 1.58 | | 4.55 | 7.48 | | 10.06 | |

# ALDEBURGH BRANCH.

## WEEK DAYS.

| | | morn | morn | Mxd | morn | morn | morn | even. | even. | even. | Mxd | even. | even. | Mxd | even. |
|---|---|---|---|---|---|---|---|---|---|---|---|---|---|---|---|
| LONDON (Liverpool St.) | dep. | 5 10 | 7 40 | ... | 8 15 | 10 16 | ... | 12 57 | ... | 3 22 | ... | ... | ... | ... | 4 25 |
| Colchester | " | 6 37 | 8 45 | ... | 9 40 | 11 32 | ... | 1 57 | ... | 4 36 | ... | ... | ... | ... | 5 40 |
| Ipswich | " | 7 17 | 9 33 | ... | 10 32 | 12 2 | ... | 2 43 | ... | 5 6 | ... | ... | ... | ... | 6 17 |
| Saxmundham | arr. | 8 10 | ... | ... | 11 23 | 12 35 | ... | 3 32 | ... | 6 1 | ... | ... | ... | ... | 7 11 |
| Lowestoft (Central) | dep. | 6 39 | 8 25 | ... | 9 53 | ... | ... | 2 28 | ... | ... | ... | 3 33 | ... | ... | 5 43 |
| Yarmouth (S.T.) | " | 6 24 | 8 25 | ... | 9 54 | ... | ... | 2 24 | ... | ... | ... | 3 23 | ... | ... | 5 30 |
| Beccles | " | 7 4 | 8 55 | ... | 10 34 | ... | ... | 2 56 | ... | ... | ... | 3 28 | ... | ... | 6 12 |
| Saxmundham | arr. | 7 46 | 9 26 | ... | 11 20 | ... | ... | 3 35 | ... | ... | ... | 4 44 | ... | ... | 7 2 |
| SAXMUNDHAM | dep. | 8 15 | 9 38 | Mxd | 11 28 | 12 42 | ... | 3 39 | ... | 6 12 | ... | 4 50 | 7 55 | Mxd | 7 17 |
| LEISTON | " | 8 25 | 9 49 | ... | 11 38 | 12 52 | ... | 3 49 | ... | 6 22 | ... | 5 8 | 8 6 | ... | 7 28 |
| Thorpeness (Halt) | " | 8 31 | 9 56 | ... | 11 44 | 12 58 | ... | 3 55 | ... | 6 28 | ... | 5 14 | 8 13 | ... | 7 34 |
| ALDEBURGH | arr. | 8 37 | 10 3 | ... | 11 50 | 1 4 | ... | 4 1 | ... | 6 34 | ... | 5 20 | 8 20 | ... | 7 40 |

### SUNDAYS.

| | | morn | morn | even. |
|---|---|---|---|---|
| LONDON (Liverpool St.) | dep. | ... | ... | 4 25 |
| Colchester | " | 9 0 | ... | 5 40 |
| Ipswich | " | 9 50 | ... | 6 17 |
| Saxmundham | arr. | ... | ... | 7 11 |
| Lowestoft (Central) | dep. | 7 10 | ... | 5 43 |
| Yarmouth (S.T.) | " | 7 0 | ... | 5 30 |
| Beccles | " | 7 38 | ... | 6 12 |
| Saxmundham | arr. | 8 22 | ... | 7 2 |
| SAXMUNDHAM | dep. | 9 55 | ... | 7 17 |
| LEISTON | " | 10 6 | ... | 7 28 |
| Thorpeness (Halt) | " | 10 12 | ... | 7 34 |
| ALDEBURGH | arr. | 10 18 | ... | 7 40 |

## WEEK DAYS.

| | | morn | morn | morn | even. | even. | even. | even. | Mxd | even. | even. | even. |
|---|---|---|---|---|---|---|---|---|---|---|---|---|
| ALDEBURGH | dep. | 7 5 | 8 50 | 10 45 | 12 5 | 2 59 | 4 11 | 5 25 | 5 45 | 6 47 | ... | ... |
| Thorpeness (Halt) | " | 7 12 | 8 56 | 10 51 | 12 11 | 3 5 | 4 17 | ... | ... | 6 53 | ... | ... |
| LEISTON | " | 7 24 | 9 3 | 10 57 | 12 18 | 3 12 | 4 24 | 5 45 | ... | 7 2 | ... | ... |
| SAXMUNDHAM | arr. | 7 35 | 9 12 | 11 7 | 12 27 | 3 21 | 4 33 | 5 56 | ... | 7 13 | ... | ... |
| Saxmundham | dep. | 8 10 | 9 38 | 11 28 | 12 55 | 3 52 | ... | 6 1 | ... | 8 5 | ... | ... |
| Beccles | " | 8 52 | 10 12 | 12 3 | 1 7 | 4 7 | ... | 6 43 | ... | 8 46 | ... | ... |
| Yarmouth (S.T.) | " | 9 31 | 10 55 | 12 40 | 1 36 | 4 40 | ... | 7 28 | ... | 9 25 | ... | ... |
| Lowestoft (Central) | " | 9 18 | 10 52 | 12 38 | 1 37 | 4 36 | ... | 7 14 | ... | 9 30 | ... | ... |
| Saxmundham | dep. | 7 46 | 9 26 | 11 20 | 1 15 | 3 35 | 4 44 | 6 47 | ... | 7 26 | ... | ... |
| Ipswich | arr. | 8 40 | 9 57 | 12 15 | 2 7 | 4 16 | 5 37 | 7 40 | ... | 7 57 | ... | ... |
| Colchester | " | 9 14 | 10 58 | 12 46 | 4 5 | 5 17 | 6 31 | 8 15 | ... | 8 38 | ... | ... |
| LONDON (Liverpool St.) | " | 10 28 | 11 30 | 1 58 | 3 58 | 5 55 | 7 48 | 9 29 | ... | 9 58 | ... | ... |

### SUNDAYS.

| | | morn | morn | even. |
|---|---|---|---|---|
| ALDEBURGH | dep. | 7 47 | ... | 6 25 |
| Thorpeness (Halt) | " | 7 53 | ... | 6 31 |
| LEISTON | " | 8 0 | ... | 6 38 |
| SAXMUNDHAM | arr. | 8 9 | ... | 6 47 |
| Saxmundham | dep. | 9 50 | ... | 7 11 |
| Beccles | " | 10 28 | ... | 7 55 |
| Yarmouth (S.T.) | " | 11 4 | ... | 8 35 |
| Lowestoft (Central) | " | 10 53 | ... | 8 20 |
| Saxmundham | dep. | 8 22 | ... | 7 2 |
| Ipswich | arr. | 9 18 | ... | 8 1 |
| Colchester | " | 10 1 | ... | 8 41 |
| LONDON (Liverpool St.) | " | 11 30 | ... | 10 9 |

**NS** Not Saturdays.  **SO** Saturdays only.

GER public timetable 1919.

| Down | | | | | Weekdays | | | | | Sun. |
|---|---|---|---|---|---|---|---|---|---|---|
| | | | | | | | | | M | |
| | | am | am | am | am | am | am | pm | pm | pm |
| Liverpool Street | dep. | | 5.00 | | 8.15 | 10.00 | 11.38* | 3.22 | 5.23 | 4.00 |
| Saxmundham | dep. | 6.23 | 8.07 | 9.38 | 11.28 | 12.47 | 3.19 | 6.06 | 7.50 | 8.05 |
| Leiston | dep. | 6.33 | 8.18 | 9.48 | 11.38 | 12.57 | 3.29 | 6.16 | 8.01 | 8.15 |
| Thorpeness Halt | dep. | 6.39 | 8.26 | 9.54 | 11.44 | 1.03 | 3.35 | 6.22 | 8.09 | 8.21 |
| Aldeburgh | arr. | 6.45 | 8.32 | 10.00 | 11.50 | 1.09 | 3.41 | 6.28 | 8.15 | 8.27 |

M Mixed. * Departs 12.30 pm Saturdays only.

By 1921 the branch passenger service had increased to pre-war standards with a weekdays service of six passenger and two mixed (SX) and seven passenger and two mixed trains (SO) in the up direction and six passenger and two mixed trains (SX) and six passenger and three mixed trains (SO) in the down direction, together with one evening train each way on Sundays.

| Up | | | Weekdays | | | | | | | | | Sun. |
|---|---|---|---|---|---|---|---|---|---|---|---|---|
| | | M | | | | | SO | SX | | M | | SO |
| | | am | am | am | pm | pm | pm | pm | pm | pm | pm | pm |
| Aldeburgh | d. | 7.05 | 8.50 | 10.44 | 12.05 | 1.29 | 2.41 | 4.11 | 5.25 | 6.47 | 8.00 | 6.32 |
| Thorpeness | d. | 7.11 | 8.56 | 10.50 | 12.11 | 1.35 | 2.47 | 4.17 | | 6.53 | 8.06 | 6.38 |
| Leiston | d. | 7.24 | 9.03 | 10.58 | 12.18 | 1.42 | 2.54 | 4.24 | 5.45 | 7.02 | 8.15 | 6.45 |
| Saxmundham | a. | 7.35 | 9.12 | 11.07 | 12.27 | 1.51 | 3.03 | 4.33 | 5.56 | 7.13 | 8.26 | 6.54 |
| Liverpool St | a. | 10.28 | 11.30 | 1.58 | 4.58 | 4.58 | 5.55 | 7.48 | | 9.29 | | 10.09 |

| Down | | | Weekdays | | | | | | | | Sun. |
|---|---|---|---|---|---|---|---|---|---|---|---|
| | | M | | | | | | M | M | SO M | |
| | | am | am | am | am | pm | pm | pm | pm | pm | pm |
| Liverpool St | d. | 5.00 | | 8.15 | 10.00 | 12.30 | | 3.20 | 4.55 | 5.23 | 4.25 |
| Saxmundham | d. | 8.07 | 9.38 | 11.23 | 12.42 | 3.38 | 4.50 | 6.12 | 7.30 | 8.36 | 7.17 |
| Leiston | d. | 8.18 | 9.48 | 11.38 | 12.52 | 3.48 | 5.08 | 6.22 | 7.40 | 8.47 | 7.28 |
| Thorpeness | d. | 8.24 | 9.54 | 11.44 | 12.58 | 3.54 | 5.14 | 6.28 | 7.46 | 8.53 | 7.34 |
| Aldeburgh | a. | 8.32 | 10.00 | 11.50 | 1.04 | 4.00 | 5.20 | 6.34 | 7.52 | 9.01 | 7.40 |

The initial LNER public timetable for summer services in 1923 showed seven passenger and one mixed train in each direction on weekdays. On the up road the first train of the day, 6.58 am ex-Aldeburgh, ran as a mixed train throughout whilst the 5.25 pm and 6.47 pm from Aldeburgh were downgraded to run as mixed trains between Leiston and Saxmundham. In the down direction the 8.07 am ex-Saxmundham ran as a mixed train, whilst the 4.50 pm ex-Saxmundham ran as mixed to Leiston and passenger train thence to Aldeburgh. On Sundays three passenger trains ran in each direction. Passenger trains were allowed 22 and 23 minutes and mixed trains between 25 and 30 minutes for the journey across the branch.

By 1924 the working timetable showed paths for seven passenger trains (SX) and eight (SO) together with one mixed train, one goods train and a light engine working on weekdays in the up direction. The mixed train departed Aldeburgh at 6.58 am and was authorized to attach cattle wagons at Leiston when required, whilst the 5.25 pm (SX) and 6.47 pm passenger services from Aldeburgh ran

# SAXMUNDHAM AND ALDEBURGH. (Single Line between Saxmundham Junction and Aldeburgh.)

## DOWN WEEK DAYS.

| Miles from Saxmundham | See page | 1 Mxd. | 2 Gds. | 3 Pass. | 4 | 5 | 6 Pass. | 7 Pass. | 8 Pass. | 9 Pass. | 10 | 11 Pass. | 12 Pass. | 13 SO Pass. | 14 NS Pass. | 15 SO Pass. | 16 NS Pass. | 17 NS Pass. | 18 SO Pass. | 19 Pass. | 20 Pass. | 21 Gds. WB | 22 Pass. a.m. | 23 Pass. | 24 Pass. p.m. | 25 Pass. p.m. | 26 Pass. p.m. |
|---|---|---|---|---|---|---|---|---|---|---|---|---|---|---|---|---|---|---|---|---|---|---|---|---|---|---|---|
| | | | | | | | a.m. | p.m. | p.m. | p.m. | | p.m. | p.m. | p.m. | p.m. | p.m. | p.m. | p.m. | p.m. | p.m. | p.m. | | | | p.m. | p.m. | p.m. |
| — | Ipswich ...... dep. | a.m. | 6 50 | a.m. | | | | | | | | | | | | | | | | | | | | | | | |
| — | Saxmundham ...... ® | 8 7 | 9 10 | 9 44 | | | 11 34 | — | 1 34 | 3 25 | | 4 50 | | 1 50 | 3 25 | 4 0 | 4 50 | — | — | 6 10 | 7 35 | 9 0 | 10 14 | | 6 35 | 8 10 | |
| — 34 | Saxmundham Jnc. ® | 8 9 | 9 12 | 9 45 | | | 11 35 | — | 1 35 | 3 26 | | 4 51 | | 1 51 | 3 26 | 4 1 | 4 51 | — | — | 6 11 | 7 36 | 9 2 | 10 15 | | 6 36 | 8 11 | |
| | Leiston (see note) ® { arr. | 8 17 | 9 22 | 9 53 | | | 11 43 | — | 1 43 | 3 34 | | 4 59 | 5 8 | 1 59 | 3 34 | 4 9 | 4 59 | 5 8 | 5 14 | 6 19 | 7 44 | 9 10 | 10 23 | | 6 44 | 8 21 | |
| 3 75 | { dep. | 8 18 | 10 45 | 9 54 | | | 11 44 | — | 1 44 | 3 35 | | — | 5 11 | 2 0 | 3 35 | 4 10 | — | 5 11 | 5 18 | 6 20 | 7 45 | 9 15 | 10 28 | | 6 46 | 8 21 | |
| 6 22 | Thorpeness Halt ...... | 8 25 | * | 10 0 | | | 11 50 | — | 1 50 | 3 41 | | — | 5 14 | 2 3 | 3 41 | 4 16 | — | 5 14 | 5 24 | 6 26 | 7 51 | * | 10 31 | | 6 52 | 8 27 | |
| 8 26 | Aldeburgh ...... ® arr. | 8 32 | 11 | 5 10 | | | 11 56 | — | 1 56 | 3 47 | | — | 5 20 | 2 12 | 3 47 | 4 22 | — | 5 20 | 5 24 | 6 32 | 7 57 | 9 25 | 10 37 | | 6 58 | 8 33 | |

=1 May attach cattle of London goods for Aldeburgh, the total number not to exceed 10. =13 Worked by engine of 5 up.

2 On Sats. to be worked by Westinghouse fitted engine. =20 May work not exceeding 2 trucks Saxmundham to Aldeburgh if the trucks are fitted

(with Westinghouse brake pipes.)

**SUNDAYS.**

## UP WEEK DAYS.

| Miles from Aldeburgh | See page | 1 Mxd. | 2 | 3 Pass. | 4 Pass. | 5 Gds. SO | 6 Gds. | 7 Pass. | 8 Pass. | 9 Pass. | 10 | 11 Pass. | 12 Pass. | 13 SO Pass. | 14 NS Pass. | 15 SO Pass. | 16 NS Pass. | 17 NS Pass. | 18 SO Pass. | 19 Pass. | 20 Mxd. | 21 Gds. WR | 22 Pass. a.m. | 23 | 24 Pass. p.m. | 25 Pass. p.m. | 26 Pass. p.m. |
|---|---|---|---|---|---|---|---|---|---|---|---|---|---|---|---|---|---|---|---|---|---|---|---|---|---|---|---|
| | | a.m. | | a.m. | a.m. | p.m. | C 55 | p.m. | p.m. | p.m. | | p.m. | p.m. | p.m. | p.m. | p.m. | p.m. | p.m. | p.m. | p.m. | p.m. | | a.m. | | p.m. | p.m. | p.m. |
| M.C. | Aldeburgh ...... ® dep. | 6 58 | | 8 50 | 10 28 | | | 12 50 | 2 50 | 4 11 | | 5 25 | 5 45 | 3 25 | 4 11 | 4 30 | 5 25 | 5 34 | | 6 54 | | 8 10 | 7 42 | | 5 52 | 7 20 | |
| 2 4 | Thorpeness Halt ...... | 7 5 | | 8 56 | 10 38 | | | 12 56 | 2 56 | 4 17 | | 5 31 | 5 53 | 3 31 | 4 17 | 4 36 | 5 31 | 5 40 | | 7 0 | | * | 7 45 | | 5 58 | 7 26 | |
| | Leiston (see note) ® { arr. | 7 12 | | 9 2 | 10 34 1/2 | 12 40 | 1 25 | 1 3 | 3 3 | 4 24 | | 5 37 | 5 46 | 3 38 | 4 24 | 4 43 | 5 37 | 5 45 | | 7 6 | 7 9 | 8 20 | 7 51 | | 6 5 | 7 34 | |
| 4 32 | { dep. | 7 17 | | 9 3 | 10 36 | 1 18 | 1 45 | 1 11 | 3 11 | | | — | 5 55 | 3 46 | 4 31 | 4 51 | — | 5 53 | | 7 8 | 7 18 | 8 28 | 7 55 | | 6 13 | 7 42 | |
| 7 74 | Saxmundham Jc. ® ... arr. | 7 26 | | 9 12 | 10 44 | 1 33 | 2 1 | 1 11 | 3 11 | 4 31 | | — | 5 54 | 3 47 | 4 33 | 4 52 | — | 5 54 | | 7 18 | 8 3 | 8 43 | 8 1 | | 6 14 | 7 43 | |
| 8 27 | Saxmundham ...... ® | 7 28 | | 9 10 10 45 | | 1 35 | 2 1 | 1 12 | 3 12 | 4 33 | | — | 5 56 | | | | | | | 7 20 | 8 45 | | | | | | |
| | Ipswich ...... arr. | | | | | 5 25 4 50 | | | | | | | | | | | | | | | | | | | | | |

=1 May attach cattle at Leiston when required.   5 Runs from 23rd July to 3rd Sept. inc.

6 To work Sizewell siding, near Leiston, and also Gas Works eng. to work 13 down & 8 up.   6 To work Sizewell siding are not to be worked same day. Aldeburgh to make necessary arrangements, and also arrange for these sidings to be cleared as required on Sats. when 6 is not running. To shunt at Leiston for 7.   6 Will not run on Sats. from 23rd July to 3rd Sept. inc.

=11 & 18 To work passenger train fish vehicles from Aldeburgh and take in all pass. train fish traffic at Thorpeness. Brake goods from Aldeburgh for up road stations may be forwarded by this train either in the guard's van or in a truck fitted with a Westinghouse brake pipe.

21 Work Sizewell Siding when required.   =24 May work not exceeding 2 trucks, Aldeburgh to Saxmundham if the trucks are fitted with Westinghouse brake pipes.

**NOTE.—Leiston.** A ballast train or goods train may be allowed to leave Saxmundham Junc. or Aldeburgh for Leiston, and there be shunted clear into the down side siding next to the main single line, until it is again required to leave Leiston. After the ballast or goods train has arrived and been shunted clear, a down train or an up train may be accepted by the Leiston Signalman provided he is in a position to do so.

After the Leiston Signalman has accepted a down train from Saxmundham Junc. he must not accept an up train from Aldeburgh. In like manner after the Leiston Signalman has accepted an up train from Aldeburgh he must not accept a down train from Saxmundham Junc.

Passenger trains must not be allowed to cross each other at Leiston Station.

LNER working timetable 1927.

forward from Leiston as mixed trains. The 5.25 pm (SX) was permitted to work passenger train fish vehicles from Aldeburgh and take all passenger train fish traffic from Thorpeness. Brake goods from Aldeburgh for up road destinations beyond Saxmundham were also forwarded by this train in either the guard's van or in a truck equipped with the Westinghouse brake. The 12.20 pm goods train from Aldeburgh was worked by an Ipswich engine and was booked 65 minutes to shunt and marshal stock at Leiston for the onwards service to Ipswich arriving there at 4.50 pm. However, on Saturdays between 26th July and 6th September only, 38 minutes was allowed at Leiston as the engine worked the 1.50 pm (SO) down passenger train ex-Saxmundham and the 2.50 pm return passenger train from Aldeburgh before continuing with the goods from Saxmundham to Ipswich arriving at the later time of 5.20 pm. The up goods services shunted Sizewell and Leiston gas works sidings provided both were not worked the same day. The 8.10 pm ex-Aldeburgh engine and brake van, if required, ran as a goods train to deliver wagons to and clear Sizewell siding before terminating at Leiston at 8.25 pm. On Sundays three passenger trains operated on the up road, the 5.52 pm ex-Aldeburgh being permitted to work not exceeding three trucks to Saxmundham provided they were fitted with Westinghouse brake pipes. In the down direction seven passenger and one mixed train worked across the branch on weekdays, the latter being authorized to work wagons of London goods for Aldeburgh provided the extra load did not exceed 10 vehicles. The 7.20 pm passenger train ex-Saxmundham could work not exceeding two trucks through to Aldeburgh provided the vehicles were fitted with Westinghouse brake pipes. The 4.50 pm SX mixed train ex-Saxmundham reverted to passenger train status beyond Leiston. The down branch goods train departed Ipswich at 8.55 am and left Saxmundham at 10.10 am but on Saturdays between 26th July and 6th September, the train departed Ipswich at the earlier time of 8.10 am and left Saxmundham at 9.55 am being worked by a Westinghouse-fitted engine as the locomotive was used to haul a passenger service in each direction. On Sundays a service of three passenger trains operated on the down road.

Services on the Aldeburgh branch were reduced as a result of the coal strike and from 31st May, 1926 four passenger trains ran each way Saturdays excepted, with an additional train in each direction on Saturdays and one return trip on Sundays. Services departed Aldeburgh at 6.58, 10.43 am, 1.55 (SO), 4.11 and 6.54 pm returning from Saxmundham at 8.07, 11.34 am, 2.42 (SO), 4.50 and 7.55 pm. On Sundays the up train departed Aldeburgh at 5.57 pm returning from the junction station at 7.46 pm.

The public timetable for July 1932 (*overleaf*) showed a service of eight trains in the up direction on weekdays with three on Sundays whilst in the down direction nine trains ran SX, eight SO and four on Sundays. The additional Sunday trains were evidence of the popularity of Thorpeness and Aldeburgh for day-trippers from Ipswich and intermediate stations on the East Suffolk line.

During the 1930s the 8.30 am Yarmouth to Liverpool Street service picked up the through coach or coaches from Aldeburgh at Saxmundham for conveyance to the capital.

The working timetable for 1935 showed a total of eight Fridays excepted (FX), nine Fridays only (FO) and eight SO passenger trains in the up direction

# Public Timetable July 1932

## Up — Weekdays

| | M | | | | | SX | SO | SX | SO | |
|---|---|---|---|---|---|---|---|---|---|---|
| | am | am | am | pm | pm | pm | pm | pm | pm | pm |
| Aldeburgh *dep.* | 7.00 | 8.49 | 10.22 | 12.50 | 2.48 | 4.11 | 4.30 | 5.20 | 5.30 | 6.58 |
| Thorpeness Halt *dep.* | 7.07 | 8.55 | 10.28 | 12.56 | 2.54 | 4.17 | 4.36 | 5.26 | 5.36 | 7.04 |
| Leiston *dep.* | 7.19 | 9.02 | 10.36 | 1.03 | 3.01 | 4.24 | 4.43 | 5.37 | 5.43 | 7.11 |
| Saxmundham *arr.* | 7.30 | 9.11 | 10.45 | 1.12 | 3.10 | 4.33 | 4.52 | 5.47 | 5.52 | 7.20 |
| Liverpool Street *arr.* | 10.30 | 11.25 | 1.13 | 3.42 | 5.54 | 7.52 | | 9.24 | 9.24 | 9.59 |

## Up — Sundays

| | | | |
|---|---|---|---|
| | am | am | pm |
| Aldeburgh *dep.* | 7.48 | 9.38 | 5.54 |
| Thorpeness Halt *dep.* | 7.54 | 9.44 | 6.00 |
| Leiston *dep.* | 8.03 | 9.51 | 6.07 |
| Saxmundham *arr.* | 8.10 | 10.01 | 6.16 |
| Liverpool Street *arr.* | 11.22 | | 9.15 |

## Down — Weekdays

| | M | | | | SX | SO M | SX | SO | | SO |
|---|---|---|---|---|---|---|---|---|---|---|
| | am | am | am | pm | pm | pm | pm | pm | pm | pm |
| Liverpool Street *dep.* | 5.00 | 8.15 | | 10.30 | 1.00 | 1.00 | 3.18 | | 4.55 | 7.30 |
| Saxmundham *dep.* | 8.07 | 9.44 | 11.25 | 1.34 | 3.22 | 3.30 | 5.02 | 6.00 | 7.35 | 10.25 |
| Leiston *dep.* | 8.20 | 9.54 | 11.35 | 1.44 | 3.32 | 3.40 | 5.12 | 6.10 | 7.45 | 10.35 |
| Thorpeness Halt *dep.* | 8.26 | 10.00 | 11.41 | 1.50 | 3.38 | 3.48 | 5.18 | 6.16 | 7.51 | 10.41 |
| Aldeburgh *arr.* | 8.32 | 10.06 | 11.47 | 1.56 | 3.44 | 3.57 | 5.24 | 6.22 | 7.57 | 10.47 |

## Down — Sundays

| | | | | |
|---|---|---|---|---|
| | am | am | pm | pm |
| Liverpool Street *dep.* | | | | |
| Saxmundham *dep.* | 8.25 | 10.11 | 6.32 | 8.14 |
| Leiston *dep.* | 8.36 | 10.22 | 6.43 | 8.25 |
| Thorpeness Halt *dep.* | 8.42 | 10.28 | 6.49 | 8.31 |
| Aldeburgh *arr.* | 8.48 | 10.34 | 6.55 | 8.37 |

M – Mixed train., SO – Saturdays only, SX - Saturdays excepted.

together with one goods working on weekdays augmented by a 'Q' path for an additional goods train. On Saturdays two empty carriage workings were operated to balance down movements. Of the passenger trains, the 7.10 am from Aldeburgh was allowed to attach cattle traffic at Leiston provided the wagons were fitted vehicles and if conveyed, the train was permitted two minutes extra running time to Saxmundham. The 5.14 pm ex-Aldeburgh was downrated to a mixed train from Leiston to Saxmundham as it worked passenger train fish vehicles from Aldeburgh and collected all passenger train fish traffic at Thorpeness and worked goods traffic from Leiston. This service was also permitted to work 'brake goods' from these stations for up road destinations beyond Saxmundham provided the commodities were in the guard's van or in a wagon attached to the train. The 12.15 pm goods train from Aldeburgh shunted Sizewell siding and also Gas Works siding, although they were not to be worked the same day, with the Aldeburgh station master making the necessary arrangements. When either siding was worked the train was permitted 10 minutes extra running time to Leiston. On Saturdays the train departed Saxmundham for Ipswich at the later time of 3.45 pm, as the dual-fitted locomotive worked an additional round trip to Aldeburgh with a passenger train. A 'Q' path was also available for goods traffic departing Aldeburgh at 8.10 pm, shunting Sizewell siding when required in addition to Leiston. The 3.15 pm ECS ran to Leiston where the engine stabled the stock and worked light to Saxmundham to take the 3.42 pm passenger train to Aldeburgh, whilst the 11.00 pm SO ECS ex-Aldeburgh to Ipswich which ran until 23rd May was the return of the 9.34 pm down through passenger train from Ipswich. The solitary passenger train on Sunday, 6.02 pm from Aldeburgh, was permitted to work not exceeding two piped wagons of important goods traffic to Saxmundham.

In the down direction the timetable offered seven FX, eight Fridays and Saturdays only passenger trains on weekdays together with one mixed train, whilst freight traffic was handled by one mandatory goods train and one 'Q' goods working. The mixed train, 8.08 am ex-Saxmundham, could work wagons from the London goods service for the Aldeburgh branch provided the total number of additional vehicles did not exceed 10 wagons, whilst the 7.37 pm (FX) and 8.22pm (FO) ex-Saxmundham could work not exceeding two piped wagons to Leiston and Aldeburgh. The 6.20 am goods train ex-Ipswich was worked on Saturdays by a dual-fitted engine, which then assisted the branch locomotive by working the 2.35 pm down passenger train and the 3.05 pm ECS return ex-Aldeburgh. After depositing the stock at Leiston the engine ran light to Saxmundham arriving at 3.28 pm to take up the 3.45 pm goods to Ipswich. The 'Q' goods train departed Saxmundham at 9.00 pm and as well as calling at Leiston, served Thorpeness siding if required. On Sundays the solitary passenger train departed Saxmundham at 7.58 pm.

The working timetable for the summer of 1939 showed eight FX, nine FO and eight SO passenger trains in the up direction on weekdays augmented by one mandatory freight train and one 'Q' conditional working. An additional passenger train, departing Aldeburgh at 5.28 pm (SO) operated in August only. The 7.14 am ex-Aldeburgh could attach cattle wagons at Leiston when required,

# SAXMUNDHAM AND ALDEBURGH.

## Single Line between Saxmundham Junction and Aldeburgh.

### DOWN WEEK DAYS.

| Miles from Saxmundham | | 1 Mxd. | 2 | 3 Gds. | 4 | 5 Pass. | 6 Pass. | 7 Pass. | 8 Pass. | 9 Pass. | 10 Pass. | 11 Pass. | 12 Pass. | 13 Pass. | 14 Pass. | 15 Pass. | 16 Pass. | 17 Pass. | 18 | 19 Pass. | 20 Gds. | 21 | 22 Pass. | 23 Pass. | 24 | 25 Pass. | 26 |
|---|---|---|---|---|---|---|---|---|---|---|---|---|---|---|---|---|---|---|---|---|---|---|---|---|---|---|---|
| | | | | 0.49 | | | | | SX | SX | | SO | | | | | FO FX | FX | | FO Q | | | SO | | | | |
| | | a.m. | a.m. | a.m. | a.m. | a.m. | a.m. | a.m. | p.m. | p.m. | p.m. | p.m. | p.m. | p.m. | p.m. | p.m. | p.m. | p.m. | | p.m. | p.m. | | p.m. | | | p.m. | |
| — | Ipswich ... dep. | | 4 45 | | | 9 50 | | | | 2 35 | 2 40 | | 3 43 | | 4 44 | 5 57 | 7 15 | 7 37 | | 8 18 | 8 0 | | 10 12 | | | 7 58 | |
| —34 | Saxmundham ... ⑤ n | 8 8 | 9 10 | 9 10 | | 9 51 | 2312 37 | | 2 36 | 2 41 | | 3 44 | | 4 45 | 5 58 | 7 16 | 7 38 | | 8 19 | 9 2 | | 10 13 | | | 7 59 | |
| | Saxmundham Jnc. ... ⑤ { dep. | 8 9 | 9 12 | 9 12 | | 9 59 | 2412 38 | | 2 44 | 2 49 | | 3 52 | | 4 53 | 6 6 | 7 24 | 7 46 | | 8 27 | 9 10 | | 10 21 | | | 8 7 | |
| 3 75 | Leiston (see note) ... ⑤ { arr. | 8 18 | 9 22 | 9 22 | | 10 0 | 3212 46 | | 2 45 | 2 50 | | 3 53 | | 4 54 | 6 7 | 7 24 | 7 47 | | 8 28 | 9 10 | | 10 22 | | | 8 8 | |
| | Leiston (see note) ... ⑤ { dep. | 8 21 | 9 22 | 10 56 | | 10 1 | 3312 47 | | 2 50 | 2 55 | | 3 58 | | 5 0 | 6 12 | 7 30 | 7 52 | | 8 33 | * | | 10 27 | | | 8 13 | |
| 6 22 | Thorpeness Halt ... arr. | 8 27 | | | | 10 11 | 4312 52 | | | | | 4 | | 5 | 6 17 | 7 35 | 7 57 | | 8 38 | 9 15 | | 10 32 | | | 8 18 | |
| 8 26 | Aldeburgh ... ⑤ arr. | 8 32 | | 11 15 | | | | | 2 55 | 3 0 | | | | 5 5 | | | | | | 9 25 | | | | | | |

=1 May work wagons of London goods for Aldeburgh, the total number not to exceed 10.

3 On Saturdays worked by dual-fitted engine.

=6 On Saturdays runs 5 mins. later.

=9 On Sats. worked by engine of 4.45 a.m. ex Ipswich. After 31st May runs Sats. only.

=10 Commences 1st June.

=17 & 19 May work not exceeding 2 piped wagons Saxmundham to Leiston & Aldeburgh.

### UP WEEK DAYS.

| Miles from Aldeburgh. | | 1 Pass. | 2 | 3 Pass. | 4 Pass. | 5 Pass. | 6 | 7 Pass. | 8 Gds. | 9 Gds. | 10 Pass. | 11 Pass. | 12 Pass. | 13 Cars. | 14 Eng. | 15 Pass. | 16 Pass. | 17 Mxd. | 18 Pass. | 19 Pass. | 20 Pass. | 21 Gds. | 22 Pass. | 23 Pass. | 24 | 25 Pass. | 26 |
|---|---|---|---|---|---|---|---|---|---|---|---|---|---|---|---|---|---|---|---|---|---|---|---|---|---|---|---|
| | | | | SO | | SX | | | C.53 | C.53 | SX | SO | SX | SO | SO | | | | FO FX | FX | | FO Q | | SO | | | |
| | | a.m. | | a.m. | a.m. | a.m. | | a.m. | p.m. | p.m. | p.m. | p.m. | p.m. | p.m. | p.m. | p.m. | p.m. | p.m. | p.m. | p.m. | p.m. | p.m. | p.m. | p.m. | | p.m. | |
| M.c. | Aldeburgh ... ⑤ dep. | 7 13 | | 8 57 | 2210 37 | 2210 37 | | 12 | 12 | 12 15 | 1 48 | 1 59 | 2 7 | 3 5 | 3 5 | 4 12 | 5 14 | | 6 41 | 7 4 | 7 41 | 8 10 | 9 35 | | | 6 7 | |
| 2 4 | Thorpeness Halt ... | 7 18 | | 10 10 | 2710 43 | | | 12 | 12 53 | 12 20 | 1 53 | 2 7 | 2 12 | 3 9 | 3 14 | 4 17 | 5 19 | | 6 46 | 7 7 | 7 45 | 8 20 | 9 40 | | | 6 12 | |
| 4 31 | Leiston (see note) ... ⑤ { arr. | 7 23 | | 2 10 | 3210 47 | | | 12 | 1 20 | 12 25 | 1 58 | 2 9 | 2 13 | 3 16 | | 4 22 | 5 24 | 5 29 | 6 51 | 7 15 | 7 51 | 8 28 | 9 45 | | | 6 13 | |
| | Leiston (see note) ... ⑤ { dep. | 7 24 | | 3 10 | 3410 48 | | | 12 | 1 | 12 57 | 1 59 | 2 10 | 2 18 | 3 27 | | 4 31 | | 5 38 | 6 52 | 7 23 | 7 52 | 8 43 | 9 54 | | | 6 21 | |
| 7 72 | Saxmundham Jnc. ... ⑤ { arr. | 7 32 | | 9 11 | 4210 57 | | | 12 21 | 1 35 | 1 37 | 2 7 | 2 18 | 2 21 | 3 28 | | 4 32 | | 5 39 | 7 0 | 7 23 | 8 0 | 8 43 | 9 54 | | | 6 21 | |
| 8 26 | Saxmundham ... ⑤ { dep. | 7 35 | | 9 12 | 4310 58 | | | 12 22 | 2 | 1 | 2 8 | 2 19 | 2 22 | | | | | | 7 1 | 7 24 | 8 1 | 8 45 | 9 55 | | | 6 22 | |
| | Ipswich ... arr. | | | | | | | 12 | 2 40 | 3 45 | | | | | | | | | | | | | | | | | |

=1 May attach cattle at Leiston in fitted vehicles when required. Allowed 2 mins. extra into Saxmundham as recovery time.

=4 Runs daily commencing 1st June.

=5 Not after 31st May.

8 & 9 To work Sizewell siding, near Leiston, and also Gas Works sidings but both sidings are not to be worked same day. Aldeburgh to make necessary arrangements. When either siding worked, to be due Leiston 12.35 p.m. on Mondays due Ipswich 5.15 p.m.

=10 Not after 31st May.

=11 Commences 1st June.

=16 & 17 To work passenger train fish vehicles from Aldeburgh and take in all passenger train fish vehicles in the guard's van or in a wagon. May work brake goods from Aldeburgh and Thorpeness Halt for up road stations at Thorpeness.

21 Works Sizewell siding when required

=25 May work not exceeding 2 piped wagons, Aldeburgh to Saxmundham.

NOTE.—Leiston. A ballast train or goods train may be allowed to leave Saxmundham Junc. or Aldeburgh for Leiston, and there be shunted clear into the down side siding next to the main single line, until it is again required to leave Leiston. After the ballast or goods train has arrived and been shunted clear, a down train or an up train may be accepted by the Leiston Signalman provided he is in a position to do so.

After the Leiston Signalman has accepted a down train from Saxmundham Junction he must not accept a down train from Aldeburgh. In like manner after the Leiston Signalman has accepted an up train from Aldeburgh he must not accept a down train from Saxmundham Junction.

Passenger trains must not be allowed to cross each other at Leiston station.

LNER working timetable 1937.

if the vehicles were fitted with continuous brake and two minutes additional running time was allowed to Saxmundham. The 5.14 pm ex-Aldeburgh was to work passenger train fish vehicles from Aldeburgh and take in all passenger train fish traffic from Thorpeness. It could also work 'brake goods' from Aldeburgh and Thorpeness Halt as previously described in the 1935 service. Some passenger services ran on specific Saturdays only in connection with Aldeburgh Regatta. The freight traffic was handled by the return of the 6.15 am down train from Ipswich running at an unspecified time which as well as calling at Leiston also worked Sizewell siding and Gas Works siding but not on the same day and with Aldeburgh station master making the necessary local arrangements. The 'Q' goods train departed Aldeburgh at 8.10 pm and worked Sizewell siding if required and Leiston to convey urgent traffic. This train did not operate when the 8.00 pm up and 8.35 pm down Fridays-only passenger trains operated. In the up direction the timetable showed paths for seven SX, eight FO and seven SO passenger trains together with a mixed train on weekdays augmented by the mandatory goods train and an additional 'Q' conditional working. The 8.09 am mixed train ex-Saxmundham was permitted to work wagons of London goods for Aldeburgh provided the total number of extra vehicles did not exceed 10. The 7.35 pm (FX), 8.18 pm (FO) and 8.35 pm (FO) down passenger services could work not exceeding two piped wagons from Saxmundham to Leiston and Aldeburgh, whilst the 5.02 pm ex-Saxmundham operated during the month of August only. The down mandatory 'bonus' goods service departed Ipswich at 6.15 am and shunted Saxmundham yard before continuing at an unspecified time to Leiston and Thorpeness, if required, to terminate at Aldeburgh. On Sundays four passenger trains ran in each direction with the 6.00 pm up train ex-Aldeburgh permitted to work not exceeding two piped wagons of goods traffic from Aldeburgh to Saxmundham.

Aldeburgh enjoyed the luxury of through coaches to and from Liverpool Street between 1906 and 1939, the coaches bearing a small destination indicator on the side of each vehicle labelled 'Saxmundham and Aldeburgh'. Typically in the early years of operation, coaches were attached during the summer timetable to the 8.47 am, 12.47, 2.01 and 4.22pm ex-Aldeburgh with return through coaches departing Liverpool Street at 10.27 am, 12.30 and 3.43 pm. A single winter through working departed Aldeburgh at 8.50 am and returned from Liverpool Street at 3.25 pm. Aldeburgh was also the regular terminus for the 'Eastern Belle' Pullman train from Liverpool Street in the summer months from June 1929 until the outbreak of World War II. The first train ran across the branch on Thursday 7th June, 1929, and from thereon each Thursday; Thorpeness and Aldeburgh were the regular destinations with timing of 2 hours 50 minutes for the 99½ mile journey. By 1933 Aldeburgh was reached in 2 hours 15 minutes and in 1935 the train departed Liverpool Street at 11.00 am on Tuesdays for Aldeburgh, returning at 7.15 pm with arrival back at Liverpool Street at 9.37 pm.

Following the outbreak of World War II on 3rd September, 1939, the LNER introduced an emergency timetable with effect from 2nd October, 1939 when the passenger services were reduced to five trains in each direction on weekdays with one train each way on Sundays retained:

| *Up* | | *Weekdays* | | | | | *Sundays* |
|---|---|---|---|---|---|---|---|
| | | am | am | am | pm | pm | pm |
| Aldeburgh | *dep.* | 7.10 | 8.25 | 10.25 | 2.00 | 6.30 | 3.40 |
| Thorpeness | *dep.* | 7.15 | 8.30 | 10.30 | 2.05 | 6.35 | 3.45 |
| Leiston | *dep.* | 7.23 | 8.40 | 10.40 | 2.15 | 6.45 | 3.55 |
| Saxmundham | *arr.* | 7.33 | 8.50 | 10.50 | 2.25 | 6.55 | 4.05 |
| Liverpool Street | *arr.* | | 12.04 | | 5.25 | 10.10 | 7.40 |

| *Down* | | *Weekdays* | | | | | *Sundays* |
|---|---|---|---|---|---|---|---|
| | | am | am | am | pm | pm | pm |
| Liverpool Street | *dep.* | | | 8.12 | 1.00 | 4.00 | 4.00 |
| Saxmundham | *dep.* | 7.50 | 9.40 | 11.05 | 4.00 | 8.00 | 7.25 |
| Leiston | *dep.* | 8.02 | 9.52 | 11.17 | 4.12 | 8.12 | 7.37 |
| Thorpeness | *dep.* | 8.09 | 9.59 | 11.24 | 4.19 | 8.19 | 7.44 |
| Aldeburgh | *arr.* | 8.15 | 10.05 | 11.30 | 4.25 | 8.25 | 7.50 |

After the initial precautions, matters improved and by April 1940 the branch passenger train service had been enhanced to six in each direction on weekdays, with the one train continuing on Sundays.

| *Up* | | *Weekdays* | | | | | | *Sundays* |
|---|---|---|---|---|---|---|---|---|
| | | am | am | am | pm | pm | pm | pm |
| Aldeburgh | *dep.* | 7.15 | 8.32 | 10.25 | 1.56 | 5.25 | 6.35 | 3.30 |
| Thorpeness | *dep.* | 7.20 | 8.37 | 10.30 | 2.01 | 5.30 | 6.40 | 3.35 |
| Leiston | *dep.* | 7.26 | 8.43 | 10.36 | 2.07 | 5.36 | 6.46 | 3.41 |
| Saxmundham | *arr.* | 7.35 | 8.52 | 10.45 | 2.16 | 5.50 | 6.55 | 3.50 |
| Liverpool Street | *arr.* | 10.45 | 11.35 | | 5.03 | | 9.41 | 6.50 |

| *Down* | | *Weekdays* | | | | | | *Sundays* |
|---|---|---|---|---|---|---|---|---|
| | | am | am | am | pm | pm | pm | pm |
| Liverpool Street | *dep.* | 4.40 | | 8.12 | 1.00 | 3.40 | 5.12 | 5.00 |
| Saxmundham | *dep.* | 8.00 | 9.40 | 11.05 | 4.05 | 6.09 | 7.55 | 8.09 |
| Leiston | *dep.* | 8.11 | 9.50 | 11.15 | 4.15 | 6.19 | 8.05 | 8.19 |
| Thorpeness | *dep.* | 8.16 | 9.55 | 11.20 | 4.20 | 6.24 | 8.10 | 8.24 |
| Aldeburgh | *arr.* | 8.21 | 10.00 | 11.25 | 4.25 | 6.29 | 8.15 | 8.29 |

From October 1940 the service was again reduced to five trains in each direction on weekdays, whilst the Sunday service was withdrawn and except for minor alterations in timings, this remained in operation throughout the war years. The timetable for 1943 showed the following service:

| *Up* | | *Weekdays* | | | | |
|---|---|---|---|---|---|---|
| | | am | am | pm | pm | pm |
| Aldeburgh | *dep.* | 7.15 | 8.35 | 12.48 | 5.25 | 6.39 |
| Thorpeness | *dep.* | 7.20 | 8.40 | 12.53 | 5.30 | 6.44 |
| Leiston | *dep.* | 7.26 | 8.46 | 12.59 | 5.40 | 6.51 |
| Saxmundham | *arr.* | 7.35 | 8.55 | 1.08 | 5.50 | 7.00 |
| Liverpool Street | *arr.* | 10.45 | 11.36 | 3.57 | | 10.15 |

| Down | | Weekdays | | | | |
|---|---|---|---|---|---|---|
| | | am | am | pm | pm | pm |
| Liverpool Street | dep. | 4.33 | 8.12 | 1.00 | 3.40 | 5.10 |
| Saxmundham | dep. | 8.00 | 11.03 | 4.05 | 6.10 | 8.07 |
| Leiston | dep. | 8.11 | 11.13 | 4.15 | 6.20 | 8.17 |
| Thorpeness | dep. | 8.16 | 11.18 | 4.20 | 6.25 | 8.22 |
| Aldeburgh | arr. | 8.21 | 11.23 | 4.25 | 6.30 | 8.27 |

By 1944 the freight train working timetable allowed for three paths in each direction with the mandatory 6.47 am ex-Ipswich departing Saxmundham at 8.17 am and terminating at Leiston at 8.25. An hour was permitted for shunting and formation of the up train before departure at 9.25 am as a through working to Melton. The 7.25 am ex-Ipswich ran as a 'bonus' working with no intermediate timings and calling at Leiston and Thorpeness siding before arrival at Aldeburgh. The outsorting and shunting was achieved as quickly as possible before the train returned to Ipswich at an unspecified time calling at Sizewell siding and Leiston Gas Works siding if required, with the station master at Aldeburgh making the necessary arrangements. An additional 'Q' path permitted an up road working from Aldeburgh departing at 8.35 pm to clear all outstanding goods traffic and calling at Sizewell siding, when required, as well as Leiston before terminating at Saxmundham. The return 'Q' run departed Saxmundham at 9.25 pm and as well as serving Leiston also called at Thorpeness when required before terminating at Aldeburgh at 9.50 pm.

The working timetable for passenger trains in 1945 showed a weekdays-only service of five trains in each direction with an additional 'Q' path departing 7.19 pm ex-Saxmundham to form the up 'Q' fish train departing Aldeburgh at 7.43 pm, the latter authorized by Norwich district control. In the up direction the 5.30 pm ex-Aldeburgh was allowed five minutes at Leiston and changed its status to that of a mixed train departing the intermediate station at 5.45 pm with arrival at Saxmundham at 5.55. The last down working of the day 8.14 pm ex-Saxmundham ran two minutes later on Mondays, Fridays and Saturdays.

The working timetable for 1949 showed a weekdays service in the up direction of six passenger trains, with the 4.50 pm ex-Aldeburgh changing status to a mixed train between Leiston and Saxmundham. The freight service, the return working of the 7.15 am 'bonus' train ex-Ipswich, ran at an unspecified time from Aldeburgh and served Sizewell siding and Gas Works siding if required as well as Leiston with the station master Aldeburgh making the necessary arrangements. Two weekdays-only Q 'as and when required' paths were available at 7.45 pm ex-Aldeburgh, for fish traffic to Saxmundham, with the district superintendent Norwich making the necessary arrangements and at 8.40 pm for goods traffic with the train serving Sizewell siding and Leiston before terminating at Saxmundham at 9.15 pm. In the down direction the six passenger trains were augmented by the 7.15 am 'bonus' goods train from Ipswich which after shunting the yard at Saxmundham ran across the branch at an unspecified time serving Leiston and Thorpeness. Two 'Q' paths were available at 7.19 pm ex-Saxmundham for empty coaching stock, to work the 7.43 pm up fish train and at 9.25 pm ex-Saxmundham for urgent goods traffic and calling at Leiston for five minutes before arriving at Aldeburgh at 9.50 pm. On Sunday evenings two passenger services ran in each direction.

# SAXMUNDHAM AND ALDEBURGH

Single Line between Saxmundham Junction and Aldeburgh.

## DOWN — WEEKDAYS / SUNDAYS

|  | No. | 1 | 2‡ | 3 | 4 | 5 | 6 | 7 | 8 | 9 | 10 | 11 | 12 | 13 | 14 | 15 |
|---|---|---|---|---|---|---|---|---|---|---|---|---|---|---|---|---|
| | Description | OP | | OP | OP | | OP | OP | ECS | OP | | | | | OP | OP |
| | Class | | B | | | | | | | | | | | | | |
| | Departs from | | Ipswich 7.25 a.m. | | | | | | | | | | | | | |
| | Previous Times on Page | L 58 | | | | | | | | | | | | | | |

|  | M. C. | am | am | am | PM | | PM | PM | PM (Q) | PM | PM (Q) | | | | PM | PM |
|---|---|---|---|---|---|---|---|---|---|---|---|---|---|---|---|---|
| — — | Saxmundham | 7 58 | * | 11 10 | 1 30 | .. | 4 5 | 6 16 | 7 19 | 8 10 | 9 25 | .. | .. | .. | 7 10 | 8 25 |
| — 34 | Saxmundham Junction (S) | 7 59 | | 11 11 | 1 31 | .. | 4 6 | 6 17 | 7 20 | 8 11 | 9 27 | | | | 7 11 | 8 26 |
| 3 75 | Leiston } See (S) | 8 7 | | 11 19 | 1 39 | .. | 4 14 | 6 25 | .. | 8 19 | 9 35 | | | | 7 19 | 8 34 |
| — — | Leiston } note | 8 9 | * | 11 20 | 1 40 | .. | 4 15 | 6 26 | 7 27 | 8 20 | 9 40 | | | | 7 20 | 8 35 |
| 6 22 | Thorpeness Halt | 8 14 | * | 11 25 | 1 45 | .. | 4 20 | 6 31 | .. | 8 25 | .. | | | | 7 25 | 8 40 |
| 8 26 | Aldeburgh (S) | 8 19 | DD | 11 30 | 1 50 | .. | 4 25 | 6 36 | 7 35 | 8 30 | 9 50 | | | | 7 30 | 8 45 |

2  To shunt Saxmundham and Leiston Yards.
8  When required District Supt., Norwich to arrange and advise all concerned.

## UP — WEEKDAYS / SUNDAYS

|  | No. | 1 | 2 | 3 | 4 | 5 | 6 | 7 | 8 | 9 | 10 | 11 | 12 | 13 | 14 | 15 |
|---|---|---|---|---|---|---|---|---|---|---|---|---|---|---|---|---|
| | Description | OP | OP | OP | | OP | OP | Mxd | OP | Fish | | | | | O P | OP |
| | Class | | | | | | | | | | | | | | | |

|  | M. C. | am | am | PM | PM | PM | PM | PM | PM | PM (Q) | PM (Q) | | | | PM | PM |
|---|---|---|---|---|---|---|---|---|---|---|---|---|---|---|---|---|
| — — | Aldeburgh (S) | 7 15 | 8 30 | 12 30 | U | 3 18 | 4 50 | .. | 6 42 | 7 43 | 8 40 | | | | 6 30 | 7 50 |
| 2 4 | Thorpeness Halt | 7 20 | 8 35 | 12 35 | .. | 3 23 | 4 55 | .. | 6 47 | .. | * | | | | 6 35 | 7 55 |
| 4 31 | Leiston } See (S) | 7 25 | 8 40 | 12 40 | * | 3 28 | 5 0 | .. | 6 52 | .. | 8 50 | | | | 6 40 | 8 0 |
| — — | Leiston } note | 7 26 | 8 41 | 12 41 | .. | 3 29 | .. | 5 5 | 6 54 | 7 51 | 8 58 | .. | | | 6 41 | 8 1 |
| 7 72 | Saxmundham Junction (S) | 7 34 | 8 49 | 12 49 | .. | 3 37 | .. | 5 14 | 7 2 | 7 58 | 9 13 | .. | | | 6 49 | 8 9 |
| 8 26 | Saxmundham | 7 35 | 8 50 | 12 50 | * | 3 38 | .. | 5 15 | 7 3 | 7 59 | 9 15 | .. | | | 6 50 | 8 10 |

|  | Arrives at | | | Ipswich | | | | | | | | | | | | |
|---|---|---|---|---|---|---|---|---|---|---|---|---|---|---|---|---|
| | Forward Times on Page | | | L 63 | | | | | | | | | | | | |

4  Return of 7.25 a.m. ex Ipswich. To work Sizewell Sidings, near Leiston, and also Gas Works Sidings. Aldeburgh to make necessary arrangements.
9  When required Dist., Supt., Norwich to arrange and advise all concerned.    10  To work Sizewell Sidings when required.

NOTE.—Leiston. A ballast train or goods train may be allowed to leave Saxmundham Junction or Aldeburgh for Leiston, and there may be shunted clear into the Down side Siding next to the main single line, until it is again required to leave Leiston. After the ballast or goods train has arrived and been shunted clear, a Down train or an Up train may be accepted by the Leiston Signalman provided he is in a position to do so.

After the Leiston Signalman has accepted a Down train from Saxmundham Junction he must not accept an Up train from Aldeburgh. In like manner after the Leiston Signalman has accepted an Up train from Aldeburgh he must not accept a Down train from Saxmundham Junction.

Passenger trains must not be allowed to cross each other at Leiston Station.

LNER working timetable 1947.

By June 1952 the BR/ER working timetable showed seven passenger trains in the up direction together with an ECS working departing at 8.14 pm. An additional ECS train departed Aldeburgh at 2.14 pm (SO). The 4.53 pm passenger train ex-Aldeburgh was down rated to run as a mixed train from Leiston for the onward journey to Saxmundham so that urgent goods traffic could be forwarded, and five minutes was allowed for attaching wagons. In the down direction, eight SX and nine SO passenger trains ran across the branch, the additional 2.50 pm (SO) service from Saxmundham being formed of the 2.14 pm up road ECS. Freight traffic was handled by the weekdays-only 'bonus' train, which departed Ipswich at 7.00 am and served Saxmundham and Leiston goods yards, and Thorpeness siding at unspecified times en route to Aldeburgh. The yard at the terminus was shunted as quickly as possible and the up train departing Aldeburgh at an unspecified time worked traffic to and from Sizewell siding and Leiston gas works siding if required as well as Leiston yard and Saxmundham en route to Ipswich. On Sundays the branch was served by four passenger trains in each direction commencing with the 9.50 am ex-Aldeburgh and finishing with the 8.45 pm ex-Saxmundham, which arrived at Aldeburgh at 9.05 pm. From September 1952 the Sunday services were withdrawn and the weekday service consisted of six trains in each direction and a class 'H' goods train each way. Up passenger trains departed Aldeburgh at 7.10, 8.30 am, 12.50, 3.30, 4.55 and 6.40 pm returning from Saxmundham at 7.53, 11.15 am, 1.30 (SO), 1.39 (SX), 4.15, 5.54 and 7.20 pm. The 'bonus' goods train departed Ipswich at 7.00 am and after calling at Saxmundham was pathed down the branch after the first passenger train, serving Leiston and Thorpeness if required. After shunting at Aldeburgh the train returned at an unspecified time pathed between the 3.30 and 4.55 pm up passenger services calling at Leiston and Saxmundham if required, and serving Sizewell siding and Gas Works sidings if there was any traffic.

The point-to-point running times of passenger trains in the 1950s were

| | | | |
|---|---|---|---|
| Down | Saxmundham and Leiston | 3 miles 75 chains | 9 minutes start to stop |
| | Leiston to Thorpeness Halt | 2 miles 27 chains | 4 minutes start to stop |
| | Thorpeness to Aldeburgh | 2 miles 04 chains | 5 minutes start to stop |
| Up | Aldeburgh to Thorpeness Halt | 2 miles 04 chains | 4 minutes start to stop |
| | Thorpeness Halt to Leiston | 2 miles 27 chains | 5 minutes start to stop |
| | Leiston to Saxmundham | 3 miles 75 chains | 9 minutes start to stop |

The time allowed for engines from departure on the locomotive shed to departure of the train from the station, yard or sidings at Aldeburgh was five minutes.

The introduction of diesel-multiple-unit workings on the branch from 1956 found the weekdays-only services operated from Ipswich, with in some cases through trains between Aldeburgh and Ipswich. The two-car unit allocated to work the branch departed as empty coaching stock from Ipswich at 6.10 am to take up the first up branch working, the 7.10 am Aldeburgh to Saxmundham and 7.53 am return. The set then returned from Aldeburgh to Ipswich at 8.24 am as a through train covering the 30½ miles in 54 minutes with five intermediate stops. A second set departed Ipswich at 10.16 am as a through train to Aldeburgh with the same five intermediate stops with a 52 minutes timing. A round trip was made to

## L24   WEEKDAYS — YARMOUTH TO LOWESTOFT, ALDEBURGH, FRAMLINGHAM, FELIXSTOWE AND IPSWICH

### UP

| M | C | M | .C | M | C | Station | No. | G (LE's) | G (LE) | K (To Lowestoft S. Side arr 8.21 am) | K | K (Q) | K | K (Oulton Broad N. arr 10.56, dep 11.23 am) | K (To Lowestoft S. Side arr 11.48 am; Lowestoft N. arr 1.0 pm) | K | G (LE) |
|---|---|---|---|---|---|---|---|---|---|---|---|---|---|---|---|---|---|
| | | | | | | | | am | am | am | am | am | am | | am | am | PM |
| 0 | 0 | | | 0 | 0 | YARMOUTH S.T. ... dep | 1 | | | | | | | | 11 30 | | |
| 4 | 1 | | | | | Belton and Burgh .. .. | 2 | | | | | | | | | | |
| 6 | 42 | | | | | St. Olaves ............ | 3 | | | | | | | | | | |
| 7 | 13 | | | | | Haddiscoe .. .. .. arr | 4 | | | | | | | | | | |
| | | | | | | ...... dep | 5 | | | | | | | | | | |
| 7 | 44 | | | | | Fleet Jn. .. .. | 6 | | | | | | | | | | |
| 9 | 27 | | | | | Aldeby ............ arr | 7 | | | | | | | | | | |
| | | | | | | .. .. dep | 8 | | | | | | | | | | |
| | | | | 2 | 52 | Gorleston on Sea .... arr | 9 | | | | | | | | 11 45 | | |
| | | | | | | .... dep | 10 | | | | | | | | | 12 40 | |
| | | | | 4 | 53 | Hopton on Sea ........ | 11 | | | | | | | | | | |
| | | | | 6 | 61 | Corton .. .. .. | 12 | | | | | | | | | | |
| | | | | 8 | 14 | Lowestoft North ...... | 13 | | | | | | | | 1 15 | | |
| | | 0 | 0 | 10 | 29 | LOWESTOFT CEN. arr | 14 | | | | | | | | 1 26 | | |
| | | 2 | 12 | | | ...... dep | 15 | 5‖32 | | | | 8 14 | | 10 48 | | | |
| | | | | | | Oulton Broad South.. arr | 16 | | | | | 8 25 | | 11 28 | | | |
| | | | | | | ...... dep | 17 | | | | | 8 35 | | 11 38 | | | |
| 12 | 46 | 8 | 40 | | | BECCLES .. .. arr | 18 | 5‖52 | | | | | | | | | |
| | | | | | | ...... dep | 19 | | | | | | | | | | |
| 17 | 11 | | | | | Brampton .. .. arr | 20 | | | | | | | | | | |
| | | | | | | .. dep | 21 | | 6‖30 | | | | | | | | |
| 21 | 7 | | | | | Halesworth .. .. arr | 22 | | | | | | | | | | |
| | | | | | | .. dep | 23 | | 6‖50 | | | | | | | | |
| 26 | 27 | | | | | Darsham.. .. .. arr | 24 | | | | | | | | | | |
| | | | | | | .. dep | 25 | | | | | | | | | | |
| | | 0 | 0 | | | ALDEBURGH .. dep | 26 | | | | | | | | | | |
| | | 2 | 4 | | | Thorpeness Halt ...... | 27 | | | | | | | | | | |
| | | 4 | 31 | | | Leiston .. .. .. | 28 | | | | | | | | | | |
| 30 | 19 | 7 | 72 | | | Saxmundham Jn. ........ | 29 | | | | | | | | | | |
| 30 | 53 | 8 | 26 | | | SAXMUNDHAM .. arr | 30 | | | | | | | | | | |
| | | | | | | ...... dep | 31 | | | | | | | | | | |
| 33 | 52 | 0 | 0 | | | SNAPE .. .. .. | 32 | | | | | | | | | | |
| | | 1 | 32 | | | Snape Jn. .. .. arr | 33 | | | | | | | | | | |
| | | 0 | 0 | | | FRAMLINGHAM .. dep | 34 | | | | | | 10 50 | | | 11 55 | |
| | | 2 | 29 | | | Parham Halt ............ | 35 | | | | | | 11 5 | | | | |
| | | 4 | 57 | | | Mariesford ............ | 36 | | | | | | | | | | |
| 36 | 46 | 5 | 46 | | | Wickham M. Jn. .......... | 37 | | | | | | | | | 12 33 | |
| 37 | 17 | 6 | 37 | | | WICKHAM MARKET arr | 38 | | | | | | | | | 12 35 | |
| 41 | 34 | | | | | Melton .. .. .. arr | 39/40 | | | | | | | | | | 12‖55 |
| 42 | 61 | | | | | Woodbridge .. .. arr | 41/42 | | | | | | | | | | |
| 45 | 62 | | | | | Bealings .. .. .. | 43/44 | | | | | | | | | | 1 10 |
| | | 0 | 0 | | | FELIXSTOWE DK. dep | 45 | | | | 9 10 | | | | | | |
| | | 0 | 66 | | | Felixstowe Beach .. arr | 46 | | | | 9 15 | | | | | | |
| | | 2 | 16 | | | FELIXSTOWE TN. arr | 47/48 | | | | | | | | | | |
| | | 3 | 67 | | | Trimley .. .. .. arr | 49/50 | | | | | | | | | | |
| | | 8 | 49 | | | Orwell .. .. .. arr | 51/52 | | | | | | | | | | |
| | | 11 | 65 | | | Derby Road .. .. arr | 53/54 | | | | | | | | | | |
| 49 | 40 | 14 | 30 | | | Westerfield .. .. arr | 55/56 | | | | | | | | | | 1 26 |
| 52 | 63 | 17 | 50 | | | Ipswich Goods Yard .. arr | 57/58 | | | | | | | | | | |
| 53 | 5 | 17 | 72 | | | IPSWICH STATION arr | 59/60 | | | | | | | | | | 1‖38 |
| | | | | | | ...... dep | 61 | | | | | | | | | | |

Notes (column annotations, reading left to right):
- G (LE's): To work 6.40 am to Lowestoft, and Beccles shunting engine.
- G (LE): To perform shunting duties at Halesworth and then proceed to Darsham about 2.35 pm for shunting, returning to Halesworth when finished.
- K: To be worked with two brakes. Calls at CWS and Kirkley Sidings.
- G (LE): After working 11.55 am from Framlingham.

BR (ER) freight working timetable 1955.

## YARMOUTH TO LOWESTOFT, ALDEBURGH, FRAMLINGHAM, FELIXSTOWE AND IPSWICH WEEKDAYS — L 25

| | K | K | K | K | J | K | K | K | K | H | K | F | E | D |
|---|---|---|---|---|---|---|---|---|---|---|---|---|---|---|
| | 11.45 am from Ditchingham | | | | 2.35 pm from Wen um Jn. | | | | | | | | | To Splashfields |
| | | | MSO | MSX | | | SX | SO | | SX | | | | |
| | PM | PM | PM | PM | PM | PM | PM | PM | PM | PM | PM | PM | PM | PM |
| 1 | | | | | | 1 20 | | | | | | | 7 40 | |
| 2 | | | | | | 1 45 | | | | | | | | |
| 3 | | | | | | R | | | | | | | | |
| 4 | | | | | | 2 12 | | | | | | | | |
| 5 | | | | | | 3 48 | | | | | | | | |
| 6 | | | | | 3 23 | 3 53 | | | | | | | | |
| 7 | | | | | | | | | | | | | | |
| 8 | | | | | | | | | | | | | | |
| 9 | | | | | | | | | | | | | | |
| 10 | | | | | | | | | | | | | | |
| 11 | | | | | | | | | | | | | | |
| 12 | | | | | | | | | | | | | | |
| 13 | | | | | | | | | | | | | | |
| 14 | | | | | | | | | | | | | | |
| 15 | | | | | | | | | | | | 4 32 | | 8 40 |
| 16 | | | | | | | | | | | | 4 42 | | |
| 17 | | | | | | | | | | | | 4 52 | | |
| 18 | 12 10 | | | | 3 39 | 4 9 | | | | | | 5 8 | 8 10 | 8 58 |
| 19 | | | | | | | | | | | | 5 20 | | 9 42 |
| 20 | | | | | | | | | | | | R | | |
| 21 | | | | | | | | | | | | | | |
| 22 | | | | | | | | | | | | 5 57 | | |
| 23 | | | | | | | | | | | | 6 32 | | 10 1 |
| 24 | | | | | | | | | | | | 6 48 | | |
| 25 | | | | | | | | | | | | 7 32 | | |
| 26 | | | Also serves Snape | Also serves Snape | | | U | U | | | | | | |
| 27 | | | | | | | | | | | | | | |
| 28 | | | | | | | R | R | | | | | | |
| 29 | | | | | | | R | R | | | | | | |
| 30 | | | | | | | R | R | | | | 7 47 | | |
| 31 | | | U | U | | | | | | | | 8 15 | | 10 18 |
| 32 | | | R | R | | | | | | | | | | |
| 33 | | | R | R | | | | | | | | | | |
| 34 | | | | | | | | | | | | | | |
| 35 | | | | | | | | | | | | | | |
| 36 | | | | | | | | | | | | | | |
| 37 | | | | | | | | | | | | | | |
| 38 | | | | R | | | | | R | | | 8 34 | | |
| 39 | | | | | | | | | | | | 9 8 | | 10 30 |
| 40 | | | R | R | | | | | | | | 9 22 | | |
| 41 | | | | | | | | | | | | 9 37 | | |
| 42 | | | R | R | | | | | | | | 9 45 | | |
| 43 | | | | | | | | | | | | 10 12 | | 10 38 |
| 44 | | | R | | | | R | | | | | | | |
| 45 | | | | | | | | 2 58 | | | | | | |
| 46 | | | | | | | | | | | | | | |
| 47 | | | | | | | | | | | | | | |
| 48 | | | | | | | | 3X 8 | | | | | | |
| 49 | | | | | | | | | | | | 4 15 | | |
| 50 | | | | | | | | | | | | 4 22 | | |
| 51 | | | | | | | | | | | | 4 40 | | |
| 52 | | | | | | | | | | | | 4 55 | | |
| 53 | | | | | | | | | | | | 5 15 | | |
| 54 | | | | | | | | | | | 4 56 | 5X25 | | |
| 55 | | 1 30 | | | | | | | | | 5 0 | 5 55 | | |
| 56 | | | | | | | | | | | 6 7 | | | |
| 57 | | 1 40 | | | | | | | | | 5 9 | 6 30 | 10 31 | 10 51 |
| 58 | | 1 54 | D | D | | | D | D | | | 5 20 | 6 45 | 10 43 | 10 58 |
| 59 | | | | | | | | | | | | | | 11 48 |
| 60 | | | | | | | | | | | | | | 11 L52 |
| 61 | | | | | | | | | | | | | | 11 L55 |

Notes (vertical): column J — "Belton and Burgh arr 1.35 pm, Fleet Jn. arr 2.27, dep 2.8 pm"; column — "After working trip from Messrs Ransomes, Sims & Jefferies Ltd Siding".

BR (ER) freight working timetable 1955 (continued).

'J15' class 0-6-0 No. 65459 pulling the Aldeburgh branch train clear of the up platform at Saxmundham before shunting the stock back over the points across the down main line and into the goods yard ready to form a return working. The train is standing on the up main line opposite the south end of the north section of the down platform with the moveable section of platform forming part of the level crossing spanning Chantry Road on 19th July, 1952. The houses in the background are in Alma Place.                                                                 *J.H. Meredith*

'B12/3' class 4-6-0 No. 61571 is deputizing for a failed 'F6' class tank locomotive as she climbs the 1 in 58 away from Saxmundham Junction with a three-coach branch train formed of Thompson 4-compartment brake/third, a lavatory composite and a third lavatory non-gangwayed stock.                                                                 *The late Dr I.C. Allen*

'F6' class 2-4-2T No. 67230 swings off the East Suffolk main line at Saxmundham Junction and on to the Aldeburgh branch with a down train formed of Gresley LNER 4-compartment brake third to diagram 64 or 65 and LNER lavatory composite with 2 x first class compartments/lavatory and 4 x third class compartments. *The late Dr I.C. Allen*

'F6' class 2-4-2T No. 67220 makes heavy weather of the climb away from Saxmundham Junction with the 4.32 pm Saxmundham to Aldeburgh train on 27th July, 1954. The leading coach is No. E21980. *G.R. Mortimer*

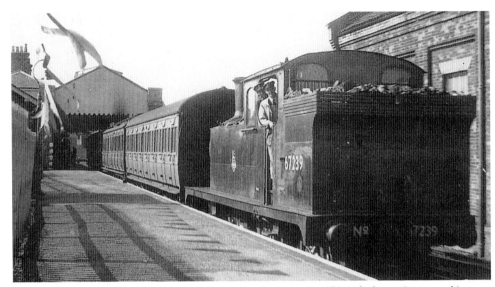

'F6' class 2-4-2T No. 67239 standing at Aldeburgh station in 1956 with the enginemen taking interest in the cameraman. The three-coach train stands with the rear vehicle under the train shed. The goods shed is to the right whilst bunting suspended between the station lamps celebrates the annual Aldeburgh Regatta.                    *Author's Collection*

'F6' class 2-4-2T No. 67239 waiting to depart from the down platform at Saxmundham with the Aldeburgh branch train.                    *Author's Collection*

Saxmundham before the unit departed for Ipswich at 12.35 pm. A third unit departed Ipswich at 1.47 pm arriving at Aldeburgh at 2.43 pm SX; three round trips were then made to Saxmundham before the dmu returned to Ipswich at 8.10 pm. Freight traffic was conveyed by a single 'bonus' trip working from Ipswich departing at 7.10 am and serving intermediate station yards to Aldeburgh as required and running at unspecified times before returning to Ipswich.

The passenger service in the summer of 1959 operated by dmus showed 10 trains in the up direction SX and nine SO, three of which worked through to Ipswich together with seven trains on Sundays, two working through to Ipswich. In the down direction nine SX and eight SO trains ran across the branch with only one working through from Ipswich. On Sundays seven trains ran with two working through from Ipswich. The winter working timetable from 2nd November, 1959 to 12th June, 1960 showed weekdays-only services drastically reduced (see overleaf).

By the summer of 1962 a reduced service was offered with eight trains in each direction on weekdays and seven trains each way on Sundays. Down trains departed Saxmundham at 6.51, 7.49, 11.28 am, 2.36, 3.53, 5.28, 6.52 and 8.03 pm returning from Aldeburgh at 7.20, 8.19 am, 12.18, 3.18, 4.56, 6.18, 7.23 and 8.33 pm. The 2.36 pm down train started back from Ipswich at 2.00 pm calling at all stations to Saxmundham, whilst the 8.19 am, 12.18 and 8.33 pm were through trains to Ipswich arriving at 9.18 am, 1.18 and 9.30 pm respectively, the latter running non-stop from Saxmundham to Ipswich. On Sundays down trains departed Saxmundham at 9.25, 10.34 am, 12.13, 1.21, 4.55, 6.33 and 8.21 pm returning from Aldeburgh at 10.00, 11.40 am, 12.50, 2.05, 5.36, 7.45 and 8.58 pm. The 9.25 am and 4.55 pm were through trains from Ipswich starting at 8.50 am and 4.20 pm respectively and calling at all stations to Saxmundham, whilst on the up road the 2.05 and 8.58 pm ex-Aldeburgh worked through to Ipswich, arriving at 3.02 pm and 9.59 pm respectively, calling at all stations from Saxmundham. The weekdays-only freight service was operated as a 'bonus' trip from Ipswich and return running at unspecified times and terminating at and starting back from Leiston, as freight facilities had been withdrawn from Thorpeness and Aldeburgh on and from 30th November, 1959.

The winter timetable for 1964/65 provided a service of seven trains in each direction on weekdays only departing Saxmundham at 6.37, 7.51, 11.51 am, 2.28, 3.51, 5.37 and 6.53 pm returning from Aldeburgh at 7.04, 8.19 am, 12.19, 2.56, 5.08, 6.16 and 7.20 pm. The 2.28 pm down train from Saxmundham started back at Ipswich at 1.54 pm, whilst the 8.19 am and 12.19 pm up trains from Aldeburgh were through trains to Ipswich calling at all stations and arriving at 9.18 am and 1.18 pm respectively. The last up working, 7.20 pm ex-Aldeburgh, was a through train to Colchester SX and Ipswich SO arriving at 8.45 and 8.20 pm respectively. The dmus were permitted between 22 and 24 minutes running time for the journey across the branch. It is interesting to note that the working timetable for the same period shown herein quoted 24 hour timings and even included half-minute arrivals, departures and passing times! This basic timetable remained in operation until the withdrawal of passenger traffic.

Occasional freight traffic, usually to Messrs Charrington, fuel depot at the former Gas Works siding, continued to be handled at Leiston with 'bonus' workings from Ipswich until the service was withdrawn on 7th May, 1984.

# Working Timetable 2nd November 1959 to 12th June, 1960

## Up

| Up | | am | pm | pm | pm | pm | pm | SX pm | SO pm | SO pm |
|---|---|---|---|---|---|---|---|---|---|---|
| Aldeburgh | dep. | 7.10 | 12.23 | 3.23 | 5.00 | 6.23 | 7.14 | 8.23 | 8.23 | 9.23 |
| Thorpeness Halt | dep. | 7.14½ | 12.27½ | 3.27½ | 5.04½ | 6.27½ | | 8.27½ | 8.27½ | 9.27½ |
| Leiston | dep. | 7a20½ | 12a33½ | 3a33½ | 5a10½ | 6a33½ | 7a22 | 8a33½ | 8a33½ | 9a33½ |
| Saxmundham Jn | pass | 7.27½ | 12.40½ | 3.40½ | 5.17½ | 6.40½ | 7.29 | 8.40½ | 8.40½ | 9.40½ |
| Saxmundham | arr. | 7.28½ | 12.41½ | 3.41½ | 5.18½ | 6.41½ | 7.30 | 8.41½ | 8.41½ | 9.41½ |
| Ipswich | dep. | 8.45½ | 12.45½ | | | | | 8.42½ | | 9.42½ |
| Ipswich | arr. | 9.18½ | 1.18½ | | | | | 9.10½ | | 10.10½ |

## Down

| Down | | am | am | pm | pm | pm | pm | SX pm | SO pm | SO pm |
|---|---|---|---|---|---|---|---|---|---|---|
| Ipswich | dep. | 6.03* | 10.20 | | | | | | | |
| Saxmundham | arr. | 6.39* | 10.53½ | | | | | | | |
| Saxmundham | dep. | 6.43 | 10.54½ | 2.59½ | 4.07 | 5.50 | 6.52 | 7.43 | 7.53 | 8.59½ |
| Saxmundham Jn | pass | 6.44 | 10.55½ | 3.00½ | 4.08 | 5.51 | 6.53 | 7.44 | 7.54 | 9.00½ |
| Leiston | dep. | 6c53 | 11a03½ | 3a08½ | 4c16 | 5c59 | 7c01 | 7a52 | 8a02 | 9a08½ |
| Thorpeness Halt | dep. | 6.57½ | 11.08 | 3.13 | 4.20½ | 6.03½ | | 7.56½ | 8.06½ | 9.13 |
| Aldeburgh | arr. | 7.01 | 11.13 | 3.18 | 4.25½ | 6.08½ | 7.08½ | 8.01½ | 8.11½ | 9.18 |

### Notes

* Class C parcels train from Ipswich to Saxmundham.
a arrives one minute earlier.
c arrives two minutes earlier.
SO Saturdays only
SX Saturdays excepted

# Table 28     SAXMUNDHAM and ALDEBURGH

## (Diesel Trains)

### MONDAYS TO FRIDAYS

| Miles | | am | am | am C | am | pm | pm | pm | pm | pm | pm |
|---|---|---|---|---|---|---|---|---|---|---|---|
| | 3 London (L'pool St) dep | .. | 4 35 | 8 30 | 9 39 | 12 39 | 1 30 | 3 39 | 4 30 | 5 30 | 6 39 |
| — | Saxmundham .... dep | 6 43 | 7 46 | 10 58 | 12 2 | 3 2 | 4 7 | 5 54 | 6 55 | 7 43 | 9 5 |
| 4 | Leiston ...... | 6 53 | 7 55 | 11 7 | 12 11 | 3 11 | 4 16 | 6 3 | 7 4 | 7 52 | 9 14 |
| 6¼ | Thorpeness.... | | 7 59 | 11 12 | 12 16 | 3 16 | 4 20 | 6 7 | | 7 56 | 9 19 |
| 8¼ | Aldeburgh ...... arr | 7 4 | 8 8 | 11 17 | 12 21 | 3 21 | 4 27 | 6 13 | 7 12 | 8 5 | 9 24 |

### SATURDAYS ONLY

| | am | am | am C | am | pm | pm | pm | pm | pm |
|---|---|---|---|---|---|---|---|---|---|
| 3 London (L'pool St) dep | .. | 4 35 | 7650 | 9 39 | 12 39 | 1T39 | 3 39 | 5 30 | 6 39 |
| Saxmundham ...... dep | 6 43 | 7 46 | 10 39 | 11 54 | 2 54 | 4 19 | 6 20 | 7 53 | 9 6 |
| Leiston . ...... | 6 53 | 7 55 | 10 48 | 12 3 | 3 3 | 4 28 | 6 29 | 8 2 | 9 15 |
| Thorpeness.......... | | 7 59 | 10 53 | 12 7 | 3 7 | 4 32 | 6 33 | 8 6 | 9 20 |
| Aldeburgh .... arr | 7 4 | 8 8 | 11 0 | 12 13 | 3 15 | 4 38 | 6 41 | 8 14 | 9 27 |

### SUNDAYS

| | am C | am | am | am | am | pm C | pm | pm |
|---|---|---|---|---|---|---|---|---|
| 3 London (L'pool St) dep | 6†15 | .. | .. | 10H 8 | 10 33 | 3 30 | .. | 5 35 |
| Saxmundham ...... dep | 9 22 | 10 17 | 11 20 | 12 36 | 1 35 | 6 20 | 7 36 | 8 58 |
| Leiston . ...... | 9 31 | 10 26 | 11 29 | 12 45 | 1 44 | 6 29 | 7 45 | 9 7 |
| Thorpeness.......... | 9 35 | 10 30 | 11 33 | 12 49 | 1 48 | 6 33 | 7 49 | 9 11 |
| Aldeburgh .... arr | 9 41 | 10 36 | 11 39 | 12 55 | 1 54 | 6 39 | 7 55 | 9 17 |

### MONDAYS TO FRIDAYS

| Miles | | am | am C | am | pm C | pm | pm | pm | pm | pm | pm C |
|---|---|---|---|---|---|---|---|---|---|---|---|
| — | Aldeburgh . .. dep | 7 10 | 8 23 | 11 22 | 12 26 | 3 26 | 5 0 | 6 23 | 7 16 | 8 23 | 9 29 |
| 2 | Thorpeness............ | 7 14 | 8 27 | 11 26 | 12 30 | 3 30 | 5 4 | 6 27 | | 8 27 | 9 33 |
| 4¼ | Leiston ............. | 7 20 | 8 33 | 11 32 | 12 36 | 3 36 | 5 10 | 6 33 | 7 24 | 8 33 | 9 39 |
| 8¼ | Saxmundham ...... arr | 7 29 | 8 42 | 11 41 | 12 45 | 3 45 | 5 19 | 6 42 | 7 34 | 8 42 | 9 48 |
| 99¼ | 3 London (L'pool St) arr | 10B 9 | 10 55 | 2 36 | 3 30 | 6 39 | .. | 9 11 | 10 19 | 12a 9 | 4a 0 |

### SATURDAYS ONLY

| | am | am C | am | pm C | pm | pm | pm | pm | pm C |
|---|---|---|---|---|---|---|---|---|---|
| Aldeburgh . .. dep | 7 10 | 8 23 | 11 26 | 12 17 | 3 20 | 5 22 | 7 4 | 8 17 | 9 41 |
| Thorpeness............ | 7 14 | 8 27 | 11 30 | 12 22 | 3 24 | 5 27 | 7 9 | 8 22 | 9 46 |
| Leiston . ........... | 7 20 | 8 33 | 11 36 | 12 28 | 3 30 | 5 33 | 7 15 | 8 28 | 9 52 |
| Saxmundham ...... arr | 7 29 | 8 42 | 11 45 | 12 36 | 3 39 | 5 41 | 7 23 | 8 36 | 10 0 |
| 3 London (L'pool St) arr | 10 5 | 10 55 | 2 39 | 3 12 | 6 39 | 8 0 | 10 18 | 12a 9 | .. |

### SUNDAYS

| | am | am | am | pm | pm C | pm | pm | pm C |
|---|---|---|---|---|---|---|---|---|
| Aldeburgh . .. dep | 9 45 | 10 46 | 11 56 | 1 0 | 2 22 | 6 53 | 8 11 | 9 21 |
| Thorpeness............ | 9 50 | 10 51 | 12 1 | 1 5 | 2 27 | 6 58 | 8 18 | 9 26 |
| Leiston . .. .. .. | 9 56 | 10 57 | 12 7 | 1 11 | 2 33 | 7 4 | 8 22 | 9 32 |
| Saxmundham ...... arr | 10 4 | 11 5 | 12 15 | 1 19 | 2 41 | 7 12 | 8 30 | 9 40 |
| 3 London (L'pool St) arr | 12L48 | 2J 5 | .. | .. | 5 20 | 9 50 | 12a12 | 4a 0 |

Tickets from Aldeburgh and Thorpeness are issued on the train

† Second class only between Liverpool Street and Chelmsford
c am
B On Mondays arr Liverpool Street 10 5 am

C Through Train from or to Ipswich (Table 3)
6 From 8th July to 26th August dep Liverpool Street 8 14 am
H Runs 25th June to 3rd September inclusive

J Not after 23rd July
L Commences 30th July
T On 9th September dep Liverpool Street 1 30 pm

BR (ER) public timetable 1961.

'J17' class 0-6-0 No. 65510 works an up freight train from Aldeburgh near Sheepwash level crossing. The 'bonus' train to Ipswich is formed of three wooden-bodied open wagons, a former Southern Railway covered van and brake van for the first leg of its journey. The locomotive is fitted with a 2,640 gallons capacity low-sided tender.                    *The late Dr I.C. Allen*

BTH/Paxman type '1' 800 hp diesel-electric locomotives Nos. D8222 and D8224 were booked to work an Ipswich to Coltishall sand train, which was cancelled and the pair worked the Leiston coal train instead. Here they are seen on the return working from Leiston to Ipswich with two empty 16 tons all-steel mineral wagons and an ex-LMS goods brake van.    *The late Dr I.C. Allen*

Thereafter atomic flask trains have been the only user of the line working to and from Sizewell siding on an 'as and when required' basis. By 1998 the train serving the branch running as 7Z58 departed Sellafield at 18.15. In 2000 the flask train ran as 7L50 Willesden Brent Sidings to Sizewell and 7M69 15.49 hours return (Mondays and Saturdays excepted). After working the Direct Rail Services Sizewell and Southminster flask trains, the pair of class '20/3' diesel-electric locomotives then ran light to Norwich Crown Point depot as 0L32 on Tuesdays, Wednesdays and Thursdays only for fuelling and returned as 0M31 10.40 on Mondays, Tuesdays and Wednesdays only to pick up their next workings. By 2002 the train ran as 7L70 09.10 Willesden to Sizewell and 7M69 16.33 ex Sizewell usually running on Wednesdays and Fridays only, although a path was available if required on other days. Despite the shutdown of Sizewell A reactor on 31st December, 2006 it was anticipated trains conveying contaminated fuel would continue for some time and the flask train ran in 2007 as the 04.46 Willesden to Sizewell and the 15.34 return although these timings were rarely adhered to. Sizewell B reactor had an unexplained shutdown on 27th May, 2008 and was then taken off line in March and July 2010 thereafter operating an 18 month operating cycle followed by one month shutdown for maintenance. On 2nd March, 2012 Sizewell B had another unplanned shutdown due to an electrical fault and was later restarted at half capacity. As of June 2012 the reactor was under carefully controlled operation. At the time of writing (2012) the service is operated by Direct Rail Services and after a period without traffic the service resumed on 6th May, 2009, following a trial run on 27th January and the visit of an inspection saloon on 19th February. Regular movements from Sellafield via Crewe and Willesden have continued varying between two and six trains per month in 2010, increasing to between two and nine in 2011. To June 2012 the number of trains has increased varying between four and eight. In all cases trains ran on weekdays only and were hauled by pairs of class '37s' or class '20s', and class '37' with a class '20' locomotives and on occasion by two class '37s' with a class '20'. Individual numbers of locomotives are given in Chapter Ten.

### Fares

In the first years of operation first, second, third and Parliamentary class fares were offered. The latter referred to travel at 1*d*. per mile, which had to be provided by at least one train in each direction on weekdays under the Act of 1844. The initial fare table from London to Saxmundham and Leiston showed separate first and second class charges for travel by express or ordinary trains, the first and second class single fare by express train to Saxmundham being £1 1*s*. 4*d*. and 16*s*. 10*d*. and to Leiston £1 2*s*. 2*d*. and 17*s*. 6*d*. respectively. Single fares by ordinary services from Bishopsgate were unchanged in 1862, and the separate express fare was no longer applicable.

| Bishopsgate to | First single | | Second single | | Third single | | Parliamentary single | |
|---|---|---|---|---|---|---|---|---|
| | s. | d. | s. | d. | s. | d. | s. | d. |
| Saxmundham | 18 | 10 | 15 | 1 | 11 | 4 | 7 | 6 ½ |
| Leiston | 19 | 8 | 15 | 9 | 11 | 10 | 7 | 10 ½ |
| Aldeburgh | 20 | 4 | 16 | 1 | 12 | 0 | 8 | 3 |

By 1882 the fares from Liverpool Street showed a slight reduction compared with two decades earlier and continued to include facilities for Parliamentary fare paying passengers.

| | First single | First return | Second single | Second return | Third single | Third return | Parliamentary single |
|---|---|---|---|---|---|---|---|
| | s. d. | s. d. | s. d. | s. d. | s. d. | s. d. | s. d. |
| Saxmundham | 17 0 | 25 6 | 13 0 | 20 5 | 10 0 | 16 0 | 7 7 |
| Leiston | 17 8 | 26 6 | 13 6 | 21 4 | 10 6 | 16 10 | 7 11 |
| Aldeburgh | 18 8 | 28 0 | 14 2 | 22 4 | 11 0 | 17 8 | 8 3 |

Local fares from Saxmundham to stations on the branch were:

| | First single | First return | Second single | Second return | Third single | Third return | Parliamentary single |
|---|---|---|---|---|---|---|---|
| | s. d. | s. d. | s. d. | s. d. | s. d. | s. d. | s. d. |
| Leiston | 8 | 1 0 | 6 | 11 | 6 | 10 | 4 |
| Aldeburgh | 1 8 | 2 6 | 1 2 | 1 11 | 1 0 | 1 8 | 8 |

Following the abolition of second class accommodation outside the London area with effect from 1st January, 1893, only first and third class fares were offered. The tariff from Liverpool Street in 1915 showed significant third class reductions compared with 1882.

| | First single | | First return | | | Third single | | Third return | |
|---|---|---|---|---|---|---|---|---|---|
| | £ | s. | d. | £ | s. | d. | £ | s. | d. |
| Saxmundham | | 17 | 0 | 1 | 5 | 6 | 7 | 8 | 15 | 4 |
| Leiston | | 17 | 8 | 1 | 6 | 6 | 8 | 0 | 16 | 0 |
| Thorpeness Halt | | 18 | 2 | 1 | 7 | 2 | 8 | 2 | 16 | 4 |
| Aldeburgh | | 18 | 6 | 1 | 7 | 9 | 8 | 4½ | 16 | 9 |

In comparison the fare structure from Liverpool Street to the branch stations in 1947, the final year of LNER operation, showed the following:

| | First single | | | First return | | | Third single | | | Third return | | |
|---|---|---|---|---|---|---|---|---|---|---|---|---|
| | £ | s. | d. | £ | s. | d. | £ | s. | d. | £ | s. | d. |
| Saxmundham | 1 | 6 | 11 | 1 | 12 | 6 | | 16 | 1 | 1 | 1 | 8 |
| Leiston | 1 | 8 | 0 | 1 | 13 | 8 | | 16 | 9 | 1 | 2 | 5 |
| Thorpeness | 1 | 8 | 9 | 1 | 14 | 8 | | 17 | 3 | 1 | 3 | 1 |
| Aldeburgh | 1 | 9 | 5 | 1 | 15 | 8 | | 17 | 8 | 1 | 3 | 9 |

Two years later fares had increased considerably as demonstrated by the charges to Aldeburgh in 1949:

| Liverpool Street to Aldeburgh | First single £ s. d. | First return £ s. d. | Third single £ s. d. | Third return £ s. d. |
|---|---|---|---|---|
| | 1  14  3 | 2  1  6 | 1  0  6 | 1  7  6 |

By 1955 fares from Liverpool Street had been restructured showing a reduction in the price of single tickets but yet further increases in the cost of return tickets.

| | First single £ s. d. | First return £ s. d. | Third single £ s. d. | Third return £ s. d. |
|---|---|---|---|---|
| Saxmundham | 1  1  9 | 2  3  6 |    14  6 | 1  9  0 |
| Leiston | 1  2  8 | 2  5  4 |    15  1 | 1  10  2 |
| Thorpeness | 1  3  2 | 2  6  4 |    15  5 | 1  10  10 |
| Aldeburgh | 1  3  8 | 2  7  4 |    15  9 | 1  11  6 |

By 1964 fares from Liverpool Street had again increased considerably.

| | First single £ s. d. | First return £ s. d. | Third single £ s. d. | Third return £ s. d. |
|---|---|---|---|---|
| Saxmundham | 1  14  6 | 3  9  0 | 1  3  0 | 2  6  0 |
| Leiston | 1  16  0 | 3  12  0 | 1  4  0 | 2  8  0 |
| Thorpeness | 1  16  9 | 3  13  6 | 1  4  6 | 2  9  0 |
| Aldeburgh | 1  17  6 | 3  15  0 | 1  5  0 | 2  10  0 |

Local fares from Saxmundham for the same period were:

| | First single £ s. d. | First return £ s. d. | Third single £ s. d. | Third return £ s. d. |
|---|---|---|---|---|
| Leiston |    1  6 |    3  0 |    1  0 |    2  0 |
| Thorpeness |    2  3 |    4  6 |    1  6 |    3  0 |
| Aldeburgh |    3  0 |    6  0 |    2  0 |    4  0 |

## Excursions

Unlike many GER branches, the Aldeburgh line was the recipient of more excursions than it generated. In the early years those that started on the branch usually required passengers to change into a main line train at Saxmundham, although in some cases through coaches attached to forwarding services at the junction station made for easier travelling. As well as London, destinations included Ipswich, Felixstowe, Lowestoft, Yarmouth and Norwich. Excursion fares were later offered to Harwich, Clacton and Walton. The first excursion offered to Yarmouth in 1860 was so crowded that the 300 passengers booking from Aldeburgh, Leiston and Saxmundham had to join a second train, the first being full and standing and a total of over 2,500 souls enjoyed the day out at the Norfolk resort.

In September 1862 a special train conveyed passengers from the branch stations to London for the Hyde Park Exhibition. Departure from Aldeburgh before 5.00 am failed to deter would-be passengers from the 3¾ hour journey and by the time the train reached Westerfield on the up journey over a thousand people were packed into the carriages. The return departing at 7.30 pm thus offered passengers nine hours in the capital.

London excursions were always popular and in 1865 a special train conveyed over 600 passengers from East Suffolk line stations and branches but generally special traffic was slow to materialize and patronage varied considerably according to the season, destination and not the least, the weather. When the line opened the wages of agricultural workers was low, so it was to the middle and upper classes that the railway excursion appealed most. Gradually alterations were made and the introduction of paid holidays and additional leisure periods brought the price of the railway excursion within the pockets of most inhabitants served by the line. During the 1870s and 1880s the most popular destinations were Yarmouth, Lowestoft and Felixstowe and to a lesser degree Clacton, Walton, Harwich and Cromer. Shorter half-day excursions were offered to the same Suffolk and Norfolk resorts but for longer excursions, through coaches from the branch were attached to and detached from main line trains at Saxmundham. In the event of a late return, a special train connected with the main line train at Saxmundham to convey passengers to the branch stations.

The ESR/ECR and later GER offered cheap excursion fares to Aldeburgh from East Suffolk line stations on Mondays during the summer months and loadings were generally good except when adverse weather precluded many from travelling. As well as running special trains, the railway company provided facilities for private parties to travel by rail. Typical of many others, in June 1865 the clergy of Worlingworth, Bedfield and Southolt organized an excursion from Framlingham to Aldeburgh for a return fare of 6d. for each person.

In the 1890s the GER offered first, second and third class Tourist, Fortnightly and Friday or Saturday to Tuesday tickets by all trains from Liverpool Street or St Pancras, and the following return fares to Aldeburgh were available:

|                                | First class | | | Second class | | | Third class | | |
|--------------------------------|------|------|------|------|------|------|------|------|------|
|                                | £    | s.   | d.   | £    | s.   | d.   | £    | s.   | d.   |
| Tourist (summer months only)   | 1    | 7    | 9    | 1    | 2    | 1    |      | 16   | 9    |
| Fortnightly                    |      | 19   | 0    |      | 15   | 6    |      | 13   | 0    |
| Friday or Saturday to Tuesday  |      | 15   | 0    |      | 11   | 0    |      | 9    | 6    |

Tourists tickets were available for return on any day up to and including 31st December in the same year of issue.

Fortnightly tickets were available for return within 15 days of issue, whilst Friday or Saturday to Tuesday tickets were available for return on the Sunday, Monday or Tuesday following date of issue.

In the years prior to the outbreak of World War I, the GER extended the offer of excursion fares for cheap travel; additional to those offered to branch stations, passengers were also offered five-, six- or eight-day excursion fares as well as continuing the Friday to Tuesday tickets, fortnightly tickets and tourist tickets from London to Aldeburgh and Aldeburgh to London, and extra-journey tickets to London from Aldeburgh. In 1911 Seaside Periodical tickets were available from Liverpool Street to Aldeburgh as follows:

|             | First class | | | | Third class | | |
|-------------|---|---|---|---|---|---|---|
|             | £ | s. | d. | | £ | s. | d. |
| 1 week      | 1 | 15 | 0 | | 1 | 6 | 0 |
| 2 weeks     | 2 | 10 | 0 | | 2 | 0 | 0 |
| 1 month*    | 4 | 2 | 6 | | 3 | 0 | 0 |
| 1 month†    | 5 | 17 | 6 | | 4 | 2 | 3 |
| 2 months*   | 7 | 1 | 8 | | 5 | 8 | 4 |
| 2 months†   | 9 | 15 | 0 | | 6 | 17 | 1 |
| 3 months*   | 8 | 0 | 0 | | 6 | 10 | 0 |
| 3 months†   | 11 | 15 | 0 | | 8 | 4 | 6 |
| 6 months*   | 17 | 0 | 0 | | 13 | 0 | 0 |
| 6 months†   | 23 | 10 | 0 | | 16 | 9 | 0 |
| 12 months*  | 34 | 0 | 0 | | 26 | 0 | 0 |
| 12 months†  | 47 | 0 | 0 | | 32 | 18 | 0 |

* Tickets not available at intermediate stations.
† Tickets available at intermediate stations also to and from Fenchurch Street by GER trains.

These were the halcyon days for the excursion programme and cheap fares were made available to many exhibitions in London, including the annual Smithfield show.

Between the two world wars the excursion programme available to residents of Aldeburgh, Thorpeness, Leiston and Saxmundham included the usual East Anglian destinations and in addition Spalding and Peterborough, although later the choice of destinations was reduced. In the years before and after World War II cheap fares were also offered to Ipswich for home games of Ipswich Town Football Club. From the late 1940s and until the withdrawal of steam traction, a through excursion train ran from Aldeburgh to Liverpool Street and return at least twice a year, with additional specials on Sundays in the summer and autumn months with a return fare of 13s. 0d. ex-Aldeburgh and 12s. 6d. ex-Leiston. For these through excursions stock was worked down from Ipswich and the train departed Aldeburgh at 9.20 am joining with the Norwich portion at Ipswich and arriving at Liverpool Street at 12.50 pm. The return departed Liverpool Street at 6.50 pm arriving at Aldeburgh at 10.40 pm after which the stock was returned to Ipswich. Additionally a regular through excursion operated to Felixstowe and back in the high summer.

## Goods Traffic

Before the advent of the railway to Leiston and ultimately Aldeburgh, the inhabitants of the towns and surrounding area were reliant on the carriers carts and wagons for the conveyance of goods and produce to and from the local markets. The carriers later extended their scope of operation, conveying commodities to and from the ESR/GER railheads. The unmade roads meant that the carriers wagons were slow and ponderous on the journey, especially in inclement weather when they sank axle deep in mud and ruts. Perishable produce, especially fish traffic from Aldeburgh, was not of the best quality by the time destinations were reached, as often journeys were made in the outward direction one day and return the following day.

Leiston was an important local industrial centre when the railway first arrived in the town in 1859 after the third Richard Garrett to bear the name, established his engineering works in the town in 1778. The works, located some 600 yards from the station had tripled in size in the 20 years between 1835 and 1855, and Garrett ever keen to take advantage of the new form of transport to export his wares, became a Director of the East Suffolk Railway. He negotiated for the branch to serve the town, together with a private tramway to serve his premises. He offered in return considerable traffic for the new line, traffic previously conveyed overland to Slaughden Quay near Aldeburgh for transportation by sea, in which the entrepreneur also had considerable interest. During the construction of the ESR Richard Garrett & Sons supplied such sundry items as lamp posts, coal, ironmongery and general ironworks to Peto and Betts, the contractors, the total value of the material amounting to £4,300.

The opening of the branch railway in 1859 was enough to spur Garrett to extend his empire and in the following year the boiler shop and major expansion of the foundry were made. From the early 1850s Garrett's were producing a considerable range of agricultural machinery and implements for planting and drilling as well as balers, reapers and steam threshers and dressing machines, horse drawn hoes and boring machines. As early as 15th October, 1862, the GER considered the traffic of importance for the Traffic Committee authorized the construction of additional machine trucks to convey 'Leiston lorries'. Later came portable steam engines to power cultivator drills, wood cutting machinery and steam hammers amongst other items, most of these being transported away by rail with raw material being imported. The establishment of the Long Shop and enlarged foundry enabled the company to develop designs of more efficient fireboxes and smokeboxes so that the products were easier to handle by artisans and unskilled workers. In the 1880s the establishment was one of the largest foundries for cast ironwork in the country and by 1907 the premises covered an area of over 20 acres. Garrett's also established its own gasworks fronting Snape Road, later renamed Haylings Road, from the early 1850s and a siding was connected to the establishment to enable wagon loads of coal and coke to be conveyed to site. Coal also arrived for the power house at the Top Works and the foundry at the Bottom Works.

The firm continued to expand its operations despite a major fire in 1914, when it was decided to build a new factory on land owned as a demonstration farm adjacent to the station. This became the 'New' or 'Station' Works later 'Top' Works – the old original works being designated the 'Bottom' Works. During World War I the firm was fully employed making shell cases, steam tractors for military use and government wagons, and after 1917 was involved in the construction of FE2B aircraft designed by the Royal Aircraft Establishment at Farnborough but by the armistice the jigs and tooling were prepared for the building of Sopwith Snipe aircraft. Garrett's were also involved with construction of railway vehicles and one such example was Rail Tractor No. 26479 for the North Eastern Railway, which left the works on 25th July, 1907.

A 3½ ton electric lorry was delivered to the GER at the end of 1916, when the railway company Directors, embarrassed by the shortage of cart horses which had been conscripted by the military authorities as replacement for animals lost in the conflict, sought alternative traction. Colonel Frank Garrett had been experimenting with electric-powered road vehicles and despite wartime restrictions, combined his work, when opportunity permitted, in a lean-to shed by the boiler shop. C.D. Cuppleditch, of the drawing office - assisted him in the venture and in December 1916 the lorry, works No. 33119 and registration No. BJ 3396, was delivered to the GER. The vehicle was originally ordered for use in the London traffic environment but was sent to Norwich for comparable trials against a Ransome's 'Orwell' 2½ ton vehicle which was used at Ipswich. Garrett considered with some justification that the trial against a 2½ ton lorry was unfair since the 2½ tons vehicle was operating with considerably less load for much of the time. Both Garrett and the GER authorities subsequently agreed the 2½ tons vehicle was the optimum capacity for the type of work envisaged. After BJ 3396 was delivered to Norwich, Cuppleditch went there on 5th December to supervise the trials when arrangements were made for the corporation power station to charge the vehicle's batteries. All was not well for on the night of 6th the men forgot to recharge the batteries so that the following morning the vehicle was limping at low speed around the streets of the Norfolk capital. The power station personnel agreed to give the batteries a boost during their lunch break but then replaced the leads incorrectly, so that after 40 minutes the batteries had been drained of 20 amp hours. Luckily the fuse had blown before any damage was sustained; Cuppleditch replaced the fuse and 30 minutes charge gave him enough to finish the duties of the day. In mid-January 1917 the vehicle was handed over to Mr Dye, the GER driver he had been training, and the lorry continued working in the Norwich district until 12th March, 1918, when it was transferred to Ipswich for further trials and replaced by the Ransome's lorry. Later Dye, who was on holiday at Ipswich, took a turn at driving the Garrett and expressed the desire to have the vehicle back at Norwich, as he much preferred it to the Ransome's lorry. During the trials, which lasted until early 1919, Cuppleditch made several visits to carry out repairs to BJ 3396, which suffered recurring faults, mainly to the motor controller supplied by Cromptons and rear tyres which rapidly wore out until it was realized they had been manufactured to the wrong specification. The steering also worked loose on many occasions although the batteries supplied by Chloride Electric Storage Co. gave no trouble. The GER had, however, opted for the Ransome's vehicles and by the end of 1918 the company was operating five flatbed lorries and two vans at Ipswich. The Garrett having served its purpose was quietly withdrawn.

In 1919 the company co-joined the Agricultural & General Engineering Ltd combine but this went into receivership in 1932 and the undertaking was purchased by Beyer, Peacock of Manchester but continued to trade as Richard Garrett Engineering. The association with the Manchester engineers resulted in locomotive chassis being built in the erecting shop of the Top Works before being conveyed on low-loader wagons to Beyer, Peacock. During World War II Garrett's works was again transformed for the production of munitions, although some agricultural work was still maintained. The firm also secured the contract with the Admiralty for construction of naval guns and for the supply of both munition and shell making lathes. Post-war saw the arrival of steel plate, pig iron, coal and foundry coke when the firm became involved with the development of automatic machinery and control equipment for launderettes, but much of the equipment was transported from the factory by road with lesser use made of railway facilities. Steel off-cuts were still dispatched by rail to Sheffield for smelting whilst Bord na Mona, the Irish peat company, purchased peat cutting and digging equipment which was transported in rail wagons. In the latter years a portion of the Top Works was let to S&S Corrugated Manufacturing Co. who awarded Garrett's licence to build cardboard box-making machines producing corrugated cardboard containers. Pye radio components were also manufactured with parcels being forwarded by the 4.55 pm Aldeburgh to Saxmundham train. By 1980 Bottom Works was closed with The Top works finally closing in 1981, the latter later becoming part of the Masterlord industrial estate.

Richard Garrett was also involved with the establishment of Framlingham College, for after the publication of a memorial to the Prince Consort from Lord Stradbroke and Edward Kerrison of Hoxne Hall conceiving the idea of a college of further education for middle classes in east Suffolk, plans were published and the scheme launched at a meeting in the council chamber at Ipswich town hall on 18th March, 1862. This was followed by a committee meeting held in the former EUR Boardroom at Ipswich railway station at which Garrett was elected Honorary Secretary.

William Henry Carr's brickworks was established on the northern outskirts of Leiston in the early 1850s on Theberton Road. After the opening of the branch railway the premises was initially served by a tramway branching off a connection to Garrett's tramway, trailing into it soon after it had bisected Station Road, and then having a rail level crossing at right angles over the Aldeburgh line to the east of the level crossing. Later the crossover leading to Garrett's was abolished and a wagon turntable provided in the main single branch line with a connection leading to a parallel siding. After the signalling and track alterations of 1892, the trailing connection for up trains on the down side of the line beyond the gates was used exclusively for the brick and tile traffic. Considerable tonnages of bricks and tiles were dispatched by rail to destinations in Suffolk and Norfolk before the works closed in March 1926. W.H. Carr also had sidings at Derby Road on the Ipswich to Felixstowe branch.

Initial freight traffic included barley, wheat, hay, straw, vegetables and root crops included potatoes, carrots, swedes, mangold wurzels and turnips. Seed potatoes came from Scotland for delivery to local growers. In addition from the early 1920s sugar beet was grown, being transferred from farmers carts and waggons to railway wagons for conveyance to the British Sugar Corporation processing factories at Ipswich, Bury St Edmunds or Cantley. By the late 1950s much of this traffic had transferred to road haulage for direct delivery from farm to factory, but until closure in 1959 small amounts of sugar beet grown at Aldeburgh Hall Farm, Church Farm, Grange Farm and Bulls Hall Farm, Knodishall was still loaded at Aldeburgh, Sizewell siding and Leiston during the beet season from November to January. Packards of Street Farm at Saxmundham loaded wagons at the up side dock. In the war years beet was dispatched subject to the permit issued to the growers by the refinery to limit wagons arriving at the factory but even then illicit practices between farmers and railway staff ensured certain wagon loads were forwarded as priority for the price of a pint or a packet of cigarettes. Beet pulp was returned to all stations for farmers to use as animal feed, the pulp at Saxmundham being unloaded in the down yard. Although farming was established around Leiston the loading of agricultural traffic was far less than at other East Suffolk line stations.

Milk was regularly forwarded to Ipswich and Halesworth in the familiar 17 gallon churns, two loads being dispatched daily from Leiston, Thorpeness Halt and Aldeburgh in the summer by an early train and then again in the late afternoon and by morning train in the winter months. The traffic was loaded into the guard's brake van on passenger services or in a van attached to mixed trains. The traffic ceased after World War II when it was lost to road haulage.

Before the advent of the railway, drovers herded animals along the roads to and from market and prices fluctuated according to the condition of the beasts. The coming of the railway meant animals could be conveyed relatively quickly to local and London markets, arriving in a much fresher condition and subsequently gaining a much better price. From the outset livestock handled on the branch was two-way traffic, as the potential of the railway for rapid transit of animals to and from local markets was realized. Horses were regularly conveyed in wagons or horseboxes attached to passenger trains and until World War II hunting horses were conveyed to and from local hunt meetings on 24 hours notice being given to forwarding stations. Cattle wagons were a common feature until the early 1950s and the branch was utilized for the conveyance of animals from Aldeburgh, Sizewell siding and Leiston to and from Ipswich market held on Tuesdays, Bury St Edmunds market on Wednesdays, Norwich and Yarmouth markets - both held on Wednesdays and Saturdays. Some traffic was also sent to Saxmundham on Wednesdays. Incoming cattle arrived from Scotland and Ireland for fattening and were offloaded at Leiston, Sizewell siding and to a lesser extent Aldeburgh. Nominated passenger trains were permitted to convey cattle wagons and this was especially useful on Ipswich market day. Pigs and sheep were also conveyed by the branch freight services but trade declined with the relaxation of petrol rationing after World War II when nearly all livestock traffic was lost to road transport. During the post-World War II period meat rationing cattle was received at Leiston from such diverse loading points as Tavistock and Banbury under government regulations, offloaded at the cattle pens and herded along the roads to the slaughterhouse in the Aldeburgh Road, there to be used by John Emsden, the local butcher. Animal foodstuff for Silcocks was off-loaded at Saxmundham where the storage shed was located between the goods shed and the signal box. Pigeon traffic was mostly received on Sundays at Saxmundham and Aldeburgh when birds were released at a convenient or predetermined time as advised by the pigeon fanciers or racers.

The Aldeburgh fishing fleet could not be compared with the huge industry maintained at Yarmouth and Lowestoft but a haven was established for small vessels and before the coming of the railway around 40 vessels were registered at the port. By the mid-1880s ten or so fishermen were plying their trade into the German Ocean. Several pilots and master mariners were also registered with vessels and regular consignments of sprats, herring, cod, sole, lobsters and other fish, reaching often 70 tons per day, were dispatched by rail to local markets and Billingsgate. The sprat, a diminutive little fish, hardly exceeding five inches in length, not unlike a herring only differing by its saw-like serrated belly, approached the Suffolk coast in huge shoals from mid-November and remained until mid-February, there to be met by the fishing smacks of Southwold and Aldeburgh before drifting south to suffer further depletion by the smacks of Brightlingsea and Tollesbury. Before the advantages of rail transport were realized much of the consignment of herring and sprats were dried and exported directly to Holland but most was destined for farmers' fields as fish manure because it was impossible to get the commodity to the lucrative Ipswich and London markets in fresh condition. By 1914 the fishing and coastal trade at Aldeburgh had all but disappeared, crippled by a shingle bank which effectively blocked entry to the harbour. In later years some consignments of locally caught herring, plaice and lobsters were dispatched by rail. If fish traffic was worked up the vehicle or vehicles on arrival at Saxmundham was shunted into Hay siding ready for collection by the next main line train for conveyance to London, usually Billingsgate.

Coal and coke traffic was regularly received at Saxmundham, Leiston, Sizewell siding and Aldeburgh as well as the Leiston Gas Co.'s works at Leiston, with consignments for the local fuel merchants from a variety of collieries including Sherwood, Newstead, Kirkley, Bestwood, Hucknall, Sheepbridge, Stanton, Shirebrook, Clipstone, Worksop, Gedley and Blidworth. Anthracite was received from South Wales and coke in the latter years came from Ipswich gas works. The wagons from the coal pits usually travelled via Peterborough where the Stanground sidings acted as a clearing-house for empty wagons returning to the collieries or loading ones destined for the branch. Other traffic came via the Great Northern & Great Eastern Joint line via Spalding to March. The coal loaded in colliery private owner wagons was then routed via Ely, Bury St Edmunds and Ipswich for onward delivery to the branch stations. In the 1920s and 1930s coke was also conveyed for horticultural purposes, but after World War II this commodity was taken by road. In the early years much of Leiston's domestic coal traffic was handled at Sizewell siding. Local coal and coke merchants receiving fuel by rail at Aldeburgh included Newson Garrett, also a corn merchant and Lloyds agent, Robert George Parker, William Skeet, Charles H. Chandler, later Charles Douglas Joy trading as H.W. Joy, Ernest Cundy, Albert Ward and Peter Knights. Thomas Moy Ltd had a coal ground and office at the station yard during the 1950s, previously trading at 112 High Street and the station from the early 1900s. At Leiston fuel merchants included William Moss, Henry Frederick Reeve, William Taylor and Smith and Coleman. Charringtons Fuels, which incorporated Moy, utilized the former gas works siding at Leiston as a coal concentration depot, whilst Leiston Co-operative Society utilized the yard at Sizewell siding for the receipt of coal and coke. Thomas Durrant coal, coke, lime and salt merchant at

Saxmundham in the 1890s was also the cartage agent for the GER. Others operating from Saxmundham goods yard included George Head, coal merchant, R. Coller & Sons, corn, cake and seed merchants, Ernest Gosling, coal merchant, and William Row & Son, maltster, corn, seed, coal, coke, lime, cement and salt merchant. Post-war merchants included Arthur Newson, Bowers, Oscar Woods and Charles Ford. Petroleum for BP was received at Saxmundham in tank wagons, which were off-loaded on the back road up side storage area, from whence it was distributed to local garages.

Smalls traffic loaded at Leiston was pulled out of the goods shed by the shunting horses and positioned on the shed road neck where the locomotive of the up train collected the wagon or wagons for conveyance to Saxmundham. Here they were deposited in the Hay siding to be collected by an up main line service.

A unique working from the Leiston goods yard was the removal of scrap metal from the airship of Zeppelin L48 shot down at Theberton on 16th and 17th June, 1917, leaving only one survivor. After the war tombstones went sent by sea from Germany to Southampton, thence by train to Leiston and on to Theberton by horse-drawn waggon so that those who died in the wreckage could be remembered. Miscellaneous scrap metal continued to be loaded on an as and when required basis at Leiston until the withdrawal of freight traffic, and in 1938 it was recorded that 1,228 tons of scrap iron was loaded and dispatched.

In the late 1920s and early 1930s many roads in east Suffolk were unmetalled, dust tracks in summer and muddy quagmires in winter. Suffolk County Council undertook a rolling programme of road improvements, which included levelling the surface before covering it with granite chippings and tarmacadam. Most of the material was delivered by rail to the branch stations from where it was offloaded and taken to site by horse and waggon. The granite and tarmacadam was then levelled by steamroller. For a short period in the 1920s a concrete factory was established near Thorpeness and the manufacturer made use of the siding for the receipt and transit of goods.

In the late 19th and early 20th century shipbuilding material was delivered by rail to Aldeburgh, for C.P. Ogilvie & Co., ship and yachting boat builders and William Edward Felgate, as well as ships stores for the various fishing and coastal vessels based at the town or at Slaughden Quay.

During World War II armaments and equipment for coastal defence was conveyed across the branch, the ammunition usually conveyed in open wagons, sheeted over to conceal the deadly cargo, although the prominent red flashed wagon labels advised 'Shunt With Care' and 'Place As Far As Possible From The Engine, Brake Van and Wagons Labelled Inflammable'. Supplies were also received at Leiston for various airfields in the area notably the United States Airforce base at Theberton as well as food supplies for the Central Food Store at Saxmundham.

The railway was used extensively for the conveyance of materials for the construction of Sizewell A nuclear power station, which began in April 1961 until commissioning in 1966, and for Sizewell B nuclear power station built and commissioned between 1987 and 1995. The Sizewell siding area was transformed by the addition of an overhead gantry crane spanning the single

The fireman of 'J17' class 0-6-0 No. 65560 holds out the hoop containing the short section of the Leiston to Saxmundham Junction split Train Staff for the Junction signalman as the up branch 'bonus' freight train for Ipswich approaches the main line. In the background the up branch home signal is clear but the Saxmundham Station branch distant signal remains at caution.

*The late Dr I.C. Allen*

View from Leiston station platform showing the signal box and Station Road level crossing with two bulk grain wagons being loaded at the dock beside the former down side goods loop. The gantry crane has been removed and the connection leading to Garrett's Bottom Works curves away to the right. *R. Kennell*

sidings which was initially used to tranship equipment from railway wagons to road vehicles for onward transit to site. Since the closure of the branch to general freight traffic, the truncated section from Saxmundham Junction to Sizewell siding has been retained for the periodic conveyance of nuclear flask traffic on 56 ton flatrol wagons to and from British Nuclear Fuels establishment at Sellafield on the Cumbrian coast, usually via Willesden, a task that is at present performed under contract by Direct Rail Services, owned by the Nuclear Decommissioning Authority who also own the flasks. Sizewell A was shut down on 31st December, 2006 and decommissioning will take several years to achieve with a regular traffic to Sellafield. Sizewell B was placed offline in March 2010 but has a life span until 2035. The construction of the proposed Sizewell C nuclear plant might well ensure regular traffic flows well into the 21st century.

The following goods facilities were available at the branch stations:

| | |
|---|---|
| *Saxmundham* | Loading gauges |
| | Loading dock |
| | Fixed crane (1 ton 10 cwt capacity) |
| | Cattle dock |
| | 2 paved cattle pens |
| | Water supply for animals in transit |
| | Truck weighbridge (20 tons capacity) |
| | Weighing machine (1 ton 12 cwt capacity) |
| | Goods shed with storage capacity for 25 quarters of grain |
| | Facility for loading vans and furniture vans on wheels, also round timber |
| | Cartage by company |
| | Latest time for same day forwarding 5.00 pm Monday to Friday and 3.00 pm Saturdays |
| | |
| *Leiston* | Loading gauges |
| | Loading dock |
| | Fixed crane (1 ton 10 cwt, later 2 x 1 ton 10 cwt capacity) |
| | Fixed crane (15 tons capacity, later 30 tons capacity) |
| | 2 Truck weighbridges (20 tons capacity each, later 1 x 40 tons capacity) |
| | Weighing machine (1 ton 12 cwt, later 2 tons capacity) |
| | Cattle dock |
| | 2 paved cattle pens |
| | 2 wagon turntables, later increased to eight, |
| | and then reduced to five by 1920 |
| | Goods shed |
| | Facility for loading vans and furniture vans on wheels |
| | Cartage by company |
| | Latest time for same day forwarding 4.30 pm Monday to Friday, 6.00 pm Saturday |
| | |
| *Sizewell siding* | Loading gauge |
| | Cattle dock |
| | 2 paved cattle pens |
| | Latest time for same day forwarding 4.30 pm |
| | |
| *Thorpeness siding* | Loading gauge |
| | Latest time for same day forwarding 4.30 pm |

| Aldeburgh | Loading gauge |
|---|---|
| | Loading dock |
| | Fixed crane (1 ton 10 cwt capacity) |
| | Weighing machine (1 ton capacity) |
| | Goods shed with storage for 100 quarters of grain |
| | Facility for loading vans and furniture vans on wheels |
| | Cartage by agent |
| | Latest time for same day forwarding 6.00 pm |

In 1865 the permitted load of the branch engine was not to exceed 10 trucks and regular goods trains 15 trucks, but from 1870 specific loadings were stipulated, with three empty trucks considered as equal to two loaded.

| | Goods trucks loaded | | Coal trucks loaded | | Gross | Net |
|---|---|---|---|---|---|---|
| | down | up | down | up | tons | tons |
| Four-wheel coupled | | | | | | |
| second class engines | 20 | 20 | 16 | 16 | 300 | 200 |
| Third class engines | 16 | 16 | 12 | 12 | 252 | 160 |
| Fourth class engines | 11 | 11 | 7 | 7 | 220 | 140 |

By 1891 the loading allowed for goods engines on the branch was:

| | Goods trucks loaded | | Coal trucks loaded | | Gross | Net |
|---|---|---|---|---|---|---|
| | down | up | down | up | tons | tons |
| Second Class Engines | 16 | 16 | 14 | 14 | 300 | 200 |
| Third Class Engines | 14 | 14 | 12 | 12 | 252 | 160 |

The permitted load limit to be hauled by goods engines between Saxmundham and Aldeburgh in 1897 was:

| | Goods trucks loaded | | Coal trucks loaded | |
|---|---|---|---|---|
| | down | up | down | up |
| First class engines | 22 | 22 | 18 | 18 |
| Second class engines | 16 | 16 | 14 | 14 |
| Third class engines | 14 | 14 | 12 | 12 |

After the turn of the century the loads for goods engines was revised as under

| Class of locomotive | Minerals | | Goods | |
|---|---|---|---|---|
| | down | up | down | up |
| A | 33 | 22 | 40 | 40 |
| B | 21 | 21 | 30 | 30 |
| C | 18 | 18 | 26 | 26 |
| D | 14 | 14 | 20 | 20 |
| E | 14 | 14 | 20 | 20 |
| F | 14 | 14 | 20 | 20 |
| G | 12 | 12 | 17 | 17 |
| H | 12 | 12 | 17 | 17 |

The following locomotives, regularly allocated to work across the Aldeburgh branch, were classified as follows:

| GER class | LNER class | Type | Classified |
|-----------|------------|------|------------|
| G58 | J17 | 0-6-0 | A |
| Y14 | J15 | 0-6-0 | C |
| M15 | F4 | 2-4-2T | D |
| M15R | F5 | 2-4-2T | D |
| G69 | F6 | 2-4-2T | D |
| C32 | F3 | 2-4-2T | E |
| Y65 | F7 | 2-4-2T | E |
| 417 | – | 0-6-0 | F |
| 477 | – | 0-6-0 | F |
| T26 | E4 | 2-4-0 | F |
| E22 | J65 | 0-6-0T | H |

When the LNER reissued the loads book, freight trains on the Aldeburgh branch were not to exceed 45 wagons on the down run and 40 wagons in length on the up run with individual loadings as follows, although trains were not to convey more than 20 wagons when starting from Aldeburgh:

*Saxmundham to Aldeburgh*

| Engine | Minerals | Goods | Empties |
|--------|----------|-------|---------|
| Class 1 | 16 | 24 | 32 |
| Class 2 | 17 | 25 | 34 |
| Class 3 | 19 | 28 | 38 |
| Class 4 | 21 | 31 | 42 |
| Class 5 | 23 | 34 | 45 |
| Class 6 | 26 | 39 | 45 |

*Aldeburgh to Saxmundham*

| Engine | Minerals | Goods | Empties |
|--------|----------|-------|---------|
| Class 1 | 26 | 39 | 40 |
| Class 2 | 29 | 40 | 40 |
| Class 3 | 32 | 40 | 40 |
| Class 4 | 35 | 40 | 40 |
| Class 5 | 39 | 40 | 40 |
| Class 6 | 40 | 40 | 40 |

A class '3' goods engine was a 'J15' class 0-6-0 tender locomotive and a class '4' was a 'J17' class 0-6-0 tender locomotive. 'F3', 'F4', 'F5' and 'F6' class 2-4-2 tank locomotives were to convey six mineral wagons less than the load shown for a No. 1 freight engine, 'D15' and 'D16' class 4-4-0 tender locomotives were to convey three mineral wagons less than the load shown for a No. 1 freight locomotive whilst a 'B12' class 4-6-0 tender locomotive could convey the load shown for a No. 3 freight locomotive.

British Railways made slight amendments to the load book for class 'J' and 'K' class freight trains:

*Saxmundham to Aldeburgh*

| Load Group | Heavy | Goods | Empties |
|---|---|---|---|
| Class 1 | 14 | 25 | 28 |
| Class 2 | 15 | 26 | 30 |
| Class 3 | 17 | 30 | 34 |
| Class 4 | 19 | 34 | 38 |
| Class 5 | 21 | 37 | 42 |

*Aldeburgh to Saxmundham*

| Class 1 | 23 | 40 | 40 |
|---|---|---|---|
| Class 2 | 26 | 40 | 40 |
| Class 3 | 29 | 40 | 40 |
| Class 4 | 31 | 40 | 40 |
| Class 5 | 35 | 40 | 40 |

Trains were not to convey more than 20 wagons when starting from Aldeburgh.
    The following were the load groups for the various classes that worked across the Aldeburgh branch.

| Tender | Group 1 | Class D15* |
|---|---|---|
|  |  | Class D16* |
|  |  | Class E4† |
|  | Group 2 | Class J15 |
|  | Group 3 | Class B12 |
|  | Group 4 | Class J17 |
| Tank | Group 1 | Class F3† |
|  |  | Class F4† |
|  |  | Class F5* |
|  |  | Class F6† |

* These classes to convey three heavy wagons or equivalent less than the loads shown for Group 1 engines.
† These classes to convey five heavy wagons or equivalent less than the loads shown for Group 1 engines.

The length limit of freight trains on the branch in 1956/57 was restricted to 20 wagons.
    After dieselization of freight services, a load limit of 45 wagons in the down direction and 40 wagons on the up road were placed on the branch services, with the undermentioned limits for individual classes of locomotive.

| Class of Train | 4, 5, 6 | 7 | 8, 9 |
|---|---|---|---|
| Class 15 800 hp | 17 | 22 | 28 |
| Class 21 1,100 hp | 20 | 26 | 28 |
| Class 24 1,160 hp | 27 | 35 | 32 |
| Class 31 1,250/1,365 hp | 29 | 38 | 36 |
| Class 37 1,750 hp | 39 | 45 | 36 |

# Chapter Ten

# Locomotives and Rolling Stock

The relatively light construction of the permanent way of the Aldeburgh branch precluded the use of locomotives with heavy axle loading and only those with light or medium axle loading were permitted. The ECR, EUR and later GER possessed ample engines of low route availability to work the branch. The LNER initially permitted class 'B4'*, 'B5/3', 'B12', 'D2'*, 'D13', 'D15', 'E4', 'J10', 'J15', 'J17', 'J19' and 'J21' tender locomotives and 'F1', 'F3', 'F4', 'F5', 'F6', 'F7', 'G5', 'J65', 'J66', 'J67', 'J68', 'J69', 'J70', 'Y1', 'Y3', 'Y5', 'Y6' and 'Y10' tank locomotives. The LNER and later BR classified the branch to route availability 4 (RA4) with additional class 'J19' with higher route availability. With dieselization the RA4 classification initially continued with classes '10/4', '11/1', '11/4', '12/2', '13/2', '16/2' and '17/1' classes of higher route availability permitted, the additional classes being restricted to a speed limit of 25 mph. Later the line from Saxmundham Junction to Sizewell was upgraded to RA7 although the sidings at Sizewell were restricted to RA5.

It appears a decision was made at an early stage to work the branch with tank locomotives, which were capable of hauling the relatively lightly loaded passenger and freight services. It is almost certain that the Saxmundham to Leiston and later Aldeburgh branch was taken over by the trio of Eastern Union Railway 2-2-2 tank locomotives with one outbased on the branch at any one time. Built by Sharp Brothers of Manchester in 1854 (Works Nos. 765, 766 and 768), they were initially allocated Nos. 29, 30 and 31 but it is doubtful if these numbers were carried for they were delivered after the ECR had taken over the operation of the EUR. The new owner renumbered the 2-2-2 tank engines Nos. 13, 14 and 15 and they were well equipped to handle both passenger and freight traffic. All were withdrawn for scrapping in November 1871.

Working turn and turn about on the branch with the above trio was the former EUR 2-2-2 well tank locomotive No. 27, built by Sharp Brothers at Manchester (Works No. 555), and delivered in 1849. When the ECR took over the running of the EUR they renumbered the engine to 16 and she was withdrawn in February 1871.

Another class regularly outbased at Aldeburgh was the Gooch designed 'B' class 2-2-2 well tank locomotives allocated to Ipswich. The class of six, numbered 7 to 12 inclusive, dated from 1853 and 1854 and before transfer to Suffolk worked the North Woolwich branch. No. 9 was evaluated on the neighbouring Eye branch in 1867 and later worked on both the Framlingham and Aldeburgh branches with No. 12. It must be assumed that others of the class worked across the line before scrapping. Nos. 10 and 11 were condemned in 1871, whilst Nos. 7, 9 and 12 were withdrawn from traffic in June, August and January 1874 respectively. No. 8 was converted to an inspection locomotive and was finally scrapped in March 1883.

---

* Provided they conformed to LNER loading gauge.

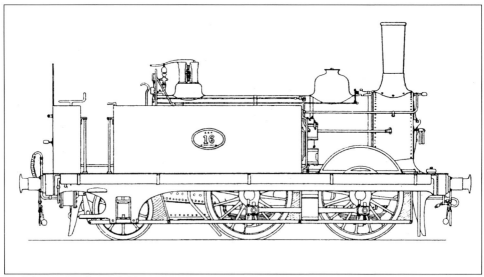

Johnson 'T7' class 0-4-2T.

S.W. Johnson's 'T7' class 0-4-2Ts were introduced into traffic between 1871 and 1875 for light branch duties. Nos. 12, 14, 82 and 84 spent some time outbased at Aldeburgh. No. 84 shown here and built in 1873 was subsequently withdrawn from traffic in 1892.          *LCGB/Ken Nunn*

The 'V' class 2-4-2 tank locomotives designed by Robert Sinclair found regular employment on the Aldeburgh branch soon after delivery. The 20 locomotives, Nos. 140 to 159, were commonly called 'Scotchmen' as they were built by Neilson & Co. of Glasgow (Works Nos. 1083 to 1102) and entered traffic between November 1864 and July 1865. The class was noteworthy as being amongst the earliest of the 2-4-2 type of tank engines and when new were employed on the London suburban services to Enfield and Brentwood, whilst others went to work on country branches. No. 146 was working the Aldeburgh branch services in the spring of 1871 when she was severely damaged in a collision with 'Y' class 2-4-0 goods locomotive No. 339 at Saxmundham. No. 146 also disgraced itself the following year when working the 11.40 am passenger train from Manningtree to Harwich by derailing at Ramsey Ray crossing between Wrabness and Dovercourt, taking her train of four coaches and a brake van with her. Nos. 142 and 151 were also known to have been outbased at Aldeburgh from Ipswich to work the branch. In 1880 Nos. 140 to 149 were placed on the duplicate list and had an '0' suffix added. Nos. 1400 and 1480 were withdrawn from traffic in 1883, No. 1420, 1450 and 1490 in 1884, Nos. 153 and 155 in 1885, Nos. 1470, 154, 156, 157 and 158 in 1886, Nos. 1410, 1430, 1440, 1460, 151, 152 and 159 in 1887, whilst the last of the class to go was No. 150 in 1880. The principal dimensions of the 'V' class were:

| | | |
|---|---|---|
| Cylinders | 2 outside | 15 in. x 22 in. |
| Motion | | Stephenson with slide valves |
| Boiler | Max. diameter | 3 ft 11 in. |
| | Length | 13 ft 6 in. |
| Firebox outside length | | 4 ft 6 in. |
| Heating surface | Tubes    143 x 1⅞ in. | 965.96 sq. ft |
| | Firebox | 68.8 sq. ft |
| | Total | 1,034.76 sq. ft |
| Grate area | | 11.7 sq. ft |
| Boiler pressure | | 120 psi |
| Leading wheels | | 3 ft 7¼ in. |
| Driving wheels | | 5 ft 7 in. |
| Trailing wheels | | 3 ft 7¼ in. |
| Length of frames | | 28 ft 10 in. |
| Wheelbase | | 17 ft 4 in. |
| Weight in working order | | 36 tons 6 cwt |
| Max. axle loading | | 9 tons 14 cwt |

When the 2-2-2 tank locomotives were withdrawn the branch services were taken over by Samuel Johnson's 'T7' class 0-4-2 tank locomotives especially built for light branch traffic. Fifteen locomotives were constructed between 1871 and 1875, although the first three engines, Nos. 81, 82 and 83, were actually prototypes included in the class total. No record exists of all the individual locomotives outbased at Aldeburgh, but Nos. 12, 14, 82 and 84 spent a period of time on the branch from 1878 to 1881. All locomotives were withdrawn by 1894.

As with many GER branch lines the 'T7' class worked turn and turn about with the 'K9' class 0-4-2 tank locomotives designed by William Adams. The class totalled 10 in number and was built in 1877 and 1878. Nos. 20, 24 and 25 were known to have worked the Aldeburgh branch at some time, the first and last being involved in

Working turn and turn about with the Johnson 'T7' class on the Aldeburgh branch were several of the 'K9' class 0-4-2Ts introduced by William Adams in 1877. Nos. 22, 24 and 25 were known to have been outbased on the Suffolk line, the first and last being involved in accidents. No. 25 later worked the initial services on the Kelvedon & Tollesbury Light Railway in Essex in 1904 and is shown at Norwich in 1905 just before withdrawal from traffic. *LCGB/Ken Nunn*

In 1889 James Holden introduced into service 10 six-coupled passenger tank locomotives of class 'E22' for light branch duties followed by a further 10 engines in 1893. Soon after introduction of the second batch, a member of the class was outbased from Ipswich to work the Aldeburgh branch to displace the 'T7' class 0-4-2Ts and work alongside the 'K9' class 0-4-2 tank engines. The 'E22' class, later reclassified to J65 by the LNER, was ousted from the branch as early as 1909. No. 7248 as GER No. 248 was one of the class which worked the Suffolk coastal branch. *Author's Collection*

accidents at Aldeburgh in October 1883. The entire class was withdrawn between 1903 and 1907. The 'K9' class were the only locomotives built at Stratford works during Adams term in office. At first only a handbrake was fitted but the class was later equipped with the Westinghouse brake. A half-cab was originally provided when the locomotives were built, but a few years later weather plates were fitted at the back of the cab and later the roof was extended to cover the footplate completely. No. 20 was transferred to the duplicate list in 1902 and renumbered 020 before being scrapped in 1906. Nos. 24 and 25, the latter working the inaugural services on the new Kelvedon & Tollesbury Light Railway when it opened in 1904, were scrapped in 1905.

When Massey Bromley succeeded William Adams as locomotive superintendent at Stratford he immediately ordered the construction of 60 0-4-4Ts which became class 'E10'. The introduction was rather protracted with Nos. 87 to 94 appearing in 1878, Nos. 51 to 57 and 95 to 102 in 1879, Nos. 58 to 60 and 231 to 244 in 1880, Nos. 572 to 574 in 1882 and 585 to 591 in 1883. Many working the London suburban area services had shorter chimneys than those working from country depots and in the early 1880s several 'E10' class 0-4-4 tank locomotives based at Ipswich spent some time on the Aldeburgh branch workings, including No. 97, which hardly distinguished itself by derailing near Leiston on 30th August, 1882. It further disgraced itself on 15th May of the following year by leaving the track between Wrabness and Parkeston on the Harwich branch. The escapades did no lasting damage for the locomotive was experimentally fitted with Holden's patent apparatus for burning liquid fuel in 1901, but this was later removed. From 1887 to 1896 locomotives were rebuilt with a new boiler and other detailed differences and most were placed on the duplicate list. No. 097 was the last to be withdrawn from traffic in 1912, having worked her days out on the Saffron Walden branch.

In 1889 James Holden introduced 10 six-coupled passenger tank locomotives into service for light branch duties and classified the engines 'E22'. The first six were sent to work on the Fenchurch Street to Blackwall services with the result they quickly earned the nickname of the 'Blackwall Tanks'. The subsequent engines on release to traffic were allocated to Buntingford and Braintree. A further 10 tank locomotives with detail differences were built in 1893 and whilst some were allocated to Blackwall the remaining engines were allocated to various GER country depots. It was during this period that one of the representatives allocated to Ipswich was outstationed at Aldeburgh. For a short period No. 156 was the regular branch engine, but was later replaced by Nos. 153, 157, 247 and 248. These engines never monopolized the branch services and in the latter years worked alongside the 'K9' class. They survived on branch duties until 1909 when they were ousted by the 'Y65' class 2-4-2 tank locomotives. The locomotives regularly allocated to the branch included:

| GER No. | LNER 1924 No. | LNER 1946 No. | BR No. | Withdrawn |
|---------|---------------|---------------|--------|-----------|
| 153 | 7153 | – | – | September 1931 |
| 156 | 7156 | – | – | August 1937 |
| 157 | 7157 | 8212 | – | November 1947 |
| 247 | 7247 | 8213 | – | February 1948 |
| 248 | 7248 | – | – | May 1936 |
| 250 | 7250 | 8214 | 68214 | October 1956 |
| 253 | 7253 | 8215 | – | May 1949 |

For a short while the 'Y65' class 2-4-2Ts, designed by S.D. Holden and introduced into service in 1909-10, were used on the Aldeburgh branch. The class never gained a monopoly on the workings, being underpowered for mixed trains and by 1913 they had been displaced by the larger 'C32' class 2-4-2Ts. No. 1311, shown at Ipswich, was later converted for auto-train working in 1914 and was withdrawn from traffic as LNER 'F7' class No. 8311 in September 1931.                    *LCGB/Ken Nunn*

For many years Holden's GER 'C32' class 2-4-2Ts were employed on Aldeburgh branch services and this was continued by the LNER, which classified the locomotives 'F3'. Here No. 1073 in full GER livery is shown near Brentwood en route from Stratford to Ipswich on 16th March, 1913.
                    *LCGB/Ken Nunn*

The next class associated with the Aldeburgh branch, albeit for only a short period was the 'Y65' class 2-4-2 tank locomotives designed by S.D. Holden and introduced into service in 1909-1910. Built especially for light branch passenger duties, they were the least successful of Holden's tank engines and after a time they were relegated to auto-train working and services on minor branch lines. Nos. 1300 to 1311 were constructed at Stratford works and their small boiler and enormous cab soon earned them the nickname 'Crystal Palaces'. Nos. 1300, 1304, 1309, 1310 and 1311 were allocated to Ipswich and were regularly outbased at Aldeburgh to work the branch. Other duties of Ipswich-based locomotives included the Felixstowe line and for short periods on the Hadleigh, Framlingham and Brightlingsea branches. As on other branches in the district the class never gained the monopoly on the Aldeburgh services, being underpowered for mixed trains, which were a regular feature of the line, and by 1913 they were displaced by the larger 'C32' class 2-4-2 tank locomotives. After leaving the Ipswich district No. 1310 was subsequently allocated to Ramsey High Street, whilst No. 1311 was converted to auto-train trials in 1914, on the Cambridge to Mildenhall and Somersham to Ramsey High Street branches, before working on the reintroduced service on the Churchbury loop line between White Hart Lane and Cheshunt during World War I. The LNER redesignated the 'Y65s' to class 'F7' and renumbered them to 8300 to 8311 inclusive. No. 8310 was transferred to Scotland in 1931 with two other members of the class to work the Gifford, Lauder and Selkirk branches and the Galashiels to Peebles line. There she was renumbered in 1942 to 7598 and again under the 1946 scheme to 7094. With the former 8308, renumbered 7093, she was scrapped as joint last member of the class in November 1948. Details of the Aldeburgh branch engines were:

| GER No. | LNER 1924 No. | LNER 1946 No. | BR No. | Withdrawn |
|---------|---------------|---------------|--------|-----------|
| 1300 | 8300 | – | – | August 1938 |
| 1304 | 8304 | 7594 | – | March 1944 |
| 1309 | 8309 | – | – | January 1931 |
| 1310 | 8310 | 7598 | 7094 | November 1948 |
| 1311 | 8311 | – | – | September 1931 |

James Holden's 'C32' class 2-4-2 tank locomotives soon replaced the 'Y65' class on the Aldeburgh branch workings. The class of 50 locomotives was built between 1893 and 1902 at Stratford works and when introduced into traffic worked principally on the longer distance semi-fast services from Liverpool Street to Bishop's Stortford and later from Liverpool Street to Southend and Southminster. Soon after the turn of the century many were displaced and sent to GER country depots. Aldeburgh shed initially had two of the class outbased from Ipswich, later reduced to one engine. The 'C32s' were reclassified 'F3' by the LNER after the Grouping and remained the mainstay on the branch workings for many years. The engines based at Ipswich also worked the Felixstowe, Framlingham, Brightlingsea and Hadleigh branches. Locomotives known to have worked from Aldeburgh shed included:

GER 'C32' class 2-4-2Ts (LNER 'F3') worked the Aldeburgh branch for several decades and were instantly recognisable by the large brass axlebox covers on the leading and trailing axles. No. 8072 is in plain unlined LNER black livery. *Author's Collection*

Ivatt GNR 'C2' class, later LNER 'C12' class 4-4-2T.

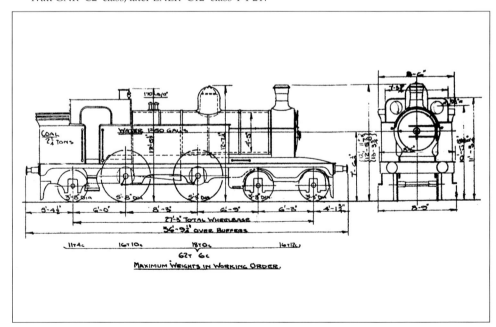

| GER No. | LNER 1924 No. | LNER 1946 No. | BR No. | Withdrawn |
|---------|---------------|---------------|--------|-----------|
| 1041 | 8041 | 7142 | – | April 1947 |
| 1042 | 8042 | 7143 | – | July 1948 |
| 1043 | 8043 | 7144 | – | November 1947 |
| 1049 | 8049 | 7150 | – | October 1949 |
| 1064 | 8064 | 7137 | – | November 1947 |
| 1065 | 8065 | – | – | March 1938 |
| 1066 | 8066 | 7138 | – | August 1947 |
| 1068 | 8068 | 7140 | – | March 1949 |
| 1070 | 8070 | 7121 | – | April 1947 |
| 1071 | 8071 | 7122 | – | November 1947 |
| 1072 | 8072 | 7123 | – | March 1947 |
| 1073 | 8073 | – | – | November 1938 |
| 1075 | 8075 | 7124 | – | March 1950 |
| 1076 | 8076 | – | – | March 1937 |
| 1077 | 8077 | – | – | August 1947 |
| 1078 | 8078 | 7126 | – | January 1950 |
| 1079 | 8079 | 7127 | 67127 | April 1953 |
| 1081 | 8081 | 7128 | 67128 | December 1950 |

In 1935 former Great Northern Railway 'C2' class, LNER 'C12' class, 4-4-2 tank locomotive No. 4016 made several appearances on the Saxmundham to Aldeburgh services, deputizing for the normal 'F3' class 2-4-2 tank engine, during her wanderings in the Norwich and Ipswich districts. The locomotive was not popular with the local crews and finally settled at Parkeston shed. The class was introduced between 1898 and 1907 for use on the GNR London suburban services and also in the West Riding of Yorkshire. On being displaced on the services from Kings Cross by the Ivatt and Gresley 0-6-2 tank locomotives, later LNER 'N1' and 'N2' classes, many 'C2s' were dispersed to country depots and it was thought that after Grouping No. 4016 was sent to the former GER section for evaluation. In later years after nationalization four of the class worked on the Saffron Walden branch whilst others saw service on the Bury St Edmunds to Long Melford and Thetford to Swaffham branches. For a short while in the early 1950s No. 67387, allocated to Yarmouth South Town shed and fitted with push-pull gear, also worked shuttle services to Lowestoft as well as Beccles and Saxmundham over the East Suffolk line. During that time she on one occasion worked one round trip to Aldeburgh and return covering for the branch locomotive which had failed because of shortage of steam caused by poor coal. Sister engine No. 67366 was transferred from New England in April 1955 as replacement for No. 67387 and worked to Saxmundham but did not work across the Aldeburgh branch.

| GER No. | LNER 1924 No. | LNER 1946 No. | BR No. | Withdrawn |
|---------|---------------|---------------|--------|-----------|
| 1016 | 4016 | 7355 | – | March 1948 |
| 1537 | 4537 | 7387 | 67387 | February 1955 |

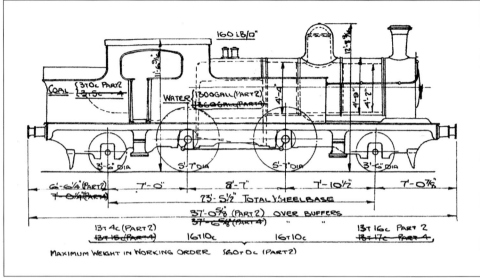

GCR class '3 Altered' 2-4-2T, later LNER 'F1' class.

Former Great Central Railway class '3 Altered', later LNER class 'F1' 2-4-2T No. 5727 was used on Aldeburgh branch services for a short period in 1938. Her performance showed no improvement on the existing "F3" class 2-4-2T and No. 5727 was soon transferred away from the Ipswich district.                                                    *Author's Collection*

The leading dimensions of the 'C12' class were:

| | | |
|---|---|---|
| *Cylinders* | *2 inside* | 18 in. x 26 in. |
| *Motion* | | Stephenson with slide valves |
| *Boiler* | *Max. diameter* | 4 ft 5 in. |
| | *Barrel length* | 10 ft 1 in. |
| *Firebox* | | 5 ft 6 in. |
| *Heating surface* | *Tubes*  213 x 1¾ in. | 1,016.0 sq. ft |
| | *Firebox* | 103.0 sq. ft |
| | *Total* | 1,119.0 sq. ft |
| *Grate area* | | 16.25 sq. ft |
| *Boiler pressure* | | 170 psi |
| *Leading wheels* | | 3 ft 8 in. |
| *Coupled wheels* | | 5 ft 8 in. |
| *Trailing wheels* | | 3 ft 8 in. |
| *Tractive effort* | | 17,900 lb. |
| *Length over buffers* | | 36 ft 9¼ in. |
| *Wheelbase* | | 27 ft 3 in. |
| *Weight in working order* | | 62 tons 6 cwt |
| *Water capacity* | | 1,350 gallons |
| *Coal capacity* | | 2 tons 5 cwt |

An unusual visitor to the branch in 1938 was former Great Central Railway (GCR) class '3 Altered', later LNER 'F1' class 2-4-2 tank locomotive No. 5727, which was transferred from Gorton shed and allocated to Ipswich from May until November. The 39 members of the class '3' and class '3 Altered' tank locomotives, the latter with larger bunkers, were introduced by the Manchester, Sheffield & Lincolnshire Railway between 1889 and 1893 to the design of Matthew Parker to improve suburban services radiating from Manchester, which had hitherto been worked by ancient 2-4-0 tank engines. The locomotives were built at Gorton works and by Neilson & Co. and later passed into the hands of the GCR and continued their suburban work well into the 1930s. Generally the class never transferred from the former parent system and during her brief sojourn in East Anglia No. 5727 was chiefly used on the Aldeburgh branch, possibly as part of an evaluation exercise to compare the class with the ex-GER 'F3' 2-4-2Ts. She was noted with the branch train formed of two GER bogie corridor coaches on 14th June then again in July, August and September 1938. Evidently No. 5727 was unpopular with local crews and showed no improvement on the performance of the 'F3s'. In November she returned to her home territory at Gorton. No. 5727 was built by Neilson & Co. in April 1892 (Works No. 4371) and was initially designated by the LNER to class 'F1/2', then class 'F1/3' in 1927 and to 'F1/4' in 1928, the main differential being the fitting of an original chimney ('F1/3') and LNER chimney ('F1/4').

| GER No. | LNER 1924 No. | LNER 1946 No. | BR No. | *Withdrawn* |
|---|---|---|---|---|
| 727 | 5727 | – | – | October 1939 |

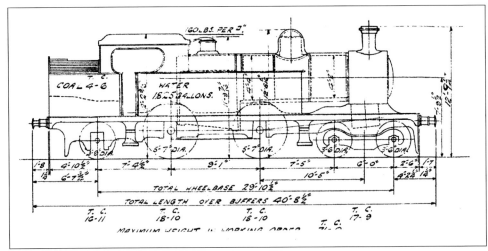

Robinson GCR class '9L', later LNER class 'C14' 4-4-2T.

'F6' class 2-4-2T No. 67230 spins along the branch near Saxmundham Junction with an Aldeburgh branch train formed of former North Eastern Railway brake/third with five compartments to diagram 503, a GER diagram 212 or 213 clerestory composite and then a Thompson LNER lavatory corridor third at the rear of the formation. With true branch line malpractice the locomotive displays no headcode.                     *The late Dr I.C. Allen*

Other former Great Central Railway interlopers made brief appearances on the Aldeburgh branch in the late 1930s when several Robinson-designed class '9L', later LNER class 'C14', 4-4-2 tank locomotives were transferred to Ipswich chiefly for use on the Felixstowe branch. A total of 12 engines were introduced in 1907 and initially saw service on the Marylebone suburban services but with the introduction of the larger GCR class '9N', later LNER 'A5' class, 4-6-2 tank locomotives from 1911 they were largely displaced and sent to country depots. After Grouping No. 6120 was transferred to East Anglia in 1934 followed by Nos. 6122, 6123, 6125, 6126, 6127, 6128 and 6129 in 1935 where four initially saw service at Bury St Edmunds before all eight were allocated to Ipswich, to be joined by No. 6130 in 1938. It was during this period that at least two, Nos. 6120 and 6126, worked on the Aldeburgh branch services standing in for 'F3' class failures, but were not popular with local enginemen. On the outbreak of World War II the engines were dispersed from Ipswich to Kings Lynn, Cambridge, Norwich and Lowestoft depots for short periods in 1940 and 1941 but by 1943 only three remained at Ipswich working on the Felixstowe diagrams until 1950 when they were displaced by the 'L1' class 2-6-4 tank locomotives.

| GER No. | LNER 1924 No. | LNER 1946 No. | BR No. | Withdrawn |
|---|---|---|---|---|
| 1120 | 6120 | 7440 | 67440 | July 1957 |
| 1126 | 6126 | 7446 | 67446 | May 1957 |

The 'F3' class was gradually superseded by members of S.D. Holden's 'G69' class, reclassified by the LNER to 'F6'. These 2-4-2 tank locomotives represented the final development of the 2-4-2 wheel arrangement on the GER. The class were originally put to work on the London suburban services but with the arrival of the GER 'L77' class 0-6-2 tank locomotives, redesignated class 'N7' by the LNER, were ousted as more of the 0-6-2 locomotives were introduced after Grouping. The 'F6s' gradually migrated to country depots and worked out their days on rural branches. The Ipswich district allocation first arrived in 1949 and was usually outbased at Aldeburgh and Framlingham, where they worked both passenger and mixed trains. Initially three locomotives were based at Ipswich but later a fourth locomotive was transferred from Yarmouth Beach as a cover. Usually No. 67220 was regular engine on the Aldeburgh branch with Nos. 67230 and 67239 covering when 67220 was not available. No. 67230 had seen better days and tended to leak after working hard and when on the Aldeburgh turn driver Runnacles asked his fireman to build up a huge fire with boiler full and blowing off fit to burst. Runnacles did not like to receive No. 67230 and constantly worried the Ipswich running foreman for a relief locomotive to replace the engine. On one occasion No. 67228 was sent down as replacement, and being in a worse condition than No. 67230 it is best left to the imagination in gauging Runnacles' reaction. On 4th August, 1951 'F6' No. 67230 failed on the branch train and the only available cover, 'J20' class 0-6-0 No. 64686, worked the service from Saxmundham to Aldeburgh and back despite being RA5 classification and officially restricted from the branch. Officialdom quickly realized they had a 'rogue' engine working the branch and purloined 'J17' class

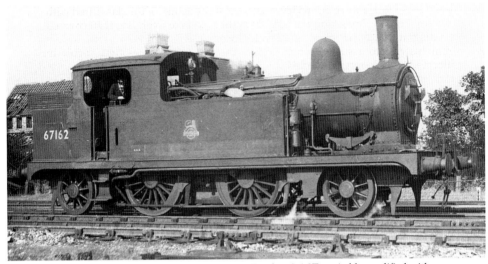

During World War II, two members of the LNER 'F4' class 2-4-2Ts, suitably modified with armour plating, worked coastal defence armoured trains over East Anglian lines including the Aldeburgh branch. Train C, which was disbanded in 1943, was hauled by No. 7214, which survived hostilities and with its armour plating removed was renumbered 7162 in the 1946 renumbering scheme. As BR No. 67162 she is shown just before withdrawal in 1955. *Author's Collection*

'F5' class 2-4-2T No. 7147 worked on the Aldeburgh branch in the 1920s. She was renumbered 7193 in the 1946 renumbering scheme and became BR No. 67193 before withdrawal in November 1957. *Author's Collection*

0-6-0 tender locomotive No. 65559, one of the few engines of the class fitted with vacuum brake for working the M&GN system, to take over. She then covered the diagram until 'J15' class 0-6-0 tender locomotive No. 65447 was sent down from Ipswich to assume branch duties. The 'F6' class locomotives regularly allocated to Aldeburgh included:

| GER No. | LNER 1924 No. | LNER 1946 No. | BR No. | Withdrawn |
|---|---|---|---|---|
| 1 | 7001 | 7230 | 67230 | May 1958 |
| 10 | 7010 | 7239 | 67239 | December 1955 |
| 61 | 7061 | 7220 | 67220 | July 1955 |
| 69 | 7069 | 7228 | 67228 | April 1958 |

During World War II, 15 class 'F4' and one class 'F5' 2-4-2 tank locomotives were loaned to the Government for hauling coastal defence armoured trains. The initial 40 members of the 'M15' class had entered service between 1884 and 1887 to the designs of T.W. Worsdell. Between 1903 and 1909 a further 120 locomotives were built, and from 1911 until 1920 the GER rebuilt 30 engines with higher boiler pressure and designated them 'M15R'. The earliest built locomotives were all condemned by 1929, whilst the LNER reclassified the 'M15s' to class 'F4' and the 'M15Rs' to class 'F5'. They were nicknamed 'Gobblers' because the original engines had a voracious appetite for coal and, although improvements were made, the name persisted. Between June 1940 and July 1943 the Aldeburgh branch together with the neighbouring Framlingham and Snape lines was regularly patrolled by the coastal defence trains, initially by train D powered by 'F4' class No. 7178 based at Ipswich, and then by train C hauled by 'F4' class No. 7214. After returning from patrols in Cornwall, train D resumed its activities on Suffolk and Essex branch lines until disbanded in July 1943. The classes were not new to the branch, for occasional use had been made on the line before the war, deputizing for the usual 'F3' class engines, and at least five 'F4' and 'F5' class locomotives were outbased at Aldeburgh in the period after Grouping and into nationalization.

| LNER class | GER No. | LNER 1924 No. | LNER 1946 No. | BR No. | Withdrawn |
|---|---|---|---|---|---|
| F4 | 74 | 7074 | 7182 | 67182 | January 1953 |
| F5 | 144 | 7144 | 7191 | 67191 | November 1955 |
| F4 | 146 | 7146 | – | – | January 1930 |
| F5 | 147 | 7147 | 7193 | 67193 | November 1957 |
| F4 | 178 | 7178 | 7173 | – | April 1948 |
| F4 | 214 | 7214 | 7162 | 67162 | August 1955 |
| F4 | 665 | 7665 | – | – | August 1926 |

In the early summer of 1949 a prominent member of the British Transport Commission was playing golf at the Thorpeness links on a fine sunny day. The usual 'F3' class 2-4-2 tank locomotive was working the branch when it stalled climbing away from Saxmundham Junction. The train was finally assisted by a light engine sent from Ipswich but unfortunately with brakes dragging the pair were making heavy weather taking the train to Aldeburgh. On passing the links

Strange motive power on the Aldeburgh branch in the early summer of 1949, in the form of ex-London Midland & Scottish Railway Ivatt class '2' 2-6-2T No. 41200 still bearing LMS on her side tanks. The engine was transferred in haste to Ipswich to work the Aldeburgh branch services after a prominent member of the British Transport Commission had his round of golf disturbed by two of the native ex-GER locomotives exuding sparks which resulted in a huge fire across the golf course. Unfortunately the new engine was not popular and only served for two summers before returning permanently to the London Midland Region.                    *The late Dr I.C. Allen*

'E4' class 2-4-0 No. 62789 standing at Thorpeness Halt with an officers' special during inspection for the best kept station garden competition. The leading vehicle is DE962451, former GER saloon No. 48 to diagram 20 coupled to an LNER Gresley corridor brake/third. The solitary siding at Thorpeness can be seen in the foreground with the station gardens between the tracks.

*The late Dr I.C. Allen*

the pyrotechnics resulted in a huge fire across the golf course. The BTC Member and his golfing companions were not amused and, no doubt highly embarrassed by the incident, officialdom demanded that the ancient steeds (with long chimneys !) should be replaced as a matter of urgency. The chain of command acted with commendable speed and ordered a suitable modern locomotive to be sent to Ipswich for specific work on the Aldeburgh branch. Thus arrived on the scene former London Midland & Scottish Railway (LMS) Ivatt 2-6-2T No. 41200 post-haste from Bangor shed still bearing the identity of its previous owner 'LMS' on the side tanks. The engine dated from February 1947 and had been introduced into service as LMS No. 1200, and Bangor footplate staff considered the locomotive 'immensely popular'. Its allocation to Ipswich especially to work the Aldeburgh branch, however, proved exactly the opposite with local staff and driver Runnacles and his companion on the opposite shift finding any excuse to report it unfit for service or fail it completely, despite the comfortable fully-enclosed cab and self-cleaning smokebox. The one real problem was coaling the high bunker at Aldeburgh. At other times No. 41200 seems to have been held as spare locomotive at Ipswich shed. Despite its unpopularity the locomotive continued to serve on the branch in the summer of 1950 but had returned to the London Midland Region by 1951.

The principal dimensions of the locomotive were:

| | | |
|---|---|---|
| Cylinders | | 16 in. x 24 in. |
| Motion | | Walschaerts valve gear |
| Boiler | Barrel length | 10 ft 9⅞ in. |
| | Max. diameter | 4 ft 3 in./4 ft 8 in. |
| Firebox | | 5 ft 11 in. |
| Heating surface | Tubes | 162 x 1⅝ in. |
| | Superheater tubes | 12 x 5⅛ in. |
| | Tubes | 924.5 sq. ft |
| | Firebox | 101.0 sq. ft |
| | Total | 1,025.5 sq. ft |
| | Superheater | 134.0 sq. ft |
| | Total | 1,159.5 sq. ft |
| Grate area | | 17.5 sq. ft |
| Boiler pressure | | 200 psi |
| Leading wheels | | 3 ft 0 in. |
| Driving wheels | | 5 ft 0 in. |
| Trailing wheels | | 3 ft 0 in. |
| Tractive effort | | 17,400 lb. |
| Length over buffers | | 38 ft 9½ in. |
| Wheelbase | | 30 ft 3 in. |
| Weight in working order | | 63 tons 5 cwt |
| Water capacity | | 1,350 gallons |
| Coal capacity | | 3 tons |

The 'T26' class 2-4-0 tender locomotives, which were later designated class 'E4' by the LNER, made occasional forays to the Aldeburgh branch. The 100 locomotives were built at Stratford works to the design of J. Holden between 1891 and 1902 and were nicknamed 'Intermediates'. The engines were utilized on cross-country routes and mixed traffic workings and were often employed on the East Suffolk main line. Details of engines known to have worked the branch or spent time outbased at Aldeburgh included in the latter years Nos. 62782 and 62789, which acted as branch locomotives in lieu of the usual tank locomotive. The employment of No. 62789 during March and April 1951 was extremely unpopular with Aldeburgh enginemen who considered tender-first working a disadvantage despite the tender being equipped with a backplate. No. 62789 later worked across the branch with an engineer's inspection train and also with a special formed of two coaches conveying judges in the best kept station gardens competition.

| GER No. | LNER 1924 No. | LNER 1946 No. | BR No. | Withdrawn |
|---|---|---|---|---|
| 413 | 7413 | – | – | October 1931 |
| 465 | 7465 | – | – | July 1928 |
| 466 | 7466 | 2782 | 62782 | November 1954 |
| 467 | 7467 | – | – | April 1937 |
| 468 | 7468 | – | – | August 1929 |
| 469 | 7469 | – | – | June 1929 |
| 470 | 7470 | – | – | May 1934 |
| 472 | 7472 | – | – | May 1938 |
| 473 | 7473 | – | – | December 1935 |
| 474 | 7474 | – | – | April 1929 |
| 475 | 7475 | – | – | May 1931 |
| 476 | 7476 | – | – | March 1937 |
| 497 | 7497 | 2789 | 62789 | December 1957 |

As excursion traffic increased, members of the LNER 'D13' class 4-4-0 tender locomotives made occasional visits to the Aldeburgh branch from around Grouping until 1935. Originally built as GER 'T19' class 2-4-0s, 110 were constructed between 1886 and 1897. Sixty were subsequently rebuilt as 4-4-0s between 1905 and 1908 and 50 of these engines entered service with the LNER. Ipswich shed had an allocation of five in 1923 but they were gradually transferred or scrapped until the last one was withdrawn from the depot in 1937. Like all tender classes the engine worked tender first down the branch to haul excursions destinations south of Saxmundham or engine first when destinations were north of Saxmundham. Locomotives known to have worked across the branch included:

| GER No. | LNER 1924 No. | Withdrawn |
|---|---|---|
| 700 | 7700 | October 1935 |
| 731 | 7731 | August 1931 |
| 737 | 7737 | April 1933 |
| 741 | 7741 | December 1935 |
| 744 | 7744 | April 1935 |
| 765 | 7765 | January 1930 |
| 1037 | 8037 | December 1934 |

The LNER 'D14', 'D15' and 'D16' class 4-4-0 tender locomotives made sporadic visits to the branch usually with excursion trains to and from Ipswich and regularly in the 1930s with the weekly 'Eastern Belle' Pullman train from Liverpool Street. The 4-4-0s however struggled with the load of seven Pullman coaches on the undulating gradients and after stalling on several occasions the instruction was issued that the 'D16/3' class required assistance when working the train between Saxmundham and Aldeburgh. The motive power authorities, however, considered this a costly exercise and 'B12/3' class 4-6-0 locomotives took over the working. Thereafter their forays to Aldeburgh were with day excursion traffic. The 111 GER 'S46' and 'D56' classes, later LNER 'D14' and 'D15' class, dated from 1900, with the last 10 emerging as class 'D16' in 1923. Throughout the years many were rebuilt and the majority that survived into BR ownership formed the 'D16/3' sub-class. Locomotives known to have worked across the branch included:

| GER No. | LNER 1924 No. | LNER 1946 No. | BR No. | Withdrawn |
|---|---|---|---|---|
| 1875 | 8875 | 2526 | 62526 | May 1957 |
| 1855 | 8855 | 2546* | 62546 | June 1957 |
| 1841 | 8841 | 2552 | 62552 | October 1955 |
| 1845 | 8845 | 2556 | 62556 | January 1957 |
| 1849 | 8849 | 2560 | – | September 1948 |
| 1819 | 8819 | 2590 | 62590 | January 1952 |
| 1780 | 8780 | 2611 | 62611 | January 1957 |
| 1781 | 8781 | 2612 | 62612 | November 1959 |

* Named *Claud Hamilton* in 1947.

From the late 1930s Gresley rebuild of Holden's 'S69' class 4-6-0 tender locomotives, the 'B12/3' class, occasionally worked across the branch on special trains for Thorpeness and Aldeburgh Regatta days when increased loadings demanded special through trains from Ipswich. They also worked Sunday excursions from Ipswich between 1951 and 1954; one excursion in 1952 was loaded to eight coaches so it was impossible to run-round the train at Aldeburgh and an unfitted 'J17' class 0-6-0 tender locomotive worked the train back to Saxmundham. This unofficial action was not repeated. Before World War II the class had largely superseded the 'D16/3' class engines on the weekly 'Eastern Belle' Pullman trains from and to Liverpool Street. The use of the 'B12/3' class did not always guarantee smooth working, for in August 1939 the 'Eastern Belle' hauled by No. 8577 stalled on the down working soon after passing Saxmundham Junction whilst climbing the 1 in 58 gradient with its heavy train. The class was first introduced in 1911 when the GER authorities were finding the 'Claud Hamilton' 4-4-0s struggling with the ever-increasing heavy trains. Known as the '1500s' from the running number of the initial locomotive, a total of 71 were built to 1921 although No. 1506 was totally written off after a fatal crash at Colchester and the number was never reused. After Grouping the locomotives were allocated to class 'B12' and a further 10 engines were introduced. With the introduction of the Gresley 'B17' class three-cylinder 4-6-0 tender locomotives from 1928, and a general improvement in motive power availability, the LNER found several 'B12s' could be made available for use on other sections of the system. Accordingly, between 1931 and

'D15' class 4-4-0 No. 8799 departing from Saxmundham with an up stopping passenger service formed of six-wheel vehicles in the late 1920s. By this date the footbridge had lost its roof but still retained its side windows. Note the miniature repeater arms on the down starter signal post to the left. No. 8799 was rebuilt to 'D15/2' class in February 1934. *Author's Collection*

'B12/3' class 4-6-0 No. 61562 darkens the landscape as she swings off the down East Suffolk main line to the Aldeburgh branch at Saxmundham Junction with a branch service. The train is formed of LNER 4-compartment brake/third to diagram 340, a GER clerestory first/third composite to diagram 212 or 231 (arranged luggage/2 x first compartments/2 lavatories and then 4 x third class compartments) built 1900 to 1906 and finally a GER 8-compartment third to diagram 430 dating from 1913 to 1915. *The late Dr I.C. Allen*

1942 several of the class migrated to the Great North of Scotland section working trains from Aberdeen to Keith, Elgin and Peterhead. Most of the class that remained on the GE section was subsequently rebuilt between 1932 and 1944 with a larger boiler and other alterations and were designated to class 'B12/3'. Ipswich depot had a large allocation and it was usually one of these which visited the Aldeburgh branch. Indeed during the first week of June 1952 No. 61535 was working the branch diagram for several days as Ipswich depot was unable to provide the usual 'F6' class 2-4-2 tank locomotive. On 19th May, 1953 an Aldeburgh to Windsor excursion was hauled on the Eastern Region by No. 61571 with No. 61569 hauling the return working. Those known to have worked across the line included:

| GER No. | LNER 1924 No. | LNER 1946 No. | BR No. | Withdrawn |
|---|---|---|---|---|
| 1533 | 8533 | 1533 | 61533 | November 1959 |
| 1535 | 8535* | 1535 | 61535 | December 1959 |
| 1537 | 8537 | 1537 | 61537 | April 1957 |
| 1561 | 8561 | 1561 | 61561 | December 1958 |
| 1562 | 8562* | 1562 | 61562 | August 1955 |
| 1564 | 8564 | 1564 | 61564 | November 1958 |
| 1566 | 8566 | 1566 | 61566 | January 1959 |
| 1568 | 8568* | 1568 | 61568 | August 1959 |
| 1569 | 8569 | 1569 | 61569 | January 1957 |
| 1570 | 8570 | 1570 | 61570 | March 1958 |
|  | 8571 | 1571 | 61571 | December 1959 |
|  | 8572 | 1572 | 61572 | September 1961 |
|  | 8577* | 1577 | 61577 | December 1959 |

* The following were renumbered in the 1942 scheme; No. 8535 to 7449, No. 8562 to 7476, No. 8568 to 7482, No. 8577 to 7491

On 2nd December, 1953 the locomotive booked to work the Ipswich six-wheel district engineer's inspection saloon on a visit to the branch failed just before departure and the only available standby was 'L1' class 2-6-4T No. 67705. Despite her RA7 route availability it was decided to allow the locomotive to propel the saloon coach as far as Leiston but not on to Aldeburgh because of weak bridges and as most of the inspection involved the trackwork leading to Garrett's siding, this proved acceptable to the inspection team and district civil engineer. The 'L1s' were introduced in 1945 to the design of Edward Thompson when the prototype No. 9000 built at Doncaster entered service. After extensive trials a further 98 engines were built at Darlington and by the North British Locomotive Co. and Robert Stephenson & Hawthorns between 1948 and 1950. Several members of the class including No. 67705 were re-allocated from Stratford to Ipswich in May 1950 and were immediately put to work on the Felixstowe branch as well as workings to Bury St Edmunds, Cambridge, Norwich and Yarmouth.

| Original No. | BR No. | Withdrawn |
|---|---|---|
| E9004 | 67705 | December 1960 |

*Left:* On 2nd December, 1953 the locomotive booked to work an officers' special to the Aldeburgh branch failed on shed at Ipswich and the only available standby engine was 'L1' class 2-6-4T No. 67705. Despite the RA7 route availability it was decided to let the locomotive take the special formed of 6-wheel saloon coach No. DE960903 as far as Leiston but not through to Aldeburgh. Here No. 67705 propels the saloon towards Leiston station with the goods yard to the left and Garrett's holding sidings to the right.

*The late Dr I.C. Allen*

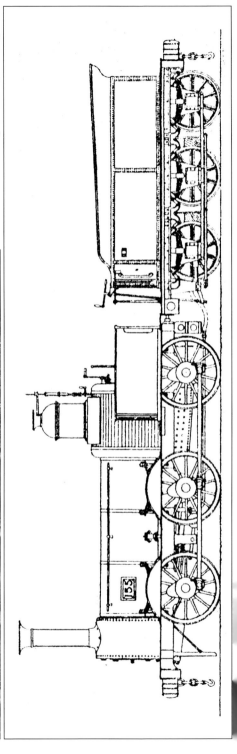

*Below:* Stothert & Slaughter 0-6-0 goods engine.

In the early years tank locomotives outbased at Aldeburgh normally handled the goods traffic but special and out-of-course freight workings brought a variety of tender locomotives to the line. The engines known to have worked the East Suffolk main line and branch freight trains included five 0-6-0 goods engines built by Stothert & Slaughter for the ECR in March and April 1846. They were originally numbered 97 to 101 but were soon renumbered 155 to 159 and were delivered with six-wheel tenders. In 1858 the tenders received new tanks with greater water capacity and although the first two locomotives were early candidates for scrapping, Nos. 157 to 159 were placed on the duplicate list in 1864 becoming Nos. 1570, 1580 and 1590 respectively. The first two were rebuilt with new boilers in 1866 and were sent away to Cambridge to work goods trains to Colchester via Sudbury and the Colne Valley & Halstead Railway. No. 1590 was condemned in April 1873, No. 1580 in August 1880 and No. 1570 in October 1883.

Another class used in the early years was Robert Stephenson & Co.'s 'Long Boiler' 2-4-0 tender locomotives, delivered to the ECR between March and September 1847. Numbered in the series 71 to 77, they regularly worked the East Suffolk line in the first decade after opening. They were the subject of several modifications and rebuildings, Nos. 71 to 77 receiving new boilers in 1860 with Nos. 72 and 75 being rebuilt in June 1867. Three were placed on the duplicate list, Nos. 71, 72 and 75 becoming 710, 720 and 750 respectively in 1876. The locomotives were scrapped as follows: Nos. 710 in May 1878, 720 in September 1877, 73 in November 1869, 74 in April 1859, 750 in April 1881, 76 in July 1868 and 77 in August 1871.

Between 1854 and 1855 Gooch introduced into service five 0-6-0 goods engines with fairly new boilers taken from five large Crampton singles which were scrapped because of lack of adhesion. The five, numbered 233 to 237, were built at Stratford works and had outside bearings. They were allocated to Ipswich for a while and worked the East Suffolk goods services. New boilers designed by Sinclair were fitted to Nos. 234 and 236 in October 1867, whilst Johnson rebuilt the remaining three locomotives in 1869 and 1870. The five engines were placed on the duplicate list in 1880 by having a cipher added to their running number but only survived a few more years in service, No. 234 being condemned in April 1882, Nos. 233 and 235 in January 1883, No. 237 in October 1883 and No. 236 in November 1884.

The next locomotives to work the Aldeburgh branch goods traffic and some special passenger services were Sinclair's celebrated 'Y' class 2-4-0 goods engines. In all 110 locomotives were provided by a variety of makers and introduced into service between July 1859 and August 1866, Neilson & Co. building Nos. 307 to 326, Robert Stephenson & Co. Nos. 327 to 341, R. & W. Hawthorn Nos. 342 to 356, Kitson & Co. Nos. 357 to 381, Vulcan Foundry Nos. 382 to 406 and Schnider et Cie of Creusot Nos. 407 to 416. Each batch had detail differences and locomotive No. 327 was displayed at the Exhibition held in Hyde Park, London in 1862. The engines worked all over the GER system on passenger, mixed and goods trains. Over the years most were rebuilt and a number converted into 4-4-0 tender locomotives for passenger work. Scrapping of the class commenced in 1882 and after 1888 surviving engines were placed on

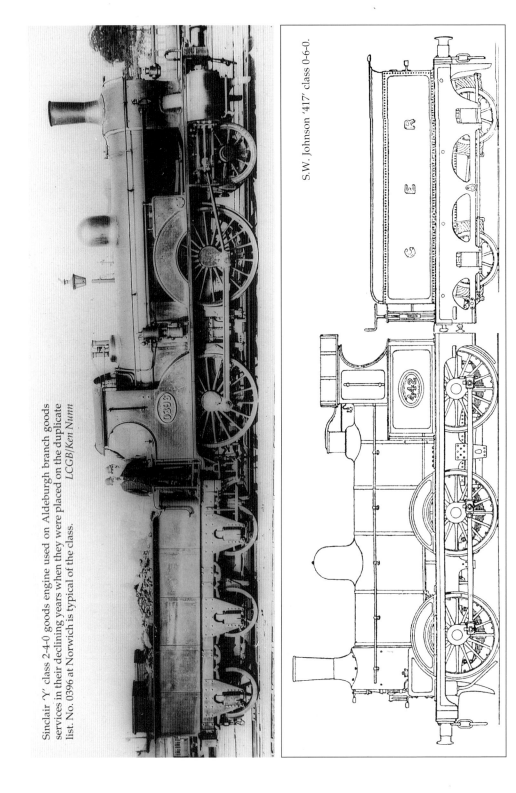

Sinclair 'Y' class 2-4-0 goods engine used on Aldeburgh branch goods services in their declining years when they were placed on the duplicate list. No. 0396 at Norwich is typical of the class.                    LCGB/Ken Nunn

S.W. Johnson '417' class 0-6-0.

the duplicate list by having the prefix '0' placed before the running number. The class only saw service on the branch in their declining years and the final batch of four was condemned for scrapping in 1894.

From the 1880s a variety of 0-6-0 tender locomotives were used on the daily freight services. The first of these was the '417' class 0-6-0s designed by S.W. Johnson and built between 1867 and 1869 by Neilson & Co. and the Worcester Engine Co. The 60 were numbered 417 to 476 inclusive and the first member of the '417' class was withdrawn in 1888. Scrapping continued every year, with the exception of 1897 until 1899. The survivors after 1891 were placed on the duplicate list by having a '0' prefix added to the number.

The Johnson '477' class 0-6-0 tender locomotives were the next class associated with the goods services to Aldeburgh. The engines came from a variety of builders, Beyer, Peacock, Robert Stephenson, Dübs, Nasmyth Wilson and the Yorkshire Engine Co. between 1871 and 1873 and were numbered 477 to 526. Most were rebuilt in their lifetime and they were withdrawn between 1897 and 1902 when members of Worsdell's 'Y14' class 0-6-0 tender locomotives were allocated by Ipswich for the Aldeburgh branch freight diagram.

After the withdrawal of the '477' class the freight traffic, when not handled by the branch locomotive, was placed in the hands of the GER 'Y14' class 0-6-0s designed by T.W. Worsdell. Introduced in 1883, these small engines were later classified 'J15' by the LNER. Such was the success of the design that building continued until 1913 with all except 19 of the class of 289 built at Stratford works, the others being constructed by Sharp, Stewart & Co. Because of their low RA1 route availability this ubiquitous class was ideal for branch line traffic and in the latter years often deputized on Aldeburgh branch passenger services including the last steam-hauled passenger train, when No. 65447 worked the 7.24 pm from Saxmundham on 9th June, 1956. Thereafter a 'J15' class engine was occasionally diagrammed on the Aldeburgh goods from Ipswich and return, although more often than not a 'J17' locomotive worked the service. The use of steam traction ended in March 1960 when the Snape goods line closed and steam engines were transferred away from Ipswich. Locomotives known to have worked on the Aldeburgh branch included:

| GER No. | LNER 1924 No. | LNER 1946 No. | BR No. | Withdrawn |
|---|---|---|---|---|
| 37 | 7037 | – | – | August 1923 |
| 38 | 07038 | – | – | September 1932 |
| 39 | 07039 | – | – | March 1933 |
| 40 | – | – | – | October 1922 |
| 509 | 7509 | 5429 | – | November 1950 |
| 510 | 7510 | 5430 | 65430 | January 1956 |
| 516 | 7516 | 5435 | 65435 | October 1956 |
| 525 | 7525 | – | – | October 1935 |
| 537 | – | – | – | August 1923 |
| 538 | 7538 | – | – | December 1938 |
| 542 | 7542 | 5470 | 65470* | December 1959 |
| 545 | 7545 | 5473 | 65473* | March 1960 |
| 546 | 7546 | 5474 | 65474* | February 1960 |
| 550 | 7550 | 5478 | 65478* | October 1961 |

With true branch line malpractice 'J15' class 0-6-0 No. 65447 carrying no headcode crosses from the main line to the Aldeburgh branch at Saxmundham Junction with a down train formed of a Thompson LNER brake/third to diagram 140, then a Thompson full third and finally an ex-GER first/third composite to diagram 237, formed lavatory 2 x first class compartments/5 x third class compartments, and dating from 1907 to 1915.                    *The late Dr I.C. Allen*

Following an inspection of the Aldeburgh branch, 'J15' class 0-6-0 No. 65459 displaying express passenger train headcode passes Wickham Market Junction with officers' saloon en route to Ipswich.                    *The late Dr I.C. Allen*

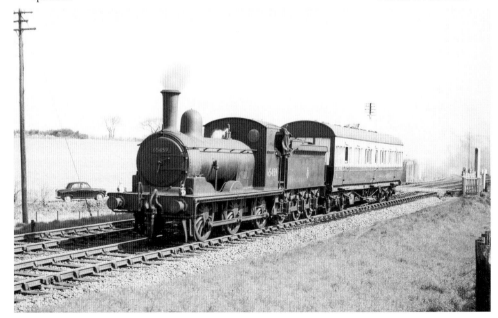

| GER No. | LNER 1924 No. | LNER 1946 No. | BR No. | Withdrawn |
|---|---|---|---|---|
| 556 | 7556 | 5454 | 65454* | May 1959 |
| 559 | 7559 | 5457 | 65457* | February 1962 |
| 561 | 7561 | 5459 | 65459* | February 1960 |
| 566 | 7566 | 5464 | 65464* | September 1962 |
| 568 | 7568 | 5466 | 65466* | July 1958 |
| 569 | 7569 | 5467 | 65467* | February 1959 |
| 570 | 7570 | 5468 | 65468* | September 1959 |
| 592 | 7592 | – | – | August 1928 |
| 593 | 7593 | – | – | December 1926 |
| 594 | 7594 | – | – | July 1926 |
| 595 | 7595 | – | – | June 1929 |
| 596 | 7596 | – | – | November 1932 |
| 597 | 7597 | – | – | April 1928 |
| 598 | 7598 | – | – | September 1926 |
| 599 | 7599 | – | – | May 1931 |
| 640 | 7640 | 5440 | 65440* | October 1960 |
| 641 | 7641 | 5441 | 65441* | October 1958 |
| 642 | 7642 | 5442 | 65442* | May 1958 |
| 647 | 7647 | 5447 | 65447* | April 1959 |
| 693 | 7693 | – | – | July 1928 |
| 694 | 7694 | – | – | October 1931 |
| 836 | 7836 | 5361 | 65361 | September 1962 |
| 866 | 7866 | 5377 | – | February 1951 |
| 875 | 7875 | 5382 | – | March 1952 |
| 883 | 7883 | 5388 | 65388 | May 1959 |
| 886 | 7886 | 5389 | 65389 | April 1960 |
| 897 | 7897 | 5396 | – | March 1951 |
| 910 | 7910 | 5404 | 65404 | October 1956 |
| 914 | 7914 | 5407 | 65407 | April 1951 |
| 915 | 7915 | 5408 | 65408 | December 1951 |
| 923 | 7923 | – | – | October 1934 |
| 933 | 7933 | – | – | March 1936 |
| 934 | 7934 | 5421 | – | March 1948 |
| 936 | 7936 | – | – | April 1937 |
| 937 | 7937 | 5422 | 65422 | July 1955 |
| 939 | 7939 | – | – | February 1936 |
| 940 | 7940 | 5423 | – | November 1950 |
| 941 | 7941 | 5424 | 65424* | December 1959 |
| 942 | 7942 | 5425 | 65425 | October 1956 |
| 943 | 7943 | 5426 | 65426 | May 1951 |

* Westinghouse and Vacuum brake fitted for working passenger trains.

The introduction of eight-coupled heavy goods locomotives on the Whitemoor to Temple Mills and other main line freight services from the 1930s gradually released other 0-6-0 tender classes for cross-country and branch line freight workings. The LNER 'J17' class was originally built to the design of James Holden and introduced from 1900 as GER class 'F48' with round-topped fireboxes. A further batch of 30 engines was produced with Belpaire fireboxes as class 'G58' from 1905 to 1911. Thereafter some of the earliest engines were

The Aldeburgh branch handled considerable freight traffic in the 1950s, especially to and from Leiston. Here 'J17' class 0-6-0 No. 65507 works a down train on the East Suffolk main line near Woodbridge.                                                                                    *The late Dr I.C. Allen*

'J17' class 0-6-0s were rarely employed on Aldeburgh branch passenger services but here No. 65559 has charge of a down service near Saxmundham Junction. The motley collection of coaching stock include, from the locomotive, LNER Gresley brake/third with four compartments to diagram 340, then GER clerestory composite to diagram 212 or 231 dating from 1900 to 1906 arranged luggage/2 x first class compartments/pair of lavatories/4 x third class compartments. The third carriage is GER 8-compartment third to diagram 430 built 1913 to 1915 and the final vehicle is an LNER Thompson lavatory first/third composite.                *The late Dr I.C. Allen*

rebuilt with Belpaire fireboxes and reclassified. After Grouping the 'F48s' became LNER class 'J16' and the 'G58s' LNER class 'J17' but by 1932 all round-topped firebox locomotives had been rebuilt with Belpaire fireboxes as class 'J17' and class 'J16' became extinct. The 'J17s', gradually replaced the 'J15' class on the branch freight workings by the outbreak of World War II and their superior tractive effort was appreciated by the footplate crews when working ammunition trains from Garrett's siding.

For a number of years from the early 1950s Ipswich retained four of the 'J17' class for working the 'bonus' goods but they were restricted to a maximum load of 20 wagons between Aldeburgh and Leiston and on climbing the 1 in 58 bank soon after Saxmundham Junction in the down direction and leaving Aldeburgh on the up road. Locomotive known to have worked the Aldeburgh branch goods services included:

| GER No. | LNER 1924 No. | LNER 1946 No. | BR No. | Withdrawn |
|---|---|---|---|---|
| 1157 | 8157 | 5507 | 65507 | September 1961 |
| 1160 | 8160 | 5510 | 65510 | March 1955 |
| 1162 | 8162 | 5512 | 65512 | December 1959 |
| 1163 | 8163 | 5513 | 65513 | March 1961 |
| 1209 | 8209 | 5559 | 65559* | November 1959 |
| 1210 | 8210 | 5560 | 65560 | June 1962 |
| 1211 | 8211 | 5561 | 65561 | December 1959 |
| 1217 | 8217 | 5567 | 65567* | August 1962 |
| 1228 | 8228 | 5578 | 65578 | March 1962 |

* Equipped with vacuum ejectors for working passenger trains.

On 4th August, 1951 due to failure of the booked 'F6' class 2-4-2 tank engine, 'J20' class 0-6-0 tender locomotive No. 64686 with an RA5 availability was substituted on the branch services. Officially barred from the line it was used until the replacement in the form of 'J17' class 0-6-0 tender locomotive No. 65559 with suitable RA4 route availability was substituted. The 'J20' class were the largest of the ex-GER 0-6-0 tender locomotives and 25 were built between 1920 and 1922 to the design of A.J. Hill as GER 'D81' class. In accordance with the GER practice the new design had cylinders, valve gear, boiler and other parts interchangeable with the Holden '1500' class 4-6-0s. When introduced into traffic the 'J20s' were the most powerful 0-6-0 freight locomotives in Great Britain and retained this superiority until O.V.S. Bulleid introduced his 'Q1' class 0-6-0s on the Southern Railway in 1942. Initially the 'D81s' and later 'J20s' worked the heavy Whitemoor to Temple Mills freight trains and although equipped with vacuum ejectors rarely worked passenger services.

| GER No. | LNER 1924 No. | LNER 1946 No. | BR No. | Withdrawn |
|---|---|---|---|---|
| 1281 | 8281 | 4686 | 64686 | August 1960 |

Another interloper on the branch was LNER 'J39' class 0-6-0 tender locomotive No. 64785 which worked an engineering train for relaying work on

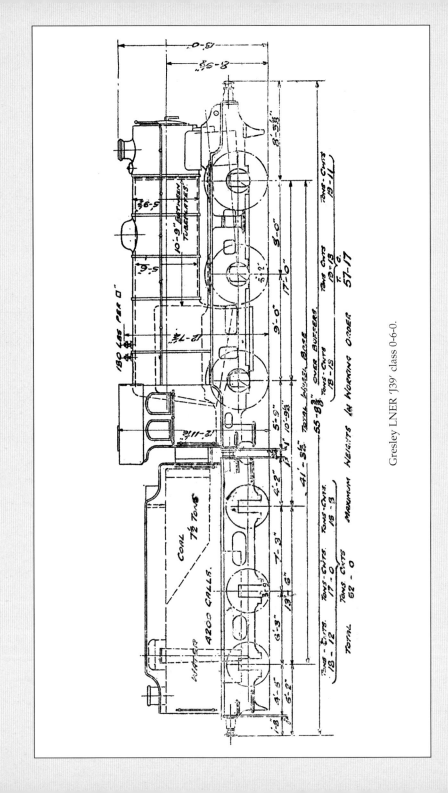

Gresley LNER 'J39' class 0-6-0.

19th February, 1951. The Ipswich running foreman must have been short of suitable locomotives of RA4 category for placing No. 64785, dating from May 1929 and of RA6 route classification, on such work could have led to complaints from the district civil engineer. A total of 289 locomotives were introduced to the design of Nigel Gresley, later Sir Nigel, between 1926 and 1941as a group standard for use on primarily goods work but they were also used on passenger duties.

| LNER No. | LNER 1946 No. | BR No. | Withdrawn |
|----------|---------------|--------|-----------|
| 2732 | 4785 | 64785 | June 1959 |

Richard Garrett & Sons utilized two locomotives to shunt wagons to and from the interchange siding at Leiston to their works. In 1925 A.F. Bennett, the works manager, approached C.W. Glaze, the manager at Stratford works, with a design for a small shunting locomotive similar to a Sentinel shunting engine, probably in the hope of enticing sales. After some deliberation H.N. Gresley, the chief mechanical engineer of the LNER, turned down the proposal and replied to Glaze, 'I think you should advise Colonel Garrett that the engine proposed is too small'. Curiously the design featured in the company's sales catalogue but a prototype was never built. After a runaway accident with wagons the withdrawal of horse power for shunting vehicles between Leiston station sidings and the works was imperative and Garrett's subsequently purchased the steam locomotive *Sirapite*. It was a 0-4-0 single-cylinder geared locomotive built by Aveling & Porter Ltd of Invicta Works, Canterbury, Kent in 1906, Works No. 6158, one of about 140 traction engines built for use on railways and chiefly used at Kent & Essex Cement Works. The locomotive, costing £985, was originally delivered to Gypsum Mines Ltd of Mountfield in February 1907 for use on their tramway where it received its name, *Sirapite* being *Parisite* with the first syllable reversed. *Sirapite* after giving several years of sterling service was found to be underpowered and was subsequently transferred to Garrett's on 2nd November, 1930, the attractions to the new owners being its small size, low appetite for coal and low gearing which was ideal for hauling wagons up the 1 in 38 incline. The engine was well maintained, painted green and the Aveling & Porter horse badge on the smokebox was later replaced by Garrett's leaping leopard motif in brass with the words 'strength - silence - speed'. The locomotive was last used during week ending 14th July, 1962 and was ultimately sold to W.H. McAlpine of Gateshead for preservation on 16th May, 1966. The diminutive machine returned to the Long Shop at Leiston in 2004 for restoration to full working order. Thanks in part to a £50,000 grant from the Heritage Lottery Fund, the work was finally completed and *Sirapite* made its debut to the public on 25th March, 2010, when it appeared in steam on the BBC *Look East* television programme. The locomotive will be used in conjunction with the Long Shop Museum, operating on a short length of track.

The replacement for *Sirapite* was a 120 hp 200 volts centre cab battery locomotive built by Electromobile (Works No. W247) in 1927 for Metropolitan Vickers of Eaglescliffe. On arrival at Leiston in April 1962 it was overhauled and

Three-quarter rear view of Richard Garrett's Aveling & Porter 0-4-0 locomotive *Sirapite* (Works No. 6158) at Leiston on 19th December, 1961.                                   *J.H. Meredith*

Garrett's 120 hp 200 volts centre-cab battery shunting locomotive in the siding at Leiston on 20th May, 1966.                                                                                    *G.R. Mortimer*

painted yellow with diagonal black stripes on each end, black underframe, roof, grab handles, buffers and coupling hooks and red buffer beams. The locomotive was scrapped on site by A. King & Sons Ltd of Norwich in August 1968.

With the withdrawal of steam traction from East Anglia, Ipswich depot used a variety of diesel-electric classes to work the branch freight services. The first were BTH/AEI 800hp Bo-Bo diesel-electric locomotives, later '8/5' and then BR class '15'. The locomotives in the series D8200 to D8243 were generally found to be underpowered for heavy goods traffic and were quickly replaced by larger locomotives. The class was used often in pairs on permanent way recovery trains after closure of the Sizewell to Aldeburgh section.

Another diesel-electric class used for a short period after introduction in 1959 was the North British Locomotive Co. (NBL) 1,100 hp Bo-Bos, of which Nos. D6110 to D6137 were allocated to Stratford and Ipswich depots. After a brief period in service in East Anglia, major technical difficulties were experienced and by September 1960 all were re-allocated to the Scottish Region, enabling them to be nearer the NBL works in Glasgow for failures and defects to be rectified.

BR Sulzer type '2' diesel-electric locomotives, initially classified '11/1', later class '24' were then used by Ipswich depot on freight and excursion passenger work for a short period. These locomotives were found to be underpowered when hauling the freight services or atomic flask trains on the undulating gradients across the branch and were only operated for a short period until replaced by Brush type '2' diesel-electric locomotives.

The '11/1' class locomotives initially worked turn and turn about with the Brush type '2' diesel-electric locomotives, class '13/2', later '31/1' on freight services. As well as working main line passenger and freight trains, the initial allocation at Ipswich, Nos. D5520-24, D5526-9, D5537-44 and D5548-54, also worked the various branch freight services including those to Aldeburgh. Later visitors included Nos. D5617, D5631, D5632, D5661, D5662, D5682 and D5699.

The English Electric class '17/3', later class '37', 1,750 hp diesel-electric locomotives numbered in the series 'D6700' occasionally worked across the Aldeburgh branch in the early years but after the withdrawal of passenger and freight services they became synonymous with operating the nuclear flask train to and from Sizewell sidings. A small number, including Nos. 37038, 37053, 37094 and 37141, were initially to be equipped with radio cab signalling to work across the East Suffolk line. Later Nos. 37138, 37140, 37144, 37216 and 37219 were fitted. Locomotives subsequently registered working on freight and atomic flask trains included Nos. 37023, 37059, 37069, 37087, 37194, 37216, 37218, 37219, 37229, 37259, 37379, 37409, 37423, 37431, 37510, 37601, 37603, 37604, 37606-12, 37682, 37684 and 37688.

The BR class '20' 1,000 hp diesel-electrics have seen increasing service in recent years on the nuclear flask trains to/from Sizewell siding and a selected few were equipped with radio cab signalling for working over the East Suffolk line. Nos. 20313, 20314 and 20315 tripled-headed the 13-coach Pathfinder Tours special 05.30 Crewe to Leiston/Sizewell across the branch on 10th March, 2007, with class '47' No. 47501 in the rear. The train returned to Saxmundham with No. 47501 leading. Class '20s' allocated to Direct Rail Services used on the atomic flask trains included all of Nos. 20301-20316. Leading dimensions are:

BTH/Paxman type '1' 800 hp diesel-electric locomotive No. D8224 standing at Leiston with the up branch freight train formed of three 16 ton all-steel mineral open wagons, a plate wagon and brake van. The signal box and connections to Garrett's sidings are still extant, but the up loop has been truncated short of Station Road level crossing.                    *The late Dr I.C. Allen*

BR/Sulzer, class '24', 1,160 hp diesel-electric locomotive No. D5049 near Station Road level crossing at Leiston propelling coal wagons to the former gas works siding. By this date the former loop line and headshunt east of the gates had been lifted but signalling is still extant with the up home signal in the background. The area in the immediate foreground beyond the gates was the site of the former crossover removed in 1892 and associated siding serving Carr's brickworks which closed in March 1926. From then until removal in the early 1950s the brickworks siding was served by facing points in the down direction on the down side of the main single line.                    *The late Dr I.C. Allen*

Brush type '2', class '31' 1,365 hp diesel-electric locomotive No. D5699 collecting three coaches for an exhibition train from the sidings at Leiston. The main single line and loop line are to the right, whilst the yard continues to be used as a coal ground by local fuel merchants.

*The late Dr I.C. Allen*

English Electric type '3' 1,750 hp diesel-electric locomotive No. D6744 stands on the former main single line, now truncated by buffer stops, beside the atomic flask unloading gantry at Sizewell siding. The class '37' is hauling a weed killing train whilst a wagon holding a single flask is stabled in the siding. At the time the locomotive propelled the stock back to Leiston before running round the stock. It was soon realised this was a time consuming and dangerous procedure and a holding siding west of Sizewell level crossing and run-round loop and additional siding were subsequently installed east of the crossing to facilitate ease of operation for the flask trains. *The late Dr I.C. Allen*

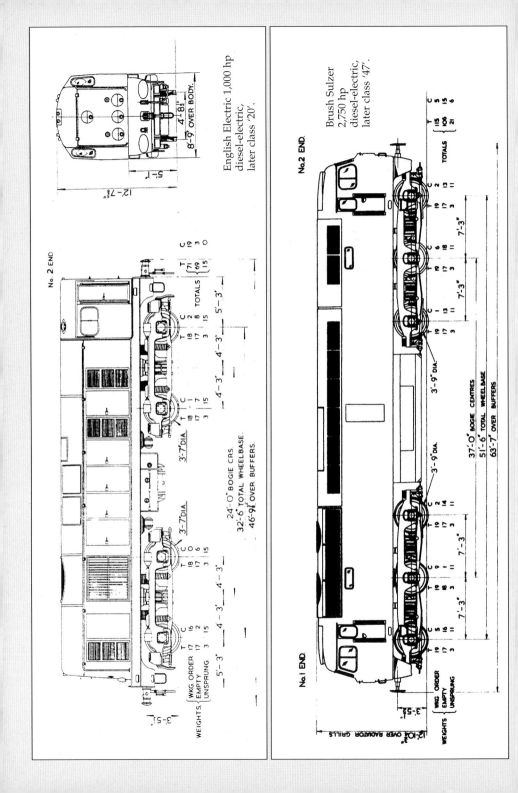

English Electric 1,000 hp diesel-electric, later class '20'.

Brush Sulzer 2,750 hp diesel-electric, later class '47'.

| | |
|---|---|
| *Type* | Bo-Bo |
| *Weight in working order* | 72 tons |
| *Tractive effort* | 25,000 lb. |
| *Wheelbase* | 32 ft 6 in. |
| *Wheel diameter* | 3 ft 7 in. |
| *Bogie wheelbase* | 8 ft 6 in. |
| *Bogie centres* | 24 ft 0 in. |
| *Width overall* | 8 ft 9in. |
| *Length overall* | 46 ft 9¾ in. |
| *Height overall* | 12 ft 7⅝ in. |
| *Minimum curve negotiable* | 3½ chains |
| *Maximum permitted speed* | 75 mph |
| *Fuel tank capacity* | 380 gallons |
| *Brakes* | Straight air and auto air on locomotive, auto air and air-controlled vacuum for train |
| *Power equipment* | 8 cylinder English Electric type 8 SVT Mark 2, 1,000 hp at 850 rpm |
| *Traction motors – 4* | English Electric EE 526/8D |

In recent years Brush Sulzer 2,750 hp diesel-electric locomotives, later class '47', with RA7 route availability have made several forays across the branch on special workings but have rarely been employed on the flask workings to and from Sizewell. On 6th June, 2005 No. 47802, allocated to Direct Rail Services and outstationed at Stowmarket, carried out RETB tests between Saxmundham Junction and Sizewell in readiness for the resumption of atomic flask trains, which had not operated for a period of three months. The test run also proved the condition of the permanent way and being a success allowed the flask trains to resume on 7th June. DRS-allocated No. 47501 worked across the branch with the Pathfinder Tours special on 10th March, 2007 on possibly the longest passenger train ever to be recorded on the line, the formation consisting of 13 coaches. The class '47' was assisted by three class '20s' at the other end of the train. No. 47501 ventured across the branch again on 26th March, 2007 with a flask train in tandem with class '20' No. 20302. The '47' had replaced class '20' No. 20304, which had incurred a brake problem at Willesden. No 47790 has also worked a flask train.

The leading dimensions of the class '47' are:

| | |
|---|---|
| *Type* | Co-Co |
| *Weight in working order* | 119 tons 9 cwt |
| *Tractive effort* | 55,000 lb. |
| *Wheelbase* | 51 ft 6 in. |
| *Wheel diameter* | 3 ft 9 in. |
| *Bogie wheelbase* | 14 ft 6 in. |
| *Bogie centres* | 37 ft 0 in. |
| *Width overall* | 9 ft 2 in. |
| *Length overall* | 63 ft 7 in. |
| *Height overall* | 12 ft 9⅝ in. |
| *Minimum curve negotiable* | 4 chains |
| *Maximum permitted speed* | 95 mph |
| *Fuel tank capacity* | 765 gallons |
| *Brakes* | Straight air and auto air on locomotive, auto air and air-controlled vacuum for train. |
| *Power equipment* | 12 cylinder Sulzer 12 LDA type 28C, 2,750 hp at 800 rpm |
| *Traction motors – 6* | Brush TH 64 - 68 |

Pathfinder Tours special train 05.30 Crewe to Leiston/Sizewell on the branch returning to the East Suffolk main line near Saxmundham on 10th March, 2007. This was probably the longest passenger train to traverse the former Aldeburgh line and Direct Rail Services class '20' diesel-electric locomotives Nos. 20313, 20315 and 20314 head the formation of 13 coaches whilst DRS class 47 No. 47501 brings up the rear. *G.R. Mortimer*

The winding nature of the branch is evident from this view of two-car Metropolitan-Cammell dmu Nos. E79066/E79282 forming the 14.57 Aldeburgh to Saxmundham train approaching Thorpeness Halt on 6th September, 1966. *G.R. Mortimer*

Diesel-multiple-units took over the branch passenger workings on and from 10th June, 1956 initially using Metropolitan-Cammell two-car units built in 1955, conveying second class accommodation only and numbered in the series E79047 to E79075 for the driving motor brake seconds, Nos. E79263 to E79291 for the driving trailer seconds. As Aldeburgh shed was closed with the abolition of steam-hauled passenger services, the dmus worked out and back from Ipswich each weekday. Unit Nos. E79066/E79282 operated the final regular passenger service on the branch on Saturday 10th September, 1966.

The leading dimensions of these two-car units were:

|  | DMBS | DTS |
|---|---|---|
| Engine | 2 x BUT (AEC) 6-cylinder horizontal 150 hp | – |
| Transmission | Mechanical cardan shaft and freewheel to 4 speed epicyclic gearbox and further cardan shaft to final drive | – |
| Weight | 26 tons 10 cwt | 25 tons |
| Length over body | 57 ft 0 in. | 57 ft 0 in. |
| Height | 12 ft 8⅛ in. | 12 ft 8⅛ in. |
| Width | 9 ft 3 in. | 9 ft 3 in. |
| Maximum speed | 70 mph | 70 mph |
| Coupling code | Yellow diamond | Yellow diamond |
| Seating (2nd class) | 57 | 71 |

Another type of two-car dmu occasionally used on the Aldeburgh branch services were built by Derby works and introduced into traffic in 1955. The vehicles were numbered in the series E79021 to E79046 for the driving motor brake seconds and E79250 to E79262 and E79613 to E79625 for the driving composite trailers with a combined seating of 109 second class and 16 first class passengers. The principal dimensions of these units were:

|  | DMBS | DTC |
|---|---|---|
| Engine | 2 x BUT (AEC) 6 cylinder horizontal 150 hp | – |
| Transmission | Mechanical cardan shaft and freewheel to 4 speed epicyclic gearbox and further cardan shaft to final drive | |
| Weight | 27 tons | 21 tons |
| Length over body | 57 ft 6 in. | 57 ft 6 in. |
| Height | 12 ft 7 in. | 12 ft 7 in. |
| Width | 9 ft 2 in. | 9 ft 2 in. |
| Maximum speed | 70 mph | 70 mph |
| Coupling code | Yellow diamond | Yellow diamond |
| Seating (1st class) | – | 16 |
| Seating (2nd class) | 56 | 53 |

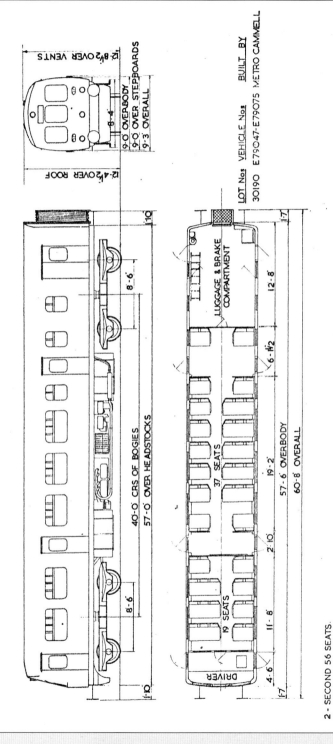

GANGWAYED MOTOR OPEN SECOND BRAKE

12-8½ OVER VENTS

9-0 OVERBODY
9-0 OVER STEPBOARDS
9-3 OVERALL

8-4

12-4½ OVER ROOF

8-6

40-0 CRS OF BOGIES
57-0 OVER HEADSTOCKS

8-6

1-10

DRIVER

19 SEATS

4-6    11-8    2-10    19-2    6-11½    12-8    1-7

57-6 OVERBODY
60-8 OVERALL

37 SEATS

LUGGAGE & BRAKE
COMPARTMENT

LOT No:   VEHICLE No:   BUILT BY
30190   E79047-E79075   METRO CAMMELL

2 × 150 H.P. BUT ENGINES

2 - SECOND 56 SEATS.
1 - DRIVERS COMPARTMENT.
1 - LUGGAGE COMPARTMENT.

Metropolitan-Cammell two-car dmu
motor brake second, later BR class '101'.

Derby lightweight two-car dmu departing Aldeburgh station for Saxmundham on 26th June, 1961 before the train shed was demolished and the signal box abolished. The lower quadrant GER up starting signal is also devoid of its decorative finial.                          *S. Creer*

Two-car Derby lightweight dmu forming a train to Yarmouth South Town departing from Saxmundham past the signal box on 24th June, 1961. Units of this type were also occasionally used on Aldeburgh branch services. Note the change in gradient on the down line behind the train. The unit is passing over the trailing crossover connecting the up and down main lines and the crossover leading to the down reception siding. The water crane for up trains is at the London end of the up platform.                          *Author's Collection*

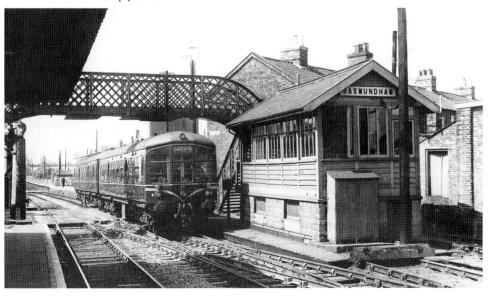

A third type of diesel-multiple-unit used occasionally on services were two-car sets built by Craven, consisting of driving motor brake second and driving trailer composite, with combined seating for 103 second class and 12 first class passengers. Initially introduced in 1956 these units were numbered in the series E51254-E51301 for the driving motor brake seconds, and E56412-E56461 for the driving trailer composites. The leading dimensions were:

|  | DMBS | DTC |
|---|---|---|
| Engine | 2 x BUT (AEC) BUT (Leyland) 150 hp | – |
| Transmission | Mechanical cardan shaft and freewheel to 4 speed epicyclic gearbox and further cardan shaft to final drive | |
| Weight | 29 tons | 23 tons |
| Length over body | 57 ft 6 in. | 57 ft 6 in. |
| Height | 12 ft 7 in. | 12 ft 7 in. |
| Width | 9 ft 3 in. | 9 ft 3 in. |
| Maximum speed | 70 mph | 70 mph |
| Coupling code | Blue square | Blue square |
| Seating (1st class) | - | 12 |
| Seating (2nd class) | 52 | 51 |

### Staff and Facilities

Ipswich motive power depot, later coded 32B by British Railways, always supplied motive power for the branch. Initially an engine shed and turnplate was provided at Leiston but these facilities were made redundant when the line was extended. As the branch was often worked by a tender locomotive an unsuccessful attempt was made in November 1859 to provide a turntable at Saxmundham but nothing came of the venture. However, tank locomotives were soon made available to work the services and the locomotive allocated to Aldeburgh was stabled in the brick-built engine shed, 60 ft in length with doors at each end, located on the down or east side of the line north of the station and served by the shed road. The shed contained an inspection pit and alongside was the oil store and messroom. On the spur leading to the shed road and behind the signal box was another inspection pit and beside that a coal stage, backed by a sleeper fence to keep the coal on the stage. Excess coal was often placed on the loading dock at the back of the platform. In the early years a small turnplate and a short stub siding with a crane was provided for coaling purposes. On 4th November, 1898 another attempt was made to provide a turntable at Saxmundham and estimates were prepared but again nothing came of the proposal. As at Framlingham, from the late 1940s the locomotive at Aldeburgh was rarely stabled within the shed in the spring and summer months and usually stood by the coaling stage. With the onset of adverse autumn and winter weather the opportunity was taken to stable the engine within the shed. Locomotives were sub-shedded at Aldeburgh for about a fortnight before returning to Ipswich and usually worked chimney first to Aldeburgh. When changeover took place the relieving locomotive from Ipswich, worked by Ipswich men, arrived and stabled on the down line at Saxmundham opposite the up platform. When the branch train arrived the locomotive pulled up alongside so the footplate crews could exchange engines. The relieved engine was then uncoupled from the train and worked back to Ipswich shed by the Ipswich men, whilst the fresh locomotive crossed to the up main line and backed on to the stock before drawing the coaches into Hay siding or into the down side goods yard before forming the next down train to Aldeburgh.

Water for locomotives at Aldeburgh was obtained from a water crane fed from the storage tank raised above the pump house and located to the north of the coal stage. Water was raised from well into the storage tank by means of a water raising cock fitted to the locomotive, and all engines working the branch were required to be fitted with this equipment. It was usual for the branch engine to stand pumping water at the end of the daily diagram in order to replenish the tank. George Airey commenced his railway career as a pumper at Aldeburgh in July 1872 before transferring to Ipswich as a cleaner in 1874 and subsequently was promoted as a driver in 1885. Later an external pump was fitted and obviated the use of engines to replenish the tank. Normally the tanks and tenders of locomotives working the branch were topped up at Aldeburgh, as facilities at Saxmundham involved engines occupying the up or down main line, which could lead to delays. At Saxmundham water cranes were located at the London end of the up platform and country end of the down platform, the cranes being fed from a water tank located on the down side of the line at the north end of the down platform, which was in turn supplied by pump from a well. In later years the topping up of tanks at Aldeburgh was avoided as the water was hard despite provision of molasses to soften the supply. Thus footplate crews preferred to top up at Saxmundham, much to the consternation of the operating department for such action occupied the main line, sometimes delaying traffic.

The coaling of engines at Aldeburgh was carried out by a cleaner or coalman on nights, working from the open coaling stage by the shed or at the back of the station platform. The fireman was responsible if the bunker or tender required replenishing during the day and, in order to facilitate coaling, the branch locomotive usually worked engine first to Aldeburgh and bunker or tender first to Saxmundham.

When the line opened to Leiston and subsequently Aldeburgh only one driver and fireman were employed covering a full 12 hour shift. A pumpman or coalman was also employed and one of these disposed of the engine after a day's duty and prepared it for the following day's service. As a result of legislation over enginemen's hours, two sets of men were later based at the shed, assisted initially by a coalman/labourer and later by an engine cleaner who was booked on nights to coal and water the engine for the next day's diagram. This was considered a thankless task, especially in winter with the cold easterly wind blowing off the sea resulting in the bangs and creaks caused by the heated engine expanding or contracting in the chilly air. A visit by the local policeman calling in for a cup of tea and a rest from his patrol often broke the monotony.

During World War I, the number of staff at Aldeburgh depot consisted of a driver-in-charge, an acting driver, two acting firemen and a cleaner. One of the acting firemen booked on duty at 1.30 am to light up the fire and raise steam on

*Above:* Fireman James (Jim) Gilbert on the footplate of a 'J15' class 0-6-0 at Aldeburgh. *Gilbert Family Collection*

*Right:* Locomotive and enginemen's workings, Aldeburgh depot 1925.

*Below:* Locomotive diagram for Ipswich 'J17' class working Aldeburgh branch goods 1953.

IPSWICH DEPOT

| Eng. Diagram No. | Engine M.P. Class | Engine Diagram | | Days Run | Train Class | Reference to Trainmen's Workings | |
|---|---|---|---|---|---|---|---|
| | | | | | | Enginemen | Guards |
| 109 | 4 | Ipswich Aldeburgh Ipswich | a.m. 7 5 | EWD | K | IPS 11 IPS 11 | IPS 35 IPS 35 |

the branch locomotive. The driver-in-charge signed on at 6.00 am and, after checking the engine and oiling round worked the first up train at 6.57 am with the acting fireman as his mate. The acting driver worked the middle turn relieving the acting fireman who then proceeded to clean the ash pit and tidy the locomotive shed yard before signing off duty at 11.30 am. At 3.00 pm the second acting fireman signed on duty and the acting driver took over the driving. After the last trip of the day the engine was connected to the water raising cock to pump water into the storage tank, a process that often took in excess of two hours.

During the coal shortage after World War I the cleaner was delegated to make briquettes from coal dust and cement to supplement the meagre coal supplies and cut up old sleepers to light the fire in the firebox. The cleaner also offloaded coal from wagons on to the coaling stage. The junior driver or senior acting fireman performed tube cleaning on the locomotives at the depot, receiving four hours Sunday rate of pay for the work. Boiler washing and other running repairs and maintenance were carried out when the locomotive returned to Ipswich shed. Engines were normally changed over on a Monday morning, with Ipswich men bringing down the relieving engine and taking back the relieved engine, the changeover being made at Saxmundham.

By 1925 the two sets of men (by now driver and fireman) worked regular turns, the first pair signing on at 5.58am on weekdays, preparing the engine before working four round trips to Saxmundham and back, then being relieved by the second set of men who signed on at 1.56 pm. These men worked the remainder of the services for the day before disposing of the locomotive on shed and handing over to the cleaner and or/coalman to water and coal the engine during the night. On Sundays the first set of men signed on at 6.42 am working one return trip to Saxmundham before being relieved by the back turn men who signed on at 2.00 pm. In the later years the two sets of men worked alternate shifts - one early turn and the other the back shift. Signing-on times varied according to the contingencies of the service and varied from 5.15 to 5.45 am to 1.45 or 2.00 pm and 1.30 to 1.45 pm to the close of service.

The senior of the two drivers at Aldeburgh was designated locomotive foreman, later driver-in-charge, and received a half day's additional pay per week for administrative duties, including the submission of driver's tickets and coal and oil returns to the locomotive shed master at Ipswich. The majority of drivers based at Aldeburgh 'signed the road' for the branch and the main line to Ipswich, with a few signing to Beccles. Some also signed for the Snape goods branch. The footplate staff based at Aldeburgh were not provided with accommodation and lived away from the railway, in the town. Ipswich depot men provided cover for Aldeburgh footplate staff during absence due to annual leave or sickness and these men 'signed the road' for the branch. In the latter years the cleaner on nights was from Ipswich and, unlikely to get a firing turn at his home depot, elected to go to Aldeburgh where he was paid night labouring rate and expenses.

Drivers at Aldeburgh in the early years included Robert Bickerdyke and James Hughes, with passed fireman Edward Howe and firemen Charles Fryer and Thomas Bell. The famous Arthur Benjamin Cage of Ipswich depot, a stocky gentleman with a 'Captain Kettle' beard and known locally as 'Chuffy', worked the '1500' class 4-6-0s on the main line up to 1912 but by 1914 was semi-retired and in

Driver Jack Runnacles on the right and fireman Maurice Holman on the footplate of 'J15' class 0-6-0 No. 65447 at Aldeburgh. *Author's Collection*

'F6' class 2-4-2T No 67230 in lined black livery standing in the down goods yard at Saxmundham between trips. Driver Jack Runnacles stands on the right with shunter Walter Brown to the left. *M. Hunt*

1916 at his own request was transferred as driver-in-charge at Aldeburgh. His fireman was Frank Cocksedge, who later fired on the 'Cross Country Continental' train from Ipswich to Manchester with 'B12' class locomotive No. 1569 and then later as driver with regular locomotive 'B1' class 4-6-0 No. 1059. Cage had worked on the Orwell river boats when aged 13, and transferred to Ipswich locomotive depot three years later. He retired on 24th April, 1924 aged 65 years and died on 17th December, 1935. In the latter years the drivers at Aldeburgh included Thurkettle and Mountel, the former retiring as driver-in-charge on 21st October, 1943. At a ceremony attended by station master Bass of Aldeburgh and station master Roe of Saxmundham, Thurkettle was presented with a wallet of money subscribed by the staff at Aldeburgh, Thorpeness, Leiston and Saxmundham. W. Mountel, who assumed the post of driver-in-charge, also made a presentation to Thurkettle on behalf of locomotive department staff. At the end George Barnett, a bachelor who was a fireman at March before World War II and then driver at Ipswich, was at the shed. He commenced his railway career in 1915 and lived at Aldeburgh and enjoyed fishing and had a laid-back approach to his job. The driver on the other shift was driver-in-charge Jack Runnacles whose life centred around the Aldeburgh branch. Runnacles was never satisfied with the locomotive allocated to the small sub-shed and was always telephoning the Ipswich running foreman for a fresh engine. He liked the fireman to have a hot fire with the engine blowing off to prevent shortage of steam. He was a conscientious man but tended to worry. Jack Runnacles took early retirement before the withdrawal of steam services due to failing eyesight and passed fireman James Gilbert was appointed to the post.

Firemen at Aldeburgh in the latter years included James Gilbert and Maurice Holman. Gilbert commenced his railway career at Langwith Junction in March 1936 being promoted to fireman in 1939 and transferred to Aldeburgh in 1941. Holman joined the railway in March 1941 as engine cleaner and was promoted fireman at Aldeburgh in 1944. After closure of the shed, like others he transferred to Ipswich and later Kings Cross where he was killed in a railway accident.

In the event of staff shortage due to illness or holidays Ipswich men covered some of the Aldeburgh turns. One of these involved leaving Ipswich in the early evening about 6.00 pm and travelling passenger to Saxmundham before catching the branch train on to Aldeburgh and lodging overnight. Crews were given lodging allowance but to save money the official lodgings were not sought and the incumbents slept in a hut by the locomotive shed during summer months. In winter this was considered too cold so the engine would be coupled to the coaching stock standing in the platform, the steam heating pipe connected and the men slept in the train. The crew then worked the branch early turn before travelling back to Ipswich, often by bus as the trains were inconveniently timed, the conductor waiving the fare if the men were in uniform. Illicit practices were not unknown with the authorities none the wiser. On some occasions at the end of the day and to save time disposing of the engine on shed the majority of the fire was thrown out of the firebox at Saxmundham or en route on the last down run. Shifts were exchanged to accommodate personal affairs of the heart or darts matches. Maurice Holman, playing for Aldeburgh Town Football Club, exchanged duties with his opposite number so that he could turn out for the team on Saturday afternoons including away matches. Such was the camaraderie that reciprocal arrangements were made as social commitments required.

*Above:* Driver Jim Gilbert standing on the footplate of ex-LMS Ivatt '2MT' 2-6-2T No. 41200 at Aldeburgh in May 1950. The locomotive was transferred from Bangor shed to Ipswich for the summers of 1949 and 1950 and often outbased at Aldeburgh shed.
*Author's Collection*

*Right:* The driver of the Saxmundham to Aldeburgh dmu leans from the cab to gather the Saxmundham Junction-Leiston single line train staff from the Junction signalman.
*R. Kennell*

Initially the locomotive working the booked branch services carried no headlamp by day and only one white light at the base of the chimney by night. Special trains only carried lights at night with the engine displaying a white light at the base of the chimney and another light on the buffer beam, if fitted with a lamp bracket, or if not, presumably attached to the coupling. By 1875 the headcode for ordinary trains was the same but special trains carried a white disc at the base of the chimney by day and two white lights at night. The headcode carried by locomotives hauling the branch trains in later GER days was a red light at the top of the smoke box by the chimney and a white light on the buffer beam. During daylight hours a circular red disc with white rim was carried under the chimney. Special trains carried an additional white light by night or white disc by day on the buffer beam. By 1890 a red disc with white rim was carried under the chimney by day, and a red light under the chimney and a white light on the left-hand end of the buffer beam by night. Special trains then carried a red disc with a white rim under the chimney and a white disc in the centre of the buffer beam by day, whilst at night a red lamp under the chimney and white light on the left- and right-hand ends of the buffer beam were stipulated. In 1903 the headcode for single line working was again changed to a red disc with white outer rim under the chimney during daylight hours and red lamp under the chimney and a green lamp on the left-hand end of the buffer beam by night. From 1910 ordinary and special trains carried the same code, red disc with white outer rim or red lamp under the chimney and a green disc with white outer rim or green lamp over the left-hand end of the buffer beam. After Grouping the LNER phased out the green lights and discs as a possible source of danger and replaced them with a purple light. From 1925 the standard stopping passenger train code of a white light or white disc at the base of the chimney was used on the Aldeburgh branch trains and remained so until the withdrawal of steam passenger services. Freight trains on the branch then carried the appropriate Railway Clearing House class headcode.

The following engine whistle codes were applicable to the branch in early GER days,

*Saxmundham Junction*

| | |
|---|---|
| Main line | 1 distinct sound |
| Up Branch Trains for Branch Siding | 2 distinct sounds |
| Branch trains to and from main line | 3 distinct sounds |

About the 1880s the whistle code was amended to,

*Saxmundham Junction*

| | |
|---|---|
| Main line | 1 distinct sound |
| Branch trains to and from main line | 3 distinct sounds |

The LNER and BR issued no specific whistle codes for the branch.

In the event of a mishap or breakdown, the Ipswich breakdown vans, later breakdown crane and vans, covered the Aldeburgh branch, latterly using GER 20 ton capacity steam crane No. 5A dating from 1908. It was later renumbered by the LNER to 961603 in the 1938 re-numbering scheme and then by BR to No. 132 before being withdrawn in 1967.

DIAGRAM Nº 14600-108

— FIRST CLASS CARRIAGE —

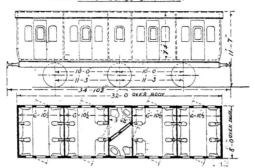

TO SEAT 22-1ˢᵀ CLASS PASSENGERS
TOTAL WEIGHT EMPTY 13-15-2    G. A Nº 9655

GER 6-wheel first to diagram 108.

CODE Nº 6135.

DIAGRAM 14600-518E    L N E R.    BUILT 1896-97-98-99-1900.

BRAKE VAN.

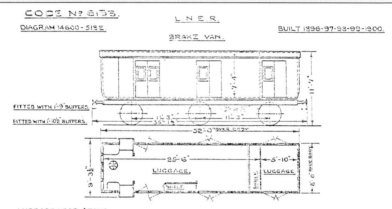

FITTED WITH 1-9" BUFFERS.
FITTED WITH 1-10½ BUFFERS.

LUGGAGE LOAD 4 TONS.
TOTAL WEIGHT EMPTY    12-2-3    G. A. Nº 9272E.
          "       LOADED    16-4-0
FITTED WITH INCANDESCENT GAS, WESTINGHOUSE BRAKE, STEAM HIS

GER 6-wheel brake to diagram 518.

CODE Nº 6141.

DIAGRAM Nº 14600-532E.    L N E R    BUILT 1901-04-06

BRAKE VAN

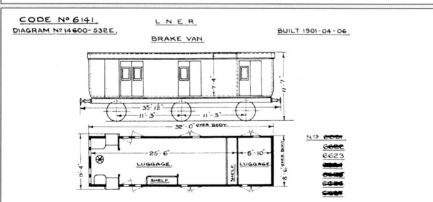

Nºs 6616
    6612
    6623
    6611
    6615
    6624
    6627

LUGGAGE LOAD 4 TONS.
TOTAL WEIGHT EMPTY    12-2-3    G. A. Nº 11513, 13743E
          -       LOADED    16-4-0    DUAL BRAKE SHEWN THUS 6618
FITTED WITH INCANDESCENT GAS, STEAM HEATING, VACUUM BRAKE.

GER 6-wheel brake to diagram 532.

*Coaching Stock*

The ECR and later GER placed no weight or loading gauge restrictions for coaching stock on the Aldeburgh branch and conventional stock was used. Initially coaching stock was very primitive four-wheel vehicles with first, second, third and Parliamentary accommodation offered, the latter travelling third class on certain designated trains. The first class vehicles had fully upholstered seats in compartments, whilst at the lower end of the spectrum the third class and Parliamentary passengers were subjected to sitting on wooden boards. Until the early 1900s the coaching stock was exclusively four-wheeled, provided with oil lighting and only latterly equipped with the Westinghouse brake.

During the 1860s and 1870s the stock allocated to the branch was Gooch and latterly Sinclair design for the ECR. The latter with four-compartment first/second composites to diagram 33, five-compartment thirds to diagram 34, both with 24 ft body length, and full brake van to diagram 39 with 21 ft body length. The branch train usually comprised four vehicles with one composite, two full thirds and one brake van as the normal formation. On Ipswich market day an additional full third was attached.

From the early 1880s the GER began drafting four-wheel vehicles, 27 ft in length, originally built for main line services during the 1870s. Trains were usually formed of up to five vehicles, two being third class to diagram 402, one second class to diagram 302, one composite to diagram 217 and a brake third to diagram 504.

The introduction of bogie stock on the principal GER trains from the late 1890s was a gradual process and the use of four-wheel coaching stock outside the London suburban area continued for many years. When replacement of stock was finally made on the Aldeburgh branch, the six-wheel vehicles dated from 1879 onwards and varied in length from 32 ft for full brake to 34 ft 6 in. for six-compartment third. The branch train was then usually formed of a composite to diagram 108, two thirds to diagram 404 or 422 and a brake/third to diagram 514, strengthened at busy periods by either a composite or full third vehicle. During the early years of the 20th century trains were often formed of a mixture of four- and six-wheel stock but gradually the four-wheel stock was withdrawn and the six-wheel vehicles served on the branch until 1936 when bogie stock was introduced.

By 1934 a single six-wheel carriage set No. 204 on weekdays was rostered for branch duties, the same set operating on Sundays as No. 206. This set was formed of brake diagram 518 or 532, full first class to diagram 108 and two full thirds to diagram No. 422. Additional carriages were attached to certain trains at Saxmundham: either a bogie composite with two first and three third class compartments with vestibule, probably to diagram 225, or a bogie brake third vestibule to diagram 222 plus a bogie composite with two first and four third class compartments and luggage compartments vestibule to diagram 221, all originally built for the Harwich to York service. The leading dimensions of these vehicles were:

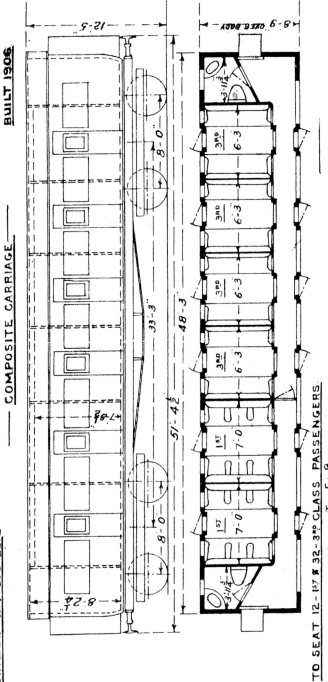

GER bogie composite to diagram 221.

**L. N. E. R.**

COMPOSITE CARRIAGE

BUILT 1906

DIAGRAM N° 14600–221E

TO SEAT 12–1ST & 32–3RD CLASS PASSENGERS.

TOTAL WEIGHT EMPTY 26–15–2    G. A. N° 14786.

FITTED WITH ELECTRIC LIGHT STEAM HEATING. DUAL BRAKE.

N°S 63572. 63573.

| Diagram | 108 | 518 | 532 |
|---|---|---|---|
| Type | 6-wheel first | 6-wheel brake | 6-wheel brake |
| Length over buffers | 34 ft 10½ in. | 35 ft 1½ in. | 35 ft 1½ in. |
| Length over body | 32 ft 0 in. | 32 ft 0 in. | 32 ft 0 in. |
| Height overall | 11 ft 7 in. | 11 ft 7 in. | 11 ft 7 in. |
| Body height | 7 ft 4 in. | 7 ft 4 in. | 7 ft 4 in. |
| Width over body | 8 ft 0 in. | 8 ft 0 in. | 8 ft 6 in. |
| Width over guard's lookout | – | 9 ft 3½ in. | 9 ft 4 in. |
| Wheelbase | 20 ft 0 in. | 22 ft 6 in. | 22 ft 6 in. |
|  | 22 ft 6 in. |  |  |
| Seating – first class | 22 | – | – |
| Seating – third class | – | – | – |
| Luggage | – | 4 tons | 4 tons |
| Weight empty | 13 tons 15 cwt | 12 tons 3 cwt | 12 tons 3 cwt |

| Diagram | 221 | 222 | 225 |
|---|---|---|---|
| Type | Bogie composite | Bogie composite | Bogie composite |
| Length over buffers | 51 ft 4½ in. | 53 ft 1½ in. | 51 ft 4½ in. |
| Length over body | 48 ft 3 in. | 50 ft 0 in. | 48 ft 3 in. |
| Height overall | 12 ft 5 in. | 12 ft 5 in. | 12 ft 5 in. |
| Body height | 8 ft 2¼ in. | 8 ft 2¼ in. | 8 ft 2¼ in. |
| Width over body | 8 ft 9 in. | 8 ft 9 in. | 8 ft 9 in. |
| Wheelbase | 41 ft 3 in. | 43 ft 0 in. | 41 ft 3 in. |
| Bogie wheelbase | 8 ft 0 in. | 8 ft 0 in. | 8 ft 0 in. |
| Seating – first class | 12 | 12 | 12 |
| Seating – third class | 32 | 37 | 24 |
| Weight empty | 26 tons 15 cwt | 26 tons 15 cwt | 26 tons 15 cwt |

From about 1937 a variety of 50 ft-long bogie stock fully replaced the 6-wheel stock used on the Aldeburgh branch, usually formed of a three-coach formation. Certainly in 1950 the carriage working showed set No. 140 allocated, comprising an 8-compartment third to diagram 430 or 439, composite to diagram 226 from the 'Norfolk Coast Express' or 227 to the same design and brake third to diagram 541. This set weighing a total of 55 tons worked the same diagram throughout the week and then worked two round trips on Sundays as diagram 197. The stock was often changed and the ex-GER vehicles were supplemented or replaced by former North Eastern Railway bogie coaches. The leading dimensions of the former GER vehicles were:

| Diagram | 226 | 227 | 430 | 439 | 541 |
|---|---|---|---|---|---|
| Type | Bogie composite | Bogie composite | Bogie third | Bogie third | Bogie brake/third |
| Length over buffers | 53 ft 1½ in. | 53 ft 1½ in. | 53 ft 1½ in. | 57 ft 1½ in. | 53 ft 1½ in. |
| Length over body | 50 ft 0 in. | 50 ft 0 in. | 50 ft 0 in. | 54 ft 0 in | 50 ft 0 in. |
| Height overall | 12 ft 5 in. | 12 ft 5 in. | 12 ft 5 in. | 12 ft 5 in. | 12 ft 5 in. |
| Body height | 8 ft 2¼ in. | 8 ft 2¼ in. | 8 ft 2¼ in. | 8 ft 2¼ in. | 8 ft 2¼ in. |
| Width over body | 8 ft 9 in. | 8 ft 9 in. | 8 ft 9 in. | 8 ft 10 in. | 8 ft 9 in. |
| Width over guard's lookout | – | – | – | – | 9 ft 1 in. |
| Wheelbase | 43 ft 0 in. | 43 ft 0 in. | 43 ft 0 in. | 45 ft 0 in. | 43 ft 0 in. |
| Bogie wheelbase | 8 ft 0 in. | 8 ft 0 in. | 8 ft 0 in. | 8 ft 0 in | 8 ft 0 in. |
| Seating – first class | 12 | 12 | – | – | – |
| Seating – third class | 32 | 38 | 80 | 96 | 24 |
| Luggage | – | – | – | – | 3½ tons |
| Weight empty | 26 t. 12 cwt | 26 t. 12 cwt | 24 t. 7 cwt | 27 t. 11 cwt | 26 t. 14 cwt |

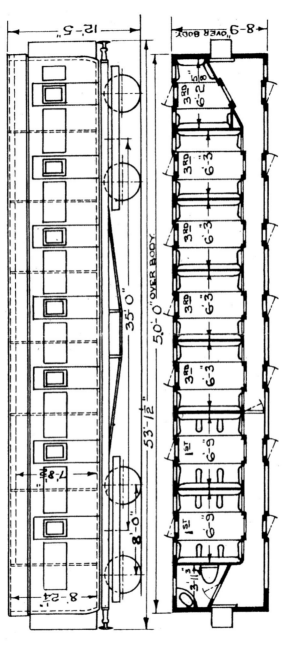

## CODE Nº 6052

### DIAGRAM Nº 14600-222E.

## L . N . E . R

## COMPOSITE CARRIAGE.

### BUILT 1906.

TO SEAT 12 FIRST AND 37 THIRD CLASS PASSENGERS.

|  | T. C. Q. |  | G. A. Nº 14785E. |
| --- | --- | --- | --- |
| TOTAL WEIGHT EMPTY | 26 - 15 - 2 | | |
| " LOADED | 29 - 16 - 3 | | |

FITTED WITH ELECTRIC LIGHT. STEAM HEATING. VACUUM BRAKE.

Nºˢ 63563. 63564. (63565)(63566). 63567. 63568.
(63569) 63570.

GER bogie composite to diagram 222.

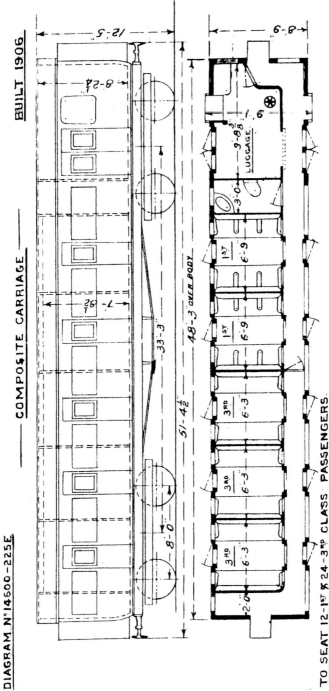

# CODE Nº 6055.

# L N E R

## DIAGRAM Nº 14600-225E

## — COMPOSITE CARRIAGE —

### BUILT 1906

TO SEAT 12-1ᔆᵀ & 24-3ᔆᴰ CLASS PASSENGERS.

TOTAL WEIGHT EMPTY 26-15-2    G.A. Nº 14788

LOADED 29-19-1

FITTED WITH ELECTRIC LIGHT. STEAM HEATING. DUAL BRAKE.

GER bogie composite to diagram 225.

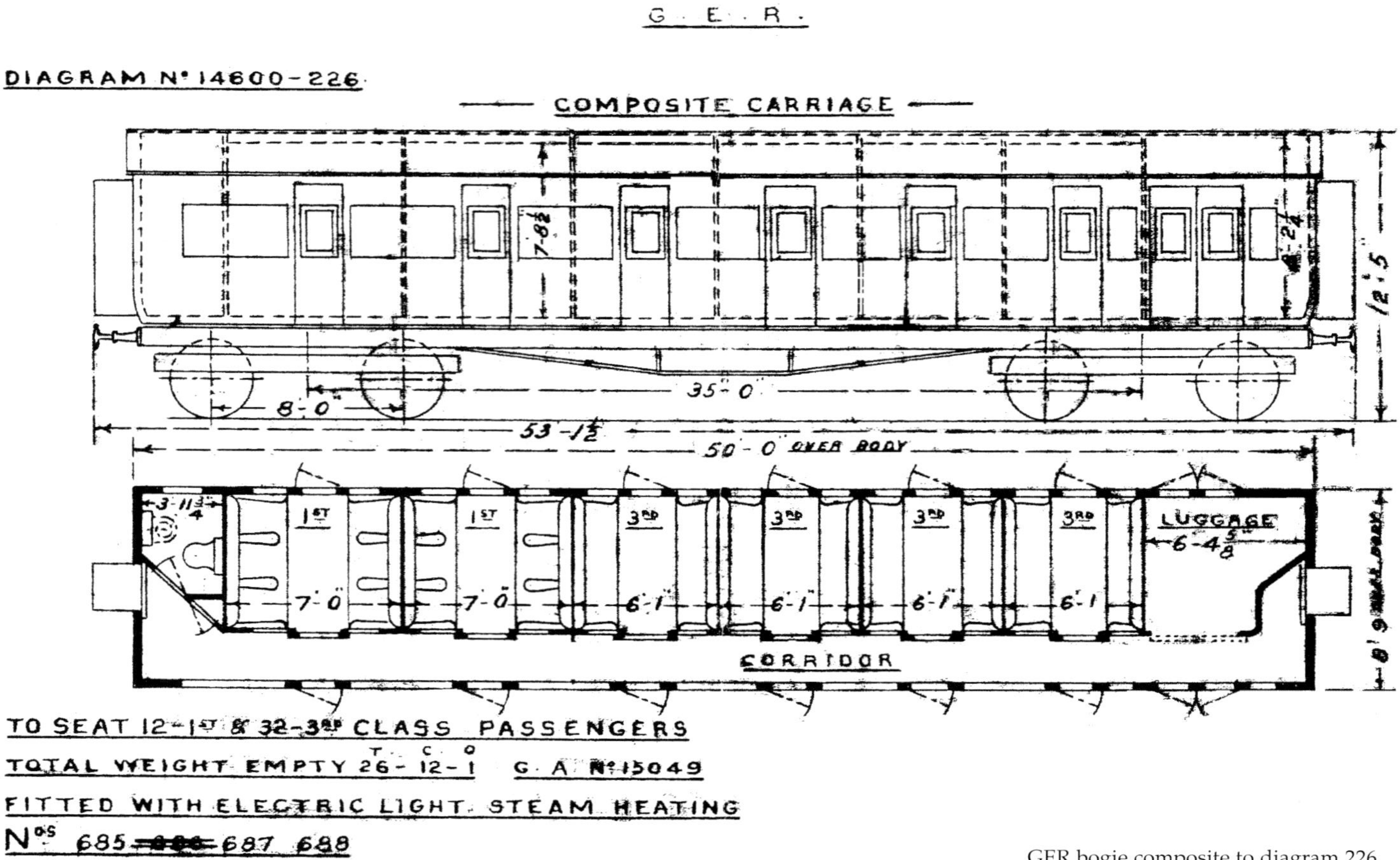

G. E. R.

COMPOSITE CARRIAGE

DIAGRAM Nº 14600 - 226.

12' 5"

8' 9" OVER DOORS

8'-2¼"

7-8½"

8'-0"

35'-0"

50'-0" OVER BODY

53'-1½"

LUGGAGE
6'-4⅝"

3ᴿᴰ  6'-1"
3ᴿᴰ  6'-1"
3ᴿᴰ  6'-1"
3ᴿᴰ  6'-1"

CORRIDOR

1ˢᵀ  7'-0"
1ˢᵀ  7'-0"
1ˢᵀ  7'-0"

3'-11½"

TO SEAT 12 - 1ˢᵀ & 32 - 3ᴿᴰ CLASS PASSENGERS

TOTAL WEIGHT EMPTY 26 - 12 - 1    T. C. Q.    G. A. Nº 15049

FITTED WITH ELECTRIC LIGHT. STEAM HEATING

Nᵒˢ 685 - 686 687 688

GER bogie composite to diagram 226.

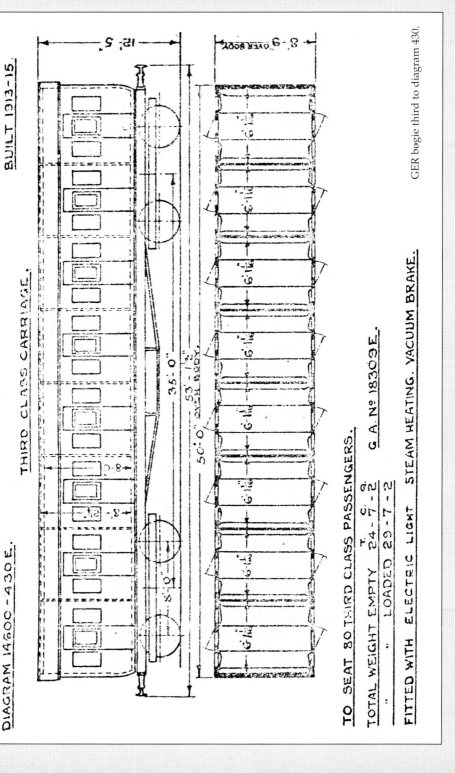

CODE Nº 6102.

DIAGRAM 14600 – 430 E.

L. N. E. R.

THIRD CLASS CARRIAGE.

BUILT 1913–15.

12'. 5"

35'. 0"

53'. 1½"

50'. 0" OVER BODY.

8'. 9" OVER BODY.

3'. 8½"     8'. 0"

8'. 0"

6'. 1½"     6'. 1½"     6'. 1½"     6'. 1½"     6'. 1½"     6'. 1½"     6'. 1½"     6'. 1½"     6'. 1½"

TO SEAT 80 THIRD CLASS PASSENGERS.

| | T. | C. | Q. |
|---|---|---|---|
| TOTAL WEIGHT EMPTY | 24 - | 7 - | 2 |
| " LOADED | 29 - | 7 - | 2 |

G. A. Nº 18309 E.

FITTED WITH ELECTRIC LIGHT. STEAM HEATING. VACUUM BRAKE.

GER bogie third to diagram 430.

CODE Nº 6111.

DIAGRAM Nº 14600 - 439 E

— THIRD CLASS CARRIAGE —

BUILT 1921 - 22

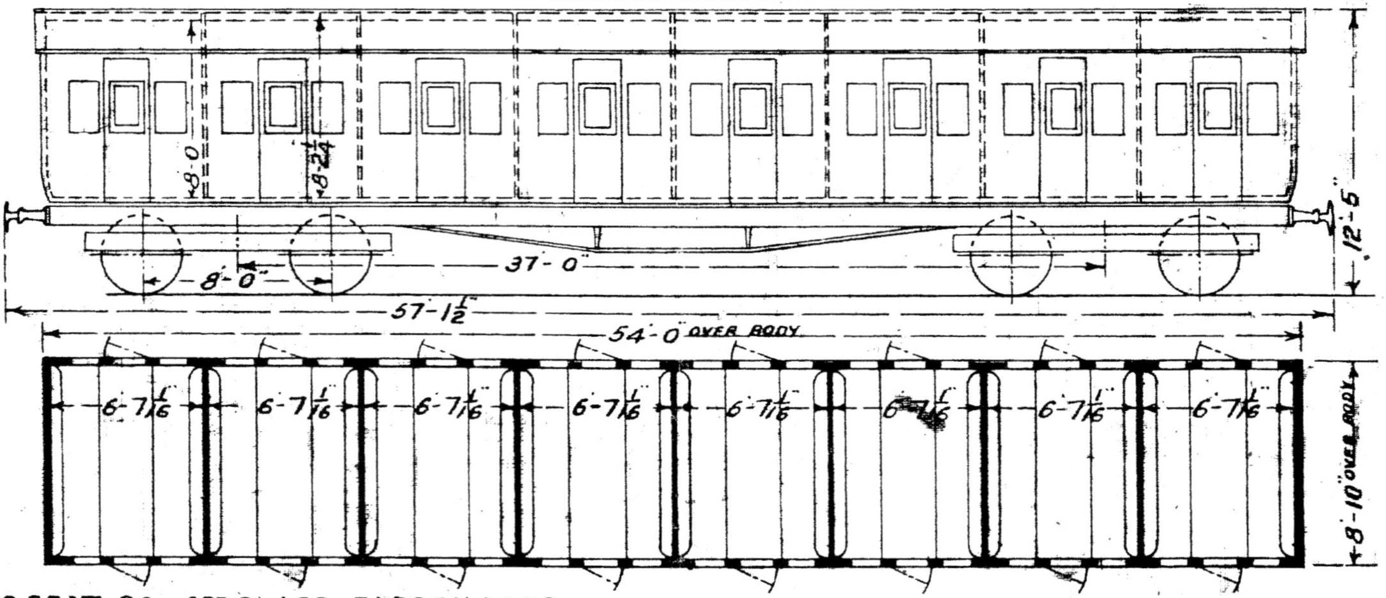

8' - 0"
8' - 0"
8' - 2½"
8' - 0"
37' - 0"
57' - 1½"
54' - 0" OVER BODY
12' - 6"
8' - 10" OVER BODY

6' - 7½"

TO SEAT 96 — 3RD CLASS PASSENGERS

TOTAL WEIGHT EMPTY 27 - 11 - 0    T C Q    G A Nº 22728 E.

FITTED WITH VACUUM BRAKE    ELECTRIC LIGHT. STEAM HEATING.

Nºs (61569) (61570) 61571 (61572) (61573) (61574) (61575) (61576)

61577 (61578) (61579) 61580

GER bogie third to diagram 439.

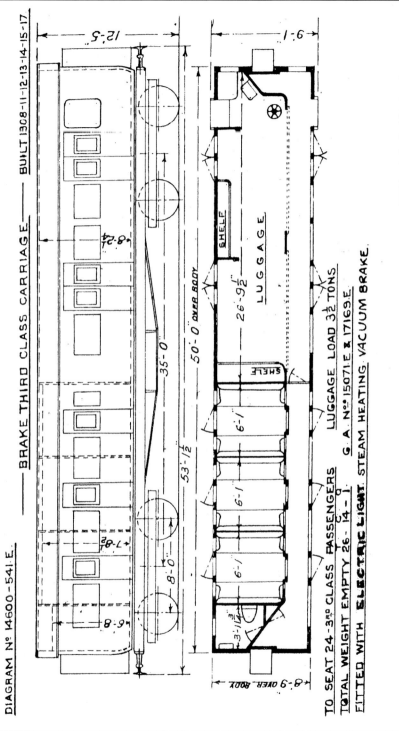

GER bogie brake/third to diagram 541.

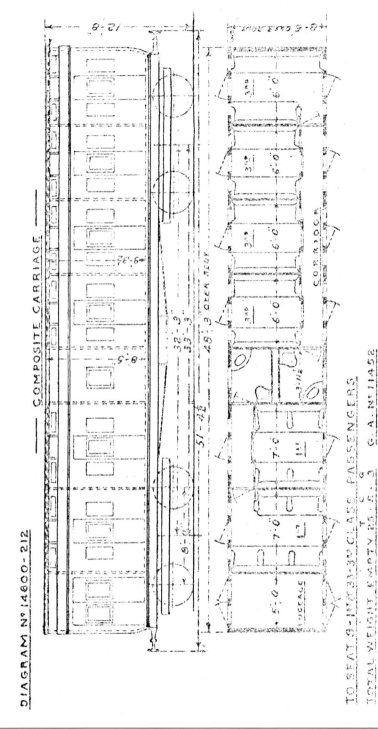

GER bogie composite to diagram 212.

Later varieties of LNER suburban bogie coaches appeared on the branch including Gresley panelled non-corridor stock. These were supplemented by Thompson steel-panelled vehicles augmented by ex-GER bogie composites to diagram Nos. 212 and 231 and ex-North Eastern Railway full thirds to diagram 503 transferred to the GE area from 1936 both before and after hostilities. These survived until the withdrawal of steam-hauled passenger services. Another interesting vehicle, which occasionally appeared on the branch, was an inspection saloon to diagram 20 built in April 1909 for the use of senior officers for inspection of the system. It was built to order No. X65 at Stratford works and was noteworthy in having wooden frames. Costing £1,210 it was numbered 48 in the GER fleet and renumbered 62 by the LNER. Gangways were provided in October 1920 but the gangway at the small saloon end was removed sometime after nationalization when it was still carrying its varnished teak livery. The vehicle later became departmental No. DE 962451, painted in maroon livery for use by the district engineer, and was withdrawn in the late 1960s.

| Diagram | 212 | 231 | 20 | 503 |
|---|---|---|---|---|
| Type | Bogie composite | Bogie composite | Bogie inspection saloon | Bogie brake/third |
| Length over buffers | 51 ft 4½ in. | 51 ft 4½ in. | 53 ft 1½ in. | 55 ft 8 in. |
| Length over body | 48 ft 3 in. | 48 ft 3 in. | 50 ft 0 in. | 52 ft 0 in. |
| Height overall | 12 ft 8 in. | 12 ft 8 in. | 12 ft 5 in. | 12 ft 7 in. |
| Body height | 8 ft 5 in. | 8 ft 5 in. | 8 ft 2¼ in. | |
| Width over body | 8 ft 6 in. | 8 ft 6 in. | 8 ft 9 in. | 8 ft 0 in. |
| Width over guard's lookout | – | – | – | 9 ft 0 in. |
| Wheelbase | 40 ft 3 in. 41 ft 3 in. | 40 ft 3 in. | 43 ft 0 in. | 44 ft 6 in. |
| Bogie wheelbase | 8 ft 0 in. | 8 ft 0 in. | 8 ft 0 in. | 8 ft 0 in. |
| Seating – first class | 9 | 9 | 29 | – |
| Seating – third class | 33 | 33 | – | 50 |
| Luggage | – | – | – | 2 tons |
| Weight empty | 25 tons 9 cwt | 25 tons 9 cwt | 30 tons 14 cwt | 23 tons 2 cwt |

The variety of LNER coaching stock used on the branch services in the latter years included corridor bogie brake third to diagram 37, coded BT, bogie composites to diagram 215 coded C and non-vestibule bogie brake thirds to diagrams 64, 65 and 340 with the following dimensions:

| Diagram | 37 | 64 | 65 | 215 | 340 |
|---|---|---|---|---|---|
| | Gresley | Gresley | Gresley | Gresley | Thompson |
| Type | Bogie brake/third corridor | Bogie brake/third non-vestibule | Bogie brake/third non-vestibule | Bogie composite non-vestibule | Bogie brake/third non-vestibule |
| Length over body | 61 ft 6 in. | 51 ft 1½ in. | 51 ft 1½ in. | 51 ft 1½ in. | 52 ft 4 in. |
| Width over body | 9 ft 3 in. | 9 ft 0 in. | 9 ft 3 in. | 9 ft 3 in. | 9 feet 3 in. |
| Seating – first class | – | – | – | 20 | – |
| Seating – third class | 40 | 40 | 40 | 60 | 40 |

On 2nd December, 1953 railway officers visited the branch for inspection of the infrastructure travelling in a 6-wheel inspection saloon hauled by 'L1' class 2-6-4T

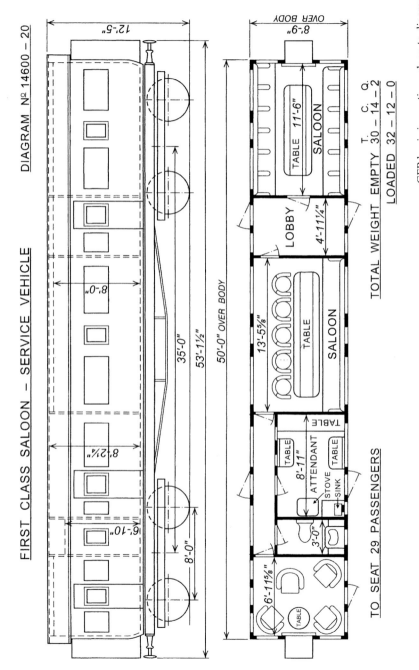

FIRST CLASS SALOON – SERVICE VEHICLE

DIAGRAM № 14600 – 20

12'-5"

8'-0"

8'-2½"

6'-10"

8'-0"

35'-0"

53'-1½"

50'-0" OVER BODY

8'-9"
OVER BODY

TABLE 11'-6"

SALOON

LOBBY

4'-11¼"

13'-5⅝"

TABLE

SALOON

TABLE

8'-11"

TABLE

ATTENDANT

STOVE

SINK

TABLE

3'-0"

6'-11⅝"

TABLE

TOTAL WEIGHT EMPTY 30 – 14 – 2
LOADED 32 – 12 – 0

T. C. Q.

TO SEAT 29 PASSENGERS

GER bogie inspection saloon to diagram 20.

No. 67705, which was officially barred from the Aldeburgh line, deputizing for a locomotive with the permitted route availability which had failed at Ipswich. The group travelled in Norwich district inspection saloon No. 960903, which had an interesting history. The vehicle was originally built to order G24 at Stratford works and completed in December 1889 as GER No. 14 in the inspection vehicle series, for use by John Wilson, the Chief Engineer of the GER, for inspection purposes. As built to diagram 11 the coach had a 27 ft 6 in. body mounted on wooden underframes with an unusually long wheelbase of 19 ft 0 in. for a four- wheel vehicle. It was also the first GER vehicle to be fitted with electric lighting when new. In 1897, then only eight years old, No. 14 received extensive alterations when the body was extended to a new length of 32 ft 0 in. A new underframe mounted on six wheels with a combined wheelbase of 22 ft 6 in. was also provided. Around 1910, in common with GER Royal and other saloons and recently built main line bogie stock, steam heating was installed. In the year prior to Grouping, internal modifications were made to the attendant's compartment whilst the door on the corridor side of the vehicle was removed and a side door to the centre saloon sealed off. It is thought the vacuum through pipes were also fitted at that date.

Under the LNER the vehicle was renumbered from 14 to 68 in the GER saloon series and in 1925 was displaced from her role as civil engineer's saloon at Stratford by the conversion of Royal saloon No. 5. No. 68 was then transferred to Ipswich where she served as the district engineer's saloon for some 20 years, occasionally travelling across the East Suffolk branches including Aldeburgh. In 1947 the saloon was renumbered 960903 but by then had been transferred to Norwich, Ipswich having acquired No. 960902, an ex-GER suburban brake third. The journey of No. 960903 over the Aldeburgh branch was almost the last in her capacity of inspection saloon for soon afterwards she was displaced by DE320042, an ex-Great Northern Railway invalid saloon No. 43087, built in 1912 and converted at Stratford in 1951 for inspection purposes. No. 960903, after use as a mobile office with the London, Tilbury & Southend and GE electrification works in the 1950s and early 1960s, was transferred to the Sheffield area before condemnation in 1973. William McAlpine subsequently purchased the vehicle for preservation. The leading dimensions of inspection saloon No. 960903 were:

| | |
|---|---|
| *Diagram* | 11 |
| *Type* | 6 wheel inspection saloon |
| *Length over buffers* | 35 ft 1 ½ in. |
| *Length over body* | 32 ft 0 in. |
| *Height overall* | 11 ft 3 in. |
| *Body height* | 7 ft 0 in. |
| *Width over body* | 8 ft 0 in. |
| *Width over guard's lookout* | 9 ft 0 in. |
| *Wheelbase* | 22 ft 6 in. |
| *Seating* | 12 |
| *Weight empty* | 15 tons 6 cwt |

The three static coach bodies which provided passenger and parcels accommodation on Thorpeness Halt platform were from the level crossing: GER diagram 302, 5-compartment 6-wheel second No. 51, 27 ft in length built at

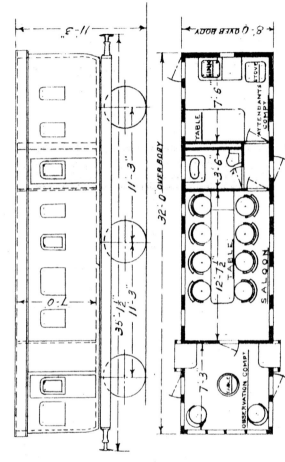

# CODE No 6004.

## L.N.E.R

DIAGRAM No 14600 – 11E

— ENGINEER'S SALOON —

BUILT 1889
SERVICE VEHICLE

TO SEAT 12 PASSENGERS

TOTAL WEIGHT EMPTY 15-5-3.   T.C.Q   G.A.Nos 7807 & 10201.

FITTED WITH ELECTRIC LIGHT STEAM HEATING. WESTINGHOUSE BRAKE

No 60.   VACUUM THROUGH PIPE

TOTAL WEIGHT LOADED 16-2-0

No. 960903

GER 6-wheel inspection saloon to diagram 11.

An unidentified 'B12/3' class 4-6-0 propels an officers' special train across the branch near Thorpeness. The leading carriage is ex-GER saloon No. 48, later LNER No. 62 and finally DE962451, to diagram 20, whilst the LNER vehicle is a 63 ft 6 in. corridor brake/third formed lavatory/5 x third class compartments/brake van to LNER diagram 37 built in 1927.

*The late Dr I.C. Allen*

Coach body of former GER 5-compartment 6-wheel second class built by Craven's in September 1880, number unknown. Converted to a 6-wheel third class some time between 1893 and 1896 and became GER No. 1480 to diagram 409, being used on main line services before withdrawal on 2nd July, 1914. It subsequently served as a booking office at Thorpeness Halt and was possibly the only accommodation when the station opened on 29th July, 1914. *J. Watling*

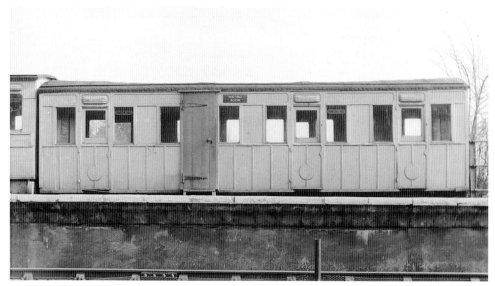

Body of former GER 4-wheel 4-compartment first No. 435 built to diagram 115 and introduced in March 1897. After withdrawal from traffic on 19th September, 1926 the body was transferred to Thorpeness Halt to act as a waiting room and is shown on 17th March, 1963.          *J. Watling*

The three carriage bodies provided as station accommodation at Thorpeness Halt on 25th August, 1965. Nearest the camera is former 4-wheel 4-compartment first class No. 435 serving as a waiting room, then former 6-wheel third class No. 1480 serving as a booking office, and finally 5-compartment 6-wheel second class No. 51 which was a parcels store.          *Author's Collection*

Side view of former GER 5-compartment 6-wheel second No. 51 built in May 1883 and withdrawn from traffic on 23rd September, 1920 and used as a parcels store at Thorpeness Halt, 17th March, 1963.                                                                        *J. Watling*

End view of GER No. 51, formerly a 5-compartment 6-wheel second to diagram 302, built at Stratford works in May 1883 and withdrawn from traffic on 23rd September, 1920, when the 27 ft body was transferred to act as a parcels store at Thorpeness Halt. The public entrance to the halt was on the right, in this view taken on 17th March, 1963.                            *J. Watling*

**140  ALDEBURGH—SAXMUNDHAM.**  T (8), CGL (2-3), BT—3 Vehs. (13 F, 71 T), 55 tons.

## WEEKDAYS

| Attach | Station | Arr. | Dep. | Detach |
|---|---|---|---|---|
| | **140** | | | |
| | | a.m. | a.m. | |
| | Aldeburgh | | 7 15 | |
| | Saxmundham | 7 35 | 7 58 | |
| | Aldeburgh | 8 19 | 8 30 | |
| | Saxmundham | 8 50 | 11 10 | |
| | Aldeburgh | 11 30 | p.m. | |
| | Aldeburgh | p.m. | 12 33 | |
| | Saxmundham | 12 53 | 1 25 | |
| | Aldeburgh | 1 45 | 3 18 | |
| | Saxmundham | 3 38 | 4 5 | |
| | Aldeburgh | 4 25 | 4 50 | |
| | Saxmundham | 5 15 | 6 19 | |
| | Aldeburgh | 6 39 | 6 45 | |
| | Saxmundham | 7 7 | | |
| | Saxmundham | | 7 17 | |
| | Aldeburgh    Q { | 7 37 | 7†13 | |
| | Saxmundham | 7†19 | | |
| | Saxmundham | | 8 10 | |
| | Aldeburgh | 8 30 | | |
| | **Works 140 MX, 197 Sundays.** | | | |

## SUNDAYS

| Attach | Station | Arr. | Dep. | Detach |
|---|---|---|---|---|
| | **197** | | | |
| | | p.m. | p.m. | |
| | Aldeburgh | | 6 30 | |
| | Saxmundham | 6 50 | 7 10 | |
| | Aldeburgh | 7 30 | 7 45 | |
| | Saxmundham | 8 5 | 8 25 | |
| | Aldeburgh | 8 45 | | |
| | **Works 140 Monday.** | | | |

Coaching stock working diagrams for the Aldeburgh branch 1950.

Stratford works in May 1883 for main line work. It was transferred to suburban services by 1893 and fitted with gas lighting but without widening of the body and was withdrawn from service on 23rd September, 1920; GER diagram 409, 5-compartment 6-wheel second with 31 ft 6 in. body length built by Cravens in September 1880, original number unknown. It was converted to a 6-wheel third sometime between 1893 and 1896 becoming GER No. 1480 and was used on main line services before withdrawal on 2nd July, 1914. The third vehicle was GER diagram 115, 4-wheel 4-compartment first No. 435 built at Stratford works in March 1897 for suburban services. The body was widened in 1904 and the vehicle was withdrawn by the LNER on 19th September, 1926. When the Halt was opened on 29th July, 1914 probably only the body of No. 1480 was on the platform.

Conversion of passenger-carrying stock from oil to gas lighting was almost completed by the early 1900s and charging of gas cylinders on carriages was carried out at Ipswich and Saxmundham. For repairs and routine maintenance the coaching vehicles were returned to Ipswich, but if minor repairs were required an examiner or fitter travelled to either Saxmundham or Aldeburgh to attend to defective vehicles.

In steam days if coaching stock required changeover it was brought down by an Ipswich locomotive - the routine being arranged where possible to coincide with the changeover of the branch locomotive.

*Wagon Stock*

The wagons used by the ECR were wooden open vehicles with side doors and were fitted with dumb buffers. Where grain, straw or merchandise was susceptible to wet weather, a tarpaulin sheet was used to cover the contents of the wagon. The brake van at the tail of the train would have been a 10 ton vehicle. In the years prior to the turn of the century the GER used four-plank-bodied open wagons with wooden frames, dating from 1882, for the conveyance of general merchandise and minerals. From 1887 these wagons were gradually superceded by five-plank, 9 ton capacity (later 10 tons) opens to diagram 16 with 9 ft 6 in. wheelbase and measuring 15 ft 0 in. over headstocks. Later 10 ton, five-plank open wagons to diagram 17, with a length of 15 ft over headstocks and 9 ft wheelbase were also used. Another variation was the use of 10 ton, seven-plank opens to diagram 55, measuring 17 ft 0 in. over headstocks and 9 ft 6 in. wheelbase for vegetable and root traffic. For fruit and perishable traffic, 10 ton ventilated vans to diagram 15 were provided, measuring 16 ft 1 in. over headstocks, with 9 ft 0 in. wheelbase and overall height of 11 ft 0¾ in. Later covered goods vans to diagram 47 were also utilized. They measured 17 ft 3 in. over headstocks, had a wheelbase of 10 ft 6 in. and were 11 ft 2 in. in height. A third variation was the 10 ton capacity covered goods wagons to diagram 72, which measured 19 ft 0 in. over headstocks whilst maintaining the 10 ft 6 in. wheelbase. The cattle and livestock traffic conveyed to and from Aldeburgh, Sizewell, Leiston and Saxmundham would have entailed the use of three types of cattle wagon on the branch. The first of 8 tons capacity was to diagram 5 and was 18 ft 7 in. over headstocks, had a 10 ft 6 in. wheelbase and was 10 ft 10¾ in. in height. The second to diagram 6 was of 9 tons capacity and measured 19 ft 0 in. over headstocks, with a 10 ft 6 in. wheelbase and overall height of 10 ft 10½ in. The third variant of cattle wagon to diagram 7 was of 10 tons capacity, 19 ft 3 in. over headstocks, with 10 ft 6 in. wheelbase and overall height of 11 ft 2 in. At the tail of the train was usually a 20 ton four-wheel goods brake van to GE diagram 56 measuring 17 ft 6 in. over headstocks, a 10 ft 3 in. wheelbase and 3 ft 1 in. diameter wheels. In addition many wagons owned by other railway companies were used to deliver and collect agricultural and livestock traffic, whilst coal and coke supplies came in private owner coal wagons. These came in two categories, those belonging to the collieries consigning the coal, and merchant and coal factors' wagons, which were loaded at the collieries.

After Grouping the GER wagons continued to be utilized, but gradually LNER standard wagons made an appearance. The most numerous were probably the 12 ton, five-plank opens with 8 ft wheelbase to code 2, and 12 ton six-plank opens with 10 ft 0 in. wheelbase to code 91, built after 1932. Later variations included 13 ton, seven-plank opens to code 162 measuring 16 ft 6 in. over headstocks and with a 9 ft 0 in. wheelbase. All were used on vegetable and sugar beet traffic. Fitted and unfitted 12 ton, 9 ft 0 in. wheelbase covered vans to code 16 conveyed perishable goods, fruit and malt and later some were specifically designated for fish traffic. Some fruit vans with 9 ft and 10 ft wheelbase saw service on the branch for malt traffic. Machinery from Garrett's at Leiston arrived and departed on the ex-GER 14 ton, 25 ft 6 in. 'Mack K12' machinery wagons to diagram 75 and later LNER builds. LNER brake vans provided for the branch traffic included 20 ton 'Toad B' to code 34 and 'Toad E' to code 64, both with 10 ft 6 in. wheelbase and measuring 22 ft 5 in. over buffers. Later 'Toad D' brake vans to code 61, with 16 ft 0 in. wheelbase and measuring 27 ft 5 in. over buffers were employed. After nationalization many of the older wooden wagons were scrapped and much traffic conveyed in open wagons was transported in 16 ton all-steel mineral vehicles. BR standard covered vans also replaced LNER vans.

In the GER era the body, solebar and headstocks of the open wagons were painted slate grey, whilst ironwork below solebar level, buffer guides, buffers, drawbars, drawbar plates and couplings were black. The LNER wagon livery was grey for non-fitted wagons and vans, whilst vehicles fitted with automatic brakes, including brake vans, were painted red oxide, which changed to bauxite around 1940. All ironwork below solebar level was black. Similar liveries continued in BR days.

Ipswich wagon repair shops carried out the maintenance and repairs of wagon stock used on the branch but in the event of the failure or defect of a wagon at a branch station, a travelling wagon examiner carried out repairs locally.

# Appendix One

# Level Crossings

| No. | Location | Mileage from Liverpool St m. ch. | Local name | Status |
|---|---|---|---|---|
| **Main line** | | | | |
| 61 | Saxmundham | 91 02 | Chantry Road | Public |
| 62 | Saxmundham | 91 07 | Albion Street | Public |
| **Branch** | | | | |
| | Junction with main line | 91 40½ | | |
| 1 | Saxmundham-Leiston | 91 58 | | Occupational |
| 2 | Saxmundham-Leiston | 92 19 | Clayhill Barn* | Occupational |
| 3 | Saxmundham-Leiston | 92 49 | Knodishall† | Public |
| 4 | Saxmundham-Leiston | 93 07 | | Occupational |
| 5 | Saxmundham-Leiston | 93 32 | West House | Public |
| 6 | Saxmundham-Leiston | 93 39 | Tyrell's | Occupational |
| 7 | Saxmundham-Leiston | 93 68 | Snowson's | Occupational |
| 8 | Saxmundham-Leiston | 94 02 | Saxmundham Road | Public |
| 9 | Saxmundham-Leiston | 94 15 | Leiston House Farm | Occupational |
| 10 | Saxmundham-Leiston | 94 33 | Coxwell's | Footpath |
| 11 | Saxmundham-Leiston | 94 39 | Harpers | Occupational |
| 11# | Saxmundham-Leiston | 94 67 | | Footpath |
| 12 | Leiston-Thorpeness | 95 05 | Leiston Station | Public |
| 13 | Leiston-Thorpeness | 95 71 | Sizewell | Public |
| 14 | Leiston-Thorpeness | 96 05 | Crown Farm | Occupational |
| 15 | Leiston-Thorpeness | 96 16 | Crown Lands | Public |
| 16 | Leiston-Thorpeness | 96 23 | | Occupational |
| 17 | Leiston-Thorpeness | 96 58 | | Footpath |
| 18 | Leiston-Thorpeness | 96 62 | Stone Cottages | Footpath |
| 19 | Leiston-Thorpeness | 97 25 | Thorpeness | Public |
| 20 | Thorpeness-Aldeburgh | 97 56 | Sheepwash | Public |
| 21 | Thorpeness-Aldeburgh | 98 09 | | Footpath |
| 22§ | Thorpeness-Aldeburgh | 98 37 | | Occupation |
| 23 | Thorpeness-Aldeburgh | 98 48 | Brick Kiln | Occupation |
| 24 | Thorpeness-Aldeburgh | 98 72 | | Occupation |
| 25 | Thorpeness-Aldeburgh | 99 13 | Northfield Covert | Footpath |

A later survey by BR increased the above mileages by between + 9 and +10½ chains.

* Also known as Brett's Black House. † Also known as Clayhill's. # Closed 1915, reopened 1970. § Closed 1922.

# Appendix Two

## Bridges

| No. | Location | Mileage from Liverpool Street (m. ch.) | Local name | Under or over | Type | Spans (No.) | Square span between abutments or supports (ft in.) | Skew span between abutments or supports (ft in.) | Depth of construction (ft in.) | Distance from road or surface of water to rail (ft in.) | Construction |
|---|---|---|---|---|---|---|---|---|---|---|---|
| *Main Line* | | | | | | | | | | | |
| 448 | Saxmundham station | 91 08 | Station footbridge | Over | Exchange and public footbridge | 1 | 37 6 | – – | 0 7 | 15 9 | Cast-iron columns, wrought-iron girders. Installed 1893. |
| 449 | Saxmundham to Darsham | 91 14 | Saxmundham North Entrance | Under | Public road | 1 | 29 10 | 33 0 | 2 6 | 18 8 | Brick abutments, brick arch. Rebuilt 1892. |
| 450 | Saxmundham to Darsham | 91 21 | Culvert | Under | Stream | 1 | 13 6 | 15 11 | 2 4 | 26 7 | Brick abutments, brick arch and parapets. |
| *Aldeburgh Branch* | | | | | | | | | | | |
| 1110A | Saxmundham to Leiston | 94 67 | Leiston footbridge | Over | Public footpath | 1 | 48 9 | – – | 0 7 | 15 8 | Cast-iron columns, wrought-iron girders. Built 1915, removed 1970. |
| 1110 | Leiston to Thorpeness | 95 37 | Valley | Under | Public road | 1 | 20 2 | 23 2 | 2 4 | 22 3 | Brick abutments, cast-iron girders. Rebuilt with wrought-iron girders 1894. |
| 1111 | Leiston to Thorpeness | 97 03 | Aldringham | Under | Occupation | 1 | 12 6 | – – | 2 0 | 13 7 | Brick abutments, cast-iron girders. Rebuilt with wrought-iron girders 1895. |
| 1112 | Thorpeness to Aldeburgh | 97 63 | Sheepwash | Under | Creek | 1 | 6 2 | – – | 3 3 | 9 2 | Brick abutments, brick arch and parapets. |
| 1113 | Thorpeness to Aldeburgh | 97 75 | Pettit's | Under | Occupation | 1 | 12 1 | – – | 1 10 | 7 4 | Brick abutments, cast-iron girders. Rebuilt with wrought-iron girders 1895. |

# Acknowledgements

The publication of this history would not have been possible without the assistance of many people. In particular I should like to thank:

| | | |
|---|---|---|
| The late A.R. Cox | The late G. Pember | R.H.N. (Dick) Hardy |
| The late W. Fenton | The late P. Proud | Peter Webber |
| The late W. Blois | The late R.C. (Dick) Riley | Les Wood |
| The late G. Woodcock | John Watling | Chris Cock |
| The late Dr I.C. Allen | Dave Hoser | Robert Powell |
| The late Bernard Walsh | John Petrie | Chris Turner |
| The late Canon C. Bayes | Alan Keeler | |

Also staff of the former Ipswich motive power depot, Ipswich wagon repair depot and many active but now mostly retired railway staff of the Ipswich district, some of who worked on the Aldeburgh branch.

Thanks are also due to the National Archives, British Railways, Eastern Region, the House of Lords' Record Office, the British Library Newspaper Library, Suffolk County Record Office at Ipswich and Bury St Edmunds, Garrett's Long Shop Museum and members of the Great Eastern Railway Society.

# Bibliography

## General Works

| | | |
|---|---|---|
| Aldrich C.L. | *GER Locomotives* | |
| Allen C.J. | *The Great Eastern Railway* | Ian Allan |
| Gordon D.I. | *Regional History of the Railways of Great Britain, Vol. 5* | David & Charles |
| | *Locomotives of the LNER* | RCTS |

## Periodicals

*Bradshaw's Railway Guide*
*Bradshaw's Railway Manual*
*British Railways, Eastern Region Magazine*
*Buses Illustrated*
*East Anglian Magazine*
*Great Eastern Railway Magazine*
*Herepath's Journal*

*Locomotive Carriage and Wagon Review*
*LNER Magazine*
*Railway Magazine*
*Railway World*
*Railway Year Book*
*Trains Illustrated*

## Newspapers

*East Anglian Daily Times*       *Ipswich Journal*       *Suffolk Chronicle*

## Other sources

*The Minute Books of the East Suffolk Railway* (Extracts)
*The Minute Books of the Eastern Counties Railway*
*The Minute Books of the Eastern Union Railway* (Extracts)
*The Minute Books of the Great Eastern Railway*
*The Minute Books of the London and North Eastern Railway*

| | |
|---|---|
| Working Timetables | ECR, GER, LNER and BR (ER) |
| Appendices to Working Timetables | GER, LNER and BR (ER) |
| Miscellaneous Working Instructions | ECR, GER, LNER and BR (ER) |

# Index